Competitiveness and Death

COMPETITIVENESS AND DEATH

Trade and Politics in Cars, Beef, and Drugs

Gary Winslett

University of Michigan Press
Ann Arbor

Published in the United States of America by the
University of Michigan Press
Manufactured in the United States of America
Printed on acid-free paper
First published March 2021

A CIP catalog record for this book is available from the British Library.

Library of Congress Cataloging-in-Publication data has been applied for.

ISBN 978-0-472-13227-0 (hardcover : alk. paper)
ISBN 978-0-472-12834-1 (e-book)

Acknowledgments

> If you were successful, somebody along the line gave you some help. . . . When we succeed, we succeed because of our individual initiative, but also because we do things together.
>
> —Barack Obama. July 13, 2012

No work of scholarship springs forth from the mind of the author without significant help from others. This book is no exception to that rule. The earliest form of this book was my doctoral dissertation. At Boston College, I would like to thank Maria McCollester, for her empathy and optimism, the Clough Center for their generous financial support, the professors of the political science department, but most of all my advisor David Deese who, along with much guidance, chose to believe in me. That meant, and still means, a great deal to me. At the European University Institute, I would like to thank my many close friends and colleagues in 2016–17 Max Weber Fellows cohort and my mentor at the Robert Schuman Centre, Bernard Hoekman. At Middlebury College, I would like to thank Cat McLaughlin, for her tireless efforts in helping me get the final version of this book across the finish line. I would like to thank the two anonymous reviewers who read this work for the University of Michigan Press for their many helpful recommendations as well as Elizabeth Demers, my editor at the University of Michigan Press. Finally, and most significantly, I would like to thank my wife Becky for her unending support. To everyone that I have mentioned here and to countless others that I have not, thank you all. Without you, this book could not have come to fruition. I did not build it on my own. You were all there at key moments. Thank you!

Contents

Digital materials related to this title can be found on the Fulcrum platform via the following citable URL: https://doi.org/10.3998/mpub.11656190

ONE

Introduction

The Centrality of Regulation to Trade Politics

Airbags, Antibiotics in Pork, and the Newest Generation of Cancer Drugs

American and European airbags are different.[1] European airbags are tested based on the assumption that vehicle occupants are wearing their seat belts. That the automakers know where the head of an occupant wearing a seat belt will be in a crash leads to a smaller, more focused airbag. Conversely, given that many Americans do not wear seat belts, U.S. airbags are tested based on the assumption that the occupants are not wearing seat belts, necessitating a larger airbag. For most automakers, it is prohibitively costly to design an airbag that meets safety requirements in both Europe and the United States. Thus automakers must either have two production lines for airbags or, if they have only one production line, forgo sales in a major market.

Another regulatory difference involves pedestrian impact testing.[2] In the United States, safety specifications revolve around just one idea: protect the people inside the vehicle. In the European Union, however, because cities are denser and because a much higher percentage of accidents involve pedestrians, automobiles must be designed and tested to reduce injury to both the vehicle's passengers and any pedestrian struck by the vehicle. One test within the constellation of regulations that accompany this goal, the child headform test, involves launching a ball into the hood of a car to simulate a small child being struck by the car. The United States does not have such a test. These differences mean that vehicles have to be produced one way for one market and a different way for another. Both the testing and airbag regulatory differences drive up the cost of trade for automakers in the two most lucrative auto markets in the world.

Pork is the mainstay meat of the Chinese diet. The average Chinese person consumes nearly 90 pounds of pork per year, with the country as a whole consuming nearly half a billion pigs annually, a number growing as living standards and demand for meat expand.[3] U.S. pork producers are some of the most efficient in the world, producing 23 billion pounds of pork annually, and would love to gain significant market share in this most lucrative of export opportunities.[4] But American pork producers give their swine ractopamine, an antibiotic, banned by China, that has the side effect of promoting accelerated growth. A regulatory barrier thus inhibits trade between the country with the world's most prolific pork eaters and that with the world's most efficient pork producers, which also happen to be the two states with the most important economic relationship in the twenty-first century.

Pharmaceutical research has now advanced to the point where medications can be made not just from synthetic components but also from living cells. The latter drugs, called "biologics," represent some of the most cutting-edge research in the pharmaceutical industry and may soon lead to medicines for maladies that currently have little or no effective treatment. Just one kind of biologic drug, PD-1 inhibitors have generated huge excitement in the medical community due to their heightened efficacy in fighting certain cancers. These drugs are a generational leap forward from their predecessors and may do for cancer therapy what AZT did for HIV. PD-1 inhibitors like Merck's Keytruda are miracles in pill form; they are also wildly expensive.[5] Biologics, even more than other drugs, can come with astoundingly high costs.[6]

Promoting innovation while controlling costs is the central dilemma of intellectual property regulation in pharmaceuticals. Trade-related intellectual property rules have generally only applied to synthetic chemical compounds, so covering biologics with intellectual property regulations requires new rulemaking efforts at the international level. For obvious reasons, pharmaceutical companies are highly reluctant to produce drugs in or import drugs into countries in which the companies' intellectual property rights will not be upheld. Differences in regulation on intellectual property thus have the power to impede the international trade in pharmaceuticals. The tension over these regulatory barriers played out between the United

States and other states in the negotiations of the Trans-Pacific Partnership (TPP), now sans America. The United States wanted to maximize the regulatory protections on biologics by granting 12 years of data exclusivity, while other states wanted 5 years or less.[7] The disagreement over that regulatory protection, perhaps the most contentious issue on the entire TPP docket, was the very last issue resolved in the negotiations.[8]

The Practical Significance of Regulatory Trade Barriers

The difference in airbag rules, the disagreement over ractopamine in pork, and the negotiations over data exclusivity in biologics are just three of the many examples of cross-national differences in regulation constituting significant impediments to international trade. These regulatory trade barriers are everywhere. They affect traded goods worth trillions of dollars annually and influence a wide range of policy areas. Regulatory and other nontariff trade barriers are becoming so important that the World Trade Organization's 2012 Trade Report was entirely dedicated to them; the WTO director-general stated that these nontariff measures "will not follow a path of diminishing relevance like tariffs have done. They will not shrink in importance. Regulatory interventions . . . with inevitable consequences for trade flows and investment are here to stay."[9] Not only are regulatory barriers important for trade, but they also affect nearly everyone's daily lives. Everyone eats, and a large portion of their food has been traded before it is consumed. The differences in national regulations affect how safe that food is and how much it costs. Everyone wears clothes, and the connection between the textiles trade and labor standards affects the conditions under which millions of people work and what it costs a consumer to be clothed. Many people take medications, and including intellectual property regulations in trade agreements influences how quickly new drugs come to the market and whether poor people in developing countries have access to medicines. Many people drive automobiles, and the safety and environmental regulations on automobiles affect the chances of a person surviving an accident, as well as the environmental impact of a driver's daily commute. In virtually all industries, by inhibiting or promoting firms' ability to sell goods in multiple markets, regulatory trade barriers impact businesses' profit margins and, in turn, workers' paychecks. Regulatory trade barriers have real-world consequences for just about everyone. This book explains the politics that surrounds them.

How This Study of Regulatory Trade Barriers Advances Scholarship in International Political Economy (IPE)

As I discuss in chapter 2 of this study, it has been well understood, since at least the 1980s, that nontariff impediments to trade, especially those that are regulatory in nature, have become more important trade barriers than tariffs or quotas. Still, notwithstanding this broad understanding, prominent theories of trade politics have failed to adequately explain the politics surrounding those trade barriers. As I explain in this chapter and in chapter 3, negotiations have not broken along cleavage-based lines as theories built on Ricardo-Viner and Stolper-Samuelsson theorems would predict.

Additionally, as I show throughout this book, activists have played a crucial and largely underappreciated role in these negotiations. The book explains what initially motivates activists to engage on regulatory trade barriers, what factors help them overcome collective action problems (and what makes those problems more difficult to overcome), and what helps them get a full hearing from government officials. Examining activists' role in these issues is crucial to building a more accurate understanding of the political negotiations over these issues. Obviously, materialist assumptions can still be part of political analyses. Even if workers and firms are understood in purely rational-materialist ways, they will still engage in political action and seek government officials' assistance. The problem is that these materialist assumptions tend to lead to an underappreciation of the importance of noncommercial motivations and of framing effects. I argue that drawing those motivations and effects into the discussion, as this book does, brings a fuller set of political explanations to bear on these questions.

Explaining, also, how government officials act on these issues, this book adds greater nuance and precision to explanations of regulatory trade barriers. Furthermore, the motivations of and roles played by government officials in the destruction, preservation, and dismantling of regulatory barriers has not been sufficiently theorized. The place of government officials in most existing analyses of trade politics has centered on the assumption that those actors represent constituencies to which they are accountable. Though surely correct, that assumption is incomplete. Government officials are more than mere conduits for constituents' interests. Their actions are driven by their government's and/or agency's institutional and staffing makeup as well as by their beliefs about the prioritization of trade expansion versus regulatory sovereignty and about their core constituency and role definitions.

Activists and government officials may have less tangibly commercial interests in regulatory trade barriers than their business counterparts, but that does not mean that they are automatically less interested in those regulations. The negotiations that surround regulatory barriers are as intrinsically political as they are economic. Of course, there will be some issues on which activists do not become highly engaged; in Chapter 3, I explain what factors are more likely to lead to that situation. On those issues, the more materialist, more traditional arguments are likely to be stronger, but I argue that framing effects and the beliefs of government officials are important even in those cases. Illustrating this dynamic are the discussions of U.S. domestic content rules for cars in chapter 4 and of the negotiation of the Agreement on Trade-Related Aspects of Intellectual Property Rights (TRIPS) in chapter 6.

Improving on Cleavage-Based Explanations

Trade politics no longer operates the way it once did. Ricardo famously argued that trade benefits countries by allowing them to specialize in producing the goods in which they have the greatest comparative advantage and then to trade that good for products in which they do not have a comparative advantage. The Heckscher-Ohlin and Stolper-Samuelson theorems built on this logic to argue that trade would help the owners of a society's abundant factor, as that abundance is what drives a country's comparative advantage. Therefore, trade would benefit the owners of capital in a capital-intensive country like the United States. The political corollary to that argument is that the owners of a society's abundant factors will favor trade liberalization, while the owners of a society's scarce factors are likely to seek protection. Thus, in the United States, the owners of capital are likely to advocate free trade, while low-skilled laborers are likely to oppose free trade.

Two of the most famous works on trade politics, Rogowski's *Commerce and Coalitions* and Hiscox's *International Trade and Political Conflict*, build their arguments on different kinds of cleavage.[10] Rogowski assumed that there are three groups in society: landowners, laborers, and capital owners.[11] In a given society, if capital and labor are abundant but land is scarce, trade will help laborers and capital owners, the holders of the abundant resources, but will hurt landowners, the holders of the scarce resource. The capital owners and laborers will form a coalition to push for greater trade, while landowners will advocate for protectionism. That society will thus have an urban-rural political cleavage. Labor and land being abundant but capital being scarce leads to a red-green coalition against the capitalists.

Hiscox added greater nuance to this framework by showing that under conditions of low factor mobility (i.e., high asset specificity), cleavages are more likely to be between different industry sectors rather than different social classes. The cleavage-based framework has been employed by others as well.[12] At its core, these cleavage-based explanations assert that trade generates economic benefits for some slice of society and shrinks the benefits that go to other slices of society, with the political struggle over trade amounting to a fight between the winners and losers from trade.

As helpful as these theories can be in explaining trade politics that are unrelated to regulation, they struggle to explain the politics of regulatory trade barriers. Because they are inclined to focus on trade's material economic implications, they tend to ignore those societal actors, such as consumer advocates and access-to-medicine activists, who have an interest in trade but are motivated by noneconomic policy goals. As trade has increasingly impacted regulations, such actors have proliferated. In many disputes over regulatory barriers, some actors, such as consumer groups, have acted in ways that are at odds with their apparent economic interests, which cleavage-based explanations expect to drive their preferences.

The cleavage-based explanations also imply that firms seeking to limit trade would advocate for greater regulatory trade barriers, but as I show in this book, firms have not tended to do that, at least since the 1980s. As I discuss in chapter 3, when businesses seek protectionism, they tend to request nonregulatory means of protection, such as antidumping duties or voluntary export restraints, because those measures offer the same benefit without limiting businesses' flexibility as would regulations.

An additional reason cleavage-based frameworks struggle to explain developments concerned with regulatory trade barriers is that they either ignore the role played by government officials or depict them as the mouthpiece of firms located in their state. Either approach is problematic. Understanding the intersection of trade and the environment, for example, requires examining the policy goals of environmental nongovernmental organizations (NGOs) as well as government officials' preferences on environmental regulation.

Cross-national differences in regulation have become the most prominent issue in trade politics and continue to grow more important. Thus the failure to explain regulatory barriers constitutes a large and expanding blind spot for cleavage-based explanations. Now that trade is inextricably bound up with regulation, the politics that surround it are new and require a new set of explanations. This study provides one of those explanations. Bringing in nonbusiness actors (i.e., activists and government officials) and examining their new actions that are less commercially oriented (i.e., issue framing around competitiveness and preventing needless death) is one of the major scholarly contributions that I hope this book makes.

Thickening the Politics in IPE: Providing a Political Companion to the New Trade Theories

Since the mid-1980s, there has been a series of theoretical improvements in scholars' explanation of the economic logics of trade. New Trade Theory (NTT), advanced most famously by Paul Krugman as well as by others, helped analysts consider the implications that increasing returns to scale, network effect, product differentiation, and oligopolistic competition could have on international trade. New New Trade Theory (NNTT) later pointed out that increasing trade could have varying implications even for different firms within an industry, helping the most efficient and challenging the less efficient. These theoretical advances were useful in explicating the reasoning underlying businesses desire to trade, and I build much of the theoretical foundation of the business part of my theory on these advances.

But NTT and NNTT are mostly devoid of politics, and in the few instances when they do consider politics, their analysis makes a key faulty assumption. NTT expects states to use disguised protectionism in an effort to become a dominant production node in high-value industries. As I show repeatedly in this book, governments do not do that. When businesses seek and governments grant protectionism, that protectionism is not regulatory in nature. Governments do, however, seek to reduce other states' regulatory barriers. Businesses either advocate for reducing regulatory barriers or stay silent. I argue that when regulatory barriers arise, they are the product not of the kind of dynamic that NTT would expect but of activists successfully pushing for specifically national regulation to address their policy concerns. Evidence in support of this claim is provided in all subsequent chapters in this study. NNTT has relatively little to say about politics, save for the implication that strong firms are more likely to seek liberalization than are weak firms. While that is true, a number of differences between businesses' politics (large versus small; eager compliers versus skeptical compliers) affect their politics as well.

NTT and NNTT struggle when they get to politics because they do not take into account that trade touching on domestic regulations brings in activists who otherwise might not care about trade but have an interest in those regulations. Government officials then have more numerous and more varied incentives and demands to juggle. One cannot understand the politics of regulatory trade barriers without accounting for activists and government officials. Trade is not just an economic phenomenon; it is also a political one. The politics involved must be theorized just as carefully as the economics.

A Hard Case for Resisting Globalization

This study uniquely demonstrates the limitations of globalization's power to compel policy adjustment in areas in which that power should be at its strongest. Globalization-driven policy convergence is especially likely to be the case in policy areas that tangibly and significantly affect other states' commercial opportunities. Such impacts lead to greater pressure from foreigners to amend state policies. This is why trade-related regulations present such an interesting test case for the power of globalization. In some ways, it is not surprising that governments' welfare, infrastructure, and defense policies do not show much convergence. In each of these cases, strong reasons for governments to jealously guard their autonomy, limited commercial gains to the state from adjusting to be more like other countries, and relatively small commercial impacts on foreigners yield relatively little objection to policy autonomy.

Trade-related policies are a different matter. When a given policy affects another state's commercial opportunities in that country, it leads to much pressure to adjust that policy. Moreover, because trade liberalization generally occurs reciprocally, adjusting that policy holds out the promise of one state benefiting from greater access to another state's market. As I show in chapter 2, domestic regulations have become the central issue in trade politics. Unlike in the case of policies that generally do not directly affect foreigners, the incentives to adjust trade regulations may be quite large. Additionally, the generally low salience of most regulations means that making these changes should be relatively easy when compared to altering policies in areas like the level of social spending. If business-driven globalization dominates anywhere, it ought to be in the area of regulatory trade barriers, but even there, the extent of policy stickiness is striking.

In IPE scholarship, there is a debate between two camps regarding globalization's impact on trade policies. In one camp are those scholars who see globalization as exerting a great deal of pressure on governments to adjust their policies in ways that make them more similar to those in other countries. In the other camp are those scholars who argue that states are likely to maintain their policy differences despite globalization's pressure.[13] This study lands squarely in the second camp, though it suggests some circumstances under which the first camp may sometimes be correct.

The Question and My Answer

When the differences between countries' domestic regulations impede trade, the states involved have three options: they can reduce those barriers, increase them, or do nothing. This book asks when states are more likely to do each of these and why. I argue that regulatory trade barriers are most likely to be reduced when firms are able to link their desire for that reduction with societal concerns about economic competitiveness, while activists are likely to succeed at increasing or defending regulatory trade barriers when they can link their desire for maintaining or increasing that barrier with preventing needless death. Reducing regulatory trade barriers may not be the same thing as reducing regulations. If regulations are harmonized upward, that is still a reduction in a trade barrier. In the present study, I am analyzing the extent to which regulatory differences impede trade, not the overall level of regulation.

Major Alternative Explanations and Case Selection

The primary alternative explanations against which I am arguing (and that I discuss in more detail in chapter 3) are the cleavage-based explanations, the idea that regulatory barriers are merely disguised protectionism, the argument that material business interests dominate, the California effect, and state-centric explanations. As Drezner points out, the paucity of good data on regulatory barriers makes statistical analysis all but impossible; case studies and process tracing are therefore the most fruitful research method and are what I employ throughout this book.[14] This work is thus broadly consistent with the "analytic narratives" research methods employed by James Shoch in his analysis of political parties' influence on U.S. trade policy in the 1980s and 1990s and with the "grounded theory" approach employed by Margaret Keck and Kathryn Sikkink in their examination of civil society activists.[15] Within my case studies, I relied on any public information I could find: industry and NGO statements, the congressional record, government reports, newspaper articles, and other secondary sources. Most of the evidence presented here is from secondary sources, in line with the scholarly literature in this research vein. Again, in terms of style but not content, I am following in Drezner's footsteps. The majority of the material he used for *All Politics Is Global* was publicly available information, as was also the case for Buthe and Mattli's *The New Global Rulers*, Shoch's *Trading Blows*, and books by Susan Aaronson.[16]

The cases that I selected for the analysis in this book help to test my hypothesis in several ways. First, they present hard cases for my argument, against each of the alternative explanations. As I mentioned above, regulatory trade barriers, perhaps more than any other policy area, should be an area where business-driven globalization dominates. Additionally, huge sums of money are at stake in these three sectors. Given these large economic stakes, we should see the politics on trade in these areas center on the economic actors involved and the cleavages between the economic winners and losers on a given issue, yet, time and again (as will be pointed out in the following chapters), the politics surrounding these negotiations does not fall along cleavage lines. Given that there are such large commercial stakes involved, one might think that state interests would be simple and straightforward and that the state-centric arguments might be adequate explanations, but this study shows that the trajectory of the politics on these issues requires going inside states. Given those large stakes and the fact that there is considerable national-level regulation in each of these industries, we should clearly see if regulatory trade barriers are disguised protectionism being pushed by import-competing rent seekers, yet that is not what happens in these cases.

Second, these cases break out into a number of subcases, meaning that there is considerable variation within these cases as well as between the three of them. There are 11 subcases analyzed in respect to automobiles, 8 in respect to beef, and 6 in respect to drugs. The comparisons between cases generate insights that can be applied to other industries, while subcase variation within each case allows for detailed process tracing and empirical depth. Using these cases means that while this book does not gain the advantages of using large-*N* quantitative analysis, it allows enough space to analyze the cases at many points in time. In this way, each case becomes many data points instead of one. We can be more confident in the hypothesis examined here if it holds in the cases at time x as well as times $x + 1$, $x + 2$, $x + 3$, and so forth. This variance also means that findings from this study are not likely to be idiosyncratic to one sector. Had I chosen three agriculture-related industries, for example, any patterns I found might simply have been due to some idiosyncrasy within that field. Collectively, agriculture, manufacturing, and advanced technology comprise three of the most important kinds of internationally traded goods. Given how varied these three industries are, it is safe to say that they are at least fairly representative of the types of goods traded internationally. Moreover, each of them is a quintessential industry in its sector. If one wants to know how regulatory barriers affect manufacturing, the automotive industry is an excellent place to start. The same is true for beef in agriculture and for pharmaceuticals in high technology.

Third, each case constitutes its own empirical puzzle. The automobile case is centered on the puzzle that regulatory barriers were reduced within Europe and within North America but not between them. The explanations that could be used to elucidate the intraregional reduction—such as economies of scale, factor-price differences, cleavage-based explanations, or business-driven globalization—would have predicted interregional reduction, yet that did not happen. Conversely, explanations that could be used to illuminate the lack of interregional reduction, such as the disguised protectionism argument or differences in regulatory strategy, would predict prevention of intraregional reduction, yet that did not happen either.

The case of the beef industry is centered on the puzzle that even though factors that scholars consider important for explaining trade politics remained static throughout the period examined (2003–13), there was still significant movement in the extent to which regulatory differences impeded the trade in beef between the United States and Japan. The institutional context remained the same, and examining cases where the institutional context is constant allows for a more accurate examination of noninstitutional factors. My argument is not that institutions have no importance but that they are not the sole entities that matter; a number of other noninstitutional factors may augment or attenuate trade barriers. The market power of each state also did not significantly shift over this time. As with institutions, choosing a case where this remains constant allows for a clearer examination of other factors.

The case of the pharmaceutical industry centers on the puzzle that despite similar power asymmetries between developing and developed countries throughout the time period analyzed, there are highly varied outcomes in the movement of regulatory trade barriers. They were significantly reduced in the TRIPS Agreement, reinforced in the Doha Declaration, subject to political draw in subsequent WTO negotiations and in India's use of TRIPS flexibilities, kept the same as part of the Free Trade Area of the Americas, and finally reduced in the Central America Free Trade Agreement. Additionally, it is puzzling that developing states agreed to TRIPS in the first place (given that TRIPS was not in their interests) and that the United States backed down in the negotiations over the Doha Declaration, despite its economic and diplomatic power.

Fourth, each case study has other attributes that augment its contribution to the scholarly literature. The automotive industry was one of the earliest sectors to be highly affected by regulatory barriers, so findings from there may preview dynamics we are likely to see in other sectors as they become entangled in these barriers. Examining the auto industry also allows for an investigation into one the most fundamental trends in trade:

the rise of regionalism. Trade in automobiles is one of the clearest manifestations of this trend; almost three-quarters of the trade in automobiles is intraregional.[17] Analyzing the auto industry thus helps illuminate why trade liberalization has progressed more at the regional level than globally.

The case involving regulations related to mad cow disease and the U.S.-Japan beef trade has not yet been thoroughly analyzed by scholars. The disputes surrounding growth hormones and genetically modified organisms (GMOs) have already received large amounts of scholarly attention.[18] If we scholars want to learn something that we do not already know and if we believe the already-examined cases were adequately analyzed, the most fruitful intellectual route is to study cases that have not already been exhaustively investigated. Chapter 5 of this book does just that.

The pharmaceuticals case is useful because it tackles regulatory barriers, such as compulsory licensing, that are becoming increasingly significant. As countries grow older and wealthier, the health care sector is likely to become that much more important. Additionally, intellectual property is one of the regulatory areas that most clearly pit developing and developed countries against each other, so examining that issue allows for an exploration of that dynamic too.

Finally, given how much is at stake economically in these cases, there is a great deal of practical significance in studying them. In 2017, trade in automotive products, food, and pharmaceuticals was valued at $1.4 trillion, $1.5 trillion, and $550 billion respectively.[19] Each of these industries affects millions of workers and billions of consumers. They are all large important industries and merit attention simply on that consideration.

How Regulations Became Central to Trade Politics

In chapter 2, I explain how national regulations became central to international trade politics. By the 1970s, six rounds of negotiations on the General Agreement on Tariffs and Trade (GATT) had reduced tariffs to a fraction of what they were in the 1940s. As tariffs receded, nontariff barriers (NTBs) became more significant. The Tokyo Round launched in 1973 was the first round of GATT negotiations to address these NTBs. The expansion of trade and national regulations, combined with the increased sophistication of traded products and the heightened level of trade within industries, further raised the significance of regulatory trade barriers. In the 1980s, states becoming more concerned with their export performance and Western businesses pushing for trade rules in new areas added to this significance.

The Uruguay Round further constrained NTBs, which made regulatory barriers more important, placed new rules on states' use of regulations that had trade implications, and brought those new rules under a more robust process of dispute settlement. As trade agreements increasingly impacted regulations, trade politics engaged labor unions, environmentalists, consumer safety activists, and access-to-medicine advocates previously uninterested in trade but interested in regulations. These activists pushed for specifically national regulations that can function to impede trade. Businesses have sought to reduce these regulatory trade barriers. Finding agreement on these regulatory barriers has been impossible in the Doha Round, which has fueled the proliferation of regional and bilateral trade deals.

Summary Preview of My Argument

In chapter 3, I present my main argument. I assert that businesses seek to reduce regulatory trade barriers when those barriers raise production costs or inhibit market access. They may, however, choose to end that pursuit if complying with those regulations is cheap or if pursuing that reduction carries reputational risk. My argument is not that businesses are reflexively antiregulation but that because businesses tend to dislike when regulatory differences between states abrade international trade, they seek to reduce the extent of that abrasion. In some instances, as in the case of emissions standards in the European Union (analyzed in chapter 4), this reduction may mean raising standards to a common high level. Contra businesses, activists defend specifically national regulations, even if those amount to regulatory trade barriers, when they perceive those regulations to be the sole effective means to address a societal problem of concern to them. They may accept a reduction in regulatory trade barriers if those barriers have low salience or if their opposition is bought out through corporate social responsibility, private standards, or some other arrangement. Government officials choose whether to side with businesses or activists based on their relative prioritization of trade and regulatory independence, their staffing, and their identified core constituency. Concerns about economic competitiveness stack these factors in favor of business more broadly and of reducing regulatory trade barriers specifically. Concerns about needless death stack these factors in favor of activists and of maintaining or increasing those barriers. This pattern can be seen throughout the cases analyzed in chapters 4–7.

Cars

In chapter 4, I examine environmental, labor, and consumer safety regulations and the international trade in automobiles in North America and Europe. I ask why intraregional regulatory trade barriers were reduced in Europe and North America but not between those regions.

Europe

From 1983 to 1988, environmentalists demanded an increase in emissions standards in some states in the European Community, regarding such increase as the most effective means of alleviating salient environmental degradation. Automakers opposed an increase in emissions standards in these European Community states because those standards would have amounted to regulatory trade barriers that would have raised their production costs and inhibited their market access. Government officials in Denmark and the Netherlands sided with environmentalists, but officials in France and Italy as well as at the European Community level were more concerned with promoting economic competitiveness and sided with the automakers. The regulatory barriers were thus not allowed to be raised.

In 1989–90, complying with higher emissions standards became cheaper for automakers in Europe, so the automakers' opposition to the standards softened. Environmentalism had continued to strengthen, and the political force pushing for higher standards had increased. Government officials still prioritized advancing the single market and agreed to prevent regulatory trade barriers related to emissions by raising emissions standards to the highest feasible level.

North America

In the United States in the early 1980s, the United Auto Workers felt that domestic content rules were the only way to stem rising unemployment in the auto industry and pushed for domestic content regulations. Automakers opposed those regulations because they would have raised production costs. The automakers linked their opposition to concerns about U.S. competitiveness. The Republican-controlled Senate and White House stood with automakers in opposing domestic content rules, so those regulatory barriers were never raised.

In the early 1980s, Mexico had domestic content rules, which were making Mexican cars uncompetitive in export markets. This problem became much more acute as a result of the Latin American debt crisis. Automakers lobbied to reduce the rules. Additionally, as a result of changes in the Mexican economy, businesses that favored trade liberalization became much more powerful over the course of the decade. The new leaders of the Mexican government at the time, President de la Madrid and President Salinas, had much tighter connections to these businesses than their predecessors had and were willing to marginalize Mexican labor unions from the trade policymaking process. This marginalization led to the reduction of regulatory barriers concerned with domestic content.

In Canada, businesses also became more favorably disposed toward trade liberalization. The MacDonald Commission Report recommended greater trade with the United States as an alleviation of Canada's economic malaise. That recommendation gave intellectual and political cover to Brian Mulroney, the Conservative prime minister, to pursue a free trade agreement with the United States, even though doing so contradicted decades of Canadian trade policy. Canadian labor unions sat out of those free trade negotiations and thus facilitated government and businesses working together to reduce domestic content regulatory barriers as part of the free trade deal with the United States.

These dynamics continued in the United States, Mexico, and Canada into the early 1990s, which led to the North American Free Trade Agreement entirely removing domestic content regulatory barriers between those three states. Meanwhile, environmentalists saw NAFTA as an opportunity to embed environmental regulations into trade negotiations, but businesses were determined to prevent environmental regulatory trade barriers from raising their production costs. Unlike in the case of labor, Mexican and U.S. officials were somewhat sympathetic to environmentalists' policy goals. To prevent the emergence of environmental regulatory barriers, government officials in these two states increased enforcement of Mexico's domestic environmental regulations and added language to NAFTA that sanctions states for not enforcing their own environmental regulations.

Automakers have not called for reduced regulatory differences between the United States and Mexico related to consumer safety, because those differences have been not only cheap in terms of compliance but also a source of profit. Mexican consumers have not pushed for increased regulations either, because they are more concerned with maintaining access to affordable automobiles than with ensuring that vehicles abide by the full range of American safety standards. Given that neither societal interest has become engaged on the issue, government officials have not been incentivized to attempt to reduce that regulatory difference.

U.S. consumer safety advocates became alarmed, however, at the difference in safety between U.S. trucks and Mexican trucks that would be allowed to enter the United States as a part of NAFTA. They were able to portray these Mexican trucks as a potentially lethal threat. Persuaded by that argument, U.S. officials banned Mexican trucks. The officials did not lift the ban until after those consumer safety advocates were satisfied with Mexican trucks and after U.S. businesses hurt by retaliatory sanctions began lobbying on the issue and arguing that the regulatory trade barrier was undermining their competitiveness in the Mexican market.

Interregional

Regulatory differences between the United States and the European Union on consumer safety issues raised production costs for automakers, who initially attempted to convince government officials to reduce those differences. Consumer safety advocates and national government officials in both places held, however, that their specific regulations were saving lives. Unwilling to potentially jeopardize that outcome for the sake of trade, the advocates and officials resolutely opposed the automakers on those regulatory barriers. Consumer safety advocates won on that issue, because they were able to portray the regulatory barriers as preventing needless death.

Beef

In chapter 5, I analyze consumer safety regulations related to mad cow disease and the trade in beef between the United States and Japan. After the first case of bovine spongiform encephalopathy (BSE) was found in the United States, Japan's more-stringent safety regulations applied to imports of beef from the United States. American cattlemen did not want to abide by these regulations that would raise their production costs, but refusing to do so cost cattlemen access to the Japanese market. Japanese consumer safety advocates robustly defended anti-BSE regulations as the only way to ensure the safety of beef. American officials at the United States Department of Agriculture and the Office of the United States Trade Representative had strong mandates to promote sales in the meat industry and American exports respectively. At the USDA in particular, a number of high-ranking officials had direct personal connections with the meat industry. U.S officials thus sided with American cattlemen and attempted to get Japan to reduce those regulatory barriers. Japanese officials at the Ministry of Agriculture and Ministry of Health had badly botched the response to Japan's first case of BSE in 2001 and needed to win back credibility with consumers on the issue, so they resisted reducing the barriers.

In negotiations from May 2004 to December 2005, Japanese consumer activists and U.S. cattlemen continued to hold their respective positions. The Japanese and U.S. governments eventually settled on a deal in which U.S. beef exports would not have to undergo universal BSE testing on exports from cattle 20 months old or younger and with all specified risk material removed. That deal took time to reach, because the regulations were highly salient for Japanese consumer safety advocates, who took the details of the regulations very seriously, and because much of the decision-making process was located in an institution, the Food Safety Commission, which was receptive to the arguments of consumer advocates.

After a U.S. producer made a serious safety mistake in January 2006, Japanese consumer groups were reenergized to push for more-stringent BSE regulations, which were opposed by U.S. producers and U.S. officials. Japanese officials ultimately allowed the resumption of U.S. beef imports but agreed to new requirements promoted by those consumer activists. In 2007, after the World Animal Health Organization improved the risk classification of the United States, beef producers in the United States sought to remove all age restrictions on nonuniversally tested exports. Japanese consumer groups opposed their removal. Some kind of compromise or buyout might have been possible, but U.S. beef producers and the U.S. government rejected that approach. Consequently, Japanese government officials sided with the consumer activists and maintained the regulatory barriers. In 2009, the Democratic Party of Japan came to power and, after having harshly criticized the Liberal Democratic Party for being too eager to compromise with the United States on these issues, could not afford to be seen as doing the same thing, especially once a basing dispute over Okinawa became more contentious. These factors ensured that the Japanese government would continue to stand with the consumer activists, and the regulatory barriers were maintained.

Beginning in 2010, the Japanese government took some initial steps to join the Trans-Pacific Partnership, which brought exporters into the negotiations over Japan's regulatory barriers on U.S. beef. The United States had concluded a free trade deal with South Korea that same year. Japanese businesses fearing that they would become less competitive in the American market relative to their South Korean rivals lobbied the Japanese government to enter into the TPP negotiations. Once regulatory barriers in beef became embedded in a larger constellation of trade issues, the Ministry of Industry, which has traditionally been less protectionist than the Ministry of Agriculture, became the leading player in formulating Japan's trade policy.

In 2012, the mood in Japan regarding the country's BSE countermeasures had begun to shift. The number of BSE cases worldwide had fallen from 37,000 to just 29,[20] and most middle-class urban consumers in Japan were accepting of American beef. The diminishing consumer hostility to relaxing the regulatory trade barriers on American beef imports was essential in giving the Japanese government the political space to agree to those relaxations. Even with Japanese export-oriented businesses pushing for the TPP, the government would have found it very difficult to relax those regulatory trade barriers on beef had the general public still been aroused in opposition. In 2013, the Japanese government announced that it would increase the age exception to universal testing to 30 months, which greatly reduced the regulatory barriers impeding American cattlemen's access to the Japanese market.

Drugs, TRIPS, and the Doha Declaration

In chapter 6, I analyze intellectual property (IP) regulations and the trade in pharmaceuticals involving the United States and India. As IP regulations in developing countries became more injurious to the interests of Western drug firms, the firms became more highly motivated to reduce those regulatory trade barriers. Activists who might have fought against the firms' efforts were not yet engaged in IP politics. With businesses promoting the Agreement on Trade-Related Aspects of Intellectual Property Rights and with activists largely silent, government officials in the United States and India faced one-sided incentives and gave businesses what they were asking for: significantly reduced regulatory trade barriers related to IP.

In the second half of the 1990s, the AIDS epidemic grew into a public health nightmare, especially in sub-Saharan Africa. Given the relative newness of the disease, practically all of the effective HIV drugs were patented and thus expensive. Poor people were dying of a disease for which effective medicines existed but were far too expensive for them to afford. Public health advocates began to take a much closer look at the connection between IP regulations and the cost of medicines and concluded that the high IP regulations mandated by TRIPS were the main drivers behind the expense of the medicines and thus complicit in widespread death. Drug companies compounded this imagery when they sued the South African government over measures it had taken to stem the AIDS crisis. Even after the drug companies dropped the suit, developing countries and access-to-medicine advocates wanted states to have more flexibility under TRIPS to institute different IP regulations. For a variety of reasons, the U.S. government, which normally would have been expected to oppose any increase in regulatory barriers on IP in pharmaceuticals, relented and accepted the Doha Declaration, which strengthened the ability of developing states to implement different IP regulations, most notably compulsory licenses.

Drugs Post-Doha

In chapter 7, I examine the negotiations over regulatory barriers in pharmaceuticals after the Doha Declaration. The Doha Declaration was a big victory for access-to-medicine advocates and developing countries, but it did not settle three issues: (1) which diseases warranted compulsory licens-

TABLE 1.1. Main Actors in Trade Politics

	Businesses	Activists	Government Officials
Cars	German, Italian, French automakers U.S. Big Three Canadian firms Mexican exporters U.S. exporters	EC environmentalists North American labor unions EU and U.S. consumer safety advocates	Danish/Dutch EC-level USTR Canadian PM Mexican president NHTSA director
Beef	U.S. cattlemen Specialty U.S. beef producers Japanese exporters in TPP negotiations	Japanese consumer safety advocates	USDA USTR Japanese Department of Agriculture Japanese Food Safety Commission Japanese party officials
Drugs, TRIPS to Doha	Research-based pharmaceutical companies Indian generic drug companies	Access-to-medicine advocates	USTR Developing states' trade negotiators Congressional Democrats State Department South African government
Drugs, Post-Doha	Research-based pharmaceutical companies Indian generic drug companies	Access-to-medicine advocates	USTR Indian, Brazilian, Central American trade negotiators SCOTUS Indian judiciary Indian PM Modi

ing, (2) what exceptions to make for states that did not have production capacity, and (3) whether nonviolation complaints could move forward. On which diseases to cover, Doha's language was never clarified to either side's benefit. On production capacity, the same flexibilities were granted to states without it as to other states. On nonviolation complaints, there has been a rolling temporary moratorium. In sum, the regulatory barriers on these issues remained static through a mix of constructive ambiguity and stalemate.

Under the provisions of TRIPS, India had to implement TRIPS-compliant IP regulations beginning in 2005. India's officials have found a number of creative policy means for relaxing their IP regulations. By using a narrow set of patentability requirements and giving greater policy access for patent opponents, they limited which drugs could get patented. They also employed novel injunction policies as well as compulsory licenses to control drug prices. All these measures made India's IP regulations differ significantly from the high IP standards wanted by the United States. All the measures were also technically TRIPS-compliant. Still, India has been judicious in its use of the measures (employing them much less than they otherwise could have), to maintain amicable relations with U.S. drug firms and U.S. businesses more generally and, by extension, to protect the competitiveness of their domestic pharmaceutical industry.

Meanwhile, the United States was negotiating free trade agreements with a number of countries, especially in Latin America. At the time of these negotiations in the middle and late 2000s, pharmaceutical firms were able to develop a much closer relationship with the Office of the United States Trade Representative than were access-to-medicine advocates, to some degree marginalizing the latter from the policymaking process. Meanwhile, the size of the American market and the potential lucrativeness of access to that market generated loud competitiveness-based claims within Latin American countries, overwhelming the political voice of access-to-medicine advocates. Regulatory trade barriers were significantly reduced by ratcheting up those countries' IP regulations related to pharmaceuticals. In the one instance where this did not happen, the Free Trade Agreement of the Americas, access-to-medicine advocates in Brazil were more effective and mobilized than elsewhere, and the government of Brazil was less concerned with competitiveness as a political issue than were governments elsewhere.

Implications of This Study for Businesses, Activists, and Government Officials

I begin chapter 8 by reviewing the evidence this book provides in support of its major claims: the power of framing issues around competitiveness and death, the need to question cleavage-based explanations, the counterintuitive paucity of using regulatory trade barriers as disguised protectionism, and the underappreciated political power of activists in this policy space. Next, I discuss this book's other theoretical implications for IPE scholarship: it qualifies the California effect, highlights the growing importance of national courts in international trade politics, helps explain the rise of regionalism, clarifies developing countries' forward options in trade policy, and points to emerging vectors in the U.S.-China relationship.[21] I then apply lessons from those cases to other cases and industries. Finally, I offer political recommendations for the businesses, NGOs, and government officials examined in this book.

TABLE 1.2. Interplay between Actors and Outcomes in Trade Politics

Subcase	Business	Activists	Government Officials	Outcome
Cars Emissions in EC, 1983–88	Opposed higher emissions standards, as they would hurt competitiveness by raising production costs and inhibiting access to states with those standards **Able to use competitiveness framing**	Pursued by activists, particularly in the Netherlands and Denmark, to combat environmental degradation **Not able to use death prevention framing**	French and Italian officials sided with automakers, Dutch and Danish officials with activists, EC officials with automakers **Officials more concerned with being competitive**	Regulatory trade barriers related to emissions standards were not allowed to be raised **RTB prevented**
Emissions in EC, 1989–90	Softer opposition because catalytic converters were cheaper and unleaded more available; thus, higher emissions standards were less threat to competitiveness **Less strong competitiveness framing**	Environmentalists had grown stronger across Europe; Danish activists were even more resolute **Not a needless death framing but stronger overall advocacy**	EC officials identified with activists; automakers wanted to forge common market and be seen as sufficiently green **Officials wanted to satisfy both groups**	Emissions standards raised to a level that required catalytic converters **RTB prevented via uniform high level of regulation**
Domestic Content, U.S.	Opposed domestic content rules, as they would raise production costs **Strong competitiveness framing**	Supported domestic content rules, to protect employment **Not able to use death prevention framing**	Trade priorities, staffing, and constituency ideas favored business **Officials side with business**	Domestic content legislation blocked **RTB prevented**
Domestic Content, Mexico	Firms wanted reduction to promote export orientation **Strong competitiveness framing**	Mexican labor unions repressed or co-opted **Weak opposition to business for multiple reasons**	Shift in trade priority level, staffing, and constituency ideas in firms' favor **Officials side with business**	Domestic content regulations reduced **RTB reduced**
Domestic Content, Canada	Same as above	Canadian labor unions sat out CUSFTA negotiations **No death framing, weak lobbying power**	Major ideational shift toward trade with U.S. **Officials side with business**	Same as above
Domestic Content, NAFTA	Firms wanted content rules to be continental **Continued competitiveness framing**	Labor implacably opposed NAFTA **No death framing, weak lobbying power**	Officials wanted NAFTA and were willing to sideline labor **Officials side with business**	Content rules were made continental **RTB between NAFTA states reduced**

Environment, NAFTA	Wanted to ensure that environmental rules did not hurt competitiveness **Medium power of competitiveness framing**	Activists wanted to prevent race to the bottom, raise Mexican standards **Low power of death framing**	Trade priorities, staffing, and constituency ideas split **Officials wanted to satisfy both sides**	Strengthened enforcement of national regulations **RTB prevented**
Consumer Safety, Mexico	Firms indifferent as different standards do not threaten competitiveness **Competitiveness framing nonexistent**	No policy entrepreneurs able to make death framing salient **Death prevention framing nonexistent**	Officials not facing pressure to reduce differences in regulations **Officials inert**	No movement of Mexican regulations toward U.S. standards **RTBs not increased or decreased**
Mexican Trucking	Firms' competitiveness not initially threatened but then hurt by retaliatory tariffs **Weak competitiveness framing that strengthens**	Activists concerned by Mexican truck safety, later satisfied by improvement in Mexican trucks **Strong needless death framing that weakens**	U.S. officials sided with activists initially but with firms later **Officials listen to death framing and then to competitiveness framing**	Mexican trucks barred from traveling more than 26 miles into U.S.; ban later dropped **RTB maintained, then decreased**
Consumer Safety, 1996–99	Firms want to harmonize regulations to reduce production costs **Competitiveness framing present**	Activists alarmed by health implications of harmonization **Strong needless death framing**	NHTSA and EU staffing and ideas favorable to activists **Officials side with activists**	Consumer safety differences remain **RTBs maintained**
Consumer Safety, Post-1999	Diseconomies of scale realized **Competitiveness framing weakens**	Activists maintain opposition **Needless death framing remains strong**	Same as above	Same as above
Beef BSE Emerges in Japan, 2001–3	New Japanese rules do not apply to U.S. producers **Competitiveness framing not yet applicable or necessary**	Activists become animated around BSE rules **Growing death framing not yet applicable to U.S. firms**	Japanese officials botch response, need to win back credibility **Adopt more pro-consumer orientation**	New stringent anti-BSE measures adopted but not applied to U.S. **RTBs stayed low**
BSE in the U.S., December 2003–April 2004	U.S. firms consider U.S. regulations sufficient and oppose Japanese rules, as they threaten competitiveness by raising costs or inhibiting access to the Japanese market **Competitiveness framing strong**	Japanese activists strongly commit to stringent anti-BSE rules **Needless death framing remains strong**	Staffing, trade prioritization, and ideas about constituency favor activists in Japan and firms in U.S. **Officials in U.S. and Japan on opposite sides**	Japanese BSE measures mean that U.S. cattlemen cannot / will not export to Japan **RTBs increased**

TABLE 1.2.—*Continued*

Subcase	Business	Activists	Government Officials	Outcome
Negotiations on Reopening Market Access, May 2004–December 2005	U.S. businesses maintain their position **Competitiveness framing remains for U.S. but not for Japan**	Activists maintain their position **Death framing remains for Japan but not for U.S.**	Japanese government accepts small compromises **Officials in two states still differ**	Special rules for U.S. beef **RTBs somewhat relaxed**
U.S. Mistakes and Diplomatic Cleanup, January 2006–April 2007	Same as above	Activists more strident after U.S. mistakes **Death framing remains for Japan but not for U.S.**	Japanese officials have to win back credibility **Japanese officials side with activists**	New requirements for BSE added **RTBs increased**
American Exceptionalism and Throttled Compromise, May 2007–August 2009	U.S. producers want age restrictions removed, as they raise production costs and inhibit market access **Competitiveness framing remains for U.S. but not for Japan**	Opposed age-restriction removal; remained animated by safety concerns **Death framing remains for Japan but not for U.S.**	Japanese officials wanted some kind of compromise; U.S. officials rejected that approach **Officials in two states disagree**	No compromise found **RTBs maintained**
Self-Tied Hands and the DPJ, August 2009–September 2010	Same as above	Same as above	DPJ takes power, with even more pro-consumer orientation than LDP had taken **Officials in two states disagree**	No compromise found **RTBs maintained**
The TPP and Confidence-Building Measures, October 2010–October 2011)	TPP brings Japanese exporters into negotiation **Competitiveness framing strong in both countries**	Concerns about BSE falling due to drop in cases **Death framing weakens**	Officials busy with recovery from earthquake, tsunami, nuclear disaster **Officials preoccupied**	RTB negotiations temporarily stalled **RTBs maintained**
30-Month Rule Implemented, October 2011–March 2013	Same as above	Same as above	Japanese government more open to firms and less eager to placate activists **Officials side with business**	Age restrictions relaxed **RTBs reduced**

Drugs				
TRIPS	U.S. firms argue that developing states' lower IP rules threaten competitiveness **Competitiveness framing strong**	Public health activists not yet engaged on IP **Needless death framing not present**	U.S. officials' idea, staffing favor business; developing countries' officials prioritized other issues **Officials side with business**	All WTO members raise IP regulations to U.S. standards **RTBs in drugs significantly reduced**
Doha Declaration	Same as above	HIV/AIDS crisis explodes; activists get engaged on IP **Death framing very strong**	U.S. officials less enamored with drug firms; developing states' officials more involved **Officials more divided**	Doha Declaration strengthens space for IP policy differences **RTBs increased**
Post-Doha WTO Decisions	Drug firms make same arguments as before **Competitiveness framing strong**	Activists still fully engaged **Death framing strong**	U.S. officials side with firms, developing countries' officials with activists **Officials split**	Constructive ambiguity and stalemate **RTBs maintained**
Indian Flexibilities	Indian firms want amicable relations with U.S. **Competitiveness framing present**	Activists push for flexible TRIPS implementation **Death framing present**	Indian officials want to satisfy firms and activists **Officials on both sides**	Measured use of novel patent, compulsory licensing, and injunction IP rules **Compromise**
FTAA	Brazilian agriculture excluded from FTAA negotiations by U.S. policy **Competitiveness framing not present**	Activists engaged and have Brazil's universal access program to defend **Needless death framing very strong**	Staffing, trade priorities, and constituency favor activists in Brazil and firms in U.S. **Officials in two states disagree**	FTAA negotiations collapse **RTBs maintained**
U.S. Free Trade Agreements with Chile and Central America	Exporters actively engaged **Competitiveness framing strong**	Activists weak and unorganized **Death framing weak**	Central American officials hear only one side **Officials side with business**	CAFTA includes TRIPS-plus provisions **RTBs reduced**

TWO

How Regulations Became the Crux of Trade Politics*

Today, the principal barrier to trade is the difference between states' regulations. Most contemporary trade negotiations are about those regulatory barriers more than anything else. That was not always the case. The centrality of regulation in trade negotiations is a relatively new phenomenon, emerging only over approximately the last 30 years. Over that time, scholars have analyzed a myriad of economic, legal, and political aspects of this trend. There is no dearth of scholarship on this issue. Still, to date and perhaps surprisingly, there is no political history of article or chapter length explaining how cross-national differences in regulation became the primary barriers to trade and the central focus of contemporary trade negotiations. This chapter contributes to IPE scholarship by doing just that. The chapter does not deeply delve into any single aspect of regulatory barriers (many of which are well covered in other works), nor does it advance a particular theoretical argument per se (as does the next chapter), but it provides a concise, unified explanation of how regulatory trade barriers came to be so important. It thus provides IPE scholars, political scientists, economic historians, international law scholars, economists, and public officials with a brief, useful account of how the trade world we live in came to be. Tracing this political history helps illuminate not only how we arrived at our current state of affairs but also how incorporating regulation changes trade politics and how increasing trade influences states' regulations. This chapter thus helps explain the historical context for the argument and cases presented in subsequent chapters.

Trade Politics Starts to Move Past Tariffs

By the 1970s, six rounds of GATT negotiations reduced tariffs to a small fraction of what they were in the 1940s. As tariffs receded, nontariff barriers became more significant. The Tokyo Round launched in 1973 continued to reduce tariffs but also addressed many of these NTBs. It established a series of "codes" that bound signatories' use of NTBs. GATT members were not compelled to sign those codes. Explicating codes but making them optional was an attempt to promote trade without undermining countries' policy flexibility. While understandable in theory, not forcing states to accept the codes as the price of GATT membership meant that the demand of the Tokyo Round agreement amounted to "Follow these rules unless you don't want to." Not surprisingly, many states, especially developing ones, did not follow them. Many developed states did sign on to these agreements, however. That they were following these codes while developing states were not contributed to developed states' rising cries of unfair trade in the 1980s.

Though the inclusion of NTBs in trade negotiations was less than universally binding, it led the U.S. Congress to demand greater review of those negotiations. When only tariffs were involved, Congress specified a range in which the executive was allowed to reciprocally reduce tariffs with other states; once trade negotiations had the potential to limit nontariff barriers, Congress wanted to place greater checks on presidential prerogative. Congress did this for three reasons. First, negotiating NTBs, especially those related to regulation, requires trade-offs that are less straightforward than when the main agenda item is tariffs. When the agenda involves nontariff barriers, the nature of an equivalent concession becomes less clear. Does country A cutting its subsidies to industry X fully compensate Country B for relaxing its rules on item Y? Because it was more difficult for Congress to know beforehand what the United States would be conceding, they were more reluctant to give the president carte blanche at the outset. Second, negotiating NTBs meant potentially negotiating away domestically approved law. This potential also increased congressional reluctance to take an institutional back seat, because a new trade deal would affect domestic law. Third, Congress received the request for negotiating authority on NTBs during the Watergate scandal in 1974. Given that context, Congress was not eager to expand executive authority. These considerations led Congress to demand and win influence at both the front end (giving the president fast-track authority) and the back end (the ability to vote up or down on the implementing legislation) in the Trade Act of 1974.

In other words, the inclusion of nontariff barriers in trade negotiations is the principal reason why we have the fast-track procedure that governs American trade policymaking today.

Meanwhile, developing countries were gaining meaningful involvement, for the first time, in trade negotiations. While they were given special treatment in previous GATT rounds, they had little voice in the negotiations, so liberalization excluded agriculture and textiles, two sectors where developing countries had their greatest comparative advantage. The erosion of tariffs on manufactured goods made this exclusion increasingly glaring. The inclusion of NTBs in trade negotiations threatened to constrain these states' development policies; subsidies, local content rules, and government procurement policies were at the heart of developing countries' efforts to support their infant industries. Angry at the exclusion of their voice and priorities from the negotiations and worried by the potential limits to their policy autonomy that trade rules on NTBs might impose, developing states blocked the ratification of the Tokyo Round until richer countries agreed to relax the agreement's requirements and pass the "enabling clause," which allowed developed countries to create preferential trading schemes with developing countries.

The Relationship between Trade and Regulation Expands and Changes

By the early 1980s, trade was increasing at a remarkable pace. As trade accounted for more of the global economy, more firms were engaging in trade and had an interest in other states' regulations. Meanwhile, as states grew richer, they engaged to a greater extent in health, environmental, and safety regulation. Later, developed states' attempts to promote greater competition in their economies required more regulation.[1] Moreover, the champions of deregulation tended not to focus on health and safety regulations they perceived to be particularly valued by society. For example, Thatcher's deregulation program did not take aim at consumer protection policies. Increasing trade created greater demand for regulation as a cushion against social dislocations generated by that increased trade.[2]

Changes in the nature of traded products meant that the expansions of regulation and trade began to intertwine. In earlier periods, basic commodities like wheat and steel were the primary traded goods. When trade primarily involved commodities, the ability to sell that good was mostly a matter of cost. Tariffs were central to costs. As traded products grew more complex, considerations beyond costs and thus beyond tariff levels took on added significance.[3]

Regulatory Trade Barriers Become Particularly Troublesome for Intra-Industry Trade

Over the course of the 1970s and 1980s, trade became less inter-industry and more intra-industry.[4] The shift to intra-industry trade meant that firms engaged in intra-industry trade were both exporters and importers. Those firms would oppose tariffs, because tariffs would raise production costs by making imported inputs more expensive.

Among NTBs, cross-national regulatory differences are harmful to intra-industry trade because they undermine product differentiation and economies of scale. One of the ways intra-industry trade benefits consumers is by expanding the array of available products. By limiting that array, regulatory barriers constrain consumers' choices. For example, European carmakers would like to sell models of subcompact cars to urban drivers in America, but they are prevented from doing so by regulatory differences between the United States and the European Union.[5] By forcing producers to maintain multiple production lines to meet different standards, regulatory differences reduce businesses' ability to leverage economies of scale, raising costs for consumers. Regulatory barriers also pose problems for intra-firm trade. To participate in global supply chains, firms' production must abide by multiple states' regulations. If the costs of complying with these different rules outweigh the savings from locating production steps in disparate locales, global supply chains stop making economic sense.

Europe Leads the Way in Splicing Trade and Regulation

The tensions at the intersection of regulation and intra-industry trade first emerged in Europe. By the late 1960s, intracontinental tariffs had been eliminated, so authorities in the European Community began to target NTBs, including regulatory barriers; throughout the 1970s, that diplomatic effort continually crashed on the rocks of national regulatory differences.[6] Moreover, as regulations expanded, the obstacles seemed to be ever increasing.[7]

In the same year that the Tokyo Round moved the GATT toward a framework for dealing with NTBs (1979), the European Community (EC) made a significant advance in dealing with regulatory barriers: the *Cassis de Dijon* decision and subsequent expansion of mutual recognition.[8] One of the plethora of regulatory differences between European states was a German rule mandating that all liqueurs have at least 25 percent alcohol (beer and wine were exempted from this rule), based on the idea that lower-alcohol beverages facilitated excessive consumption. The French producer of Cassis de Dijon liqueur, with 20 percent alcohol, wanted to export to Germany but was blocked from doing so. In 1979, the French government took the case to the European Court of Justice, which ruled in France's favor. What made this ruling important was not that it untangled specialized liqueur sales across the Rhine but that it established the doctrine of mutual recognition. Rather than force the European Commission to elaborate innumerable and politically impossible common rules on all traded products, European states were now obliged to allow the importation of any product that had been legally produced in another member state. Exceptions would only be made if the regulatory barrier was instituted to achieve a legitimate objective of public policy and if it used the available regulatory means that least restricted trade.

Mutual recognition was supplemented by the "new approach" to regulation, which augmented EU states' and citizens' confidence in their neighbors' regulations by adding agreed-on minimum requirements. The hope was that mutual recognition with the new approach would promote trade without forcing states to alter their policies. Differences in regulation nevertheless continued to dog intra-European trade relations throughout the early 1980s.

To alleviate these regulatory barriers, EC states signed the Single European Act (SEA) in 1986, setting 1992 as a goal for completing the common market. The SEA helped remove regulatory barriers, by changing requirements for EC-wide rulings from unanimous to a qualified majority and by expanding the European Commission's regulatory authority into consumer safety, health, and environmental policy. After the SEA and certainly after the Maastricht Treaty (1992), regulation was primarily the prerogative of Brussels. To the extent that regulation is made on a continent-wide basis, regulation stops being an intracontinental trade barrier. Thus European integration represents one end of the spectrum in dealing with regulatory trade barriers: delegate regulatory authority to a supranational government to the benefit of trade but at the cost of sovereignty.

While it reduced regulatory barriers between EC states, integration did nothing to reduce regulatory barriers that European firms faced abroad. In fact, because it raised regulations, it increased barriers between Europe and the rest of the world in many ways. To expand exports, a more comprehensive attenuation of regulatory barriers was needed. Firms in other states and thus those states' governments were increasingly paying attention to these barriers. For a variety of reasons, states had long sought to export more than they imported; this desire took on greater significance in the 1980s and elevated the importance of regulatory trade barriers.

Everybody Wants to Be an Exporter

Since the 1950s, East Asian states had made export promotion a core component of their development strategies. By the 1980s, other developing states were turning away from the development model of import substitution industrialization (ISI) and starting to follow the example of those East Asian states. Export-oriented development strategy could work only if their goods could be purchased in developed countries. Thus, by threatening to cut off market access, developed countries' growing product regulations presented a portentous hurdle to those countries' attempts to develop.

Western businesses and governments were becoming more interested in exports too. Much as the increasing interconnections of global markets undermined ISI, forcing developing states (particularly in Latin America) to seek export-led growth, it also contributed to the crisis of Keynesianism in Europe and pushed those governments to promote exports. As Helen Milner demonstrates, leading businesses had become so internationally oriented by the late 1970s that their response when faced with an economic downturn was to push not for protectionism, as their forebears had done in the late 1920s, but for greater trade liberalization.[9] Instead of attempting to solidify their domestic market share, they pursued increased sales in foreign markets. This situation also ties into the decline in the use of regulation as disguised protectionism. Regulatory trade barriers inhibited businesses' access to foreign markets while also limiting their flexibility and raising production costs. New rules pertaining to manufactured goods and to food and agriculture (the Technical Barriers to Trade Agreement and Sanitary and Phytosanitary Agreement, discussed below) inhibited states ability to use regulation as disguised protectionism, which thus declined as a phenomenon starting in the 1980s, because businesses largely abandoned it as a lobbying request and because states were more constrained in their ability to deliver that kind of protectionism anyway. The disguised protectionism argument is discussed further in the next chapter.

The perceived need to win global market share and the increasing interconnections of the global economy gave American businesses a powerful rhetorical tool in their quest to alter regulations: competitiveness. The language of competitiveness allowed businesses to argue that the U.S. government should do more to aid American businesses and that domestic regulations had to be reduced, not just because they hurt firms' profits, but also because they were making America itself sclerotic in the global economy.[10] In Great Britain and Germany, the deregulatory aspects of competitiveness also fell on receptive ears in the Thatcher and Kohl administrations.

That the United States was experiencing higher trade deficits than its policymakers considered healthy aided this framing's persuasiveness; in addition to promoting greater protectionism, a second perceived solution was to promote exports to states where U.S. firms had not traditionally had much market share.[11] That approach was especially apropos in the case of Japan, for two reasons. First, imports from Japan were rising, contributing to the U.S. trade deficit, and were particularly salient in economically and culturally important sectors, such as automobiles. Second, Japan often used regulations to exclude foreign firms.[12] Their agriculture minister's claim that U.S. beef was inappropriate for Japanese consumers because Japanese people have longer intestines is a classic example of Japanese trade obstructionism.[13] Japan's liberalization of other policies, such as quotas and tariffs, made these regulatory barriers more significant and more apparent.[14] The increased preoccupation with exports meant that businesses and the governments representing them wanted to ensure their full access to other countries' markets and had a greater interest in the extent to which those countries' regulations inhibited market access.

Western Business Pushes for Trade Rules in New Areas while Developing Countries Resist

As the extent to which regulation limited trade became obvious to businesses and governments inclined to consider other states' regulations protectionist, businesses began to pressure their governments to attempt to reduce those regulatory barriers. Monsanto was one of the first corporations to recognize how its revenue was being hurt by foreign regulations. In the late 1970s, Monsanto was losing millions of dollars annually because Hungary was violating its patents.[15] At first, Monsanto's attempts to insert intellectual property into U.S. trade policy met with limited success. Jim Enyart, the Monsanto representative who was the point man in that effort, recalled, "At the time everyone said: 'oh gee, patents are highly technical, very esoteric things. What do they have to do with trade?' . . . the minute you would say 'patent' everybody's eyes would glaze over."[16] Still, Monsanto was able to resolve its Hungarian difficulties with congressional help and, joined soon thereafter by Pfizer and IBM, was able to bring intellectual property into U.S. trade policy and get it onto the Uruguay Round agenda in 1986.[17] These three companies found allies among other corporations based in the United States and Europe.[18] U.S. and European corporations also wanted to see liberalization in services and investment. The array of national regulations in banking and services constituted an enormous trade barrier for those corporations. Developing countries had a decidedly different perspective on bringing these new policy areas and negotiations over sensitive domestic regulations into trade talks.

Developing countries' involvement in the Uruguay Round was much deeper than it had been in previous rounds. On the one hand, many developing states were hostile to including services, investment, and intellectual property in a new GATT round and were concerned that NTB rules would become obligatory. On the other hand, such states acknowledged that if a new GATT round could liberalize agriculture and textiles and if the services and investment provisions could be watered down, perhaps a more institutionalized and open trading system would benefit their countries. Developing states also feared that if a multilateral agreement could not be reached, Western countries, especially the United States, would pursue trade liberalization bilaterally and regionally, denying those developing countries the benefits of increased market access; likewise, the developing states hoped that a stronger WTO could curtail the increasing penchant of the United States for using unilateral trade sanctions.

The Uruguay Round negotiations that created the WTO produced an ambitious agreement built on compromises between developed and developing countries. Developing countries won concessions in the reduction of export subsidies and quantitative restrictions in agriculture, abolition of the Multi-Fibre Arrangement in textiles, tighter rules on safeguards measures, and softening of trade-related investment rules. Developed states won inclusion of services under the General Agreement on Trade in Services (GATS), inclusion of intellectual property based on developed-country standards under the TRIPS Agreement, and a stronger dispute settlement mechanism and greater compulsion to follow GATT/WTO rules such as the Tokyo Round codes on NTBs. The Uruguay Round also fundamentally changed how trade and national regulation coexisted.

The Uruguay Round Raises the Salience of Regulatory Trade Barriers

The Uruguay Round was a watershed in trade and regulation. The GATT dispute settlement lacked real enforcement; one of its most conspicuous weaknesses was that panel rulings had to be unanimous, meaning that a state accused of violating trade rules could veto decisions against it. In contrast, the WTO dispute settlement cannot be blocked by the accused, proceeds more quickly, possesses a greater ability to enforce decisions by sanctioning retaliation, and has more formalized panel proceedings. The WTO also more fully restricted the use of nonregulatory NTBs. This restriction, combined with further tariff reductions, more stringently constrains trade barriers and further raises the salience of regulatory barriers. The Uruguay Round was not silent on regulations either. While it did not mandate harmonization, it strengthened the Tokyo Round codes pertaining to food and agriculture and to manufactured goods, by making them requirements of WTO membership. The central idea behind the Sanitary and Phytosanitary Agreement (SPS) on food and agriculture and the Technical Barriers to Trade Agreement (TBT) on manufactured goods is that states have a right to set regulations for legitimate purposes, but the use of these regulations as disguised protectionism ought to be curtailed.[19] One of the central claims of this book is that these curtailment efforts have largely succeeded, in a subtle but significant victory for trade cooperation over protectionism.

The SPS and the TBT have three central provisions. First, if a state bases a regulation on the international standard as defined by a designated standard-setting body, such as the International Organization for Standardization (ISO) or the World Organization for Animal Health (OIE), that regulation is considered WTO-compliant. Second, if a state sets regulations that differ from the international standard, those regulations must have a scientific basis. Third, states' must use policies that are no more trade-restrictive than necessary to achieve their regulatory goals. Once again, the framers of the global economic order were attempting to encourage trade while respecting national sovereignty. This laudable goal meant that while there was enough policy wiggle room for states to continue enacting regulations that had profound impacts on trade, there was also sufficient juridical structure in the WTO for other states to challenge those regulations as illegal under international law, if those regulations imposed costs on them. Up to this point, this chapter has been about how regulation became part of trade politics. As the tension between policy space and trade-promoting rules came to a head with the creation of the WTO in 1994, trade became central to regulation politics.

Had the increasing connection between trade and regulation gone unnoticed by activists, the politics at the intersection of trade and regulation might have remained technocratic to the point of vapidity for all but the corporate lawyers and academic superspecialists, but that was not to be the case. During roughly the same period when the Uruguay Round negotiations were dominated by business, activists started becoming interested and involved in trade policy to a greater degree. Their attempt to gain greater influence over trade policymaking is one of the most important trends in global economic politics over the last three decades.

Prior to the 1980s, Western activists had little interest or influence in trade policy.[20] In the 1980s, those activists started to see trade as integral to achieving their goals. The idea that trade could be used for nontrade goals was not new; the central point of mercantilism was that trade could be used to aggrandize the state. Even in modern times, governments sometimes used trade to advance geostrategic goals. What was new was that civil society groups more fully realized that they too could use trade policy to pursue their political goals.

Labor Finds a Party and Starts to Focus on Regulations

Organized labor was the first nonbusiness civil society group to recognize the growing impact trade was having on regulations, specifically labor standards. In the United States, the political geography of the early 1970s dampened unions' ability to gain trade protection. Import-competing industries and unionized workers were concentrated in the Midwest and Northeast and were generally represented by Republicans, while export-oriented industries and less unionized workers were concentrated in southern districts represented by Democrats.

The political upheaval of the 1960s and 1970s led the two parties to switch positions on trade. By 1980, the Republican base was in the export-oriented South and interior West, while Democrats controlled the protectionist Midwest and Northeast. This shift meant Republicans now favored labor regulation rollback as well as trade expansion. To unions, trade liberalization and deregulation were no longer separate battles but linked tools in the Reagan administration's arsenal for weakening labor. Furthermore, the ascendant rhetorical frame of competitiveness alarmed labor as much as it pleased business because it suggested that workers had to bear the costs of America adjusting to a postindustrial economic landscape.

Unions believed they were in a contest for jobs with the workers of developing countries and argued that the conditions of those workers constituted an unfair advantage for businesses operating there. In 1984, labor activists were able to use that rhetoric to link trade concessions for developing states to labor standards.[21] They feared that even if firms did not move to those countries, they could bully workers and governments by threatening to do so. Human rights activists joined unions in their crusade to link labor and trade, with the most dramatic example being their drive for trade sanctions against apartheid South Africa.[22]

Consumer Skepticism Expands

Consumer activists too were becoming more skeptical of multinational firms. The modern consumer movement grew out of citizens' perceptions that firms had failed to supply goods of sufficient quality and that governments had, at best, failed in their duty to regulate and, at worst, colluded with business at consumers' expense. The U.S. consumer movement won regulatory protections against what they saw as businesses' depredations; consumer victories included the Fair Package and Labeling Act, the National Traffic and Motor Vehicle Safety Act, and the Consumer Product Safety Act, as well as numerous local and state ordinances.[23] The 1960s and 1970s also saw an expansion of consumer mobilization efforts in Europe that yielded significant political victories, such as the establishment of the Office of Fair Trading and the National Consumer Council in Britain, implementation of quality contracts in France, and the establishment of an information-based consumer protection system in Germany.[24] In Japan, though producer interests continued to dominate, consumer groups gained more consistent influence in regulatory policymaking through the creation of a consumer affairs divisions in government as well as the enactment of the Consumer Protection Basic Law.[25]

In the 1980s, consumer groups began to recognize the extent to which trade policy impacted their regulatory goals, adding suspicion of imports to their already acute qualms about business. Precisely these fears led the European Community to ban hormones in beef in 1985, a move that inhibited U.S. beef exports to Europe, marking the first time consumer organizations' political activism led to a trade dispute.[26] The Single European Act (1986) further augmented the power of European consumer organizations by strengthening the European Parliament, which was more open than the other major European Community institutions to the concerns of nonbusiness interests.[27] Meanwhile, consumer groups in Japan and the United States were gaining greater influence in their country's trade policies as well.

Much of these groups' demands rested on the argument that how a product is made is as important as the product's characteristics. One of the two pillars undergirding postwar trade rules was "national treatment," the idea that a state could not treat an imported good differently than a domestic one. The legal language used by the GATT and the WTO is that governments are not allowed to discriminate against "like products." For most of the GATT's history, the definition of like products was based on products' characteristics and thus straightforward; a soccer ball is a soccer ball. As activists became more engaged in trade politics, they advanced a new definitional framework: process characteristics. To a labor activist, a soccer ball is not to be regarded as a soccer ball if it is made by a worker toiling under deplorable conditions; because the processes by which such balls are made differ in their consequences for labor rights, they are not "like products," and a state may discriminate against the morally odious good. In the Tuna-Dolphin case, the GATT established that, for the most part, only product-based barriers are legal.

Environmentalists Become Interested in Trade Policy

In the 1960s and 1970s, environmentalists in the United States and Europe focused primarily on domestic issues. Even when the environment was discussed at the international level, such as at the 1972 Stockholm Conference, the focus was on organizing state action to combat pollution. In the late 1980s, these activists became influential actors in trade politics.

European integration brought environmental activists into EC trade debates, especially after the Single European Act.[28] At roughly the same time, environmentalists in the United States began to take a greater interest in trade policy, based on three beliefs: the potential efficacy of trade sanctions, the GATTzilla menace, and the race to the bottom. The first belief was that, under the right conditions, trade sanctions could be used to protect the environment. They could be applied unilaterally through rules granting access to the U.S. market based on meeting environmental standards or could be used to enforce multilateral environmental treaties, such as the Montreal Protocol. The second belief was that, under the wrong circumstances, trade obligations could run roughshod over states' efforts to protect their environments. This fear was stoked by the 1991 Tuna-Dolphin case that aided environmentalists in depicting the GATT as a "GATTzilla."[29] Third, many environmentalists believed that even when not being pushed by an institution like the GATT/WTO, trade could encourage a race to the bottom.[30] The idea was that if environmental regulations placed costs on businesses and if businesses were free to relocate, they would move to states with lax environmental regulations, which would create an incentive for states to relax their existing environmental rules or, at the very least, give them pause before enacting new regulations. The efficacy of sanctions, the bias or not of international trade institutions, and the existence or not of races to the bottom are beyond the scope of this work, but important for the purposes of this discussion is recognizing that these beliefs led environmental activists to engage in trade politics to a greater extent than they had before.

NAFTA and BSE Solidify Society-Demanded Regulations as Trade Issues

The NAFTA debate was a pivotal moment for labor and environmental rules in U.S. trade policy. The prospect of competing with workers in developing countries with little regulatory protection crystallized for labor when the U.S. government began negotiating America's first free trade deal with a developing country. For environmentalists, NAFTA's implications were more ambivalent, with some groups in support and others opposed. Both sets of activists were able to attract more attention to their priorities in NAFTA than in the simultaneously occurring Uruguay Round because NAFTA was more salient and more intuitive; as the secretary-treasurer of the American Federation of Labor and Congress of Industrial Organizations put it, "GATT is something nobody understands and NAFTA is something everybody understands."[31] Much of the NAFTA opposition was not explicitly protectionist per se but was concerned that NAFTA could undermine Americans' regulatory preferences. Two ecological economists summarized this point best by saying, "Protecting hard won social gains from blind standards lowering competition, that is what we are interested in—not the protection of some inefficient entrepreneur who wants to grow mangoes in Sweden."[32]

Labor and environmental activists succeeded in expanding the scope of what was considered a "trade" issue. They forced Presidents Bush and Clinton to accept that labor and environmental standards had to be part of NAFTA negotiations. These groups were able to put their concerns at the center of the opposition to NAFTA,[33] which did eventually include side agreements on the environment, as well as labor standards that were stringent enough to gain at least some support from environmental groups, though still not enough to satisfy labor.

The inclusion or not of such side agreements in future negotiations became a point of contention between the two parties. Republicans and their business allies resented that these policy areas, which they still did not consider to be "real" trade issues, had been included in NAFTA, and they were determined to prevent such issues from contaminating future trade deals. Democrats, conversely, considered their inclusion the new normal; they would take a dim view of any future agreements that did not include such provisions. Adding regulation to the trade policy mix thus activated the partisan polarization that was starting to ossify American politics more broadly. Though NAFTA indelibly added environmental and labor regulations to the docket of trade policy, it did not raise consumer protection regulations to the same level of trade salience. A significant governmental failure across the Atlantic two years later did that.

In March 1996, the British government announced that, contrary to what it had been saying for years, bovine spongiform encephalopathy (BSE), also known as mad cow disease, which had been found in many British cows, could be transmitted to humans and cause a deadly, incurable virus, variant Creutzfeldt-Jakob disease. Europeans who had consumed British beef in the previous five years could potentially have been infected. A political firestorm ensued. Fear and indignation were widespread.[34] Because the UK government had so badly failed in its obligations to protect consumers and because the increase in trade engendered by European integration had exposed consumers across Europe to potentially fatal British beef, the mad cow crisis damaged the notion that Europeans were better off federalizing regulation and trade policy. The collective experience of the mad cow crisis was so searing that trade liberalization in regard to food safety became viewed with deep suspicion.[35] The fallout from the BSE crisis directly contributed to European consumers' rejection of allowing the use of BST (a hormone given to milk cows) or the sale of GMOs in Europe.[36] These decisions created serious trade disputes with the United States, because both of those products were allowed in America.

Where Civil Society and Trade Stand Today

Consumer groups do not have the same financial resources as business associations. Nevertheless, when the former become engaged on an issue, they can be a powerful lobbying force because they deliver legitimacy by disseminating trusted information and representing respected broad-based groups. Consumer groups have an image of defending ordinary citizens. This framing is so powerful that when businesses oppose consumer advocates' demands, those businesses are forced to justify their position as being better for consumers than the advocates' position.[37]

Consumer advocates in developed countries contend that without government regulation, international businesses will make substandard products to increase profits. Moreover, developed states and their citizens generally view developing countries' regulations as flimsy or unenforced.[38] They demand that products sold in the markets of developed countries meet their standards, not the standards used in developing countries. Those demands and the regulations that emanate from them can inhibit trade. The difficulty in resolving the tension between consumer protection and trade is exemplified by an increasingly employed regulation: labeling requirements.

Requirements in labeling have long been a major thrust of consumer protection regulation. In the 1980s, labeling began to have significant trade impacts. GATT rules meant states were bound to employ the regulations that least distorted trade. GATT panels have often cited labeling as a preferred option because it is presumed to be less protectionist than an outright ban. On the one hand, it could be said that governments began to use labels as a means of encouraging consumption of domestically produced items over imports; for example, the German government used its labeling requirements to compel a British sausage manufacturer to label its product not as sausage but as "pork-filled offal tubes."[39] On the other hand, governments can respond that they are merely helping consumers. Parsing out which is the real motivation can be difficult. Consumer advocates and governments think they are protecting the public; foreign export-oriented producers think this kind of consumer advocacy is a smoke screen for protectionism.

As with consumer advocates' wishes, the intent and appropriateness of labor activists' trade demands is deeply contested. Among the American public, respondents generally favor more (rather than less) inclusion of labor standards in trade agreements.[40] Every major piece of trade legislation since NAFTA has been accompanied by a debate on whether and how to attach such standards to trade deals. In 2007, Republicans and Democrats settled on a set of basic principles on environmental, labor, and intellectual property rights in trade negotiations, known as the May 10th Agreement; still, on the details, there remained significant disagreement between the parties through the end of the Obama administration.

Notwithstanding this disagreement, the parties were able to collaborate in using trade sanctions to punish other states' human rights abuses.[41] Human rights continue to be the primary emphasis in EU positions on trade and labor rights.[42] While Europe and the United States have tried to connect labor standards and trade, developing countries have adamantly opposed it. Low-cost labor is frequently the primary comparative advantage of developing countries, so they tend to see these connections as protectionism dressed in new rhetorical garb.

Finally, the growing recognition of climate change heightened the salience of the connection between trade and the environment. Environmentalists remain concerned by the impact increased trade may have on environmental protection, but they do not oppose all trade liberalization; for most activists, the challenge is not to limit trade but to ensure that trade accommodates environmental goals. The EU has sought to include environmental standards in its trade positions. In the United States, inclusion of environmental provisions in trade agreements has divided the parties in a way similar to labor rules. Underlying all these demands for trade-encompassing protections for consumers, laborers, and the environment is a strong preference for domestic (rather than international) regulation; developed states' citizens not only distrust developing countries' regulations but consistently prefer their own country's regulations over those of other developed countries.[43]

International Businesses Want International Rules

Multinational corporations want international standards rather than a new rule for every state. Since the 1980s, international businesses have pushed their governments to reduce the extent to which national regulations inhibit their ability to profit from trade. It bears repeating here that businesses are not necessarily antiregulation but seek to minimize the extent to which regulation abrades trade. This regulation trend, like those before it, took place in Europe first. Businesses formed the vanguard in reducing regulatory barriers, with respect to promoting both mutual recognition and the Single European Act.[44]

European and American businesses that were internationally oriented worked together to promote the Uruguay Round. They were the main supporters of strengthening procedures used to address NTBs. The new SPS Agreement for example was a boon for international firms in three ways. First, it promoted the use of standards set by organizations such as the Codex Alimentarius. The rule that regulations matching Codex standards would be considered WTO-compliant generated a powerful incentive for states to adopt Codex standards. The more states adopt Codex standards, the more uniform regulations are across different states, so that fewer regulatory barriers abrade trade. Second, by forcing regulations that differed from standards set by these bodies to be based on science, the SPS and TBT Agreements constrained states' ability to create blatantly protectionist regulatory barriers.[45] They also helped export-oriented businesses by alleviating the acute difficulties that regulatory barriers present for intra-industry trade. Third, business controls the lion's share of Codex representation; the more decisions are made at a forum dominated by business, the more influence business has over those regulations.[46]

Businesses that are internationally oriented have been the leading proponents of regional trade agreements. They seek these reductions to take advantage of economies of scale and the efficiency gains from locating disparate production steps in different states. The Canadian debate over a free trade agreement with the United States pitted environmental and consumer activists, opposed to what they saw as American regulatory imperialism, against Canadian businesses, eager to gain access to the massive U.S. market.[47] North American businesses strongly supported the successor of the Canada–United States Free Trade Agreement, NAFTA.

In all these cases, firms pushed back against labor, consumer, and environmental activists opposed to trade liberalization. Businesses have not rushed en masse to locations with lower environmental and consumer protection regulations, nor have they uniformly pushed for reduced standards in their home states.[48] Instead, they fought against those groups' demands for specifically national regulations that force firms either to maintain two production lines or to forgo sales in a lucrative market. Businesses like to portray these regulatory differences as unnecessary red tape. When they push for regulatory barrier reduction, they focus on examples of seemingly pointless differences, such as Canada's deodorant rules that force Proctor and Gamble's factory to maintain separate production just for the Canadian market, regarding which they ask, tongue in cheek, whether "Canadian underarms [are] so different that we need two sets of regulations?"[49] Civil society groups respond with examples of national regulations that must be maintained to protect the citizenry.

The new, more robust WTO rules have heightened the drama of this regulatory struggle between businesses and advocacy groups by raising the stakes for all parties with an interest in the connection between trade and regulation. Under the GATT, even if a state was found to have violated GATT rules, the lack of enforcement capabilities meant that such a ruling could often be prevented from having any material costs on that state. In contrast, the new WTO rules can force a state to change its regulations on threat of retaliation.

Developing Countries Remain Wary of Further WTO Expansion

The Uruguay Round left developing countries disillusioned with trade rules. Though there was agricultural liberalization, developing countries believed (with justification) that agriculture in the Global North received too much protection.[50] They perceived the new WTO rules--especially the TRIPS Agreement, the GATS, and the Agreement on Trade-Related Investment Measures—as limiting their regulatory flexibility to a greater extent than they had initially feared, and they believed that developed states were implementing their concessions in agriculture and textiles as slowly as possible.[51] Given these beliefs and that they were facing greater domestic difficulty in implementing these new policies than they expected, they were reluctant to agree to another WTO round that would further expand the list of regulatory areas where they would be constrained by trade. Thus, when President Clinton announced in 1999 that labor and environmental regulations should be part of the trade regime and that sanctions should be used to enforce high standards in those areas, developing countries walked out of negotiations, refusing to allow the launch of another WTO round.

Despite this rebuff, developed countries hoped to launch a new round. Recognizing that agriculture remained highly protected, they agreed that a new round, the Doha Round launched in 2001, should focus on agriculture and other development-related issues. In return for concessions on these issues, the EU and the United States demanded further regulatory constraints in four areas, known as the Singapore issues: government procurement, investment, competition policy, and trade facilitation. Developing countries refused to include the first three issues in the negotiations. Given this blockage, the EU and Japan perceived that they would not receive enough in return for compliance and had little incentive to make difficult agricultural reforms. The Doha Round has collapsed and shows little sign of reaching a breakthrough on any issue other than the Bali Agreement (on relatively minor rules of trade facilitation), and a major reason behind that collapse is that the round attempted to reduce regulatory trade barriers at a global level.

Regulation's Increased Salience Pushes Promotes Trade Regionalism

The increasing centrality of regulation in trade negotiations thwarts global multilateralism and promotes regionalism. In the post–Cold War era, regional trade agreements have proliferated at a remarkable rate. Given the lack of progress in the Doha Round, developed states have pursued liberalization bilaterally and regionally. These bilateral and regional agreements provide states with large markets a greater opportunity to graft their regulatory preferences onto smaller states. The regulatory changes that these smaller states have been coaxed into making are more stringent than those mandated by the WTO and are often referred to as WTO-plus or TRIPS-plus provisions. Regulation is more central to these trade negotiations than it has been for previous trade agreements, regional or multilateral. Though they eventually floundered, the negotiations over the Trans-Pacific Partnership (TPP) and the Transatlantic Trade and Investment Partnership (TTIP) combined regulatory barriers with trade regionalism.

The politics of the TPP significantly revolved around regulation. Public health advocates squared off against tobacco producers over tobacco regulation in Southeast Asian states.[52] Unions remained skeptical of the labor standards that were a component of the TPP.[53] There was also concern that the TPP would undermine various countries' financial regulations. In Malaysia, there was apprehension over whether the TPP's chapter on government procurement would invalidate the country's efforts to assist underprivileged minorities.[54] Consumer groups worried that regulations in food safety would be weakened.[55] The intellectual property provisions reflected the regulatory preferences of the pharmaceutical and entertainment industries, to the dismay of access-to-medicine advocates.[56] Conversely, business organizations argued that regulatory harmonization was among the TPP's biggest benefits.[57]

The U.S. Chamber of Commerce highlighted regulatory convergence as the single largest benefit of the TTIP.[58] U.S. civil society groups were more ambivalent toward the TTIP than toward the TPP. Labor unions were more receptive to the former as well.[59] Some consumer activists contended that regulatory cooperation was acceptable, especially if harmonization was upward, while other activists expressed concern that mutual recognition will lower standards.[60] This greater comfort with the TTIP than the TPP has two explanations. First, TTIP negotiations did not reached the same level of salience in the United States as TPP negotiations. Second, the United States and the EU are at similar levels of development and generally have similar levels of regulatory protection; the same could not be said for many of the TPP negotiating partners of the United States. American labor and consumer activists trust European regulations more than they trust Vietnamese regulations.

Conclusion

As tariffs and other nonregulatory measures fell, the extent to which cross-national differences in regulation impeded trade became clearer, especially to multinational firms. Once regulations became the subject of trade negotiations in the 1980s, civil society groups with a vested interested in those regulations became involved in trade politics to a greater degree than before. Cross-national differences in regulation are the centerpiece issues in trade politics today, which is likely to continue being the case for the foreseeable future.

The political history offered in this chapter reveals several dynamics that drive the international negotiation over regulatory trade barriers. First, the erosion of nonregulatory trade barriers has made regulatory trade barriers more apparent and more significant. Second, regarding trade and regulation, there have been significant divisions between developed and developing states. Developed countries have often led the way in pursuing reductions in regulatory trade barriers, while developing countries have been wary of being locked into adopting developed countries' regulatory preferences. Third, businesses have been a major driving force behind efforts to reduce regulatory trade barriers. Fourth, the incorporation of sensitive domestic regulations into trade negotiations led environmental, labor, and consumer groups to engage in trade politics to a greater extent. Fifth, the sensitivity of these regulations made reaching multilateral agreements more difficult and contributed to the trend toward regionalism that has become so prevalent in global trade politics. Sixth, the intent of a regulatory trade barrier is often in the eye of the beholder; where one group sees vital domestic regulation meant to protect citizens, another group sees disguised protectionism meant to coddle underperforming but politically connected businesses.

THREE

Competitiveness and Death

Explaining the Negotiations over Regulatory Trade Barriers

When the differences between countries' domestic regulations impede international trade, the states involved have three basic options. They can reduce those regulatory barriers, they can increase them, or they can do nothing. This chapter explains when states are more likely to do each of these and why. My explanation involves examining the motivations of and interactions between three sets of actors: businesses, activist groups, and government officials. I argue that businesses are likely to succeed at reducing a regulatory trade barrier when they can link their desire for that reduction with broader concerns about economic competitiveness, while activist organizations are likely to succeed at increasing regulatory trade barriers when they can link their desire for maintaining or increasing that barrier with preventing needless death.

In this chapter, I explain why the negotiations around regulatory trade barriers are essentially bargains between businesses and activists. I first discuss why businesses seek to reduce regulatory trade barriers and what can get them to end that pursuit. I then examine why activist groups seek to increase or defend regulatory barriers and what can get them to accept a reduction in those barriers. I investigate government officials' two primary roles in regulatory trade bargaining, that of the champion and that of the marginalizer. Finally, I discuss which political entities are likely to prevail in this bargaining and why. That discussion lays the theoretical expectations for later chapters.

The Trade Strategy of Businesses: New Trade, New New Trade, and Regulation

Businesses are the main actors that push for regulatory trade barriers to be dismantled or reduced, because those barriers constitute major impediments to their competitiveness. Firms in the food industry have been the primary supporters of efforts to reduce regulatory barriers in food through the Codex Alimentarius.[1] The Motion Picture Association of America has been the biggest promoter of coordinating international copyright regulations.[2] Pfizer led the charge to harmonize regulations on intellectual property in pharmaceuticals.[3] A timber firm (the Ecological Trading Company) and a British retail chain in home improvement (B&Q) were the early leaders pushing for green certification schemes and the creation of the Forestry Stewardship Council, which has coordinated international regulations on timber.[4] Chemical companies like Dow and Dupont have consistently pushed for reducing regulatory barriers in the chemical industry.[5] These are just a few of the many examples of this trend.[6]

New Trade Theory and the Changing Economic Logics of Trade

New Trade Theory helps to explain some crucial developments in the economic logics underpinning how contemporary businesses approach trade. In the late 1970s and 1980s, Paul Krugman, among others, advanced NTT, for which Krugman would later win the Nobel Prize. NTT brought a much richer set of assumptions than the Ricardian and Hecksher-Ohlin models had. Specifically and significantly, NTT assumed increasing returns to scale and network effects, product differentiation, and the possibility of oligopolistic (rather than perfect) competition.[7] Emphasizing that trade could be intra-industry, NTT implied that the need for economies of scale, augmented by the power of network effects, meant that certain locations would dominate the production of certain goods. Two of the classic examples used by NTT proponents were the rivalry between Airbus and Boeing and the preponderance of movie production in Hollywood.

While they may seem obvious now, these three aspects (returns to scale, intra-industry trade, and product differentiation) were not as obvious then, and NTT pioneers deserve credit for highlighting them. My explanation builds on their work. Economies of scale, product differentiation, and intra-industry trade have become more important in shaping how businesses maintain their competitiveness. Economies of scale have grown in significance as globalization has progressed. That firms have become increasingly capital intensive and must market differentiated products heightens the importance of economies of scale in trade.[8] Firms in many industries have grown larger and more multinational, as evidenced by expanding global value chains and production networks, increased foreign direct investment, and more extensive intra-firm trade.[9] The increase in intra-industry trade in particular has created greater opportunities and incentives for firms to become more politically engaged.[10]

The increasingly international nature of commerce, greater need for economies of scale, and more extensive capital intensity mean that more businesses have a greater degree of multinational asset specificity (i.e., possessing resources that are multinational in character but specifically geared toward one kind of economic endeavor). As firms have come to rely on greater economies of scale and cumulative learning effects and have gone further in multinational asset specificity, their ability to gain access to many national markets has become more important, and so has their interest in reducing the regulatory trade barriers that inhibit that access.[11] As discussed in the last chapter, the imperative to market different products and the prevalence of intra-industry trade have also grown.

All these dynamics are stymied by regulatory trade barriers. The barriers threaten to deny businesses access to a lucrative market, thus undermining their global competitiveness. The multiplicity of regulations can be burdensome even if businesses are skilled at handling regulation. In pharmaceuticals, for example, the need to separately file for market access in disparate countries can add hundreds of millions of dollars in costs and consume valuable patent time, depriving a firm of significant revenue.[12]

At the very least, regulatory barriers can force firms to have multiple production lines. These barriers can force businesses to engage in bizarre, efficiency-destroying behaviors. For example, a combination of tariff barriers and regulatory differences forces Mercedes-Benz and Freightliner to build their cargo vans in Germany, take them off the assembly line and test drive them in Germany, partially disassemble them, and then ship them to and reassemble them in the United States.[13] Obviously, there is zero business rationale for constructing a vehicle twice before it goes to the dealer.

New Trade Theory, the Political Logics of Trade, and the Paucity of Disguised Protectionism

This book's explanation parts ways here with New Trade Theory. While NTT proponents clarified factors driving firms to engage in trade, they said little to nothing about businesses' political behavior. Assertions they did make about trade politics were and still are incorrect when those politics involve regulation and regulatory trade barriers. In short, the economic logics that NTT proponents suggest are sound, but the political logics need revision.

NTT implies that because production in some goods will concentrate in certain locations and because that production brings with it good employment and other economic benefits, governments will compete to become the home of those production locations, dominate the world market in that production, and reap the concomitant benefits. Governments may thus engage in a variety of neoprotectionist policies to pursue that goal. Again, the battle between Airbus and Boeing is a classic example. The NTT argument may or may not be the case with regard to nonregulatory trade issues like subsidies or tariffs, but once the issue at hand is regulatory in nature, its predictions become less accurate.

NTT would expect businesses needing government assistance to seek protectionism, but that is not, generally speaking, what they do. Unlike more nationally based predecessors that sought protectionism from governments in earlier periods, contemporary businesses are more likely, due to their much more extensively international character, to ask for government assistance in gaining access to foreign markets.[14] A good example of this is Kodak's response to stiff competition from its Japanese archrival, Fuji; instead of pushing for the U.S. government to grant Kodak protection to help it strengthen its grip on the U.S. market, Kodak chose to lobby the U.S. government to reduce trade barriers that were impeding its ability to compete in the Japanese market.[15] This dynamic played out in the semiconductor industry as well.[16] The upshot to this approach is that businesses in the contemporary era pressure their home governments to get other countries to reduce regulatory barriers, instead of pressuring those home governments to increase their own regulatory barriers.

NTT would also expect businesses to seek protectionism, regulatory and otherwise, even if they are not in trouble, to help them solidify their location as the dominant production node in their industry and ensure their position in the global market. Broz and Werfel have found that industry demands for protectionism are closely linked with threats to competitiveness, but those demands take the form of antidumping petitions, not regulatory barriers.[17] Business thinks differently on regulatory trade barriers than on nonregulatory matters. Even when import-competing businesses seek protectionism, they are much more likely to ask for nonregulatory means of protectionism, like antidumping duties or voluntary export restraints, because those measures offer the same benefit without limiting the flexibility of businesses as regulations would. For example, when U.S. sugar producers seek protectionism, they do not ask Congress for a special regulation on sugar production but, instead, lobby to maintain a trade scheme built on tariff rate quotas and market allotments. Another example comes from the auto industry. When the Big Three in U.S. auto manufacturing (Ford, GM, and Chrysler) were facing increased competition from Japan, they sought voluntary export restraints, not regulatory barriers. Disguised protectionism is demanded less often and occurs less often than one might expect and than scholars like Moonhawk Kim imply.[18]

Moreover, even if we assume that trade becomes concentrated in the manner that NTT expects, once a dominant node of production becomes established, regulatory trade barriers in other states threaten to deny that node the commercial rewards it would otherwise enjoy. The firms located in that node will thus pressure their home country's government to attempt to negotiate a reduction in the foreign country's regulatory barrier. This threat, along with the paucity of disguised protectionism, means that the lion's share of business pressure will be for reduced (rather than increased) regulatory barriers.

NTT's expectations of government officials also go unmet. NTT would expect the officials to use regulations to help businesses in their constituency establish their location as the dominant node. Where that is not possible, NTT expects government to use regulatory barriers to protect businesses from competition emanating from the dominant node. As I argue later in this chapter, government officials' motivations and incentives surrounding regulation and trade are more varied and more nuanced than this expectation would predict.

Finally, again as I argue later in this chapter, regulatory barriers are a by-product of activism. That relationship helps explain how it can simultaneously be true that there are more regulatory trade barriers in democracies and that businesses do not tend to seek disguised protectionism via regulatory barriers. Daniel Kono argues that democracy increases the availability and clarity of information about tariffs and core nontariff barriers, such as quotas, over regulatory trade barriers.[19] Because the price effects for consumers of tariffs and core NTBs are easier for politicians to explain and understand than the price effects of regulatory trade barriers, politicians are incentivized to reduce tariffs and core NTBs but increase regulatory barriers. According to Kono, this incentive, which he terms "optimal obfuscation," is why we see more regulatory barriers in democracies. I agree that regulatory barriers are more likely in democracies, but I contend that democracies have more regulatory barriers because democracies are more open to activists. Activism around regulatory matters, not optimal obfuscation, leads democracies to have more regulatory barriers than nondemocracies.

New New Trade Theory, Firm Differentiation, and Opposition to Regulatory Trade Barriers

Like New Trade Theory, New New Trade Theory further refines the commercial logics underpinning trade.[20] NNTT shifted the focus to individual firms rather than industries.[21] Increasing globalization opens greater opportunities to the most efficient firms but subjects the less efficient firms to withering competition.[22] Over time, globalization thus strengthens the most efficient, most pro-trade firms and weakens the least efficient, most protectionist firms. Additionally, those firms that engage in greater levels of foreign direct investment have a strong disincentive to initiate trade disputes involving states in which they operate. These political forces lubricate international trade.[23]

I share NNTT's appreciation of the differences between firms. Because of other differences between them, businesses can be generalized as seeking reduced regulatory trade barriers. There are three distinctions between firms that can be made with regard to regulatory barriers: strong versus weak, large versus small, and eager compliers versus reluctant compliers.

The distinction most closely associated with NNTT is the first, strong and efficient firms versus weak and inefficient firms. Because the efficient firms want to engage in greater trade, they hope to dismantle regulatory barriers. For the reasons discussed above, the inefficient firms are less likely to pursue a disguised protectionism via regulatory barriers than to pursue more traditional nonregulatory protectionism. In Song Kim's findings on the trade lobbying of businesses (albeit with regard to tariffs rather than regulatory trade barriers) support this point.[24] This situation means that business as a whole pushes for liberalization and does not provide much, if any, of the political power behind defending regulatory barriers. One example of this imbalance in mobilization can be found in the negotiations over the Transatlantic Trade and Investment Partnership, where there was almost no opposition from businesses of any kind; its main opponents were nongovernmental organizations worried about TTIP's regulatory consequences.[25]

The second distinction to be made among firms in regard to trade barriers is size. Large firms are likely to oppose regulatory barriers because, as NNTT points out, they are the firms most likely to engage in trade.

Small firms will want regulatory barriers reduced too, though, because compliance costs often comprise a greater percentage of their overall costs. Such costs are why some smaller foreign toymakers were forced to pull out of the United States completely when the U.S. government created greater regulatory trade barriers in toys with the Consumer Product Safety Improvement Act of 2008,.[26] Small firms may seek protection, but they are less likely to want that protection to be regulatory, given the greater burden that regulatory compliance costs comprise for them.

The third distinction delineates eager compliers from reluctant compliers. For different reasons, both eager and reluctant compliers worry about the effects that different standards can have on their competitiveness, so both want one standard. The eager compliers want it to be a single high standard, so that less-scrupulous businesses do not gain a competitive advantage and to generate greater confidence in their particular industry and their firm. For example, European businesses that were forced to maintain public disclosure statements on environmental protection fought for and won requirements (through the International Organization for Standardization) that forced non-EU businesses to maintain similar statements.[27] There is no need to assume bad faith or nefarious motives on the part of businesses to recognize that, if given the choice, they would rather meet one standard than six different standards. As previously mentioned, businesses are not reflexively antiregulation but seek to reduce the extent to which regulatory differences abrade trade. Reluctant compliers want a single standard set at a low level, to avoid increased production costs. For example, the shipping firms that value costs over safety, labor, and environmental standards have supported a flag-of-convenience system that amounted to a very low level of regulation.[28]

When thinking about trade lobbying, it is important to keep in mind not only these three distinctions between firms but also that these distinctions result in business as a whole being structurally in favor of reducing regulatory barriers. To borrow a line from Osgood's research on firm heterogeneity, product differentiation, and trade, we see "strong support for liberalization by a select group of winners that spans the competitiveness spectrum and dominates the politicking on trade."[29] In sum, many modern firms have operations in multiple states, have large economies of scale, are capital intensive, have high multinational asset specificity, market differentiated products, engage in intra-industry trade, and are more interested in gaining access to global markets than in barricading themselves inside their own national market. These businesses do not tend to seek regulatory protectionism but, instead, push for a reduction in regulatory trade barriers, because those barriers make them less competitive, by (1) raising their production costs and (2) inhibiting access to lucrative markets.

Considerations That May Provoke Business Apathy on Regulatory Trade Barriers

Though businesses have often pursued reduced regulatory barriers, they have not done so always and everywhere. Several considerations may convince them to simply accept a difference in regulation that raises the cost of trade. Complying with the regulation may be easy. The Canadian requirement that new cars come with owners' manuals in English and French is straightforward, reasonable, and cheap in compliance. Attempting to reduce such regulatory differences is a waste of resources and risks making a business that does so appear implacable and extreme. As Woll and Artigas point out, "Regulatory trade lobbying rests on government solicitation of expertise, so the criteria for success or failure are different. Firms have to prove to the government that they are valuable partners, which requires credibility, reputation, and constructive cooperation."[30]

Another potential check discouraging businesses from taking political initiative on regulatory barriers is that the consequences of regulatory changes in the context of international trade are often unclear. For conglomerates, in particular, a regulatory change may help one part of the firm while hurting another.[31] If a business cannot confidently say that a regulatory change will improve its competitiveness, there is no reason for it to pursue that change.

Pushing for a reduction in a regulatory trade barrier also risks generating a backlash if that reduction is seen to be undermining a highly valued goal of public policy. Given firms' growing reliance on branding to differentiate and sell their products, reputational damage is becoming a profound risk for businesses.[32] Similarly, businesses may view a particular regulation as so firmly entrenched that political resources expended in trying to reduce the regulatory barriers are wasted. There is no point in attempting the impossible.

Even if an existing regulatory framework is not the ideal solution from a business perspective, it is sometimes good enough to elicit acceptance from business. An example of such acceptance involves the Safe Harbor Arrangement, which governed early iterations of e-commerce between the United States and Europe. While American businesses would have preferred regulatory harmonization based on U.S. law, the Safe Harbor

Arrangement was acceptable to U.S. businesses because its reduction of regulatory barriers on data privacy occurred on a firm-by-firm basis.[33]

All of these factors mean that businesses will lead the charge to reduce regulatory trade barriers in many instances. But they may remain undecided or apathetic when faced with trade-impeding cross-national regulatory differences. To summarize, firms choose not to push for regulatory barrier reduction if (1) complying with those regulatory differences is cheap or (2) attempting to reduce them would have severe reputational consequences.

Business Motivations to Seek Reduced Regulatory Barriers
1. Raises production costs
2. Inhibits market access

Factors That Weaken Business Motivation to Seek Reduced Regulatory Barriers
1. Cheap compliance
2. Potential reputational consequences of reduction attempts

Why Activist Groups Seek to Raise Regulatory Trade Barriers

Just as businesses grow in specific political and regulatory contexts, so do activist organizations. Many citizens advocate for greater environmental protection because they sense the need to clean up the air and water around them. Such concerns were central to promoting the environmental movements in the United States and Europe in the 1960s and 1970s. Many citizens get involved in consumer advocacy when they perceive that some product they have purchased endangered them because the company that made it was malfeasant. That kind of concern facilitated the rise of the consumer movements in the United States and Europe in the 1960s and 1970s. Labor unions focus on local and national grievances. Activist organizations exist to lobby governments for greater regulatory protection.

National governments' leadership in regulation means that citizens who care about a given regulation or lack thereof are incentivized to organize nationally. The smog in Los Angeles in the 1960s was so thick that it was practically chewy. The Cuyahoga River in Cleveland was so polluted that it caught on fire multiple times. The entity with the power to do something about those problems was the U.S. federal government. Environmental protection in other states also tends to be built on national-level laws. The same is true for regulation on consumer protection and labor. This dynamic is not a product of a bygone era. As new technologies arise today, they create similar calls for regulation. Almost as soon as firms started employing nanoscale particles and compounds in the twenty-first century, activist groups became concerned about the risks they posed and lobbied governments to tightly regulate them.[34]

The chief regulations that exist are not promulgated by the United Nations or other supranational organizations, which have little power to regulate except where they have the cooperation of national governments. Of course, international organizations like the World Trade Organization affect trade and regulation, and nongovernmental organizations do seek to interact with the WTO.[35] But states still take the lead in regulation. Thus, even when international organizations like the WTO and the Codex Alimentarius are involved in regulating, the chief targets of regulation-promoting activist groups are national-level government officials.[36] Even when activists go "beyond borders," their primary aims are usually to change national laws.[37] For example, when European and Japanese environmentalists wanted to increase regulatory barriers on tropical timber to protect the rain forests, their primary target was the Malaysian government.[38] As one of the leading scholars on nongovernmental organizations has found, even NGOs with an international orientation are "deeply tied to national environments," and despite their attempts to go global, their strategies "are driven by resources, institutions, and norms within their home countries."[39]

A crucial point here is that given national government's centrality, activist groups that exist to promote regulation do so largely at the national level. The differences across state's laws mean that even though activists are not really trying to create trade barriers, they do exactly that as a by-product of their demand that national governments increase regulation. Their pursuit of specifically national regulation, not their pursuit of higher regulatory standards per se, creates regulatory trade barriers. Still, activists often face collective action problems, so it is not automatic that they will be able to effectively push for the preservation or construction of a regulatory trade barrier on a given issue. Four factors lead activists to pursue specifically national regulation that can create regulatory trade barriers.

First, regulations are often the most effective, enforceable means for activists to promote their causes. Consumer campaigns rely on a series of assumptions: that consumers will receive the messaging, that they will understand it, and that they will act on it.[40] These assumptions often fail.[41] Few consumers are willing to pay more for goods produced in socially responsible ways.[42] Activists tend to lack the resources to monitor firms' compliance with private standards.[43] The amount of media attention a boycott or threatened boycott receives is another important factor here; when that attention is lacking, firms feel less pressure to alter their practices.[44] Campaigns' general rarity of success in getting consumers to punish irresponsible firms means that activists often need to get government to force businesses to change their behavior.

Second, activists are often suspicious of business. They often maintain strong skepticism that businesses will behave responsibly if not forced to do so. Activists led the opposition to the Multilateral Agreement on Investment (MAI) precisely because they feared it would empower firms to advance their interests over citizens' well-being.[45] Consumer watchdogs exist to ferret out businesses' misdeeds. Some environmental activists have adopted adversarial positions against firms, focusing on naming and shaming rather than collaboration.[46] Doctors Without Borders and other access-to-medicine advocates contend that drug companies are so obsessed with profit that they will readily sacrifice the lives of millions of poor people.[47]

Third, raising the level of regulatory protection by emulating the state with the highest protection or convincing multiple states to adopt the same regulations would not create as many regulatory barriers, but this situation happens infrequently, because activists tend to distrust foreign standards at least as much as, if not more than, those of their own country.[48] For example, most Americans want to ban unpasteurized milk even though Europeans generally accept it, and Europeans want to ban hormones in beef that raise considerably less alarm in the United States.[49] This consumer distrust extends to other regulations as well. When asked about U.S. and German regulations in data privacy, food safety, environmental protection, and automobile safety, citizens of both states trusted their own country's regulations more than the other's.[50]

Some of these consumers see regulatory cooperation in trade agreements as a threat to specifically national cultural touchstones and traditions. Polling has shown that emphasizing the ways in which investor-state dispute settlement may be used to challenge a country's domestic regulations can be an effective way to persuade citizens to oppose a trade agreement they otherwise support, generating greater mobilization against an agreement.[51] Citizens of developed states are especially mistrustful of the rules in developing countries, as exemplified by some of those citizens' views on China. When asked what percentage of Chinese imports they believed violate U.S. safety standards, the mean guess among U.S. citizens was 45 percent, and 74 percent of respondents reported being very or somewhat concerned about the safety of food imports from China.[52] This skepticism toward China can be found in Europe too.[53]

Fourth, activists often do not prioritize trade expansion or believe that threatening to curtail trade is an effective way to promote their policy goals. Environmentalists have sometimes associated trade liberalization with environmental degradation even though the evidence on that association is mixed.[54] When they have advocated for linking trade and the environment, they have tried to use the threat of trade reduction as leverage to compel compliance.[55] Examples of this include the Convention on the International Trade in Endangered Species, the International Whaling Commission, and the Montreal Protocol.[56] Activists have successfully inserted human rights clauses in the EU's trade agreements.[57] Unions, labor activists, and consumer groups have employed similar tactics.[58] An activist group's trade views play a role too. If a group views trade positively, a small attenuation in a regulation may seem to be a reasonably small price to pay. If a group already views trade negatively, reducing that regulatory trade barrier is a sacrifice that serves only to facilitate the additional hardship of liberalized trade.

Consumer groups are an interesting manifestation of activists not valuing trade because they generally represent a group of people who, at least superficially, should support trade liberalization. After all, one of trade's biggest benefits is that it lowers prices and increases choice, which benefit consumers. Why, then, do consumer groups often advocate for greater regulation at the cost of trade? That paradox can be explained by Gunnar Trumbull's research on narratives. He argues that consumer advocacy groups rely on two main kinds of argument: "narratives of access," which call on the state to increase consumers' access to certain goods, and "narratives of protection," which call on the state to protect consumers from the dangers posed by certain goods.[59]

Consumer organizations have historically rested on a foundation of affluence and have been primarily concerned with issues that motivate their more well-off members.[60] The affluence of those consumers means that they generally perceive access to goods as less of a problem than the potential dangers of substandard goods. With regard to trade, consumer groups operating with this perception tend to be much more interested in narratives of protection than in narratives of access, and narratives of protection lead them to ask for more specifically national regulation.

These factors lead activists to seek specifically national or (in the case of the EU) regional regulations, regardless of the consequences for trade. U.S. consumer groups have demanded country-of-origin labeling, which, in effect even if not in intent, disproportionately harms Canadian meat suppliers.[61] Greenpeace's campaign against phthalates (chemicals that make plastic toys softer) led to the creation of more-stringent safety regulations on toys in Europe, which created regulatory barriers in the toy trade between the United States and the EU.[62] Greenhouse gas regulations backed by European environmentalists have created regulatory trade barriers in refrigerators.[63] Again, these are just a few of many potential examples.

To summarize, activist organizations push for a regulatory barrier increase for two main reasons. First, they want to redress a societal problem and believe that they cannot achieve their goals through nonregulatory means. Second, they prefer to use trade curtailment (over liberalization) to achieve their policy aims.

Factors That May Provoke Activist Apathy on Regulatory Trade Barriers

As in the case of businesses, activists' positions on regulatory barriers are shaped not only by their material interests but also by their historical memories, their ideologies, and the way they define themselves. Activists often seek increased regulatory barriers, but sometimes they choose to not care about a particular regulatory barrier. One reason they may choose not to act is if an issue has low salience, so that people are not aware of it. The bleakness of the view of Anthony Downs that "most people are almost totally uninformed about most public issues" does not make it entirely untrue.[64] A major source of activists' political power when they interface with firms is the possibility that they can turn the public against the firm. If their ability to do so is low because the issue at hand is low in salience, that power is reduced.[65]

Relatedly, activist groups have limited resources. If few of a group's members care about an issue, that group is unlikely to expend resources defending that barrier. For example, prior to the 1970s, shipping regulations were not particularly salient for environmentalists, so they did very little lobbying on them. However, the growth in ships' size combined with several high-profile spills to elevate the salience of those regulations, so environmentalists began seeking more-stringent shipping rules.[66] Similarly, labor standards gained greater salience with the expansion and heightened publicity of the anti-sweatshop campaign in the 1990s.

The salience of a regulation depends on how tangible it is, how it gets framed, and how direct the connection is between citizens' lives and the regulation.[67] If citizens cannot understand a regulation or estimate how it might affect them, that regulation is likely to remain unpoliticized. For example, when U.S. and EU-based stock markets moved to reduce the regulatory differences between their accounting standards, activist groups took little, if any, notice and said nothing, mostly because, for those who do not already work for accounting firms, regulations on accounting standards can be almost incomprehensibly technical and perhaps a little boring.[68]

Low salience can be compounded when regulations are made internationally. Because the process of rulemaking in international forums is further removed from the public eye, the ability of a regulation to gain salience may be undermined. There can be a self-fulfilling character to this form of networked governance. Regulatory coherence provisions in trade agreements such as the Comprehensive Economic and Trade Agreement and the now-defunct Trans-Pacific Partnership are mostly meant for and apply to matters so technical that activists are unlikely to care about them, and by regulating through these coherence frameworks, those issues are even more unlikely to gain salience, which further reduces activists' access. Yet some institutions that have traditionally not had much public involvement, such as the Codex Alimentarius, have been making efforts to more fully include NGOs.[69] Some research also suggests that when activists routinely engage with the WTO, they gradually become socialized into becoming more technocratic and trade-promoting.[70]

How an NGO and the society in which it is embedded perceive risk can also affect which risks must be regulated against and which can be tolerated. NGOs and societies that adopt more group and hierarchy-based orientations are often more predisposed to risk mitigation through regulation than are those that adopt more individualistic perspectives.[71] Relatedly, much also depends on just how adversarial the particular NGO is to business. Friends of the Earth, Public Citizen, and Greenpeace have been more adversarial toward business than the National Wildlife Federation and the Environmental Defense Fund.[72] Some activists are willing to work with business. Others decry the reforms of many businesses as "greenwashing," a thin public relations veil that delivers undeserved legitimacy to activities that are still fundamentally dirty.[73] This "good cop, bad cop" routine gives NGOs leverage. David Baron's research has found that the greater the threat from confrontational activists is, the more firms want to work with cooperative activists.[74] Moreover, when activists repeatedly target the same firm, that firm is more likely to adopt defensive management practices that increase the firm's receptivity to activism.[75]

Strategic Interplay between Businesses and Activists

An NGO's acquiescence to a reduction in regulatory trade barriers can be effectively purchased by firms accepting a higher standard in exchange for that standard being unified or may be purchased through some combination of corporate social responsibility, self-regulation, and/or industry codes of conduct. Activist acquiescence bought by business agreeing to accept a higher level of regulation in exchange for a unified standard is especially likely to occur in areas where businesses care more about the multiplicity of regulation than the level of regulation and where what constitutes an upward movement in regulatory protection is clear to all parties. The movement in regulatory trade barriers on automobile emissions (covered in chapter 4 in this book) demonstrates that kind of dynamic.

Environmentalists have been able to design and promote specific regulations themselves,[76] which gives them the ability to choose from an array of regulatory options. There is significant evidence that when they have designed standards for which compliance is cheaper, they have been more effective at eliciting cooperation from business and thus protecting the environment.[77] When businesses work with NGOs to promote reform through codes of conduct or private regimes, NGOs often do not press for government regulation.[78] Indeed, what defines a private regime is that it is not state-enforced.[79] Such regimes have grown considerably over the last two decades.[80] Some examples of NGO-business partnerships that avoid government-enforced regulations include the Fair Labor Association, the Marine Stewardship Council, and the Fairtrade Labeling Organization.[81]

Importantly, activist pressure pushes businesses to agree to these partnerships.[82] Issue areas where there is significant NGO activity comprise a huge share of all private standard regimes.[83] Firms that engage in self-regulation are similarly attempting to preempt state regulation.[84] Often, firms self-regulate because they are trying to undermine an activist campaign against them.[85] The self-regulation is sometimes little more than a flimsy sham designed to serve as a public relations campaign, as in the case of the chemical industry's Responsible Care scheme after a major accident in Bhopal, India.[86] In other instances, such as in the self-regulation done by Body Shop and Levi-Strauss, self-regulation can actually be quite robust.[87]

Corporate social responsibility (CSR) activities have moved beyond philanthropic gestures and have become more political, in that firms now often provide public goods and contribute toward society's achievement of regulatory goals.[88] As with private standards, most cases of these activities are not pure altruism. Scholars have found that activists' demands are the primary stimuli that provoke firms into implementing CSR.[89] In other words, CSR is a way of buying off activists. For example, Swedish retailers were able to prevent environmentalist NGOs from undermining their sale of imported seafood by agreeing to sell only those products that had been caught sustainably.[90] A successful buyout of activists usually amounts to a buyout of government officials as well. Government officials respond to pressure. If environmentalists accept a regulatory barrier reduction, why should the Environmental Protection Agency stop it?

Activists are able to demand these buyouts by presenting businesses with the choice of accepting regulatory changes that increase costs or facing significant reputational damage.[91] For instance, Global Witness, an NGO that works on resource extraction in war zones, was able to get DeBeers to accept responsibility for keeping conflict diamonds out of the supply chain rather than foisting that responsibility onto regulators.[92] By acquiescing to NGO demands, DeBeers was largely able to avoid severe reputational damage and was able to shape the regulatory agreement known as the Kimberley Process Certification Scheme in ways that alleviated the extent to which the agreement raised trade costs.[93]

NGOs can force firms to desist with some form of commerce that the activist group, through a public relations campaign, has made too risky for their reputation. This is how the Free Burma Coalition was able to get Adidas and Costco to stop doing business in Myanmar.[94] They can also pressure a company to join a certification scheme in which the firm's reputation is safeguarded as long as it meets the requirements of an independent third party.[95]

All of these mechanisms rely on leveraging a firm's concern for its reputation. These strategies are thus especially effective in situations where a company relies on its brand and where there is a direct connection between its production methods and consumption.[96] A low-profile intermediate supplier may be somewhat less vulnerable, but a high-profile scandal involving a well-known brand can cost that firm a lot more than the cost associated with simply changing its production practices. When reports of forced child labor on cocoa farms in the Ivory Coast surfaced in 2000, Hershey's and Cadbury's were quick to work with NGOs to end those labor abuses.[97] The absolute last thing Hershey's and Cadbury's wanted people thinking about when they purchased chocolate was a child in slavery harvesting their bars' main ingredient.

Activist groups that employ these strategies in an attempt to win a buyout are aided by the fact that attempting to silence activist groups can easily backfire. For example, the attempts of Boise Cascade Lumber Company to have the Internal Revenue Service revoke the tax-exempt status of the Rainforest Action Network and to intimidate its funders with lawsuits only served to increase the profile and funding of the RAN.[98] Activist groups do have to give up total control over the regulatory process if they want businesses to participate. An early environmental labeling push (Green Seal) excluded businesses, which meant that Consumers Union loved it, while firms such as Proctor and Gamble opposed it.[99]

The key point is that businesses and activist groups may become engaged over a regulatory trade barrier but can also be convinced to remain politically inert on that issue. Should one of these sets of actors remain apathetic on a given issue, it becomes much easier for the other to dominate policy on that issue. To summarize, activist groups choose not to resist a regulatory trade barrier reduction because (1) the regulatory barrier is of such low salience that it does not justify expending resources to defend it or (2) their opposition is bought out by business through private standards, self-regulation, corporate social responsibility, or a higher international regulatory standard.

Activist Motivations to Defend Regulatory Trade Barriers

1. Perceive a problem that cannot be addressed in a nonregulatory way
2. Prefer trade curtailment to trade liberalization as a policy tool

Factors That Weaken Activist Motivation to Defend Regulatory Trade Barriers

1. Low salience
2. Concerns mollified through strategic interplay with business, via private standards, corporate social responsibility, or a higher international regulatory standard

Marginalizers and Champions: Government Officials in Regulatory Trade Politics

The involvement of officials in negotiations over a regulatory barrier means that businesses and activists both care about that barrier and were not able to reach agreement on some sort of private standard or buyout. In other words, the strategic interplay between activists and firms has reached some sort of impasse. At this point, they are both lobbying the government for policy support. Each of them is attempting to convince government officials to marginalize the other. Because activists and businesses are often so suspicious of each other, they would, in many cases, rather seek assistance from government first and cooperate with each other only as a last resort. Faced with these cross-pressures, government officials have three basic choices. First, they can champion business and marginalize activists. Second, they can champion activists and marginalize business. Third, they can refuse to take sides and instead encourage a buyout.

Officials may seek to promote domestic firms' interest, such as when the Federal Reserve supported more-stringent capital regulations in the Basel Accords while the Securities and Exchange Commission opposed more-stringent capital requirements on securities under the International Organization of Securities Commissions.[100] Officials may oppose firms, however, if defending them would incur reputational costs. Even though Nestle is a Swiss company, the Swiss government voted in favor of the World Health Organization's code of conduct on milk formula, out of concern for Switzerland's international reputation.[101] The relative political power of firms and NGOs can have a big impact on officials' incentives. Summarizing the literature on business lobbying in Washington, Coen, Grant, and Wilson note that "no group in the United States—certainly not the groups such as unions or public interest groups—that might be expected to clash with business commands anything like equal resources."[102] Yet activists provide information, deliver legitimacy, and may mete out electoral rewards and punishment.

The challenge of variation in politicians' constituencies is not a novel one but is made still more difficult by the ideational motivations explained here. Despite different pressures from their constituents, officials are more than just blind ropes following wherever they are tugged hardest. There are four major sources of officials' agency: institutional indeterminacy, competing imperatives, staffing decisions, and officials' beliefs about their core constituency. These sources of agency are exogenously given, making it difficult to formally model officials' stances on regulation and trade. Still, they matter a great deal in explaining the outcomes in negotiations over regulation and trade. Finding a way to model these motivations could be one avenue for future research on regulation and trade.

Domestic Institutional Indeterminacy

Officials are not locked in place by their institutions. Those institutions with opaque, closed decision-making can facilitate industry capture but also provide a means to marginalize firms should officials want to do so.[103] Networked governance is prone to this marginalization, given that networks tend to inhibit broader participation.[104] Institutions with open, transparent decision-making are assumed to be friendlier to NGOs, however; many access points may give firms more opportunities to shape regulations to their benefit.[105] Institutions may shape government officials' constituencies. There is evidence that officials with national constituencies tend to be more pro-trade, while officials with more parochial constituencies tend toward protectionism.[106] Party discipline also seems to push officials toward greater support for trade.[107]

Institutions vary in other ways that may hinder or promote reducing regulatory barriers. They vary in their ability to provide timely information to key stakeholders, which impacts the effectiveness of those stakeholders, usually businesses, in attempting to shape regulations being forged in international regulatory organizations such as the International Organization for Standardization.[108] There is also the issue of equality in institution's regulatory capacity. When one state has a highly developed regulatory capacity, it is more likely to impose its regulations on products from other states that do not, and it is more likely to engage in regulatory cooperation with other states that have a similar level of capacity.[109]

Competing Imperatives

One of the reasons why government officials' behavior in regulation and trade cannot be easily predicted is that, within the realm of regulatory trade politics, they are often attempting to balance competing imperatives. South African officials, for instance, have struggled with how to best balance the need to attract foreign capital to promote employment growth and black economic empowerment while also increasing labor standards.[110] Within governments, there are often contradictory impulses toward business. U.S. politicians have routinely advocated reducing the regulatory burden on business, yet the tradition of adversarial legalism pushes the entire governing structure toward conflict with businesses over regulations.[111] Another example of these impulses is the desire within many industrialized countries to accompany promotion of market competition with detailed and comprehensive regulations that govern commercial activity within the markets.[112]

There are also contradictory impulses toward NGOs. Sometimes, NGOs can be seen as quite helpful. Environmentalists helped the Environmental Protection Agency be a real player in NAFTA negotiations, despite the fact that they normally had no meaningful role in trade negotiations. But officials can sometimes be suspicious of NGOs' motives and annoyed by their activities.

Furthermore, government officials' ideas about the process of making regulation can have big effects on the character and strength of the political participation of business and activists. U.S. officials tend to promote more open and transparent processes, anticipating that this allows for more and better input while limiting corruption. The EU, fearing that such transparency simply opens the door for greater, unacceptably high levels of business influence, disagrees with the U.S. approach. This disagreement ties back into the issue of regulatory coherence. Government officials are more likely to push such salience-reducing mechanisms when they value the input of business more than that of activists.

Expertise and Staffing Decisions

Bureaucracies may develop their own systems of information gathering and expertise creation, apart from the regulated interest. The type of people that a bureaucracy hires has significant implications for these processes. The U.S. Forest Service generally hires and promotes scientists, whereas the U.S. Park Service hires few scientists; this difference leads those two departments to have different cultures and to take dissimilar positions on how best to manage wilderness areas.[113]

Hiring practices can have significant implications for government agencies' positions on trade. A good example is the staffing of the Office of the United States Trade Representative (USTR) on issues that relate to intellectual property (discussed in chapter 7). The USTR hires people from IP-intensive businesses, and those same businesses hire USTR alumni, in what appears to be an epitome of a revolving door.[114]

The practice of "cleared advisers" on this issue shows a similar dynamic. Cleared advisers are people who are allowed to view confidential negotiating documents. Firms have had many of their representatives named as cleared advisers; however, when asked about cleared advisers from nonbusiness groups, a USTR spokesperson could not name a single cleared adviser from a public interest group or activist NGO.[115] There is nothing illegal or corrupt in this relationship between the USTR and IP-intensive firms, but it is unquestionably a cozy relationship. It is not surprising, then, that the policy preferences of these firms enjoy serious clout within the USTR. When government officials believe that they need businesses' expertise in trade-related regulatory matters, they are more likely to adopt a more consultative approach to business, thus giving business greater access to the policymaking process.[116]

Beliefs and Self-Identity

How government officials define their role can have a great deal of influence in terms of which constituencies they listen to most, how much they value generalized welfare against more particular interests, who they think is supposed to be helped by a regulation, and what the proper relationship between business and government ought to be.[117] Compared to their Swedish counterparts, American officials in the Occupational Safety and Health Administration tend to be much more legalistic and to have a much more adversarial relationship with business.[118] Government officials also can define for themselves what their job is. USDA officials resisted being put in charge of nutritional assistance programs (i.e., food stamps).[119] In the 1980s, judges in the European Court of Justice sought to include themselves in adjudicating disputes over intra-European nontariff barriers.[120] These role definitions can be drivers of officials' policy disposition. The USTR (at least prior to the Trump administration) traditionally had a culture that prized free trade, so that office has been more apt to promote the interests of U.S. exporters than to look for ways to create barriers to imports.[121]

Government officials may choose to do businesses' bidding if they believe that pleasing business is a prerequisite for the economic well-being of their constituents. They may also have an ideological commitment to free trade. There is an international component to that commitment. The internationalization of epistemic communities through networks can promote common understandings of regulatory issues and can thus lead government officials to work toward reducing regulatory trade barriers.[122] Cross-national differences in institutional arrangements and cultural beliefs about the underlying regulatory issues can thwart efforts to reduce regulatory barriers, even in areas, such as software patents, where other considerations suggest policy convergence.[123]

To summarize, government officials side with business and marginalize activists if (1) the officials care more about commercial expansion than regulatory independence, (2) their staffing favors business, and/or (3) they identify business as a core constituency. Government officials side with activists if (1) the officials care more about regulatory independence than trade, (2) their staffing favors activists, and/or (3) the officials identify NGOs as a core constituency.

Factors That Motivate Government Officials to Side with Businesses

1. Care more about trade than regulatory independence
2. Staffing and expertise favor business
3. Identify business as a core constituency

Factors That Motivate Government Officials to Side with Activists

1. Care more about regulatory independence than trade
2. Staffing and expertise favor activists
3. Identify NGOs as a core constituency

The Sequencing of Negotiations on Regulatory Trade Barriers

On many occasions, the political negotiation over a given regulatory trade barrier is begun by business and influenced by a series of motivation sets, included in the flowcharts in tables 3.2 and 3.3. In those negotiation scenarios, if motivation set A outweighs motivation set B, businesses will seek to reduce regulatory trade barriers. Once businesses seek to do this, the motivations of activist groups determine whether or not they will resist the reduction. If motivation set D is equal to or greater than motivation set C, activist groups will not resist the regulatory barrier reduction. If motivation set C outweighs motivation set D, they will resist that reduction. In the last scenario, the position of government officials becomes the determining factor. If motivation set E outweighs motivation set F, government officials will side with business and reduce the regulatory barrier. If motivation set F outweighs motivation set E, government officials will side

TABLE 3.1. Summary of Motivations in Trade Politics

Set A. Business Seeks Reduction	Set B. Business Inert
1. Regulations raise production costs 2. Regulations inhibit market access	1. Reputational consequences 2. Firm culture and leader values
Set C. Activists Seek Increase	**Set D. Activists Inert**
1. Perceive regulations as sole means 2. Prefer trade leverage over expansion	1. Low salience 2. Acquiescence purchased
Set E. Government Officials Side with Business	**Set F. Government Officials Side with Activists**
1. Care more about trade 2. Staffing favors business 3. Identify business as core constituency	1. Care more about regulating industry 2. Staffing favors activists 3. Identify NGOs as core constituency

with the activist groups and maintain the regulatory barrier. If government officials hold the two motivation sets roughly equal to each other, they will promote a buyout between business and activists. On other occasions, the political negotiation over a given regulatory trade barrier is begun by activists. In those scenarios, the ordering of businesses and activists is simply reversed. The regulatory outcomes associated with the choices influenced by the motivation sets are also included in figures 3.1 and 3.2.

This depiction of the weighing of different motivations is more nuanced than many of the standard accounts of political economy discussed later in this chapter. As I explained in chapter 1, the cleavage-based explanations would not sufficiently include activists and would oversimplify government officials' motivations. The state-centric explanations would paper over virtually all of the complex strategic interplay between the three groups. The arguments of disguised protectionism and domination by business would, in my view, oversimplify the motivations of business and underappreciate the role of activists. The motivations depiction also helps show how negotiations that go on within one state impact the dyadic relationship between states. Activists and firms often initially conduct their political activities in a single state, but their actions reverberate internationally and affect firms, activists, and government officials, who then react. That reaction point is where the interplay between the three sets of actors spans state lines.

Competitiveness and Death: Explaining Who Wins and Why

Businesses are likely to succeed at reducing a regulatory trade barrier when they can link their desire for that reduction with broader concerns about economic competitiveness. Activist organizations are likely to succeed at increasing regulatory trade barriers when they can link their desire for maintaining or increasing that barrier with preventing needless death. Those linkages augment one group's motivation to engage in the political fight, weaken the other side's resolve, and present government officials with a situation in which the majority of incentives and ideas flow in one direction.

Competitiveness

As I discussed earlier in this chapter, businesses become motivated to lobby on regulatory trade barriers when those barriers raise production costs and/or inhibit market access, both situations that directly undermine

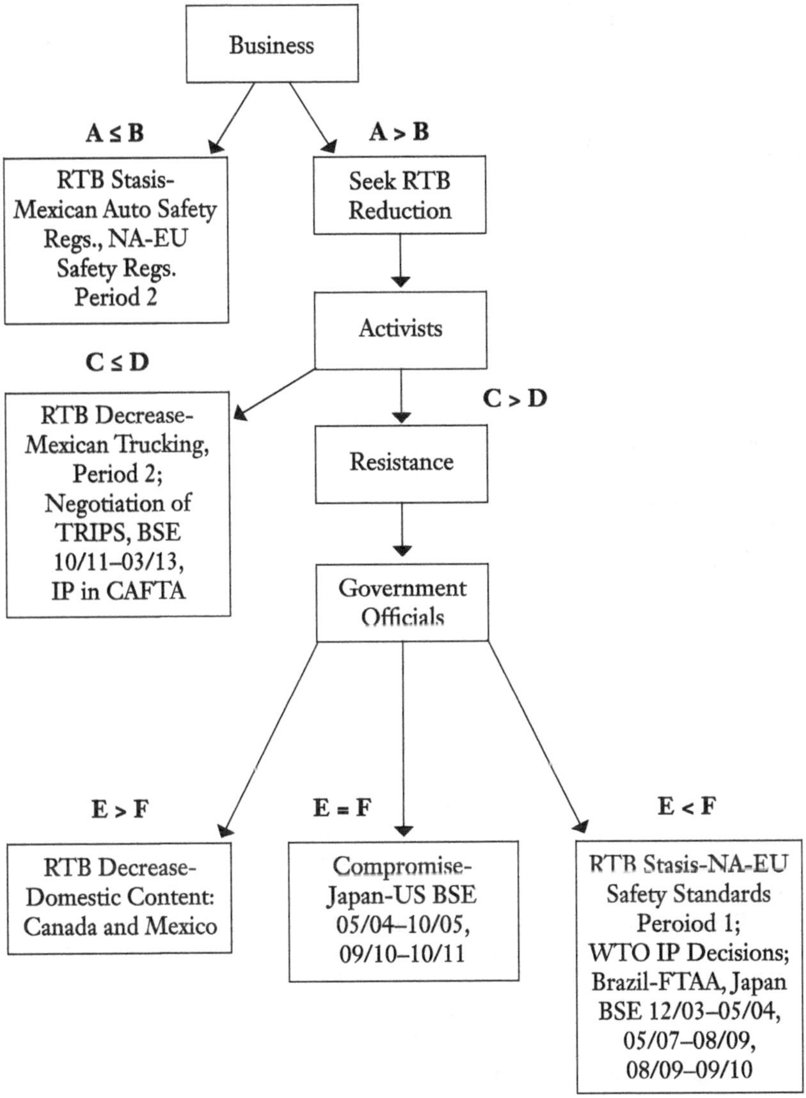

Fig. 3.1. Regulatory choices and outcomes when business moves first

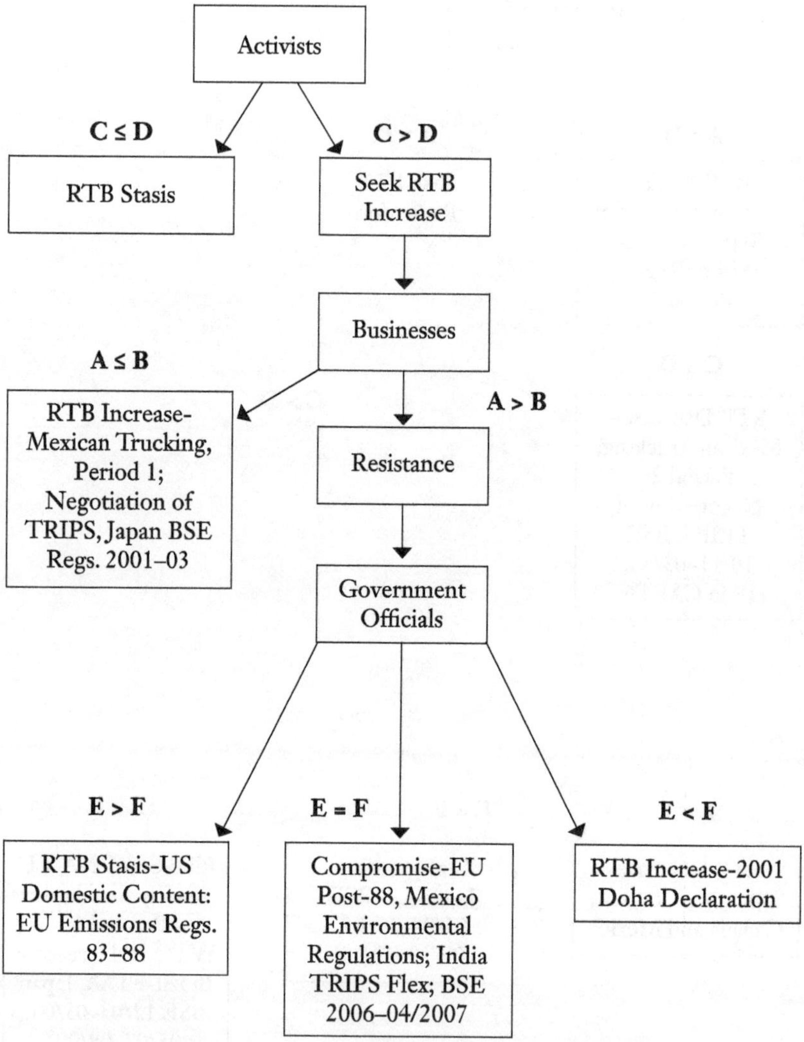

Fig. 3.2. Regulatory choices and outcomes when activists move first

businesses' competitiveness. The factors that reduce this motivation, cheap compliance and reputational concerns, are also related to competitiveness. Cheap compliance means that a regulatory barrier has little to no effect on a firm's competitiveness, while reputational concerns mean that despite the financial costs of a particular regulatory barrier, attempting to reduce that barrier could besmirch a firm's reputation and thus do even more damage to that business's competitiveness. Businesses will lobby the hardest on regulatory barriers related to competitiveness.

This relationship between regulatory lobbying and competitiveness occurs throughout the cases analyzed in the following chapters. In the early 1980s, Ford, General Motors, and Chrysler fought hard to reduce labor-backed regulatory trade barriers concerned with domestic content, precisely because those regulatory barriers were making them less competitive vis-à-vis Japanese automakers. In Europe, companies that specialized in small cars (e.g., Fiat and Peugeot) fought hard against increased environmental regulatory barriers, because those barriers threatened to annihilate their competitiveness in states like Denmark, the Netherlands, and Germany. Those companies relaxed their opposition only after a series of developments made increasing environmental regulations no longer a throttle on their competitiveness. In the mid-2000s, U.S. beef producers stridently resisted Japanese safety-related regulatory barriers on beef, because those barriers effectively prohibited the U.S. producers from competing in the Japanese market and because acquiescing to Japanese demands could have made U.S. beef products less price-competitive against other forms of meat, such as chicken and fish. Western pharmaceutical firms became highly engaged in attempting to reduce developing countries' IP-related regulatory barriers precisely because those barriers were corroding their international competitiveness.

Crucially, competitiveness concerns are also significant in driving government officials to side with business in reducing regulatory trade barriers. When businesses can link their request for reduced regulatory barriers with broader concerns about national economic competitiveness, reducing those barriers no longer appears to be a favor to business. Instead, it is a proactive, jobs-creating, economy-boosting decision. Not only does the competitiveness argument smoothly portray doing what is best for business as doing what is best for the country, but it rhetorically delegitimizes opposing that reduction, because if a regulatory barrier is perceived to be a matter of competitiveness, defending that barrier makes the country less economically competitive.

The narrative of competitiveness is effective because many people, including government officials, see economics as a fundamentally competitive activity.[124] Economists would disagree, pointing to the innumerable ways in which economic activity is positive-sum. That nature of economic activity does not change the fact that many people, including government officials, find the language of competitiveness intuitively appealing with regard to international economics.

Furthermore, competitiveness often gains salience on the political agenda during a time of acute economic distress. Concerns about competitiveness during such times take on an air of crisis requiring government action. Relatedly, government officials are more capable of reducing regulatory barriers during those times because moments of economic distress create policy windows in which altering trade policy becomes easier.[125]

The case studies analyzed in subsequent chapters demonstrate this distress pattern as well. Worries about continued economic malaise drove attempts of officials in the European Community to reduce intracontinental regulatory barriers in automobiles in the 1980s. Concerns that Korean firms would gain a competitive edge over Japanese firms in terms of exports to America contributed to the willingness of Japanese government officials to reduce the regulatory barriers in the U.S.-Japan beef trade in 2013. U.S. government officials connected stringent intellectual property rights with American firms' competitiveness during the negotiation of the Uruguay Round and were eager to reduce the regulatory barriers between developed and developing countries. These same competitiveness-based motivations led U.S. government officials to work with the Big Three automakers to marginalize labor unions and reduce regulatory barriers concerned with domestic content. All of the most significant reductions in regulatory trade barriers in the cases analyzed in this book were accompanied by competitiveness concerns. More than anything else, competitiveness explains when regulatory trade barriers get reduced.

Preventing Needless Death

Some regulations touch on matters more favorably presented as preventing needless death. For example, as discussed in the next chapter, transatlantic differences in safety regulation were much easier to frame as preventing needless death than were domestic content regulations, a situation that goes a long way toward explaining why the former were maintained whereas the latter were reduced. When regulations touch on life-and-death matters and can more easily be framed as preventing needless death, regulatory trade barriers are much more likely to be defended or increased, because then activists tend to become more motivated and stronger, businesses become inert or skittish, and government officials tend to become more receptive to activists' demands. As I discussed earlier in this chapter, activist groups may remain inert on a particular regulatory trade barrier if that barrier has low salience or if their opposition can be bought off through private standards, corporate social responsibility, or some other arrangement in which businesses are not directly regulated by government. When activist groups perceive a regulation as being necessary to prevent needless death, neither of those conditions is likely. To state the obvious, death grabs attention and concerns citizens more than almost any other thing. Death raises the salience of an issue. It is clear and tangible and motivating, especially when the time line and the causal connection between a regulatory mistake and needless death are short. The shorter that time line and causal connection are, the more available framings based on preventing needless death are likely to be.

Death does not just motivate activist groups. It also shifts the political terrain in ways that fundamentally increase activists' chance of lobbying success. Not only does death motivate activists, but it can cow businesses by presenting them with severe reputational risks, weakening the political force that might oppose activists' call for greater regulatory barriers.

Many of governments' core responsibilities revolve around preventing unnecessary deaths. The threat of such deaths is why we have armies, health care systems, government-funded cancer research, policemen, firemen, food inspection, building codes, water treatment facilities, the National Weather Service, bridge standards, and consumer safety warnings. Preventing death is what government does. The birth of modern regulation in the late nineteenth and early twentieth centuries centered on food and drug safety because business ineptitude and (in some cases) mendacity led to people dying. Activist groups and citizens are unlikely to accept the notion that the government should stand by and do nothing when, through regulation, it could prevent needless death.

Government officials are people too. At least in decently run places, those officials do not want their citizens to die needlessly, so their motivation to maintain preventive regulations is increased. The pressure that activists can bring to bear on these issues is unlikely to be lost on those government officials. Furthermore, on regulations that pertain to preventing death, those officials are more likely to value regulatory independence over trade and, given the engagement of activist groups, are more likely to identify NGOs as their core constituency. In summation, when a regulatory trade barrier is perceived to pertain to preventing needless death, activists get motivated, businesses get quiet, and government officials get involved.

The case studies analyzed in subsequent chapters bear out this pattern. The primary regulatory barriers in auto manufacturing that were reduced within Europe and North America were related to emissions in the case of Europe and domestic content in the case of North America. Neither of those concerns had to do with preventing death. The principal regulatory barriers between the regions, on safety differences, have been maintained.

They have everything to do with preventing death. Consumer advocacy groups and government officials on both sides of the Atlantic have fought to maintain those regulatory barriers.

When humans consume beef from cows infected with bovine spongiform encephalopathy, a neurological disease in cows, they may get variant Creutzfeldt-Jakob's disease, which is fatal and has no known cure. When Japanese consumer groups were defending Japan's stringent anti-BSE countermeasures, they were doing so to prevent needless deaths. Only when BSE became more fully contained and when concerns about BSE and needless death subsided were Japanese consumer groups and government officials more willing to reduce regulatory trade barriers in the U.S.-Japan beef trade.

The AIDS crisis in sub-Saharan Africa yielded death on a massive scale. Access-to-medicine advocates held that stringent intellectual property regulations, as enforced by the TRIPS Agreement, were making drugs too expensive for AIDS victims and were causing needless death. Those activists and officials in developing countries fought vigorously to solidify policy space in the Doha Declaration to increase regulatory trade barriers related to intellectual property, thereby increasing international regulatory diversity in the policy area.

In the cases analyzed in this book, the most resilient stasis in regulatory trade barriers and the most significant increases in those barriers were distinguished by serious concerns that relaxing those regulatory barriers would lead to needless death. More than anything else, the threat of needless death explains when regulatory trade barriers get maintained or increased. To be clear, many regulatory barriers cannot easily be connected to preventing needless death. My argument is not that they all can be but that those that can be shift the political terrain so that those barriers are more likely to be effectively defended or increased.

The contrasting motivations discussed earlier in this chapter help explain when framings of competitiveness and preventing death are more or less likely to succeed. A business trying to advance competitiveness framings is likely to have more difficulty doing so if it is opposed by activists armed with their own framings of preventing death or if interacting with officials who deeply value regulatory independence, who have staffing arrangements that favor NGOs, and/or who view activists as a core constituency. An activist organization trying to advance framings of preventing needless death is likely to have more difficulty doing so if it is opposed by firms that can marshal competitiveness framings or if interacting with officials who prize trade promotion more than regulatory independence, who have staffing arrangements that favor business, and/or who view business as a core constituency.

Alternative Explanations

A number of existing theories seek to explain trade politics. They all struggle to fully capture the dynamics that surround regulatory trade barriers.

Cleavage-Based Theory

As I discussed in chapter 1, cleavage-based explanations struggle to explain trade politics that involve regulations. As I showed in chapter 2, cross-national differences in regulation have become the most prominent issue in international trade politics and continue to grow even more important. Thus the failure to explain regulatory trade barriers constitutes a large and expanding blind spot for the standard cleavage-based explanations.

Business Dominates

Some theorists offer the explanation that large corporations able to effectively lobby governments drive trade policy.[126] We might call that explanation the "business dominates" hypothesis. The imagery of a businessman puppeteering government officials to deliver protectionism goes back to one of political science's earliest works on trade, Schattschneider's *Politics, Pressures, and the Tariff*.[127] In its modern manifestations, especially among antiglobalization activists, that explanation ignores the fact that officials are capable of telling business "no" when they wish.

Government officials do sometimes adopt positions that help business, but to assume that must happen is an exaggeration of businesses' political power. Activist organizations can exert significant pressure on government officials, as exemplified by the collapse of the Multilateral Agreement on Investment. Businesses wanted the MAI very much, but the trade negotiators from the United States and European Union were forced to abandon the MAI when activist organizations were able to successfully portray it as a giveaway to big business.[128] Activists' pressure was critical to the 2016 stymieing of the Transatlantic Trade and Investment Partnership and to the downfall of the Anti-Counterfeiting Trade Agreement.[129]

In some ways, regulatory barriers might even be seen as an easy case for the "business dominates" hypothesis, because businesses are often seen as the primary drivers of regulatory politics.[130] Because regulatory trade barriers should be an easy set of cases for the hypothesis, its failure to adequately explain them, as I show in the case studies to come, constitutes particularly damaging counterevidence against it. To be clear, I am not arguing that the political power of business is low. Rather, I argue that its political power is more contingent than is commonly believed.

Disguised Protectionism

Another argument is that regulatory trade barriers are nothing more than clever means of protecting domestic businesses from foreign competition.[131] The WTO limits tariffs and other nonregulatory trade barriers to such an extent that when a government wants to protect a domestic business from international competition, cleverly written regulations that hamper foreign firms more than domestic firms, but with a specious justification based in public safety, are one of the few efficacious tools of trade protectionism left to governments. This line of argument is quite common, because it comports with the cynical view of the political process held by many people. Government officials delivering protectionism to favored local constituencies and then pretending they were motivated by nobler, less parochial goals sounds like exactly the kind of thing we expect politicians to do.

Despite its intuitiveness, there are two reasons to be skeptical of this argument. First, as I discussed earlier in this chapter, businesses do not tend to seek protectionism via regulatory barriers. Second, even if businesses did so, trade rules are much more effective at preventing sly protectionism than they once were. Regulation did occur as disguised protectionism in the 1970s and 1980s, and many of the most famous examples of transparently protectionist regulations are from that period. For instance, in an effort to boost Japan's nascent industry in ski equipment, the Japanese government attempted to ban foreign equipment on the grounds that Japanese snow was "special" and that this "special" snow fell on every mountain in Japan.[132] That Ontario's environmental rules on bottles were designed more for the purpose of curtailing American beer imports than for protecting nature is transparent because those rules were not applied to soda.[133] New WTO rules under the Tokyo and Uruguay Rounds largely curtailed disguised protectionism.

John Braithwaite and Peter Drahos explain the change under the new WTO rules well and are worth quoting at length.

> Under the old regulation of national sovereignty, it would be common for South Korea, for example, to do the regulatory bidding of Hyundai in a smoke-filled room when Hyundai wanted a new non-tariff barrier. The national sovereign would not be required to provide good reasons; there was no risk that its reasoning might become known to consumer groups, let alone excoriated by their critiques. The post-1980 global regulatory order no longer works this way. South Korea will have to give reasons for the regulation, in Geneva. These reasons will be exposed to critique by hostile foreign firms, by independent professionals from non-manufacturing states or from the Society of Automotive Engineers, and by consumer advocates. If the standard is a spurious one, the South Korean public will find out by Consumers International passing the information to Korean consumer groups. South Korea will risk a WTO complaint and panel hearing over the non-tariff barrier and it may jeopardize type approval of its vehicles in states that have performance standards which are deliberatively defensible.[134]

Given that businesses in the contemporary context are unlikely to demand regulatory protectionism and that government officials are far less capable of granting that protectionism than they once were, the argument of sneaky protectionism may not be a particularly helpful explanation, despite its intuitive appeal.

The California Effect

David Vogel argues that rather than creating a race to the bottom, trade can encourage states to raise their environmental and consumer safety standards.[135] This explanation is called the "California effect," after an eponymous example in his book. After California set high standards in auto emissions, German automakers manufactured their cars to meet those standards and then, because they did not want to maintain two production lines or be disadvantaged in competition with domestic-only firms, successfully lobbied the German government to raise its emissions standards to the California level.[136]

There are three central elements to the California effect.[137] First, businesses will support stricter regulations when those regulations make them more competitive. Second, richer states with higher standards force producers in other states to raise their standards to export to them, thereby raising foreign standards. Third, trade agreements give richer states with higher standards leverage to pressure other states to raise their standards to the level of the richer states. The theory of the California effect was an important advance in this research space, but discrepancies between the expectations of the theory and empirical realities have shown that Vogel's explanation, though quite good, is incomplete.

That the California effect largely ignores government officials' beliefs is problematic, given that those officials are the people who write the regulations and do the negotiating over international trade agreements. Government officials must evaluate the utility of raising regulations, the utility of promoting commerce, and the relationship between those two goals. Official belief that raising regulations and liberalizing trade are mutually reinforcing (rather than conflicting) goals is likely to have a huge impact. Official belief that potential increases in regulation are wrongheaded and/or represent an unacceptable curtailment of commerce is also likely to matter a great deal. Societal actors can persuade government officials on various matters, provide useful information, and exert political pressure on officials, but that does not imply that those officials do not have ideas or that those ideas have no influence.

The California effect also largely undertheorizes the construction of a state's regulatory trade preferences. Why exactly is a "greener" state greener? Construction of preferences often gets addressed within the case material covered in Vogel's *Trading Up*, but within the theory of the California effect itself, it is nowhere to be found. The demands on the state for stricter regulations come from somewhere, and that somewhere needs to be explained. By ignoring activist organizations, the California effect discards a variable that may be critical to explaining which regulations a state wants to raise and on which regulations it is willing to compromise for the sake of trade liberalization.

Finally, the California effect overemphasizes the role of market power in regulatory trade politics.[138] The theory of the California effect asserts that market power matters because it gives states leverage, in the form of threatening to deny another state and its businesses access to a lucrative market. The underlying thrust of the argument is that even a smaller state that wants to fight hard on its regulatory preferences will eventually yield to the richer state's demands, because access to the richer state's market presents such an enormous economic opportunity for the poorer state's exporters. Undoubtedly, there is some truth to this argument: trade agreements do present exporters with significant opportunities in market access, and those exporters are likely to press their governments to pursue that access. Still, the argument based on market power overestimates the pliability of states' regulations. As all three cases presented in the following chapters show, even the United States, the country with the most leverage in market power, is constrained in its ability to deploy that power.

Labor, environmental, and consumer regulations are sensitive topics. Changing those regulations within a trade context may sometimes have the backing of activist organizations, as it did when Mexican environmentalists supported changes in their country's environmental regulations under NAFTA (as discussed in chapter 4). In many other contexts, though, attempts to change regulations within a trade context may run into strident opposition. Government officials changing regulations for the sake of trade promotion risk being labeled sellouts or lackeys.

The argument based on market power also assumes that officials prize promoting commerce over regulatory independence. Again, that assumption may be the case, but it is far from automatic. Finally, one must keep in mind that there are limitations to just how much the state with stricter regulations is able to demand from other states in a trade negotiation. If a state with higher standards in one issue wants to complete a trade agreement with a state that has lower standards in that area, will it really be willing to jeopardize the success of that trade negotiation over a disagreement on a regulation in that policy area? The California effect hypothesis cannot answer that question.

In summation, the theory of the California effect can be improved in three ways. Completing the theory requires adding the beliefs of government officials to the analytic mix, building a more substantial explanation of state preferences in regulatory trade politics, and shrinking (though not eradicating) the emphasis placed on market power. The explanation I offer in this book does all three.

State-Centric Explanations

Stephen Krasner and Joseph Grieco depict the intersection of trade and regulation as a distributional conflict, with the winner determined by political power.[139] In their depiction, states spar to see who can write the rules, with the winning state framing them in such a way as to benefit itself directly or, at least, its businesses.[140] Following their state-centric explanation, societal actors can be ignored, and the state's preferences can be assumed.

That state-centric depiction is parsimonious, but it assumes away many factors that may have a profound effect on the outcome of an international negotiation at the intersection of trade and regulation. If the only overarching objective a state is assumed to have in mind is to win the struggle to write the rules, it logically follows that the state will pursue that objective single-mindedly. To make that assumption, it helps tremendously to speak of country A wanting *x* and of country B wanting *y*, theorizing away the cacophonous debates that accompany political decision-making. Assuming that each of multiple unitary states wants to "win" leads almost inescapably to the conclusion that the winner is determined by which state is stronger.

Those assumptions oversimplify matters too much. At the intersection of trade and regulation, states do not have one primary goal, to win; they have two, economic benefits and autonomy in social regulation. States want both the economic benefits that derive from trade and the autonomy that comes with being able to set regulations independently. These two goals are frequently in tension. Agreeing to reduce regulatory trade barriers with another state delivers economic benefits at the cost of having specifically national regulations that can be changed on a political whim. Erecting regulatory barriers creates more regulatory independence at the cost of trade-related economic benefits. States have these multiple goals because their societies have multiple actors who make disparate and often contradictory demands on government officials. The multiplicity of demands means that states' international behavior and outcomes in international negotiation are likely to vary with the intensity and effectiveness of the societal demanders as well as with the proclivities of the governmental demandees.

The influence of state-centrism is shared by Dan Drezner's revisionist theory of international regulatory outcomes. Drezner argues that the distribution of great power preferences and the distribution of preferences between the great powers (the United States and the European Union) and other international actors (smaller states and NGOs) are the key independent variables in explaining regulatory outcomes.[141] For Drezner, domestic actors are important only insofar as they raise the adjustment cost to regulatory coordination. In Drezner's telling, on a given issue, government considers pursuing regulatory coordination, and domestic actors become important only to the extent that they make government pay a price for pursuing that coordination. This scenario fits with his approach of generally dismissing societal actors' importance. He specifically argues that NGOs and businesses "function as intervening variables, not as underlying causes," as well as that "corporations and transnational activist networks do not appear" in the accurate causal story on regulatory outcomes.[142]

On this point, Drezner's view is flawed. Firms are important domestic constituencies. When they care about an issue, their preferences matter. Indeed, in a review of international regulatory schemes, Abbott and Snidal find very few instances in which businesses' preferences were not significant factors.[143] Though they are often (but not always) outgunned by business interests, activist organizations such as consumer groups and environmental NGOs matter as well. An explanation of trade and regulation requires taking into account the preferences and political strategies of those groups directly affected by that regulation. Ignoring societal actors is unhelpful, as it leads to a serious undertheorization of state's preferences.

Potential Drawbacks of My Explanation

I contend that my explanation for the variation in regulatory trade barriers is an improvement over the alternative explanations, but I admit that its strengths come at some cost. The preferences of each of the three sets of actors involved are advanced based on inductive reasoning, stated ex ante, and exogenously given. The complex interplay among the motivations of businesses, activists, and government officials means that it is extremely difficult to deductively derive a formal model of the decision-making of any of those actors within that policy space, much less of the interaction between those actors. Hopefully, future research can provide more formalized theoretical foundations for each set of actors.

Moreover, the strategic interplay between the three sets of actors has been somewhat simplified. For example, businesses, activists, and governments may choose from a range of different options for promoting regulatory cooperation as it relates to international commerce (binding agreements, mutual recognition, networked governance, private standards, and self-regulation), and this study does not conceptually differentiate between those options.[144] There is inevitably a trade-off between parsimony and accuracy, and I hope the explanation offered in this book has struck the right balance between them. To add any more parts to my explanation would, I fear, render it unwieldy. To take parts of it away to make it more theoretically parsimonious would, I fear, make it less nuanced.

Conclusion

To summarize, businesses seek to reduce regulatory trade barriers when those barriers raise production costs or inhibit market access. They may choose to end that pursuit if complying with those regulations is cheap or if pursuing their reduction carries major reputational risk. Activist groups defend regulatory barriers when they perceive those regulations to be the sole effective means to address a societal problem of concern to them. They may accept a reduction in regulatory barriers if those barriers have low salience or if their opposition is bought out through private standards, corporate social responsibility, or some other arrangement in which businesses are not directly regulated by government. Officials in government choose whether to side with businesses or activist groups based on the officials' relative prioritization of trade and regulatory independence, their staffing arrangements, and whom they identify as their core constituency. Concerns about competitiveness stack these factors in favor of reducing regulatory trade barriers. Concerns about needless death stack them in favor of maintaining or increasing those barriers.

FOUR

Automobiles and Regulatory Regionalism in North America and Europe

By almost any measure, the automotive sector is massive in scale and significance. It accounts for $3 trillion of global economic output per year.[1] Auto manufacturing employs close to a million people in the United States without even counting dealers and mechanics.[2] A car is among the most important purchases many people make. Given the international nature of automobile production and the sheer volume of the trade in automobiles and parts ($1.4 trillion in 2017),[3] automobiles are inextricably bound up in trade politics. Automobiles are also highly regulated. From the horn's decibel level to the exhaust's content, essentially everything about a car is regulated in one way or another. The contrasting ways in which cars are regulated in different countries has big implications for the trade in automobiles.

In 1980, Europe's auto market sat atop a checkerboard of conflicting regulations that impeded the intracontinental vehicles trade. At that time, regulatory barriers also hampered the trade in cars between the three North American states. By 1996, regulatory trade barriers within both regions had been almost totally reduced. In Europe, environmental barriers were maintained from 1983 to 1988 but were reduced in 1989–90. In North America, domestic content barriers were reduced in both Mexico and Canada. Domestic content barriers were blocked from existing at all in the United States. They were then eliminated in NAFTA.

In contrast to this intraregional attenuation, interregional regulatory barriers related to consumer safety have not been reduced between

North America and Europe. Therein lies the research enigma that motivates this chapter: why were regulatory trade barriers in the automotive sector reduced within Europe and North America but not between those regions? As I point out throughout this chapter, the alternative explanations to my argument are not particularly effective at explaining these differing outcomes.

Environmental Regulatory Trade Barriers in Europe, 1983–88

Background

During the 1970s, European businesses, especially automakers, became increasingly regional and more frustrated by intra-European trade barriers.[4] After Ford began selling on a continental basis, other automakers followed suit, creating a continental vehicle market that made intraregional regulatory barriers more irksome.[5] While this market creation was occurring, the European Community began to regulate automobiles with an eye toward liberalizing the continental market in vehicles.[6] Beginning in 1970 and then in 1972, the EC began regulating automobiles' air pollution.[7] EC 70/156 established a type-approval process for automotives and

TABLE 4.1. Outcomes of Regulatory Trade Barriers in Automobiles

European Case	
Environmental, 1983–88	Pursued by environmentalists but stymied by EC and automakers
Environmental, 1989–90	Prevented via higher unified standard
North American Case	
Domestic Content, Mexico	Reduced at behest of automakers and new government
Domestic Content, Canada	Reduced by Mulroney's government as part of CUSFTA
Domestic Content, U.S.	Sought by unions, prevented by GOP Senate and White House
Domestic Content, NAFTA	Reduced via regionalizing content rules
Environmental, Mexico/U.S.	Prevented via strategic interplay between the three main actors
Consumer Safety, Mexico	Inert due to lack of activism or industry opposition
Mexican Trucking	Maintained at behest of safety advocates, then reduced once they are satisfied and firms pursue reduction
Interregional Case	
Consumer Safety, 1996–99	Maintained at behest of safety advocates
Consumer Safety, Post-1999	Inert due to lack of industry efforts and continued safety concerns

emphasized the imperative of promoting a common market.[8] EC 70/220 established the first limits on carbon monoxide and hydrocarbons (environmentally damaging emissions).[9] EC 72/306 established the first emissions limits on diesel engines. Finally, EC 78/611 set maximum lead levels in gasoline and specifically cited both the environment and public health as justifications, as well as promoting the single market.[10] These directives set the basis for the EC's automotive environmental regulations to come.

As I discussed in chapter 3, one factor motivating government officials to pursue reduced regulatory trade barriers is their greater concern for promoting international commerce than for preserving national regulatory independence. Regarding auto manufacturing, EC officials were specifically trying to pool regulatory authority in order to promote intracontinental trade at the expense of each EC state having regulatory autonomy. Starting to stitch together EC-wide regulation would help EC-based firms by organizing production continentally and would aid automakers in achieving economies of scale, which were becoming more important and more difficult to achieve. The minimum volume for a firm to survive in the auto industry leaped from 800,000 in the 1970s to 2 million in the early 1980s.[11] Continental production would ease this challenge by allowing for further specialization. Instead of having one production line for vehicle X in three markets, the automaker could have one of those lines produce vehicle X for all three markets and the other two lines produce vehicles Y and Z. Greater scale would help reduce costs through standardizing output while increasing the variety of goods produced. Greater scale could assist modularization, which involved demanding that suppliers make more complex parts (e.g., a seat rather than just the fabric) and deliver those parts to the automakers within minutes of when they were needed to curb inventory costs.[12] For economies of scale and modularization to function, automakers needed to organize continentally, and regulatory barriers can get in the way of that organization, thereby raising production costs.

The movement toward EC trade liberalization that was gaining momentum in the late 1970s and early 1980s held out the promise of helping automakers achieve continental organization, which is why automakers formed the vanguard in promoting regional trade liberalization. In fact, the European Business Roundtable, the peak organization for the largest European businesses, originated from discussions in 1982 between Pehr Gyllenhammer, the chief executive officer of Volvo, and Etienne Davignon, the vice president of the European Commission.[13] As trade liberalization was gaining momentum in the early 1980s, emissions regulations were also becoming more politically salient.

Environmentalists and Emissions Regulations in Western Europe

By the 1980s, environmentalists were strengthening in several EC states.[14] In 1983, the West German Green Party surpassed, for the first time, the threshold of 5 percent needed for Bundestag representation. The next year, environmental protection gained greater salience as it became clear that one-third to half of the country's forests were being badly damaged by acid rain.[15] Not just the trees were being hurt. By this point, it was widely understood that lead in gasoline had significant public health effects. One potential response, imposing speed limits on the autobahn, was sure to be controversial and politically costly for the West German government.[16]

The emissions standards that environmentalists wanted were not achievable without the use of catalytic converters, but for reasons discussed below, requiring catalytic converters would have created a major regulatory trade barrier.[17] As I discussed in chapter 3, activists pursue specifically national regulations, amounting to regulatory trade barriers, when regulation seems to be the sole means by which the activists can achieve their goals. Without regulations that required catalytic converters, there was no way that West Germany would be able to cut automotive pollution to the level that environmentalists wanted.

At first, German automakers did not join environmentalists on the issue of catalytic converters, but they also did not oppose the environmentalists about converters as they did on speed limits.[18] That apathetic landscape incentivized the West German government to announce that it would make catalytic converters mandatory.[19] Only when automakers became concerned that other states' retaliation could hamper their market access did they push against environmentalists' attempts to raise these regulatory barriers.[20] This pressure from automakers convinced the West German government to drop its unilateral approach.[21]

Denmark too had developed a strong environmental movement that wanted to raise emissions standards, but unlike West Germany, Denmark had no domestic automakers, so the Danish government never faced countervailing pressure against environmentalists who were pushing for increased regulatory barriers with respect to emissions.[22] Indeed, support for environmental protection was so widespread in Denmark in 1984 that 71 percent of Danes then prioritized protecting the environment over economic growth.[23] The Netherlands also had a strong environmentalist movement and no indigenous manufacturers, making it another state willing to push strict environmental regulations even when automakers opposed them.[24]

Alternative Explanations

No domestic automakers in Denmark or the Netherlands would have benefited from these regulatory trade barriers. Clearly, the barriers were implemented not to protect some nonexistent firm but to promote environmental goals. That promotion is the first piece of evidence these cases offer against the notion that regulatory barriers are a disguised means of protectionism. Activists' engagement in the politics surrounding trade and emissions regulations also underscores the limitations of cleavage-based explanations of trade politics. The cleavage here was not between a sector of society that profited from trade and a sector that lost but between a sector (automakers) that had an economic stake and a sector (environmentalists) that wanted to prioritize noneconomic policy goals. This example of emissions regulation illustrates how cleavage-based explanations, by focusing exclusively on economic considerations, ignore the extent to which trade increasingly animates actors with normative concerns once regulations get added to the equation.

Emissions Standards and Competitiveness

The specter of mandatory catalytic converters constituted a nightmare for Fiat, Peugeot, and Renault.[25] Catalytic converters work by rearranging the oxygen and hydrocarbon molecules in car exhaust into the less environmentally damaging chemicals carbon dioxide and water. In the 1980s, they were a new, costly technology, adding about $500 to the price of a car.[26] For a luxury car, such as a Mercedes Benz, that additional cost was relatively small as a percentage of the car's total cost; it could be absorbed more easily by Mercedes' more affluent consumers.[27] But for the small cars in which Fiat, Peugeot, and Renault specialized, the additional cost of converters was a much greater portion of overall costs and could seriously crimp sales if it pushed those vehicles out of reach for consumers who were less well-off.[28] Those automakers were adamant that emissions standards not be allowed to create regulatory barriers within the single market.[29]

Vehicles equipped with catalytic converters required unleaded gasoline because lead makes catalytic converters malfunction. The problem for French and Italian automakers was that unleaded gasoline was difficult to find in their countries, unlike in Germany and Denmark.[30] For Fiat, Peugeot, and Renault, mandatory converters meant producing cars that no one would be able to drive as soon as they needed their first gasoline refills. Thus the French and Italian governments could not accept emissions standards so high that they required catalytic converters as the basis for continent-wide regulations.[31] They also could not accept a situation in which other countries' governments required catalytic converters, as that would prevent France and Italy from exporting their products to those countries. In other words, automakers advocated lower standards precisely because higher standards constituted a significant regulatory barrier for them. Even carmakers that already operated continentally, such as Ford, argued that they needed a single market to remain competitive and that Europe needed to finish the project of developing a single market to bolster its overall competitiveness.[32]

At the same time and again in contrast to West Germany, Denmark, and the Netherlands, environmentalists in Italy and France were still quite weak.[33] Government officials there thus faced the opposite incentives in their domestic arena as their counterparts in West Germany, Denmark, and the Netherlands.[34] Furthermore, by undermining domestic automakers, the regulatory barriers on emissions threatened to undermine their national economic competitiveness. Given this situation, governments sided with their automakers in opposing the higher emissions standards.

An Alternative Explanation

The trajectory of events regarding emissions standards in Europe undermines state-centric explanations of trade politics. EC governments' stances were not independently designed. They came about as a result of lobbying by societal actors. The positions of Denmark and the Netherlands were a product of the strength of environmentalists there. The positions of France and Italy were a product of the strength of automakers in those countries. One cannot explain the positions of any country without first examining the societal actors within that state.

The Common Market Gets Prioritized

While EC officials in the 1980s were not hostile to the call for environmental protection, they saw creating a common market as their primary responsibility.[35] The link between Europe's national economies had grown tighter over the course of the 1970s.[36] Europe's economic recovery in the mid-1980s was much weaker than the recoveries in the United States and Japan.[37] Trade liberalization was seen as a way of boosting the competitiveness of European companies and, by extension, European states, with the goal of ending Eurosclerosis.[38]

High emission regulations that created intra-EC trade barriers were thus seen by EC officials not as an innocuous regulatory difference but as a throttle on competiveness and on EC officials' ability to deliver prosperity through the advancement of the internal market. Thus the officials sided with France and Italy. The 1985 agreement raised emission standards but, to environmentalists' chagrin, excluded small cars, necessitating a future negotiation over those cars' emissions.[39] The agreement was vetoed by the Danish government, which was still beholden to its environmentalists who wanted higher standards, come what may, in terms of trade.[40]

Danish officials, still facing pressure from only one direction domestically, continued to block the compromise. The Green Party had made significant gains in local elections in November 1985, which made Danish officials even more convinced that caving on emission standards was out of the question.[41] Denmark's minister for the environment made it clear where the battle lines were drawn: "Denmark will not accept this level. We have here a collision between environmental and business interests."[42] Danish objection persisted into 1987,[43] in another example of noneconomic interests having a significant impact.

In the meantime, the EC had passed the 1986 Single European Act, which set the end of 1992 as the goal for fully establishing a common market, codified environmental policy goals at the EC level for the first time, and changed the requirements for EC-wide regulatory rulings from being unanimous to a qualified majority.[44] In July 1987, the new regulatory procedure was used for the first time by other EC states to pass the regulations agreed to in 1985 over the objections of Denmark.[45] After the accord was reached, Denmark made it known that it planned to enact its own higher emission standards anyway, which was sure to invite a legal challenge from other EC states.[46] This challenge had to be addressed, as did emissions regulations for the smaller vehicles excluded from the 1985 compromise. The start of negotiations on small car emissions in January 1988 was not promising, as France blocked any real discussion of toughening regulations on small cars.[47] Jacques Calvet, the hard-line chairman of Peugeot, attacked increased emission standards as a demagogic barrier to intra-EC trade.[48] The French government subsequently abandoned a compromise deal on small car emissions that had been tentatively worked out in June 1988.[49]

Harmonization of Emissions Standards, 1989–90

By 1989, it became apparent that two developments had altered the configuration of interests around emissions regulations. First, environmentalism had strengthened across Europe. Picking environmental fights with Brussels continued to be a political winner domestically in Denmark.[50] Sweden's election in 1988 demonstrated the continued growth of environmentalism there too.[51] The Dutch government, which was keener on environmentalism in 1988 than at any time since 1982, defied the EC by going ahead with a tax scheme incentivizing the purchase of cars that emitted such low emissions that they required catalytic converters.[52] Environmentalists also gained strength in countries where they had previously been relatively weak. In Italy and the United Kingdom, the salience of green issues had grown substantially.[53] The growth of environmentalism made it politically dangerous for EC officials to be seen as insufficiently green. They now had to take activists as seriously as they did business constituencies. Growing environmentalism also made it clear that reducing regulatory barriers by implementing a common low level of emissions standards was infeasible.

Second, technological advances led automakers to relax their resistance to higher standards. In 1984, the EC had mandated that all EC states had to ensure the widespread availability of unleaded gasoline by 1989.[54] By 1988, it was clear that states would meet their obligation to do that.[55] It also became clear that other approaches to emissions could not match the effectiveness of catalytic converters.[56] Unlike in 1985, consumers in 1988 were highly in favor of catalytic converters.[57] The fear that cars with catalytic converters would become useless once they needed a refill subsided. Automakers and gasoline providers had achieved technological innovations that greatly reduced the performance penalties that had accompanied the use of catalytic converters a few years earlier.[58] Catalytic converters also became much cheaper to produce and install because automakers figured out how to replace the platinum in them with palladium, which cost one-tenth as much.[59] Makers of small cars no longer perceived mandatory converters to be a death knell.[60] Onetime opponents of converters, such as Fiat and Renault, had begun selling cars with converters in the Netherlands.[61] Thus those automakers no longer believed that converters would substantially raise their production costs or inhibit market access.

European Community officials identified with environmentalists and automakers and were eager to promote some sort of arrangement between them. The European Parliament was continually pushing for greater environmental protection by this point.[62] European commissioner for the environment Carlo Ripa Di Meana openly advocated for the adoption of higher standards and was soon joined in that advocacy by European commissioner for transport Karel Van Miert.[63] One European Community official noted that the European Commission serving in 1989 was, as a whole, "definitely a lot greener than the last."[64]

The common market was a central mission of the EC and preoccupied its officials at least as much as environmental protection. By this point, those officials wanted one standard, any standard, as long as it was a common one, and the 1992 deadline grew more looming with each passing month.[65] Environmentalists and the states aligned with them were not backing down. Given automakers' desire for one standard, environmentalists' push for a high standard, and the advances in catalytic converters, high uniform standards became a way to liberalize trade. That outcome is a useful reminder that firms are not uniformly opposed to regulation per se and that reducing regulatory barriers does not necessarily mean that regulations themselves are lowered.

In April 1989, the European Commission proposed new, higher emission regulations that effectively mandated catalytic converters.[66] The European Council voted to approve the new standards in the summer of 1989.[67] That reduction in emissions-based regulatory barriers opened the way for similar reductions in other regulatory barriers. Automakers hoped for region-wide standards on these issues for the same reasons that they wanted uniform emissions standards. There is no evidence that activists objected to reducing those regulatory barriers.

European Community officials were committed to completing the single market. Martin Bangemann, European commissioner for the internal market, had previously been the leader of the Free Democratic Party in Germany and the German economic minister, so the negotiation of technical standards was guided by a politician who had led a pro-trade party in a pro-trade country. It is not surprising that he provided the leadership to reduce other intra-EC regulatory trade barriers. In June 1989, European Community officials announced a mandatory technical standards regime for the entire EC, agreed to in March 1990.[68] As part of the construction of the single market, that agreement effectively completed the regionalization of European auto production.

Domestic Content Regulatory Trade Barriers in North America

Background

Although there were differences in safety and environmental regulations between Canada, the United States, and Mexico in the 1980s, they did not generally constitute significant regulatory barriers. Automakers had to meet U.S. standards for vehicles destined for the United States, but for vehicles produced for the Canadian and Mexican markets, they could meet either that state's standard or the American standard, at their discretion. The major regulatory barriers to continent-wide auto production were domestic content regulations,[69] which stipulated that a certain percentage of automakers' sales had to come from domestically produced parts and domestic labor. A domestic content requirement does not help firms, because it limits their flexibility and raises their production costs. Automakers oppose such rules even when they seek protectionism, because there are other means that achieve the same protectionist goal without limiting producers' flexibility. A domestic content requirement does help workers, by maintaining domestic auto employment. Mexico and Canada had domestic content regulations but reduced them over the course of the 1980s and early 1990s. The United States never had them; labor unions wanted them but were rebuffed in that attempt.

In 1981, the North American auto trade was stymied by domestic content regulations, and auto production was organized on a national basis. By the mid-1990s, domestic content regulations between the United States, Canada, and Mexico had been effectively eradicated, and auto production was organized on a regional basis. This shift began in the late 1970s, when the Big Three in U.S. auto manufacturing faced ballooning labor costs, new environmental and safety regulations, energy crises, and stagflation. None of these developments were popular in Detroit, and they became an existential crisis for the Big Three, because they intensified the competition they faced from Japanese automakers. At the time, Japanese cars used less gasoline, were produced more efficiently (which meant they were cheaper), and had fewer defects (which meant they lasted longer and needed fewer repairs).[70]

In this fraught moment for the Big Three, Chrysler almost collapsed, while Ford and General Motors posted record losses.[71] In response to Japanese competition, U.S. automakers needed to cut production costs and began exploring the possibility of relocating labor-intensive production steps to Mexico, where labor costs were 31 percent of those in the United States.[72] In addition, automakers were having difficulty getting unions to accept new methods such as modularization, and moving abroad could help manufacturers get around that challenge.[73] Automakers were also hoping to benefit from greater economies of scale for the same reasons as had prevailed in Europe. By pushing up the dollar's value, the tight monetary policy of U.S. Federal Reserve chairman Paul Volcker made producing a good abroad and importing it more profitable. The problem for the Big Three in this endeavor was the set of regulations on domestic content.

U.S. Domestic Content Rules, 1982–84

The confluence of factors hurting U.S. automakers in the early 1980s hit autoworkers hard. Employment in auto assembly plummeted from 760,000 in 1978 to 490,000 in 1981.[74] A Buy American campaign sprung up among the rank and file of the United Automobile Workers but did little to stem the rising tide of Japanese imports, so the UAW began pushing for Congress to mandate a Buy American regulation, domestic content rules in auto production.[75] The proposed regulations, which mandated that all models with sales over 100,000 vehicles had to have at least 25 percent of their content made in the United States, employed a sliding scale that called for all models with sales over 500,000 vehicles to have 90 percent domestic content.[76] In 1981–82, domestic content legislation in the auto industry was the top priority of the UAW and the American Federation of Labor and Congress of Industrial Organizations but was opposed by automakers.[77] Ford and General Motors were just as much a target of these UAW-proposed regulations as Japanese automakers; UAW president Doug Fraser argued, "Content legislation not only will address the savaging of the American economy by the Japanese. . . . It will also confront the exporting of American jobs and capital by General Motors and Ford."[78]

A number of management's decisions made an already difficult situation for workers feel like management was using competition from Japanese automakers as an excuse to profit at labor's expense. In 1982, the same day that General Motors convinced workers to accept wage freezes and fewer holidays, executives received bigger bonuses.[79] Into the late 1980s, GM persisted with the antagonizing practice of having segregated bathrooms for hourly workers versus management.[80] When an enormous Persian rug bought by Ford's bosses for their executive suite was too large to install because it could not fit in any of the building's elevators, the bosses did not return the extravagant rug but had windows temporarily removed so that it could be installed via helicopter.[81] Workers were incensed. It is little wonder that unions saw management as just as much their enemy as foreign competition.

Though the UAW wanted domestic content requirements, U.S. automakers decidedly did not. GM and Ford representatives testified against the bill before Congress.[82] Thomas Atkinson, a GM executive, summarized automakers' position by saying, "We wish these laws had never been invented, and would not like to see them increased or created in countries where they don't exist now."[83] The central rhetorical framing executives used to oppose domestic content was that it would make U.S.-built cars less competitive.[84] Their argument provides evidence for a point I made in chapter 3: when businesses seek protection, they are unlikely to ask for regulatory protectionism, because regulations limit their flexibility in ways that nonregulatory trade barriers do not. In the case of domestic content, the protectionism automakers sought was not regulations on domestic content but a quota-based agreement with the Japanese to restrain exports.[85]

In the meantime, Volcker's tight monetary policy was driving up the value of the dollar and made American exports that much more expensive, which only compounded concerns about U.S. competitiveness.[86] As evidence of how serious U.S. officials were taking these competitiveness concerns, both the Senate and the White House set up special commissions on economic and industrial competitiveness.[87] To the delight of the Big Three and the infuriation of the UAW, the Reagan administration was resolutely opposed to domestic content regulations. John Danforth, the chairman of the lead Senate committee on trade, attested that many members of the Senate viewed domestic content as "perfectly ridiculous," while U.S. trade representative Bill Brock called it "the worst piece of economic legislation since the 1930s."[88] Brock was a dyed-in-the-wool free trader so stoutly hostile to labor unions that he was appointed secretary of labor in Reagan's second term.

Brock's effectiveness against domestic content regulation is a good example of why it can be difficult to model government officials' behavior with respect to regulatory trade barriers. If Missouri's prominent Democratic senator Dick Gephardt, the most high-profile supporter of domestic content, had been president during this regulatory battle, his administration would most likely have taken a very different line than that of the Reagan administration. Even with the same president, a different trade representative might have been less hard-line and tried to mollify the UAW with domestic content regulations set at a very low level.

With no support from the trade representative or elsewhere in the executive, the domestic content bill died in the Republican-controlled Senate. One of the unions' central problems was that they were not able to use the frame of preventing needless death, as such framing might have been politically helpful. It was clear to all parties that labor activists complaining about their bosses' rug had little to do with preventing needless death and everything to do with wages and benefits. In sum, union attempts to create a significant new regulatory barrier to the trade in cars were defeated by the combined efforts of the automakers and government officials who opposed the erection of those barriers.

Mexican Domestic Content Rules, 1982–89

The Latin American debt crisis, which started in Mexico in 1982, augmented automakers' opposition to Mexico's domestic content rules. The decrease in domestic demand that occurred as a result of the debt crisis meant that the attraction of building in Mexico for the domestic market had evaporated. Vehicles produced there now had to be competitive internationally, which could not happen without changes in Mexican policy. Mexico's domestic content rules limited production flexibility for Ford, which aggressively lobbied Mexico for changes in domestic content and ownership regulations; one group of scholars even argues that the policy changes adopted by Mexico were a direct result of Ford's lobbying.[89] At the very least, it is fair to say that Ford was pushing hard for reduced regulatory barriers. At this point, U.S. automakers were joined by Mexican businesses organized under the Business Coordinating Council, a newly constructed superlobby that united the two most prestigious business confederations. They collectively pushed the Mexican government to take a less active role in the economy and to adopt policies to help exporters.[90]

The debt crisis softened Mexican officials' support for the domestic content rules. They no longer had the same leverage over automakers but wanted to maintain manufacturing jobs and to promote exports to improve the country's trade balance. To emerge from this debt crisis, their manufactured goods had to be competitive in export markets. One positive side effect of the crash was that it devalued the peso, which made exports more attractive. The domestic content regulations again stood in the way of exports, though, by making supply chains less flexible.

In 1983, Mexico took its first steps away from import substitution industrialization (ISI) and toward promoting exports.[91] The Border Industrialization Program, also known as the maquiladora program, was reformed and expanded, and the Trade and Industry Ministry, which had long been protectionist, was reorganized and given a staff dedicated to trade liberalization.[92] The expansion of the maquiladora program allowed firms to import goods tariff-free if they were used to make products that were then exported, and it allowed automakers to have less domestic content in cars produced for export.[93] The number of auto maquiladoras consequently increased from 51 in 1984 to 129 in 1988.[94] A Ford executive cited the decree as "a major reason" for the company's decision to construct a new half-billion-dollar facility in Hermosillo that year.[95]

Given that domestic demand had collapsed, a Mexican business had to find markets abroad to thrive. Major business organizations grew more assertive toward the government and more eager to push the government to pursue further liberalization.[96] This shift was major for business; less than a decade earlier, the composition of the business lobby was much more protectionist and had successfully blocked Mexico's accession to the GATT.[97] There was also a shift in the relative power of businesses in different regions of Mexico. Given their proximity to the United States, businesses in northern Mexico had favored trade liberalization more than had businesses in central Mexico that owed their ascendancy to state-led ISI policies.[98] The collapse of ISI weakened the latter group to the benefit of the former.

Starting around 1986, trade liberalization had created its own vested interest among the businesses that wanted more liberalization.[99] Compared to earlier periods, business leaders in the mid-1980s had a greater commitment to free trade and greater access to like-minded government officials.[100] Unions remained either repressed or co-opted and controlled by the government through the Confederation of Mexican Workers (CTM). They were in no position to offer meaningful resistance to reducing domestic content requirements, especially in the auto industry.

As I discussed in chapter 3, the staffing of government posts can make a big difference in how government interfaces with firms and activists. In the mid-1980s, the Mexican government was headed by President de la Madrid, who had nearly unanimous backing from big business.[101] Madrid's stacking of his cabinet with free traders[102] coincided with the rise of the *technoburocrata*, a cadre of younger, more pro-market officials within the government.[103] In 1984, the Mexican government sold its shares in Renault and Mexican automaker VAM, meaning it no longer had a vested interest in protecting its two least-competitive producers.[104] This made officials even more willing to listen to calls for reductions in regulatory barriers. Given this configuration of interests, Mexico moved rapidly toward trade liberalization, deciding to join the GATT in 1985 and signing the Tokyo Round's codes on nontariff barriers in 1987.

Those moves accelerated the growth of export-oriented auto manufacturing. Though auto production for the domestic market fell 36 percent for 1983–87 compared to 1978–82, production for exports increased 184 percent.[105] At first, the exports were mostly parts, but then automakers realized they could produce sophisticated components in Mexico with the same level of quality as in the United States.[106] Trade liberalization, more specifically reduction or removal of the domestic content regulations, was key to that manufacture because it meant that steel of higher quality than that produced in Mexico could be imported, which was critical in making feasible the most quality-dependent and capital-intensive processes.[107] After this discovery, the Big Three lobbied the Mexican government to adopt a new auto decree that would reward production of sophisticated components.[108] The 1989 Auto Decree completed Mexico's abandonment of ISI and reduced requirements for local content.[109]

Canadian Domestic Content Rules, 1982–88

While Mexico's auto industry had been transforming, the politics of regulatory barriers had also been unfolding in Canada. The rules requiring 60 percent domestic content and impeding auto trade between the United States and Canada in the early 1980s were a result of the 1965 Auto Pact. Canadian businesses were more eager to push for trade liberalization in the early 1980s than they had been a few years prior. In the Tokyo Round that ended in 1979 and through reforms on nontariff barriers, Canada was forced to accept tariff reductions on industrial goods that most other countries had taken in the Kennedy Round, which led to an import surge.[110] The 1981–82 global recession hit Canada particularly hard and augmented the need to tap global markets.[111] Due to Paul Volcker's tight monetary policy that increased the U.S. dollar's value, the Canadian dollar, which was worth one dollar in 1976, traded at 80 cents in 1982, making Canadian exports more competitive in the United States and lessening the vulnerability of Canadian importers to competition from U.S. exports.[112]

Faced with this import penetration, with the need to gain better access to foreign markets, and with a currency-related advantage in U.S. markets, firms began to lobby for trade liberalization, especially with the United States.[113] The Canadian Manufacturers Association, the Business Council on National Issues, and the Canadian Chamber of Commerce began calling for a free trade agreement with the United States.[114] In addition to becoming more proactively in favor of trade liberalization, Canadian firms had grown in political power and organization.[115] Canadian business leaders were slightly ahead of their government counterparts in their turn toward trade liberalization but would not have to wait long to be joined by them.

A Turn in Canadian Trade Policy

The turn in Canadian policy in the 1980s flew in the face of decades of Canadian trade policy. The Canadian government had historically adopted a protectionist line going as far back as the late nineteenth century. Indeed, high tariffs were essential in early Canadian political development. The 1879 National Policy was the Canadian government's attempt to economically unify Canada by promoting domestic east-west trade rather than international north-south trade with the United States. Before that policy, it was easier for a businessman in Winnipeg to do business with Minneapolis than with Ottawa, so Canadians often had closer connections with Americans than with each other. High tariffs changed that situation.

When Wilfrid Laurier, who had held power as prime minister since 1896, pursued greater trade with the United States in 1911, he was quickly chased from office. As Michael Lusztig notes, "the lesson that emerged was clear and lasting, free trade was a political nonstarter in Canada."[116] Even in the 1960s and 1970s, Canadian support for GATT trade rounds was more about multilateralism than about a deep-seated love of free trade.[117] With regard to the United States in particular, the Liberal government under Pierre Trudeau advocated the Third Option policy, which took an economically nationalist line, even to the point of antagonizing the behemoth to the south. The clearest example of that policy was the 1979 National Energy Program, which, in an attempt to subsidize energy in Ontario and Quebec, curtailed energy exports to the United States at the exact moment it was suffering from an energy crisis.[118]

As late as 1983, Brian Mulroney, the Conservative Party leader who later championed the Canada–United States Free Trade Agreement, said, "Don't talk to me about free trade, that issue was decided in 1911. Free trade is a danger to Canadian sovereignty, and you'll hear none of it from me now during this leadership campaign or at any other time in the future."[119] But the utility of greater trade with the United States was starting to percolate through the Canadian bureaucracy, and many Canadian government officials were beginning to seriously question the protectionist policy orientation. Ed Lumley and then Gerald Regan, two trade ministers sympathetic to both trade reforms and business interests, conducted a stem-to-stern review of Canadian trade policy; their final analysis, released in August 1983, advocated for greater trade and somewhat unexpectedly signaled that bilateral negotiations with the United States might be an option in addition to Canada's traditional commitment to the GATT.[120] Their report and the media attention it received sparked the most open trade discussion Canada had seen in a very long time.[121] In many ways, it laid the groundwork for what would become probably the most consequential Canadian report on trade policy.

In its encapsulation of the political zeitgeist and as an intellectual defense for a policy response to a problem fixating the nation, the Macdonald Report was as important for Canadian trade policy in the 1980s as George Kennan's writings were for U.S. Soviet policy in the 1940s. In 1982, the Canadian government set up a Royal Commission to diagnose Canada's economic malaise. Its mandate was the economy in general, and there was little expectation that it would focus on trade.[122] The commission's report criticized Trudeau's policies that shifted political and economic attention away from the U.S. relationship, arguing that those policies hurt Canada's economy.[123] The report's signature recommendation was for Canada to pursue freer trade, especially with the United States.[124] The one representative of labor on the Macdonald Commission was its strongest opponent of free trade.[125] That objection notwithstanding, when the report was released in 1985, it delivered instant intellectual and political cover for a politician who wanted to unlearn the lesson of 1911.

Getting CUSFTA

The year before the Macdonald Report, the Conservatives led by Mulroney defeated the Liberals who had been the champions of leftist nationalism. Mulroney's base was the business community economically and the Western provinces geographically, both of which wanted trade liberalization. His political instincts were to improve relations with the United States, and trade, almost by definition, had to be a major part of that effort.[126] After months of political planning, consultation with business leaders, and the release of the Macdonald Report, Mulroney announced his intention in September 1985 to seek a free trade agreement with the United States.

Once the negotiations for the Canada–United States Free Trade Agreement (CUSFTA) got under way, automobiles became an enduring subject, given their economic importance. The automakers wanted an end to Canada's domestic content regulations.[127] The lead negotiators also believed the domestic content regulations were expendable.[128] Labor formed the vanguard of CUSFTA opposition and argued vociferously against reducing domestic content requirements.[129]

While businesses had been strengthening, Canadian labor unions, much like their American counterparts, had seen their political power wither due to a decline in unionization, a fragmentation of unions' organizational structure, and the transition to a more service-based economy.[130] They also made a major strategic error. Fearing their participation would give CUSFTA legitimacy, labor refused to participate in the negotiations and thereby undermined their own influence.[131] In labor's absence, there was no one at the negotiating table to push against the competitiveness framing. In the end, automakers and government officials got what they wanted. CUSFTA, signed in 1987, eliminated Canada's domestic content requirements; content could now originate in Canada or the United States, and the level of required content was lowered to 50 percent.

NAFTA and Domestic Content

As I showed earlier, Mexico was even more predisposed to pursue trade liberalization by the late 1980s than it had been earlier that decade. The firms most committed to protectionism had been undermined by the economic crisis.[132] The major business associations were in favor of greater liberalization and, for the first time, were joined in that opinion by small businesses.[133]

President Salinas, who took office in 1988, was as pro-trade as his predecessor—especially vis-à-vis the United States, after he received tepid interest from EC firms and officials when he pursued a trade deal with the EC. In addition to his pro-trade and pro-business instincts, Salinas had an electoral incentive to pursue liberalization, as that would help Mexico's Industrial Revolutionary Party (PRI) by appealing to pro-liberalization firms that had defected to the National Action Party.[134] Salinas also tapped a Kimberly-Clark executive as his economic adviser, while arresting a union boss.[135] In 1990, business and government leaders created the Coordinating Body of Foreign Trade Business Associations to be the link between them in the formation of Mexican trade policy.[136]

In the NAFTA negotiations, Mexican officials and businessmen cooperated so closely that they would meet before and after each session during the talks; businesses were even allowed to set up in the adjacent room with a system that allowed them to monitor what was being said by whom.[137] Government-business collaboration during this period was frequent and close,[138] a relationship reflected in negotiations concerned with the auto industry. One Mexican official said that the Big Three in U.S. auto manufacturing were just as influential in guiding Mexico's positions as they were for the Canadian and U.S. teams.[139] Clearly, business and government officials were cooperating to marginalize labor.

The government-affiliated Confederation of Mexican Workers toed the government line and dutifully endorsed NAFTA.[140] Another union, the Revolutionary Confederation of Workers and Peasants, took an ambivalent approach, welcoming the agreement because they believed it would generate employment and better wages, but also lobbying for special treatment.[141] Other unions, along with nationalists, were opposed to NAFTA but were systematically marginalized by the coalition of business and government leaders pushing for trade liberalization.[142]

With content regulations combined for Canada and the United States, the final step to creating a regional production network for automobiles was folding Mexico's domestic content into the regional content with the other two states. For automakers, the NAFTA negotiations were a fortuitous window for pushing exactly this kind of regulatory alteration. Canadian and U.S. negotiators closely consulted with the Big Three throughout the negotiations.[143]

U.S. and Canadian unions advanced proposals that would reinforce domestic content requirements in all three countries, essentially taking the region back to where it was in 1982.[144] Those proposals had no chance of gaining support from automakers or the respective government officials. The unions knew that the regionalization of content requirements would be an inevitable result were NAFTA to pass. Their hope was to stop NAFTA altogether. Given that everyone knew unions would oppose practically any agreement, their preferences carried little weight.[145] Unions were further hampered, as business was further helped, by the fact that Conservatives were in power in Canada while Republicans were in power in the United States, as both parties were ideologically sympathetic to business and ideologically hostile toward labor. With business advocating for reduced regulatory barriers and with governments in all three countries aligning with business and marginalizing labor, NAFTA replaced domestic content with regional content.[146] With content regulations organized on a regional level, they no longer impeded intraregional trade.[147] In all three of these states, the state-centric approach fails to explain why these states took the positions they did. This failure is further evidence that to understand states' policies on regulatory trade barriers, societal actors must be examined.

Environmental Trade Barriers in North America Preempted

NAFTA also dealt with environmental rules that had the potential to create regulatory barriers. If access to the U.S. market was conditioned on meeting standards not achievable at Mexican plants, those plants could no longer be used, and the regionalization strategy would no longer deliver the cost savings that were its reason for being. That effect was not an impossibility. Environmentalists had recently brought it about in the tuna industry.[148] Environmentalists' concern was that Mexico's lax rules would badly pollute the border region.[149] They also worried that the looser rules would attract industries eager to evade regulation and would thus throttle regulatory improvements in the United States.[150] Experienced from the fight over CUSFTA, environmentalists saw NAFTA as an opportunity to embed environmental protection into trade deals.[151] Mexican environmentalists saw NAFTA as a way to strengthen their country's regulations.[152]

Firms were determined to prevent regulatory differences from impeding trade.[153] They were not opposed to environmental protection per se, but such protection could not be allowed to raise trade costs, so they pushed for the requirement that states employ the regulation that was "least trade-restrictive."[154] The U.S. and Mexican governments were willing to accept some environmental language in the agreement, so long as it did not create trade barriers.[155]

Unlike their responses to labor, U.S. and Mexican officials were sympathetic to environmentalists' goals. As I discussed in chapter 3, staffing and officials' relative prioritization of different goals are a key predictor of the position that a government takes on regulation and trade. On environmental concerns, those factors played a major role in the strategic interplay between firms, activists, and officials. EPA administrator William Reilly was a major proponent of linking trade and environmental issues and was able to use his contacts with U.S. trade representative Carla Hills to advance that position, even though the EPA is usually not a major player in trade policy.[156] Hills appointed the leaders of the National Wildlife Federation, the National Audubon Society, the Natural Resources Defense Council, and the Nature Conservancy to key trade advisory committees.[157] Additionally, over 200 congressmen signed a letter supporting linking environmental and trade goals.[158] Mexican officials accepted the environmental agenda of their NGOs. Staffing was again an important factor: Mexico's environmental ministry was relatively new, staffed by young professionals eager to improve environmental protection, open to change, and accepting of NGOs.[159] Given the imperative to liberalize trade, staff sympathy toward environmentalists, and the cheapness of improving environmental protection practices, Mexican officials hoped to satisfy environmentalists while also pursuing NAFTA.

To achieve that balance, the U.S. and Mexican governments needed to emphasize Mexico's commitment to the environment, especially among the maquiladoras, and to demonstrate to the U.S. public that Mexico was neither sending pollution across the border nor attempting to attract firms with lax regulations. To those ends, they increased inspections and shut down noncompliant maquiladoras in the lead-up to NAFTA.[160] They also announced a plan to clean up the border.[161] Such inspections and shut downs had not been long-standing practices. The Mexican government rarely inspected its industrial plants prior to the NAFTA debate but conducted more than 11,000 inspections in 1992 and 1993, which suggests that satisfying environmentalists was the main impetus for those inspections.[162]

The heart of environmentalists' complaints about Mexican regulations was not that they were poorly written but that they were unenforced.[163] Given that focus, the major thrust behind NAFTA's environmental provisions was not to change regulations but to ensure enforcement. The primary sanctions mechanism under NAFTA's environmental side agreement thus occurs when a state repeatedly fails to enforce its own environmental regulations. That approach alleviated trade impediments while respecting Canadian and Mexican sensitivities. Even though business leaders and government officials in those countries had shifted to seek increased trade with the United States, their concerns over America imposing its regulatory will had not evaporated. It was not politically possible for Canada and Mexico to accept U.S. hegemony over setting regulatory standards for all three states to fully integrate the North American market, nor was it at all likely that the United States would cede much real authority to an EU-style supranational institution.

Thus, in liberalizing North American trade, there was a greater need to minimize the number of regulatory alterations, which is why the environmental side agreement leaves so much room for interpretation. Article I stipulates that the point of the side agreement is to avoid new trade barriers, while Article III stipulates that the three states can set their own regulations as long as they ensure high levels of environmental protection. These articles satisfied a significant portion (though not all) of American environmental NGOs, which thus supported NAFTA.[164] By satisfying at least some of the environmental groups, business interests and government officials prophylactically stopped the emergence of new regulatory trade barriers.[165] Environmental regulations were not allowed to interrupt the intraregional trade in automobiles. Once again, the proposed barriers to environmental regulatory trade were sought for normative reasons and by activists, not by businesses that wanted trade protection. That situation is yet more evidence that regulatory trade barriers are generally not disguised protectionism.

Consumer Safety Regulations in North America

The Absence of a Mexican Ralph Nader

Whereas domestic content regulations were regionalized and whereas regional environmental regulations were formulated to encourage environmental protection along with trade liberalization, consumer safety regulations did not change. The degree of difference between the United States and Mexico on consumer safety was as great in the late 1990s as it was in the early 1980s.[166] Even today, Mexican automobiles are not required to have safety features such as antilock brakes and electronic stability controls that Americans take for granted, which is almost certainly one of the main reasons why, adjusted for miles traveled, the automobile fatality rate in Mexico is more than three and a half times higher than the U.S. rate.[167] This lack of convergence is interesting because the need for two production runs to satisfy different standards is often used by business as a primary justification for reducing regulatory trade barriers. Why, then, are automakers not producing their cars for Mexico in the same way they are producing cars for the United States and Canada? Why have regulatory standards not converged in North America as environmental standards did in Europe? In other words, why was there no California effect?[168]

The North American firms were not advocating for reduced regulatory differences, and unlike in the case of European emission standards, no activists were pushing for increased standards, which might have lead to regulations being harmonized but at a higher level. For U.S.-based automakers, the regulatory differences have been a source of profit rather than a barrier to trade. Even though it requires a different production process, not including regulated safety features in vehicles boosts the automakers' profit, since they sell their less-safe Mexican versions at the same price point as their American versions.[169] There was no indigenous Mexican automaker for which the regulatory difference constituted a barrier to the U.S. market. There was no company that was meeting the American standard but being undermined by a purely domestic competitor. In other words, the regulatory difference did not pose a regulatory barrier for the U.S. Big Three even though it likely would have posed a barrier for the hypothetical Mexican firm. That situation demonstrates an important point: a cross-national regulatory difference may be a trade barrier for one firm but not for another in the same sector.

Furthermore, whereas there were environmentalists pushing for higher regulations in Europe, there was no such group trying to increase Mexican safety standards. There was no Mexican political entrepreneur like Ralph Nader, able to make a political issue out of safety standards. Consumers have actually been resistant to more safety regulations, due to a widespread perception that such standards would make cars unaffordable.[170] That resistance is in marked contrast to the approach of Japanese consumer groups to safety standards involving beef, discussed in chapter 5. Gunnar Trumbull's argument based on narratives of access and narratives of protection helps explain the political behavior of both those consumer groups.[171] Whereas Japanese consumers were more concerned with being protected from the potential harm of American beef, Mexican consumers were more concerned with ensuring continued access to affordable cars. The Mexican government has been reticent to fight for higher safety regulations because it does not want to throttle a sector that generates significant employment and revenue.[172] Had consumer groups effectively mobilized around the issue, perhaps government officials may have felt pressured to improve Mexico's safety regulations, but that has not happened.

Safety Standards Differences and Mexican Trucking

The one area where there was regulatory movement on safety involved an issue on which U.S. activists and officials were eager to increase regulatory barriers and leave it to Mexican firms to meet them. NAFTA allowed Mexican trucks' access to the United States for the first time, but as the 1995 date for opening that access drew closer, highway safety advocates and other activists urged the Clinton administration to delay allowing Mexican trucks full access.[173] State officials in Texas and California began loudly criticizing the safety of Mexican trucks.[174] There had also been reports of a spill of hazardous material from a Mexican truck, allegedly involving a sixteen-year-old, uninsured truck driver whose truck had faulty brakes and bald tires.[175] No U.S. firms would be immediately affected if Mexican trucks were barred from the road, so there was no entity to make competitiveness claims that would have served as a countervailing force against the critics. Given the potential for fatal auto accidents even when safety rules are being followed, there was a chance that these trucks could become a public relations nightmare for the Clinton administration; as one official put it, "All we need is one big environmental disaster, or one of these trucks plowing into a school bus, and all of a sudden NAFTA is going to look like a pretty disastrous idea."[176] Deaths related to such incidents would have been seen as preventable. President Clinton thus banned Mexican trucks from traveling farther than 26 miles from the border.[177] As a 2001 NAFTA panel report makes clear, prior to the opposition of activists and to the rise of safety concerns, officials in the Clinton administration had shown nothing but eagerness to finalize full access for Mexican trucks.[178]

In August 2010, after the dispute had dragged on for over a decade, Mexico began leveling retaliatory tariffs affecting $2.6 billion in American products, hurting U.S. export competitiveness in Mexico; that retaliation got U.S. exporters as well as a number of congressmen to quickly and strongly push in favor of reducing regulatory trade barriers in the United States.[179] Meanwhile, a pilot safety program running from 2007 to 2009 had shown that Mexican trucks were just as safe as U.S. trucks by that time.[180] In 2011, less than a year after the Mexican tariffs were levied, with businesses screaming for a reduction of regulatory barriers and with highway safety advocates largely satisfied with Mexican trucks, the United States and Mexico agreed to allow access for Mexican trucks in exchange for removal of Mexican tariffs.[181] When the regulatory barriers surrounding Mexican trucks were a matter of preventing needless death, those barriers were maintained. When that fear subsided and when those barriers were a matter of competitiveness, they were reduced.

Consumer Safety Regulatory Barriers in the Transatlantic Auto Trade

Background

By 1996, North America and Europe were each unified regions in terms of regulation and the trade in automobiles. For the previous 15 years, the organization trajectory of the auto market had bent toward greater scale and internationalization. Reducing the regulatory barriers that inhibited trade between Europe and North America seemed the next logical step, and automakers initially adopted a strategy suggesting they believed so. Carmakers, especially Ford, attempted to create "world cars" that could satisfy consumers in multiple markets,[182] which seemed like a real possibility, at least at first. Nontariff barriers had been greatly reduced, as had domestic content rules. U.S. and European environmental standards were now much closer than they had been. The problem for automakers was the extent to which differences on the bevy of regulations related to consumer safety inhibited trade.

European safety standards began to be promulgated on a regional level in the late 1950s, under the aegis of Working Party 29 of the United Nations Economic Commission for Europe.[183] In 1970, the European Community established a type-approval system in which design plans automakers submitted for a type of vehicle would be either rejected or approved. Using the EC 70 type-approval system and coordinating work on technical standards under Working Party 29 helped European standards alleviate potential regulatory trade barriers that might arise from different safety rules and attract extraregional adherents as well.[184] The type-approval system carried through to the 1990s.[185] The United States never joined it. In the lead-up to the creation of the National Highway Transportation Safety Administration (NHTSA), the U.S. Congress decided that European regulations were insufficient and that the United States should develop its own standards.[186] The United States moved toward a self-certification system: automakers certify that they have met government standards, and automobiles are recalled if they are found to be noncompliant with those standards.

Interestingly, the NHTSA used a system of rule promulgation similar to type-approval from its inception in 1966 to 1974.[187] That system proved too difficult to follow, given the penchant for adversarial legalism in the United States. A recall-based approach was much easier to implement and to uphold in court when challenged by automakers. In fact, the NHTSA lost half of the cases that were brought to court under the rule system but lost only a single case under the recall system.[188] As with type-approval in Europe, the U.S. recall approach persisted into the 1990s. The different systems meant that safety standards in the two markets developed independently from one another. By the 1990s and even up to today, there are numerous differences in how automobiles are regulated in the two markets. For example, the U.S. roof crush standard is multiple times higher on an average vehicle than the European standard, the European offset crash test has the car hit a deformable barrier at 40 miles per hour while the U.S. test has the car hit a rigid barrier at 25 miles per hour, and the European side impact test uses a lighter impact sled at a lower speed than the U.S. test.[189]

Consumer Safety Regulatory Trade Barriers, 1996–99

Starting in 1995, firms on both sides of the Atlantic joined to create the Transatlantic Business Dialogue (TABD), an international lobby to push for trade liberalization. Automakers were major players in the TABD.[190] Some estimates claimed that harmonizing regulations could save $3,000 per car in production costs.[191] Regulatory cooperation in autos was a core pursuit of the TABD starting with their first meeting in Seville.[192]

In 1996, with the support of the TABD, automakers called for their governments to "eliminate completely the barriers to trade resulting from unwarranted differences in vehicle regulation."[193] As a start, they proposed harmonizing regulations for five auto parts for which they thought aligning standards would be easy (windshield wipers, defrosters, seat belts, head restraints, and headlamp encasings).[194] To their surprise, regulators did not agree to make any changes to the requirements for any of those parts.[195]

The 1996 TABD disagreement happened because the other interested parties chose to stridently resist businesses' attempts to reduce regulatory barriers. American consumer groups, accustomed to extensive access during regulation comment periods and public hearings in the United States, were angry that the discussions going on under the auspices of the TABD systematically excluded them.[196] European regulators chafed at automakers appearing to call the shots, saying that European officials, particularly French ones, "don't accept that businessmen can sit down and set policy."[197]

Safety Advocates Enter the Fray

Among the loudest critics of the TABD's efforts was Ricardo Martinez, the head of the NHTSA. He argued that the TABD was too willing to sacrifice the public's safety for the sake of trade: "I have great concerns that the perspective is not broad enough to respect the real issues of safety and health . . . The dialogue so far has been very much one way."[198] Martinez was not a former auto executive. He was a former ER doctor who frequently had to deal with the consequences of car accidents.[199]

That lack of industry background for the head of the NHTSA was not anomalous. A previous NHTSA chief, Joan Claybrook, was a former chief executive of Public Citizen, the advocacy group founded by Ralph Nader.[200] In many ways, the NHTSA's relationship with automakers is the diametric opposite of the USDA's relationship with beef producers, discussed in chapter 5. Whereas the USDA sees its mandate as protecting public safety and promoting sales in the meat industry, the NHTSA sees it mission as only protecting consumers. The NHTSA was set up in 1966 to monitor automakers precisely because those automakers were perceived to have valued profits over passenger safety. As I discussed in chapter 3, one of the major factors driving the choices that government officials make on these issues is who the officials identify as their core constituency. From the beginning, the NHTSA saw their constituency in consumers, with their need for safety, rather than in automakers, with their drive for competitiveness.

Moreover, the NHTSA's early decision to staff itself primarily with engineers, rather than economists or industry representatives, created an institutional outlook at the NHTSA that promoted the use of design specifications (i.e., safety regulations) with little if any regard for automakers' profit margins.[201] That stance carried into the 1990s and meant that the NHTSA remained skeptical of automakers' attempts to harmonize regulations to boost trade. Furthermore, changing those regulations would have required them to turn against regulations that they believed were just fine. Robert Zoellick, the former head of the World Bank, explained, "A lot of the regulatory authorities are sensitive to their prerogatives. They think 'we are doing it the right way, and why should we change?'"[202] Indeed, when asked about specific regulations such as airbag size, U.S. and European regulators each insist that their standard is superior and saves lives.[203] They both fervently believe that the regulations they laid out are necessary and effective; for them to believe otherwise would be tantamount to admitting to doing their jobs poorly, which they are obviously reticent to do.

Alternative Explanations

The regulatory barriers proposed by the TABD were promoted by activists for normative reasons and were not means of disguised protectionism. By ignoring those actors who engaged in trade politics for normative reasons rather than economic ones, cleavage-based explanations are not able to explain the politics surrounding those environmental regulations and trade. Furthermore, the TABD case demonstrates that the political power of business is more limited than is often estimated. As with regulatory barriers related to bovine spongiform encephalopathy and consumer safety, analyzed in the next chapter, the barriers proposed by the TABD seemed to involve the kind of technical, low-salience issues that should allow for easy cooperation between governments, especially when business interests are pressuring them to do so. Nevertheless, when these regulatory barriers take concrete form and seem to be protecting lives, consumer safety advocates can effectively defeat large businesses.

Consumer Safety Regulatory Trade Barriers, Post-1999

As it was becoming clearer to automakers that they would face greater resistance to reducing transatlantic regulatory barriers than they originally believed, automakers also realized that the gains from transitioning from region-based to globally-based production were not likely to produce the level of benefits that they had envisioned. That realization centered around three considerations. First, economies of scale often have a diminishing marginal return. At a certain point, the fixed costs that drive economies of scale become small enough that firms encounter diseconomies of scale where increased size hurts profits. Those diseconomies can emerge from a host of issues, ranging from specialization getting too narrow to organizational decision-making becoming sclerotic and unwieldy.[204] Automakers had already reached an effective size at the regional level to achieve helpful economies of scale. They did not need to reorganize globally to get those, and if they did attempt such reorganization, they might encounter costly diseconomies of scale.

Second, the just-in-time inventory systems pioneered by the Japanese firms in the 1970s and adopted by other automakers in the 1980s and 1990s required that supplier networks and automakers' production processes be at least somewhat near each other. To state the obvious, just-in-time inventory is much easier when there is not an ocean in the way. In addition, shipping finished vehicles is very expensive given their size and the need to handle them with care, which motivates firms to complete final production stages near where the vehicles will be sold.[205]

Third, consumer preferences between North America and Europe were becoming so different that attempting to create a single vehicle for both markets might be a losing proposition even without being held up by regulatory trade barriers. Differences in consumer tastes between the two regions obviously did not begin in the 1990s. but they did become more significant over that decade. In North America, light trucks and SUVs became popular, growing from 30 percent of the market in 1990 to around 50 percent in 2001.[206] In Europe, diesel cars increased from 19 percent market share in 1990 to 42 percent in 2001, whereas their share of their North American market share remained close to zero.[207] Attempts at "world cars," such as the Ford Mondeo, had a habit of being successful in one of the regions while tanking in the other.[208]

As it became more apparent that changing from a regional to a global orientation would be less lucrative and more difficult than expected, automakers stopped expending political energy advocating for reduced regulatory barriers. There were no serious efforts to harmonize regulations after 1999. Businesses had stopped pushing for reduced regulatory barriers, while consumer organizations and regulators were ready to push back if businesses again started to call for reduction.

Some discussion of renewed regulatory cooperation in automobiles accompanied negotiations of the Transatlantic Trade and Investment Partnership.[209] Automakers hoped that those talks would reduce regulatory barriers in their industry.[210] The negotiations have stalled for now, but even if TTIP negotiations resume at some point, the skepticism that U.S. and EU officials have toward each other's regulations are likely to impede progress.[211] German consumer groups became quite alarmed and activated when they found out that the TTIP could potentially lead to imports of U.S. chicken that, unlike German chicken, is put through a series of chlorinated rinses.[212] U.S. consumer groups likewise worry about areas in which standards in the EU are lower than those in the United States.[213] Such dynamics would arise again if and when TTIP negotiations resume.

It would be foolhardy to try to predict exactly which car-related regulation would become the focus of consumer groups, but given that car regulations have life-and-death consequences, it is not difficult to envision those groups considering some regulatory change in a TTIP proposal to be a public safety sacrifice in the name of trade expansion. One plausible scenario involves the regulatory differences on child safety restraints between the United States and Europe.[214] It is not too difficult to imagine a policy entrepreneur convincing a group of American parents that the reductions a TTIP deal would make to regulatory trade barriers would endanger their children. There is a decent likelihood that NHTSA officials would take the side of the policy entrepreneur, adding further fuel to the criticism that the Office of the U.S. Trade Representative would be getting. The only way to circumvent that criticism would be to have all of the harmonization go upward, but unlike in the case of environmental regulations, the various regulators and consumer groups involved with safety regulations cannot agree on what "upward" even means or on whose regulations are higher than whose. Unless automakers can find some way of mollifying or marginalizing consumer advocacy groups as well as regulators, reducing safety-related regulatory trade barriers in the transatlantic auto trade appears unlikely.

Alternative Explanations

The case of regulatory trade barriers in consumer safety since 1999 undermines the disguised protectionism thesis as well as the state-centric and cleavage-based explanations. Regulatory differences were not promoted by automakers as a way to reduce competition. Instead, they wanted those differences reduced. Both purely state-centric explanations that ignore societal actors and cleavage-based explanations that ignore actors with normative motivations fail to explain the politics behind the negotiations over these safety-related regulatory barriers.

Concluding Remarks: Wealth Generation and Regulatory Autonomy

The generation of wealth is a worthy goal for societies. Many of societies' other goals depend on its accomplishment, which trade liberalization helps accelerate. That function of liberalization is why concerns about competitiveness are so instrumental in reducing regulatory trade barriers. Competitiveness links the particular interests of businesses with society's broader goal of wealth generation. Still, wealth generation is not the only goal societies have. They also want to protect their environments, their laborers, and their consumers. Pursuing those goals leads states to jealously guard their regulatory autonomy, especially when the potential or actual removal of a regulatory barrier has clear negative consequences as it relates to government protection of citizens. A focus on preventing unnecessary death links the particular interests of activists with society's broader goal of protecting people. As long as regulation and trade intersect, regulatory trade barriers will continue to affect both societies' attempts to generate wealth and their attempts to protect citizens. The politics surrounding regulatory barriers in the automobile trade has been about these two imperatives since the 1980s and is likely to continue be so for the foreseeable future.

FIVE

Mad Cow Regulations and the U.S.-Japan Beef Trade, 2003–13

Beef exports are a lucrative business for American cattlemen. The largest export market for American beef is Japan, the recipient of 1.4 billion of the $6.5 billion in beef exported by the United States in 2014.[1] Beef exports have not just been remunerative. They have also been highly variable. The dollar value of U.S. beef exports to Japan was 1.2 billion in 2003, just 80 million in 2004 and 2005 combined, 439 million in 2008, and 1.3 billion in 2013.[2] The tariffs and other nonregulatory trade barriers faced by U.S. exporters remained constant throughout that period. The changes in regulatory trade barriers faced by U.S. beef exporters were the major driver of the variability. Those regulatory barriers were increased at some times and were reduced or stayed the same at others. This chapter explains the political negotiations that drove that variation in regulatory trade barriers.

As this chapter will show, the state-centric and cleavage-based explanations, the "business dominates" hypothesis, and the argument of disguised protectionism do not adequately explain the trajectory of those negotiations in in the U.S.-Japan beef trade. I contend that the argument framed by competitiveness and death prevention, presented in chapter 3, better explains this case. The reaction of Japanese consumers to the spread of bovine spongiform encephalopathy (BSE) was so strong that Japanese officials were forced to increase regulatory differences between the United States and Japan despite protests from U.S. officials and cattlemen. Competitiveness concerns explain both the cattlemen's position and the U.S. officials' stance. Meanwhile, Japanese consumer groups were motivated

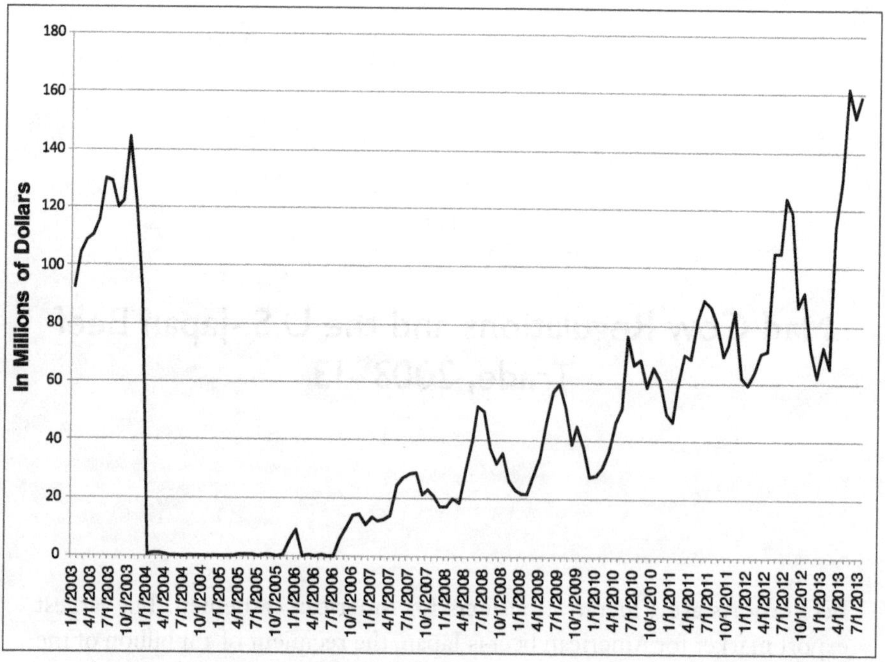

Fig. 5.1. U.S. Beef Exports to Japan, 2003–13

enough and strong enough to ensure that any compromises made that allowed renewed market access for American beef came with significant regulatory commitments. All along the way, the framing of preventing needless death motivated Japanese consumer activists and persuaded Japanese government officials. Only when those consumer groups became less alarmed, when the death framing thus became less powerful, and when the Trans-Pacific Partnership (TPP) brought Japanese producer interests and concomitant competitiveness framings into the negotiations did U.S. cattlemen regain nearly full market access.

Beyond the within-case variation just discussed, this chapter gains further analytic leverage by holding constant both the institutional setting and the relative market power of the states involved. It also presents a hard case for my argument against the "business dominates" hypothesis. Put simply, if businesses dominate anywhere in the trade and regulation space, they should do so in a case in which businesses have a powerful government acting on their behalf and in which the businesses' opponents are not other businesses but consumer activists, a preeminent example of a diffuse group. Moreover, regulatory barriers seem like the kind of technical, low-salience issues that should allow for easy cooperation between governments, especially when businesses are pressuring them to cooperate. As I mentioned in chapter 1, this chapter presents the first study of this case. Understanding the negotiations between the United States and Japan on this issue is, in and of itself, valuable to trade scholars.

Overview of the Case

In the wake of discovering BSE (commonly referred to as mad cow disease) in their country in September 2001, Japanese government officials instituted the world's strictest beef safety regulations. They did not apply those regulations to beef imports from countries that had never had a case of BSE, which, at the time, included the United States. Once the first case of BSE was discovered in the United States in 2003, Japan's strict regulations did apply to U.S. beef. Those regulations were markedly tougher than the regulations beef producers were accustomed to operating under in the United States. Because the U.S. producers could not or would not abide by the Japanese regulations, that cross-national difference in regulations constituted a major regulatory trade barrier for U.S. beef.

Negotiations between the United States and Japan in 2004–5 resulted in a compromise in which U.S. beef producers regained some market access but could only ship certain kinds of beef (only from cows under 20 months old and with all specified risk materials removed). A U.S. producer's major safety mistake in 2006 led to a renewed ban and, subsequently, to another round of negotiations, in which U.S. producers regained market access for a second time, but with even more regulatory strings attached. A 2007 decision by the World Animal Health Organization (OIE) led the United States to take a more hard-line stance; the two sides could not reach an agreement, so the regulatory trade barriers remained in place. Just when a compromise seemed within reach, the Liberal Democratic Party of Japan (LDP) was replaced by the Democratic Party of Japan (DPJ), which was much less willing to compromise on the issue. The Japanese government's initial steps to join the TPP led to some softening on the issue but were halted by farmer protests and the need to focus on recovering from the 2011 tsunami/nuclear disaster. Finally, negotiations that stretched from the fall of 2011 to March of 2013 led to a nearly full reopening of the Japanese market for U.S. beef producers, almost a decade after that access had been originally shut.

Cultural, Historical, and Scientific Background

In terms of political activity, the stereotypical view of Japanese consumers is that they are docile accomplices of producers or are bullied into submission by the combined strength of business interests in league with the Japanese bureaucracy.[3] By the start of the BSE case in 2003, reality was far more nuanced than that depiction suggests. To understand why Japanese consumers cared as much as they did in the BSE case requires me to lay out some important context.

First, in Japanese culture, the customer has traditionally been considered socially superior to the retailer, a view that has fostered high standards but encouraged consumers to be detail-oriented and unforgiving of merchants' mistakes.[4] Postwar Japanese businesses amplified this trend by advocating consumer education and promoting greater information provision as a means of protecting consumers without adding costs to themselves.[5] The upshot of that social context was that strict regulations had become foundational to Japanese consumer protection policy by the 1970s.[6] Furthermore, because consumers had fewer avenues for recompense through the court system than had their U.S. counterparts, they were more reliant on protection through regulation, and Japanese law does not allow liability lawsuits from advocates who were not themselves hurt by a product.[7] The Japanese system is designed to prevent defects beforehand, whereas the U.S. system often relies on compensating victims after the fact.[8]

Second, Japanese consumer groups were particularly animated by food safety issues. They had been highly engaged in food safety as far back as the 1970s and 1980s.[9] They have aggressively lobbied in favor of stringent labeling requirements and against the use of synthetic additives and postharvest pesticides, both commonly used in the United States.[10] Augmenting that lobbying was frequent newspaper coverage of food sto-

TABLE 5.1. Outcomes of Regulatory Trade Barriers in the U.S.-Japan Beef Trade

BSE Emerges in Japan, 2001–3	Stasis
BSE in the U.S., December 2003–April 2004	Increase
Negotiations on Reopening Market Access , May 2004–December 2005)	Compromise
U.S. Mistakes and Diplomatic Cleanup, January 2006–April 2007	Compromise
American Exceptionalism and Throttled Compromise, May 2007–August 2009	Stasis
Self-Tied Hands and the DPJ, August 2009–September 2010	Stasis
The TPP and Confidence-Building Measures, October 2010–October 2011	Stasis
30-Month Rule Implemented, October 2011–March 2013	Decrease

ries, because such stories involving issues that readers could easily digest made good copy.[11]

Third, Japanese citizens have been suspicious of foreign safety measures in general. Japanese consumer groups have tended to assert that safety inspections, even based on similar regulations, will not be carried out as carefully in other states as they would be in Japan.[12] Those groups have favored stricter regulations even when such regulations limit the variety of products available to them.[13] That contaminated blood from the United States was one of the major sources of the spread of AIDS in Japan only compounded Japanese suspicions of imports from America.[14]

Fourth, Japanese consumer groups grew in strength in the 1990s. The LDP's loss of power in 1993, its first since the 1950s, weakened producers' stranglehold on the political process and strengthened consumer activists by creating more access points and leading to augmented consumer protection laws.[15] Consumer groups have punished parties for mistakes on other occasions too.[16] Compared to other civil society groups, such as environmentalists, the consumer movement is organizationally strong and politically influential.[17]

Fifth, the strength of consumer groups was and continues to be supplemented by the great extent to which government officials have dreaded the public outrage that can ensue from a scandal. As one minister put it, "We have to be very careful to prevent incidents because the newspapers really go after you when you slip up."[18] By 2000, businesses were still well represented in the halls of Japanese power but no longer dominated the political process to the exclusion of consumer groups in the manner they once did, especially with regard to food safety regulations. As that change was occurring, Japan was also rapidly increasing its imports of U.S. beef.

Finally, Western food had become more prevalent in the Japanese diet but was nevertheless viewed with suspicion. Beef was a significant part of that trend. Japan began importing large amounts of U.S. beef in the late 1970s, but the imports were subjected to a highly protectionist quota system.[19] In 1991, the quotas were replaced with tariffs, which were further reduced in the Uruguay Round. Consequently, Japanese imports of U.S. beef increased in the early 1990s and then surged again in the late 1990s.[20] That increase notwithstanding and even though imported foods were once highly prized, domestically produced foods had become associated with higher quality and safety by the 2000s.[21]

For all these reasons, Japanese consumers have generally shown more concern with food regulations than have their U.S. counterparts. Japan's demands on BSE regulation in the 2000s are embedded within that cultural and regulatory dynamic. In that context and amid the increase in beef imports, BSE gained notoriety in 1996, especially in Europe, and led to calls for regulatory action to prevent its spread. BSE is a neurological disease in cattle. If someone eats meat from a cow infected with BSE, even meat cooked thoroughly, that person can contract variant Creutzfeldt-Jacob disease (vCJD), which is fatal within one to two years after onset and has no cure.[22] BSE is correlated with a cow's age, which is why many regulations designed to combat BSE have an age component. Because the disease clusters in the cow's brain and spinal cord, those parts are deemed "specified risk materials" that should be removed from cattle older than 30 months at the time of slaughter, according to the OIE, the international standard-setting body for regulations used in the meat industry.

BSE in Japan but Not in the United States: September 2001–December 2003

In September 2001, the first case of BSE was discovered in Japan. Japanese governing bodies—especially the Ministry of Agriculture, Forestry, and Fisheries (MAFF) and the Ministry of Health, Labor, and Welfare (HLW)—were widely perceived to have badly botched their response, because the infected cow had inadvertently been processed into bone meal and distributed to pork and chicken farmers.[23] Pigs and chickens cannot contract BSE, but that incident still alarmed consumers and created a perception of an ineffective safety system.[24] One Japanese consumer said, "I don't think there is any concrete logic to say that meat is safe . . . when you hear that the cow was not actually destroyed, what can you believe?"[25] The MAFF was criticized for not banning meat-and-bone meal for cattle feed, as the OIE had recommended.[26] The HLW, the ministry responsible for conducting the BSE tests, came under severe criticism for contributing to the slow response, because its officials forgot to inform their counterparts in the MAFF that a BSE case had been found.[27]

The opposition political party at the time, the DPJ, condemned the ruling LDP's handling of the situation and engaged in some rhetorical outbidding, advocating for a total ban on the use of bone meal.[28] Shortly thereafter, it came to light that the government had not just ignored but suppressed a report on the risk of BSE coming into the Japanese market via imports of meat-and-bone meal from Europe.[29] The discovery of that suppressed report only added to consumer groups' outrage.[30]

As I discussed in chapter 3, consumers are much more likely to fight for increased regulatory trade barriers when they believe that national regulation is the only means to achieve their policy goals. A series of scandals shortly after the BSE discovery further reinforced consumer groups' belief that strict regulations were needed to prevent producers from engaging in unsavory behavior. One company had falsely labeled imported beef as domestic and had sold meat to the government well past its expiration date in order to take advantage of a government insurance program, a maneuver that an MAFF official called "heinous beyond imagination."[31] Subsequent investigations revealed that at least two other companies had falsified information regarding their products too.[32] A number of smaller-scale frauds accompanied those revelations and convinced consumer advocates that those deceptions were "only the tip of the iceberg."[33] Those episodes fueled calls for greater traceability and more exacting labeling requirements for meat, and some of those calls directly accused the government bureaucracies of being too cozy with producers.[34]

Those events in Japan, though not directly related to U.S. beef, had two consequences for later negotiations on regulatory trade barriers between Japan and the United States. First, they convinced consumer activists that stringent regulations were absolutely necessary, so the activists became more rigid in defending Japan's BSE countermeasures. Their conviction helped birth a traceability system in which shoppers could view a cow's breeding history, the inspection certificate showing the cow to be free of BSE (as well as its species, breed, sex, and slaughter date) and the name of the inspector, and even a photograph of the farmer who sold the animal to the slaughterhouse.[35] Once Japanese consumers considered that level of transparency the norm, the argument made a few years later that U.S. producers should not have to keep records of or identify a cow's actual age—the factor most strongly correlated with BSE—struck those consumers as unreasonable and flippant.

Second, as I argued in chapter 3, government officials are led to defend regulatory barriers when they identify activists as a core constituency. These scandals so thoroughly embarrassed the MAFF that it became highly incentivized to aggressively pursue and enforce food safety regulations in order to win back credibility in the eyes of the public. After these incidents, Japanese agriculture minister Tsutomu Takebe said that the MAFF would begin implementing regulations "from the standpoint of the consumer."[36] Demonstrating the extent to which this issue was being taken seriously across the Japanese government, the Fair Trade Commission, though not the central target of consumers' ire, said that it too would take a stronger stand on consumer protection regulations.[37]

To reestablish its credibility on food regulation, the government implemented the world's strictest BSE countermeasures. All cattle would be tested for BSE, and all specified risk materials would be removed. Later, in 2003, when the OIE recommended that vertebrae be considered a specified risk material, Japan changed its regulations to match the OIE's guidance, a move suggesting that the Japanese government was not as contemptuous of international standards as the United States would later claim.[38] Because the regulations were not applied to beef imported from states that had never had a case of BSE, beef imports from the United States, which still had not had a BSE case, were not subjected to the regulations. Such exemption is further evidence that the Japanese government was not attempting to use BSE regulations as a disguised means of protectionism. If a government were using regulations as disguised protectionism, it would not exempt imported products from the regulations imposed on domestic producers.

During this time, U.S. producers organized a promotional campaign to extol the safety of U.S. beef.[39] They ostentatiously labeled their products as imported from America and even had U.S. agriculture secretary Ann Veneman tour Japan, giving cooking lessons prominently featuring U.S. beef to Japanese children.[40] By May 2003, Japanese beef consumption had returned to 86 percent of its pre-BSE level, and U.S. producers were set to resume their billions of dollars in annual beef exports to Japan, if the United States could remain BSE-free,[41] which did not happen.

The Discovery of BSE in the United States and Initial Reactions: December 2003–April 2004

In December 2003, the first case of BSE was discovered in the United States. In response, Japan suspended U.S. beef imports until an investigation could be undertaken, as is standard international practice when a country reports its first BSE case. That BSE discovery had two effects. First, it increased Japanese consumers' skepticism of the adequacy of U.S. food safety regulations and the safety of U.S. beef in particular.[42] Those concerns were especially acute because by the time the test results from that first U.S. case came back showing that the cow in question did have BSE, that cow had been slaughtered, and its meat had been mixed with 10,000 pounds of meat from other cattle, and shipped to supermarkets in eight states.[43] The BSE discovery raised considerably more alarm in Japan than in the United States.[44] Second, if U.S. producers wanted to regain market access, they now had to meet Japan's strict BSE countermeasures.

Notably, the Japanese government declared that U.S. producers would not have to implement a Japanese-style traceability program and said that, by making this exception, they were hoping to avoid erecting an unnecessary trade barrier, statements suggesting that they were not attempting to use regulations as disguised protectionism.[45]

After the BSE discovery, U.S. producers fought virtually all of the regulatory changes designed to curtail BSE in the United States on the grounds that the changes would raise production costs; they successfully blocked a number of proposed regulations.[46] The USDA implemented some new safety measures, however. For example, it stopped allowing downer cows (i.e., cows too sick or injured to walk) to be slaughtered and enter the food supply, and it instituted a rule that if a cow was tested for BSE, its meat could not be sent to retailers until after the results were known.[47] The USDA did not, however, institute universal testing or the removal of specified risk material for all cows.

U.S. consumer groups, who criticized both the meat industry for adopting this approach and the USDA for acquiescing to industry demands, were no match for an industry with a direct interest in regulations and a close connection with regulators, especially since the consumer groups were unable to galvanize the wider public.[48] The situation resembled what James Q. Wilson called "entrepreneurial politics," in which a diffuse interest squares off against a concentrated interest.[49] For the diffuse interest to prevail, a successful political entrepreneur must be able to garner attention and sympathy from the wider public, which U.S. consumer groups were not able to do in this case.

The U.S. regulatory changes were not enough for Japanese politicians or consumers who saw no reason why U.S. producers should not have to abide by the same regulations as Japanese producers.[50] Japan's prime minister, Junichiro Koizumi, stated that all beef imported from the United States had to pass "the same measures taken in Japan to secure safety and peace of mind such as removal of specified risk materials and inspection on all cows."[51] The Japanese government did, however, introduce an exception to blanket testing. The youngest cow found to have BSE in Japan was 21 months old, so the Japanese government stated that beef from cows slaughtered at 20 months or younger did not have to be tested for BSE as long as producers implemented a traceability system.[52] Though any producer could theoretically take advantage of the 20-month age exception to universal testing, only U.S. producers could use it, because only U.S. cattle are raised and fattened quickly enough (through intensive grain feeding) for slaughter at or before 20 months.[53] Japanese cattle are not ready for slaughter until they are roughly 27–30 months old.[54] Basically, Japanese regulators were saying that U.S. producers could avoid a traceability system or avoid blanket testing, but not both. That seeming good-faith effort to make Japanese regulations less burdensome for U.S. firms counts as further evidence that the Japanese government was not using BSE regulations as disguised protectionism. If it had been doing so, the last thing it would have done would be to create a regulation exemption that only benefited imported products.

Despite this attempt at flexibility, U.S. producers balked at Japan's demands. They were less interested in assuaging Japanese consumers than in getting the Japanese government to allow them to sell their products under a regulatory framework more to their liking. Roger Evans, the president of the Colorado Cattleman's Association, stated, "This thing has to be producer-friendly," adding, "I want it to be in the private sector that way someone is accountable to the producer."[55] Note the extent to which this cattleman either did not understand or did not care that food safety regulations are usually thought of as being primarily for consumers' benefit.

Explaining the Absence of a California Effect

U.S. producers could have chosen to adopt the higher Japanese standards and to lobby the U.S. government to raise U.S. standards accordingly, thus creating a California effect. Had they done so, they would have immediately regained access to the Japanese market. Market power gives states with high standards the ability to force foreign firms to raise their standards.[56] Japan was the largest export market for U.S. producers, so if any state had the market power to create a California effect in U.S. beef, it was Japan. One small producer, Creekstone Farms, attempted to adopt universal testing, but the USDA blocked it from doing so, as it was concerned that one firm testing all of its beef would lead to consumer demands that all firms do the same, thus adding production costs for major producers.[57] In other words, the USDA was implementing its regulations with the intent of undermining consumer activism on those regulations.

As I mentioned in chapter 3, one of the major factors influencing government officials' disposition on regulatory issues is their staffing. The penetration of beef industry insiders at high levels in the USDA made it more likely that the USDA would identify with producers. Alisa Harrison, Secretary Veneman's spokeswoman, and Dale Moore, Veneman's chief of staff, worked for the National Cattlemen's Beef Association prior to their time at the USDA.[58] Michael Taylor (who did not have a connection to the meat industry) recalls that when he took office as head of the USDA Food Safety and Inspection Service in 1994, he was perturbed that the phone in his new office already had two numbers on speed dial, both for producer organizations.[59] As Taylor explains, there was "a culture [in the USDA] that has developed over the years at the political level, the food safety program at the USDA thinking of the industry as the customer rather than the consumer."[60]

Regardless of the USDA's position, U.S. producers' opposition to adopting Japanese standards even though that resistance cost them access to their largest export market demands explanation. Two factors explain their intransigence. First, their rhetorical strategy for criticizing Japanese BSE regulations hardened their position. Because they disagreed with Japan's regulations and because regulations need to be justified on scientific grounds, U.S. producers repeatedly impugned Japanese BSE rules as "unscientific."[61] Over time, those derisions created an echo chamber among producers and reinforced their position.[62] Producers were also philosophically opposed to regulation and government intervention in markets in general. From 1990 through 2014, three-quarters of their over $60 million in campaign contributions went to Republicans; relatedly, the 15 largest recipients of campaign contributions from the livestock industry in the 2014 cycle were Republican.[63] Since the 1980s, the meat industry has also been stridently anti-union.[64] During the BSE episode, the industry as a whole was not predisposed to accepting higher regulations it deemed unnecessary.

Second, universal testing would have required U.S. beef firms to go against the primary strategy of their business model, aggressive cost cutting. The meat industry's primary focus at that time was on getting meat to market as cheaply as possible; every other consideration was secondary.[65] Adding costs, especially costs emanating from a regulatory approach they deemed unscientific, was not something producers were willing to do, even if such a stance lost them export business. Beef producers were not only in competition with each other; they were also in competition with the producers of all other foods, especially other forms of meat. Even if the costs of new testing requirements were spread evenly across beef producers, thus ensuring that none of them were disadvantaged relative to one another, those producers still would have lost out by having their product become more expensive relative to chicken, pork, and fish.

The BSE episode suggests a few caveats to the California effect. First, while market power does matter, it does not automatically override other concerns. As committed as U.S. cattle producers were to regaining access to Japan's market, they were even more committed to promoting a regulatory regime that operated on their policy terms. Second, unlike European automakers in their interaction with the environmental regulations discussed in chapter 4, U.S. beef producers believed that they had another option besides conforming with Japan's stricter regulations and then pressing the U.S. government to raise its standards to match Japan's. As will be shown in the following section of this chapter, they believed that they could get the U.S. government, specifically the U.S. trade representative, to successfully pressure the Japanese government into allowing imports of U.S. beef under a special arrangement that exempted U.S. beef producers from Japan's more onerous regulations.

Japanese market power could not make U.S. producers adopt stricter regulations, but U.S. political and economic power could tempt them into trying to strong-arm the Japanese, which did not work either. In the BSE case, economic and diplomatic power impeded progress more than it helped. That economic power backfired in a situation where it arguably should have been effective suggests that power-based explanations may be less efficacious than is commonly assumed and that the domestic politics over regulation can be highly sensitive.

Age Verification, Elections, and the Crawl toward Market Access, May 2004–December 2005

With U.S. producers refusing to accept either Japanese standards or permanent exclusion from the Japanese market, their only other option was to lobby the U.S. government to pressure the Japanese government to allow U.S. beef imports under a special arrangement. Through the fall of 2004, the U.S. trade representative pressured the Japanese government to allow a resumption of imports from the United States under regulatory terms U.S. firms could accept, showing that it was not just the USDA siding with producers. Allen Johnson, the chief U.S. agricultural negotiator, alluded that the United States might take the case before the World Trade Organization, and U.S. Senator Max Baucus and Vice President Dick Cheney urged the Japanese government to reopen its market.[66] In June, Secretary Veneman and President George W. Bush implored Prime Minister Koizumi to reestablish market access for U.S. producers as soon as possible.[67] Those entreaties grew more insistent as the U.S. presidential election loomed. President Bush badly wanted to be able to declare victory on this issue in order to gain support in key swing states with large agriculture sectors, such as Colorado, Missouri, and Florida.[68]

The lead negotiators in the case were in the Office of the United States Trade Representative. Two dynamics incentivized the USTR to vigorously defend the interests of U.S. beef exporters. First, the USTR is strongly pro-trade in its culture, its personnel, and its mission.[69] Second, the USTR wants good relations with Congress. In some cases, those two imperatives are in tension. Congressman X wants to protect the industries in his or her district, while the USTR wants to promote trade, which may come at the expense of those industries. However, when a congressman's efforts to protect industry entail not raising U.S. trade barriers but, instead, reducing another state's barriers, the USTR's two bureaucratic interests dovetail.

The barriers the USTR would be trying to reduce were not part of a larger trade deal. Thus USTR officials need not worry that another congressman would object to the USTR's backing of the beef industry while not demonstrating the same fealty to an industry in their district. Additionally, the USTR had no bureaucratic or ideational interest in the content of America's domestic beef regulations. The dispute with Japan over beef regulations provided the USTR with a rare opportunity to simultaneously pursue trade liberalization and good relations with Congress, and there was no countervailing interest mitigating those incentives. As I discussed in chapter 3, the three biggest drivers of officials advocating for reduced regulatory barriers are when they care more about trade than regulatory autonomy, when their staffing favors business, and when they identify business as their core constituency. All three drivers were present in this case.

Meanwhile, MAFF and HLW officials worried that a resumption of U.S. imports under looser regulations than those imposed on domestic beef would be perceived as the government sacrificing public health in order to appease the United States.[70] By October 2004, it was clear that, for the time being, Japan would not back down from its offer of a 20-month age exemption from universal testing and removal of specified risk materials from all cattle.[71] U.S. negotiators had already accepted a plan close to that one as a first step, so it seemed as if the two sides were close to reopening at least some access for U.S. producers.[72] The only real difference between the U.S. and Japanese plans was how to measure the cattle's age to ensure that they were not older than 20 months. Japan wanted the United States to institute a cattle-tracking system. The United States wanted to be allowed to estimate the cattle's age based on the cow's skeleton, even though that method had a greater margin for error than met Japanese regulators' comfort.[73]

The Bush administration decided to accept the Japanese terms and declare victory less than two weeks before the presidential election.[74] It presumed that the age-verification details could be worked out later and that this temporary agreement would be superseded after the United States won still greater access to the Japanese market.[75] In Japan, the timing of the agreement led the main opposition party (the DPJ) and a number of consumer groups to mistrust the reopening of imports, as they saw the agreement as Prime Minister Koizumi's gift to President Bush.[76]

To the consternation of U.S. producers, the dispute over age verification and thus the exclusion of U.S. beef from the Japanese market dragged into and throughout most of 2005. The MAFF and HLW accepted new U.S. proposals for age verification in February 2005, but they did not have final say on the matter.[77] To implement the agreement, an official end of the universal testing policy and the acceptability of the U.S. age-verification system had to be recommended by the Food Safety Commission (FSC), an independent, politically insulated panel of experts created in July 2003 to make scientific judgments on food safety.[78] MAFF and HLW officials argued, probably correctly, that any attempt on their part to force the commission to quickly make the decision that the MAFF/HLW wanted would have generated a storm of outrage.[79]

After the Japanese government had publicly stated its intention to create the 20-month exemption, the FSC came under intense pressure from consumer groups to maintain universal testing.[80] Those groups argued that the FSC should not allow a resumption of U.S. imports, because safety procedures at U.S. meat facilities did not meet Japanese standards.[81] In March 2005, restaurants that needed specifically U.S. beef began lobbying the government to find some way to expedite the FSC's decision.[82] For the first time, the Japanese government received significant business lobbying in favor of reducing the regulatory barriers.

U.S. producers and government officials believed that the October 2004 agreement amounted to a Japanese commitment to allow a resumption of U.S. beef imports and that the delay was foot-dragging, if not reneging.[83] U.S. officials became more aggressive in their pressure. Industry organizations and congressmen began demanding that sanctions be leveled against Japan if it did not allow imports of U.S. beef.[84] That pressure made any relaxation seem to be a Japanese capitulation to U.S. demands. In its zeal for sanctions, Congress actually made reducing the barriers harder, by delegitimizing Japanese officials' attempts to change their country's regulations in ways that would have facilitated renewed U.S. beef imports. Framing mattered a great deal to the situation, and power backfired more than it helped.

Despite the threats, filing suit before the World Trade Organization on behalf of beef producers was never a real option for the U.S. government.

A ruling in favor of the United States could have created a perception that Japan was being forced to accept imports of unsafe beef. Besides generating diplomatic tension, that perception could lead consumers to shun U.S. beef, thus negating the regained market access. That situation points to a limitation to the power of the WTO's mechanism for settling disputes over regulatory trade barriers. The sensitivity of domestic regulations means that an exporter is constrained in its ability to make a WTO case out of a barrier, because forcing a state to change its domestic rules risks destroying the exporter's reputation and profits in the importing country.

Throughout 2005, consumer groups remained convinced that U.S. standards did not pass muster and said so loudly.[85] In Japan, the DPJ criticized the ruling LDP for disregarding consumer safety and for kowtowing to the United States.[86] It was a sensitive time for the DPJ to make such accusations, because there was a general election coming up in September. Before the election, Koizumi and the LDP wanted to avoid making a concession that would incur consumer groups' wrath. To get the FSC to approve U.S. beef after the election, the LDP-led government ordered the commission to perform its risk-assessment based on the assumption that U.S. producers would follow Japanese regulations.[87] In October 2005, the FSC approved a resumption of U.S. imports under that assumption but presciently noted skepticism that stringent adherence to Japanese standards would actually occur.[88]

Throughout this period, contra to the expectations of state-centric theories that presume that security issues predominate, neither side sacrificed its position on regulatory trade barriers in beef to realize gains on other security-related issues, such as Japan's participation in the war in Iraq, talks with North Korea, China's military growth, or basing issues in Okinawa.[89] Relatedly, even though the United States and Japan were key security allies, neither side was willing to allow the other to have its way on this issue. In fact, the beef issue overshadowed security matters at certain points during bilateral talks.[90] The pattern of beef-related tensions predominating security concerns would be repeated at later points as well.[91] That the United States could not get Japan to yield on these regulatory barriers suggests that the benefits in political leverage gained from providing security benefits to a regional protégé are highly limited once regulations are involved. It has long been presumed that delivering security benefits gained the United States diplomatic capital that it could spend in other policy areas. Throughout the Cold War, trade policy was often subservient to geopolitics, but that was a time when trade policy generally did not impact regulations. Now, trade policy very much does affect regulation. Looking forward, the United States should not presume that security assistance will coax other states into bending in negotiations over regulatory trade barriers.

In December 2005, U.S. beef was allowed to be exported to Japan.[92] The regulatory standards under which U.S. beef producers regained access to the Japanese market (an age limit of under 20 months and removal of all specified risk materials) still constituted a significant regulatory barrier, but at least renewed access meant some access. If U.S. producers had demonstrated the safety of their product, perhaps those regulatory barriers could have been reduced still further.

The resumption of imports was severely criticized by Japanese consumer groups.[93] The notion that U.S. meat facilities might not always abide by the rules was not a figment of Japanese consumer groups' imagination; a USDA audit found 1,036 violations of regulations on specified risk material from January 2004 to May 2005, and the rules violated were not even as strict as those in the U.S.-Japan agreement.[94] MAFF and HLW officials, as well as Prime Minister Koizumi and the LDP, had staked their reputations in public health policy on the safety of U.S. beef. If U.S. producers had adhered to the requirements in the agreement, they could have reestablished healthy, growing sales. But, to put it mildly, U.S. producers failed to follow those regulations.

Careless, Stupid Mistakes and Diplomatic Cleanups: January 2006–April 2007

In January 2006, Japanese inspectors found a serious lapse in U.S. beef producers' implementation of the safety protocols, which resulted in Tokyo resuspending U.S. beef imports.[95] In one of the boxes of U.S. beef, Japanese inspectors found vertebrae and a spinal cord.[96] It would be difficult to overstate just how much of a blunder that was. BSE clusters in the cow's nervous system, making the spinal cord an especially risky specified risk material. The *American News*—published in Aberdeen, South Dakota, and as probeef a publication as one is likely to find anywhere—called the inclusion of these materials "a careless, stupid mistake."[97] Mike Johanns, the new U.S. secretary of agriculture, said it was "an unacceptable failure."[98]

The contrition of Johanns was undermined by other U.S. officials and suppliers. The National Cattlemen's Beef Association downplayed the mistake, pointing out that the inclusion of spinal cords from cattle less than 30 months old was not actually illegal in the United States, as if somehow that obviated Japanese concerns and regulations.[99] In a similarly undiplomatic vein, the U.S. undersecretary of agriculture, J. B. Penn, compared the risk of contracting vCJD from eating U.S. beef to the risk of being hit by a car on the way to purchase the beef.[100] From an actuarial standpoint, he may have been correct, but the remark was tone-deaf. In any case, comparing the consumption of one's product to being struck by a vehicle does not conjure up images of safety and wholesomeness. Congressmen who immediately began calling for retaliatory sanctions after Japan's reimposition of the import ban compounded the perception of insensitivity.[101]

Meanwhile, Japanese consumer activists that had objected to allowing U.S. beef imports all along were furious over the mistake and vindicated in their suspicion of U.S. regulatory effectiveness. The Food Safety Citizen's Watch declared their "great anger" and reminded everyone that they had "pointed out again and again . . . there is indeed a danger to us Japanese consumers [from U.S. beef]."[102] The mistake shook Japanese consumers' trust in U.S. beef as badly as, if not worse than, the original discovery of BSE in the United States.[103] As one official put it, "In the opinion of the Japanese consumer, this is like a new scandal being revealed."[104] The DPJ party leadership pounced on the scandal, portraying it as indicative of the LDP's insufficient concern for consumer safety and pointing out that it had opposed the agreement opening market access.[105]

Consumer groups demanded that, at minimum, the United States should have to allow Japanese regulators to inspect and decide for themselves which facilities to approve and that Japanese inspectors should be allowed to accompany their U.S. counterparts when they conducted surprise inspections.[106] Japanese consumer groups demanded reinforced protection rather than continued access. In this case, what Gunnar Trumbull has called "narratives of access" (arguments in favor of the state increasing access to certain goods) were less powerful than "narratives of protection" (arguments in favor of the state protecting consumers from the dangers posed by certain goods).[107]

Narratives of access had little power to encourage relaxations of the Japanese regulations on U.S. beef exports, because consumers knew their demand for beef could still be satisfied by other sources. A Japanese shopper interviewed after the spinal cord discovery argued that "the government should stop importing dangerous beef from the United States as (a supply shortage) could be averted with beef from Australia."[108] For their part, Australian beef importers expressed astonishment at the maladroitness of the American blunder but were happy that their competition, after fighting so hard to regain access, had managed to fritter it away so expeditiously.[109]

Japanese officials again faced a serious threat to their credibility on food safety. What made matters worse for the MAFF and HLW was that the day before the spinal cord discovery, Japanese officials had, on camera, assured consumers of U.S. regulatory effectiveness.[110] To retain the public's trust, they had no choice but to reimpose the ban on beef not universally tested for BSE and to insist on the two policy demands that had been advanced by the consumer groups. As the owner of a Japanese slaughterhouse pointed out, "MAFF took the USDA at its word and it let them down. Because they look foolish, it would be some time before trade resumes."[111] The MAFF also decided to increase inspection of U.S. beef should imports be resumed.[112] If these policies meant trade friction, that would be Prime Minister Koizumi's problem.

Koizumi thus needed to demand tougher rules on U.S. beef but also not start a trade row. He did not want to be seen as caving to U.S. pressure and argued that the decision was in the MAFF's hands. When asked about U.S. imports resuming, he said, "Specialists are discussing this matter. I'll follow their opinion."[113] Importantly, by April, MAFF officials were satisfied with the increase in safety rules placed on U.S. producers. They also believed that Japanese consumers' concerns had become overwrought; one FSC official said, "As specialists here at the ministry, we regard the consumers' reaction as extreme."[114]

The United States acceded to Japan's demands, and in May 2006, the two governments reached an agreement to restore U.S. producers' access to the Japanese market.[115] That restored access came with stricter oversight that gave foreign regulators inspection rights over U.S. firms located entirely in the United States, an uncommon arrangement, to say the least. Moreover, the HLW also began inspecting every box of imported U.S. beef rather than just a random sample.[116] The agreement restored access to its December 2005 level, with which U.S. cattlemen were never satisfied. U.S. beef had not yet reached Japan before the U.S. government was already pushing Japan to further reduce its regulatory barriers, specifically to raise the age exception on universal testing to all cows 30 months and younger.[117] That pressure continued into 2007.[118]

Throughout this period, U.S. producers continued to make basic errors in complying with the U.S.-Japan beef agreement. For example, they included unapproved thymus glands in one shipment, erroneously shipped beef that did not abide by Japan's age limits on multiple occasions, and included yet another spinal column.[119] Those mistakes did not make the Japanese more eager to alter their regulations to match U.S. preferences. Still, Japanese officials believed that U.S. safety standards were effective enough on the whole, and instead of imposing broader import restrictions as they had after the earlier spinal cord mistake, they chose to decertify the offending facilities individually.[120] In April 2007, the United States agreed to allow Japan to conduct more audits of American meatpacking plants in exchange for Japan agreeing to loosen its policy of inspecting 100 percent of all beef boxes.[121] In addition to these amity-producing developments, the OIE would soon issue new estimates that encouraged Japanese regulators to have even more confidence in U.S. regulations.

American Exceptionalism and Throttled Compromise: May 2007–August 2009

In May 2007, the OIE reclassified the United States from being a country with "unidentified BSE risk" to being a country with "controlled BSE risk." That classification, though nonbinding in international law, endorsed U.S. BSE regulations as effective enough to support the U.S. ability to export beef regardless of age.[122] In response to the OIE ruling and after an internal review, Japanese officials announced that they were willing to relax their testing regulations and exempt all cattle 30 months and younger.[123] In effect, this meant adopting the age threshold the United States had been advocating all along.

In other words, Japanese officials were agreeing to implement the regulations U.S. beef producers and policymakers had spent the previous three years saying they wanted. Had U.S. officials accepted that offer, the confrontation over regulatory trade barriers in beef between the United States and Japan would have been over. Japan would have been able to maintain the regulations it preferred, and U.S. producers would have had what amounted to a 90–95 percent opening of the Japanese market, as that is the percentage of U.S. cattle slaughtered between 15 and 24 months.[124] U.S. officials rejected the Japanese offer.

The same change in OIE guidelines that softened the Japanese government's approach led the U.S. government, particularly the USDA, to adopt a more ambitious goal of convincing the Japanese government to remove all of its age restrictions to cattle.[125] Immediately after the OIE change was made, Secretary Johanns said that the United States would "use this international validation" to pry open the Japanese market for all American beef products.[126] Thereafter, U.S. officials all the way up to President Bush pressured Japan to remove all of its age-related regulatory trade barriers.[127] Making the American position transparently inconsistent and easier for the Japanese to disregard was the fact that the United States held up the OIE as the source of the definitive "scientific" international standard in this particular instance but continued to ignore OIE standards on other matters related to beef regulations, calling those recommendations "unscientific." The United States would not fully align its beef regulations with OIE recommendations until March 2012, over three years into the Obama administration.[128]

Three reasons lay behind the U.S. government's decision to reject the Japanese offer of a 30-month age limit. First, USDA officials and American producers did not accept the legitimacy of Japan's regulatory preferences (dismissing them as "unscientific") and did not accept that they needed to bend at all.[129] Second, the United States was attempting to fully open Japan's beef market so that it could use that as a lever to open the South Korean market in the free trade negotiations taking place between the United States and South Korea.[130] Third, a maximalist approach fit the Bush administration's modus operandi in negotiations. Bush administration officials tended to conflate compromise with capitulation. The dispute thus dragged into 2008.[131]

International standards bodies like the OIE, the International Organization for Standardization, and the Codex Alimentarius are often credited with facilitating cooperation, and there is considerable evidence that they do exactly that. This part of the case study, though, suggests a potential limitation to that facilitation. When these bodies issue recommendations that support a claimant, they can make that claimant more rigid in its position. In situations in which the willingness to compromise is more important than coordination difficulties (arguably a huge proportion of disputes on regulatory trade barriers), making one party more immutable may hamper cooperation more than the recommendations facilitate cooperation through the enunciation of potentially common standards.

Barack Obama's rhetoric showed that, like President Bush, he saw his role as supporting U.S. producers. Like Bush, he chalked up the regulatory differences to disguised protectionism, saying, "You can't get beef into Japan and Korea, even though, obviously, we have the highest safety standards of anybody, but they don't want to have that competition from U.S. producers."[132] Austan Goolsbee, the chairman of Obama's Council of Economic Advisors, likewise argued, "Two facts are not in dispute. Japan and Korea retain rules that prevent imports of U.S. beef, rules that other countries don't have, and in countries that don't have those rules, U.S. beef exports have returned to higher levels than before. So you've got to be highly suspicious at the outset."[133] The Obama campaign may have phrased its position on Japan's beef regulations more politely than the Bush administration, but that position was still based on the same hubristic premise. The underlying assumption behind Goolsbee's and Obama's statements as well as the Bush administration's position is that American businesses and, by extension, America are so unfailingly excellent that if they cannot effectively compete in a foreign market, the only logical explanation is that there must be some form of disguised protectionism preventing them from doing so.

When the policy position of the National Cattleman's Beef Association on negotiating with Japan changed, so did President Obama's. In January 2009, the NCBA asked its members to consider changing the association's position to support an incremental approach vis-à-vis Japan.[134] Instead of pushing for the removal of all age restrictions, as was their preference before, the beef industry was willing to accept the 30-month position that Japan had signaled it would accept after the OIE's 2007 ruling. In May 2009, the NCBA adopted that position, and the U.S. Meat Export Federation joined in promoting the incrementalism.[135]

In the intervening period between January and May 2009, the Obama administration's position remained unchanged from its predecessor's.[136] After the industry's preference shift, the Obama administration adopted the incremental approach; by July, even Republicans were taking that position.[137] That the Obama administration's position did not change upon taking office but did shift after the industry's position changed suggests that this policy adjustment was not simply a manifestation of campaign rhetoric being jettisoned in the face of the realities of governance. Rather, it was a manifestation of policymakers defining their role as promoting the beef industry, from which they would take policy cues. That the GOP's position changed too and aligned with the Obama administration's further supports that explanation. State-centric explanations would have serious difficulty explaining that shift. The state's preference here was not independently designed but, rather, the product of lobbying by domestic political actors.

The problem for U.S. policymakers in the summer of 2009 was that a Japanese election was approaching in August, and the ruling LDP did not want to implement compromises until after September.[138] The LDP had been in power for all but 11 months since the 1950s (which is why Japan has often been held up as an exemplar of a single-party democracy), so there was some sense that the issue could be dealt with after the election. The LDP's loss of power to the DPJ in August 2009 buried any chance of such a resolution.

The DPJ and Beef Imports: August 2009–September 2010

The DPJ had spent years castigating the LDP as subservient to the United States and insufficiently protective of consumers.[139] The opposition party had portrayed every concession that the LDP had made to the United States as craven and had called for a tougher approach to U.S. beef imports. Even if LDP leaders had wanted to compromise with the United States on beef, such a naked about-face, would have been a humiliating climb down, with little domestic upside, at least in the near term. Moreover, the divisions within the DPJ, which was created in 1998 as a merger of several smaller parties, continued to shine through on trade. Though the party had used the beef dispute as a cudgel against the LDP and though some DPJ members opposed trade liberalization, other members were in favor of a trade agreement with the United States as a way to promote exports and were thus willing to consider a relaxation of Japan's regulatory barriers against U.S. beef if it were part of a trade deal.[140] Though that willingness created some room for compromise, it also meant that addressing the beef issue jeopardized splitting the already fractious party. Percolating disputes with the United States over other agenda items made the issue even more politically fraught for the DPJ.

In 2006, the LDP had signed an agreement to move the U.S. base at Okinawa, which was highly unpopular with local residents, to a less populated area of the island. During the 2009 election, DPJ leader Hatoyama had promised to move the Futenma base off the island of Okinawa completely.[141] After the DPJ won, Okinawa residents believed that they would finally be rid of the base. When the DPJ ultimately had to allow the base to remain, large protests ensued. The public relations damage was so bad that Hatoyama was forced to resign.[142]

Once again, trade considerations were not made subservient to security concerns; neither the Japanese nor the American government attempted to barter away its position on beef regulations to win concessions on the basing dispute. In light of the Futenma dispute, the DPJ believed it could not afford to be seen caving to American demands regarding an issue as sensitive as consumer safety.[143] The basing controversy not only left the DPJ with even less political room for appearing to compromise with the United States but also led to leadership changes that added an additional hurdle to resolving the beef trade dispute.

The new prime minister, Naoto Kan, largely left the cabinet the same, but one of the few changes he did make affected policy related to trade and beef regulations. Kan's choice to head the MAFF was Masahiko Yamada, a devoutly protectionist beef farmer who had written a book titled *America Will Destroy Japan's Food Industry* and a dystopian novel titled *The Japan-US Food War: When Japan Goes Starving*.[144] Yamada's position meant he would play a major role in determining how much the government compromised with the United States over BSE regulations and trade in beef. Kan chose him because he had been close to Ichiro Ozawa, a longtime power broker within the DPJ who had been forced to resign with Hatoyama, and Kan wanted to hold the factions in his party together.[145] Kan's situation is another example of both how much staffing matters and why it can be difficult to formally model officials' behavior on regulation and trade; a different official, even from the DPJ, might have taken a different stance on these issues.

In fact, that is exactly what happened. Later that year, when Ozawa attempted to usurp Kan's leadership of the DPJ, Kan was able to beat back the challenge to his leadership and consolidate his control over his party. Soon thereafter, he sacked Yamada, replacing him with a free trade advocate and installing Akihiro Ohata, another proponent of trade liberalization, as the head of the Ministry of Economy, Trade, and Industry.[146] U.S.-Japan discussions over the beef issue ensued directly after this shake-up, though nothing was agreed to in an immediate sense.[147] To signal its seriousness in considering relaxing the regulatory barriers, the new Japanese leadership asked the United States to provide the data Japan would need to conduct the internal risk assessment that would be the first step in that process.[148] The new leadership's tentative steps toward meaningful negotiation augured well for compromise on the beef trade issue. At this point, the nascent Trans-Pacific Partnership began to gain salience in Japan, bringing hitherto uninvolved domestic actors into the negotiation of regulatory barriers in beef.

The TPP, Farmer Protests, and the Triple Disaster: October 2010–October 2011

The Trans-Pacific Partnership negotiations began in 2005 as a free trade agreement between New Zealand, Brunei, Chile, and Singapore. By 2010, it had been joined by Peru, Malaysia, Australia, Vietnam, and the United States and had thus grown immensely larger in geographic and economic terms. Until that point, the main actors in the beef case were Japanese consumer organizations, Japanese policymakers, U.S. beef producers, and U.S. policymakers—the four groups that had an interest in beef regulations and trade. The attenuations and increases in the regulatory trade barriers in beef were based on their respective positions. The TPP gave Japanese beef producers and Japanese exporters an interest in those regulatory trade barriers.

Japanese beef producers had never really entered the contestation over those regulatory trade barriers because their competition was not U.S. beef imports in particular as much as imports generally. As long as Australia and other states could provide beef to fill the lost American supply, Japanese producers' incomes were not really affected by the regulatory trade barriers.[149] Perhaps, had the Japanese regulations been disguised forms of protectionism that excluded all imports, Japanese beef producers would have been major defenders of those regulations. Given that the regulatory barriers did not erect tariff-like walls that affected all imports, beef producers had no reason to expend political capital on regulations. Instead, they saved their organizational strength for the policy fights that did matter to them, tariffs and other nonregulatory trade policy, exactly the policy fights that the TPP was creating.

Throughout this period, whenever negotiations over beef involved tariffs or other nonregulatory trade barriers, Japanese beef farmers loudly opposed any trade liberalization. At their behest, the government chose not to end safeguard tariffs early, despite the fact that they were seen as unnecessary and were raising consumer prices.[150] Farmers blocked trade talks with the United States in 2007 and an agreement with Australia in 2008.[151] In those episodes, the negotiations over regulatory and nonregulatory trade were always kept separate. That separation would not be the case for the TPP. The farmers understood that the United States would demand compromise on beef regulation as a price of Japanese entrance into the TPP. In other words, beef farmers saw relaxation of regulatory barriers as paving the way for the TPP, which would lower tariffs and threaten their sales. They saw those regulatory barriers as a roadblock to that threat and wanted to ensure that the roadblock stayed in place. Just days after Prime Minister Kan began to signal that the government was considering joining the TPP, thousands of farmers rallied in Tokyo against it.[152]

Meanwhile, the conclusion of a trade agreement in December 2010 between the United States and Korea gave other Japanese businesses an augmented interest in getting Japan to join the TPP.[153] Two goods, cars and machinery, comprised 70 percent of Japanese and South Korean exports to the United States.[154] Japanese businesses, especially in those two areas, feared that the Korea-U.S. free trade agreement had given their Korean rivals a significant competitive advantage and that Japan now needed a free trade agreement with the United States to compete in the lucrative U.S. market.[155] Fortunately for them, the TPP presented just such an opportunity, if only they could get the U.S. government to acquiesce to Japan's inclusion in the TPP. Like Japanese farmers, those businesses recognized the extent to which the regulatory barriers in beef functioned as a roadblock to that inclusion. Unlike those farmers, they wanted that roadblock removed.

The addition of nonagricultural issues to the trade docket also had a big impact on the Japanese government's approach. In principal, the Ministry of International Trade and Industry (MITI) controls Japanese trade policy. However, when the trade policy at hand is agricultural, the MAFF is given primary responsibility in that negotiation. As long as the negotiations over regulatory barriers on beef remained isolated from other trade issues, the MAFF controlled Japan's position. Once regulatory barriers in beef became embedded in a larger constellation of trade issues, MITI became the leading player. MITI is much less inclined toward protectionism than the MAFF.[156] Also, MITI's core constituents, unlike those of the MAFF, are export-oriented businesses, the very entities making competitiveness claims vis-à-vis their Korean rivals.

That exchanging one trade concession for another did not generate the political blowback threatened by exchanging agreement on the beef issue for nontrade concessions suggests something interesting about the nature of cross-issue linkages in trade negotiations. Which issues are getting cross-linked matters a great deal. How citizens and policymakers think about concessions is central to which concessions can be made. Linking other trade-related issues to the beef regulation dispute created greater space for compromise, because both sides in a trade negotiation recognize that concessions are a prerequisite for the successful conclusion of the negotiation. Conversely, linking security-related issues was, at best, a nonfactor in the negotiation over regulatory trade barriers and, at worst, made finding a resolution more difficult.

While the deliberations surrounding joining the TPP were occurring, Japan was struck in March 2011 by the triple disaster of an earthquake, a tsunami, and a subsequent nuclear crisis. Progress on compromise over the regulatory trade barriers in beef was slowed by the simple fact that the catastrophe understandably pushed all other agenda items to the margins while recovery and reconstruction began in earnest in the spring and summer of that year.

The 30-Month Compromise: October 2011–March 2013

By fall 2011, Yoshihiko Noda had replaced Kan as prime minister. Noda's trade positions were the same as his predecessor's, but by this point, the mood regarding BSE had begun to shift. *Yomiuri Shimbun*, Japan's most widely circulated newspaper, which had opposed earlier efforts to relax the regulatory barriers in beef, now supported such a move.[157] Even admonishing consumer groups for continuing to oppose relaxation, the paper provided cover for officials who wanted to advance that position.[158] Public sentiment toward relaxed rules had softened as the global number of cattle found with BSE had fallen to 29 from a high of 37,000 cases.[159]

By this time, most middle-class consumers were accepting of U.S. beef.[160] The diminishing consumer hostility to relaxing the regulatory trade barriers on U.S. beef was essential in giving the government the political space to agree to those relaxations. Even with Japanese export-oriented businesses pushing for the TPP, the government would have found it very difficult to relax those barriers on beef had the general public still been aroused in opposition. This change suggests that Japanese consumer organizations were not only critical in promoting the augmentation of regulatory trade barriers but also key in allowing an attenuation of regulatory trade barriers, through their acquiescence. In October, the Japanese government announced that it intended to revise its BSE regulations, which clearly signaled that it was strongly contemplating relaxing the age regulations on beef.[161] Soon thereafter, Japan announced its intent to join the TPP talks.

Alternative Explanations

This case complicates the "business dominates" hypothesis. Throughout the case, U.S. producers pushed for a relaxation of regulatory barriers and had a cozy relationship with U.S. officials who fought hard for their policy positions. Still, time and again, in terms of international negotiation outcomes, they lost that fight. Despite their constant efforts, it took them a decade to regain full market access, at the cost of billions of dollars. At no point were they defeated by a competing business interest. Instead, their losses came at the hands of consumers groups, the interest frequently held up as the exemplar of diffuse, weak interests. Only when consumer fears had subsided were American businesses, the interests most often held up as the most powerful private interests, able to enact their policy preferences.

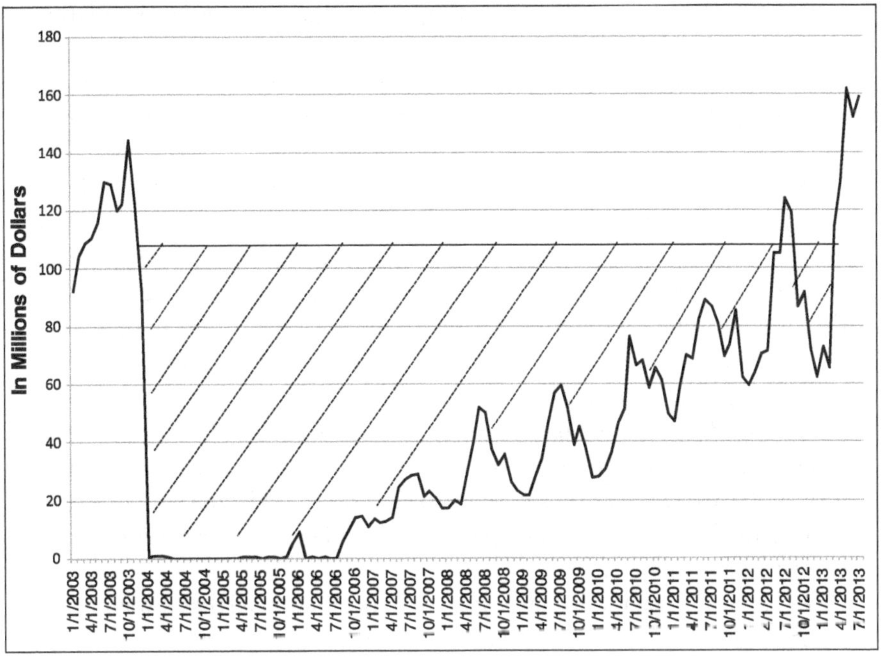

Fig. 5.2. Losses from U.S. Beef Exports to Japan, 2003–13

The hypothesis might carry more weight had U.S. exporters been able to maintain the market access they had prior to December 2003. Beef exports to Japan averaged $118.2 million per month for the first 11 months of 2003.[162] The shaded region in figure 2 represents the lost exports of those beef producers from December 2003 to March 2013. That lost revenue totals $9.2 billion.[163] If business truly does dominate, it does not lose $9.2 billion in revenue at the hands of the paragon of diffuse interests defending regulations those firms perceive to be illegitimate.

U.S. officials welcomed the Japanese announcement but made it clear that in the context of the TPP, they expected actual movement on the regulatory barriers in beef, not signals and promises of future movement.[164] The next month, Tami Overby, the vice president for Asia of the U.S. Chamber of Commerce, echoed that sentiment: "Now we need to see action. Not words, action." She called on Japan to enact three "confidence-building measures" to show Tokyo's readiness to participate in TPP talks.[165] The USTR soon adopted this very position, even using Overby's phrase "confidence-building measures."[166] With regard to beef regulations, the National Cattlemen's Beef Association announced its support for Japan's entrance to TPP negotiations, contingent on Japan relaxing its regulatory barriers on U.S. beef.[167]

In September 2012, Tokyo took another step toward moving the 20-month rule to 30 months, pleasing the U.S. Meat Export Federation and the USTR.[168] The LDP, which took power in December 2012, contained even fewer opponents of the regulatory alterations than the DPJ.[169] Even though they did not oppose relaxing regulatory trade barriers in beef, many LDP Diet members did oppose Japanese participation in the TPP as a whole, because they did not want to see reductions in agricultural tariffs; they even specifically stated that their opposition stemmed from their concern for the farming sector.[170] Given that many LDP members wanted to engage in protectionism of some kind on behalf of farmers, opposing this relaxation of regulatory barriers would have been a perfect opportunity to do just that, so their response undermines the idea that these regulatory trade barriers were disguised protectionism. This episode also contradicts the behavior we should have seen based on the expectations of the cleavage-based explanations.

In January 2013, the Japanese government announced that it was changing its regulations to the 30-month age limit. U.S. beef producers now had essentially 90–95 percent access to the Japanese market. They could finally resume their roughly billion-dollar level of annual exports to Japan. Once the regulatory relaxation was fully implemented in March, the National Cattlemen's Beef Association endorsed Japan's involvement in TPP negotiations "as soon as possible."[171] After Japanese prime minister Shinzo Abe officially announced that Japan would be seeking entrance to the TPP, the U.S. government supported, for the first time, Japan's inclusion in the TPP.

The Counterintuitive Difficulty of Finding Compromise on Regulatory Trade Barriers

There was a certain frustration to the negotiations over the regulatory barriers in beef. Just when U.S. and Japanese negotiators thought they had found a compromise, the negotiations would fall apart. The negotiators thought they had an agreement in fall 2004 but were stymied by age-verification techniques. In 2006, the negotiators again thought they were making progress, only to be thwarted by slapdash producers allowing spinal cords to find their way into beef packages. In 2009–10, hopes for agreement were dashed first by a stunning election result and then by an unrelated controversy over the location of a military base. Those events had the power to block progress toward compromise on regulatory barriers that were embedded in sensitive domestic politics. Finding agreement on issues that affect consumers' health and safety required engaging in a laborious and contentious process. Given that sensitivity, any number of trends and dynamics had the potential to act as roadblocks.

Nesting the negotiation over these regulatory trade barriers within a milieu of other issues undermined as often as facilitated compromise. Adding issues to the agenda is often considered an avenue toward reaching a deal because it increases options and gives each side a greater ability to find some concession on an unrelated matter. The more issues there are on the table, the easier it is to find some concession on issue Y that can be exchanged for movement on issue X. This logic has underpinned conducting trade negotiations in a single undertaking. Such bargaining occurred in the context of the TPP, but in other instances, more agenda items, such as the base dispute, made compromise harder, because Tokyo felt that it could not be seen as capitulating to the United States on two issues at once. That complication suggests that embedding multiple issues in a single undertaking, a maneuver that was quite effective at promoting liberalization in tariffs and other nonregulatory measures, may actually backfire when applied to some regulatory trade barriers.

As I mentioned earlier in this chapter, regulatory barriers seem, at first glance, like the kind of technical, low-salience issues that should allow for easy cooperation between governments, especially when businesses are pressuring them to cooperate. Businesses want to reduce those regulatory barriers and think they can easily do so because they perceive themselves as the only interested entities. Governments, responding to business entreaties, explore cooperation over those regulatory barriers and then find, to their surprise, that reaching compromise is not so easy, because activists also care about those barriers. Prior to deal exploration, most people do not get excited when they hear the word *regulation*. When talked about in the abstract, trade regulations seem remote and almost painfully boring. But when the regulations being discussed take concrete form and affect citizens in a tangible, easy-to-understand way, some of those citizens get animated. Only when activist opposition can be prevented, either through persuasion or political marginalization, can negotiators pursue their policy prey unimpeded. This dynamic is why finding a mutually acceptable attenuation of regulatory trade barriers requires Sisyphean perseverance.

SIX

Small Details, Enormous Consequences (Part I)

Regulation and the Trade in Pharmaceuticals, TRIPS to Doha

Perhaps more than any other product, pharmaceuticals distill the complex interplay between commercial interests and noneconomic public policy goals that is at the center of regulation and trade politics. The global trade in pharmaceuticals is worth approximately $550 billion annually.[1] Drugs generate massive sales because they are indispensable in promoting the health of huge numbers of people around the world. Almost everyone will take some form of medication at some point in their lives. Governments have an interest in promoting the health of their citizens and access to safe, effective medications. Drugs were thus among the first products to be closely regulated by governments.

Across the globe, societies are aging and developing and are likely to spend greater shares of their GDP on health care, which means that the trade in pharmaceuticals is likely to continue growing larger and more geopolitically significant. Given the increasing extent to which different states' disparate regulations on pharmaceuticals impact this trade, the content of those regulations is becoming a central issue in trade negotiations. The last issue resolved and one of the most contentious issues raised in the Trans-Pacific Partnership negotiations was what length of data exclusivity to give to patented biologic drugs.[2]

Pharmaceutical companies are highly reluctant to produce drugs in or import drugs into countries in which their intellectual property will not be respected. Though different from the health, safety, and environmental regulations that are the more intuitive and traditional regulatory barriers to trade, refusing to protect a firm's IP constitutes a trade barrier because it prevents that firm from reaping gains from trade and effectively prohibits them from engaging in international trade. With the power to impede the trade in pharmaceuticals, differences in regulation on IP thus constitute regulatory trade barriers.[3] Those regulatory barriers are becoming the centerpiece issues in the geopolitical negotiations that surround the trade in pharmaceuticals. I further contend that because they affect the incentives to innovate and the speed with which cheaper generic drugs can come to market, they can fairly be considered health and safety regulations as well.

The United States and India are two of the central players in the geopolitics of drugs. The United States is home to some of the world's largest, most advanced drug companies. It has been a leader in using regulation to promote an efficient pharmaceutical sector. More controversially, it has attempted to get other states to adopt IP regulations similar to its own. It leads the camp that wants IP regulations set at high levels.[4] Without the U.S. pharmaceutical firms, many of the miraculous drugs we have today would not exist, and millions of people would have had shorter, less fulfilling lives. India has been a leader in using IP regulations to promote access to medicine for even the poorest of citizens. It has led the camp that wants IP regulations set at lower levels. Without India's efforts, many millions of people would have had shorter, less fulfilling lives, not because the drugs they needed did not exist, but because those drugs were too expensive.

The extent to which states' regulations on IP differ has varied over time. The negotiation of the Agreement on Trade-Related Aspects of Intellectual Property Rights (TRIPS) in the 1980s and early 1990s significantly reduced those regulatory differences. The Doha Declaration in 2001 strengthened the flexibilities in TRIPS and gave states greater policy room to re-expand those regulatory differences. Subsequent decisions of the World Trade Organization from 2003 to 2015 amounted to a stalemate that preserved the regulatory differences. After 2005, India found ways to creatively interpret TRIPS provisions to further increase the differences but selectively employed those flexibilities in ways that balanced the interests of activists and drug companies. The negotiations between the United States and Brazil that were part of the push for a Free Trade of the Americas Agreement completely broke down, largely due to disagreements on IP policy. Meanwhile, just the opposite happened in the negotiations of the Central America Free Trade Agreement (CAFTA) between the United States and Central American countries, where the parties agreed to CAFTA and the TRIPS-plus provisions that came with it. This chapter and the one that follows explain that variation.

In this chapter, I focus on the negotiations over the TRIPS Agreement and the Doha Declaration. I explain their varying outcomes by examining the relevant political bargaining between pharmaceutical companies, access-to-medicine advocates, and government officials. In the TRIPS negotiations, two key factors gave pharmaceutical companies and the U.S. government officials identifying with them the ability to significantly reduce those regulatory differences. First, activists were not yet engaged on the issue, so those firms and officials had the negotiating terrain to themselves. Second, pharmaceutical companies were able to successfully link their policy requests with broader societal concerns about economic competitiveness.

In the negotiations leading up to the Doha Declaration, activists were able to wage a highly successful public relations campaign and to work with officials of developing countries to force drug firms and their allies in Western governments to accept an increase in those differences. They were able to do this by linking uniform IP regulations with needless death, specifically the AIDS crisis in sub-Saharan Africa. Chapter 7 examines negotiations over these issues after the Doha Declaration.

Beyond the practical significance of the pharmaceutical sector in and of itself, this case involves one of the regulatory areas that most clearly pits developing versus developed countries, one of the most important divides in the trade and regulation policy space, so examining this case allows for an exploration of that dynamic. Furthermore, despite similar power asymmetries between developed and developing countries throughout this case, there are highly varied outcomes in the movement of regulatory trade barriers in the various subcases. This case is also analytically useful because the pharmaceutical sector is one area in which businesses are said to especially dominate, yet even here, as I will show in this chapter and the next, businesses' power is more limited and contingent than is commonly argued.[5] Finally, this case challenges cleavage-based explanations, because the main

TABLE 6.1. Outcomes of Regulatory Trade Barriers in Pharmaceuticals

TRIPS	Decrease
Doha Declaration	Increase
WTO Decisions	Compromise
Indian Flexibilities	Compromise
FTAA	Maintained
U.S. Free Trade Agreements	Decrease

opponents of the research-based pharmaceutical firms in the case are not generic drug manufacturers but access-to-medicine activists.

A Primer on Intellectual Property Regulations

TRIPS structures those IP regulations that have trade implications. One set of those regulations concerns patents and thus shapes the trade in pharmaceuticals. At their heart, the IP regulations that surround patents are an attempt to balance the desire to limit both monopoly and free riding. The intellectual work that goes into a product has to be protected from being imitated before the creator can be appropriately compensated. Doing nothing to prevent that sort of free riding undermines the incentive to innovate and leaves society worse off, particularly when there are large up-front research and development costs. If it costs a billion dollars to develop a new drug but the marginal costs of producing every additional pill is one cent, a second company can copy the drug and sell it for far less because it never incurred that cost. The first company would be foolish to invest in that new drug unless there is a mechanism to prevent the second company from undercutting it. That mechanism is a patent.

Patents give businesses the exclusive right to market their invention for a given period of time; in other words, patenting gives them a temporary monopoly. Patents are granted for inventions that meet three criteria: novelty, nonobviousness, and usefulness.[6] The stronger patent regulations are (i.e., the longer the patent lasts and the more effectively it prevents free riding), the greater the commercial incentive is to invest in new drugs. Pharmaceutical executives point to stunning improvements in health outcomes for patients with diseases such as HIV and hepatitis C and contend that the profitability of drugs for those diseases is the major incentive driving innovation.[7] In fairness to the drug companies, society now has a vast array of highly effective medicines that are now off-patent and incredibly cheap. Those medicines were expensive when they first came out, and pharmaceutical companies created them out of profit-seeking motives rather than philanthropic ones, but it can still be credibly argued that the stringent IP regulations that the United States employs built that storehouse of wonder drugs. Pharmaceutical companies also contend that despite high costs, some drugs actually save the overall health care system money by preventing more expensive procedures such as transplants and extended hospital stays.[8]

Because the catalog of available medicines continues to improve, the benchmark that drug companies must exceed to create new medicines continues to get higher. The first person to invent aspirin could patent it; the second person had to invent something better than aspirin; the third person had to invent something that was better still and even more difficult to produce. That every generation of scientists makes the next generation's job harder is yet another reason why firms want patents to be as strong as possible. If it is getting ever harder to invent patentable products, firms want to ensure that products that get patented are revenue bonanzas.

Pharmaceutical companies do not just want to expand patent regulations. They also want a high regulatory standard for data exclusivity, especially for biologics, today's cutting-edge medical products that cost far more to develop than traditional small-molecule drugs. When research-based pharmaceutical firms attempt to get their product approved by regulators such as the FDA, they must provide extensive amounts of data demonstrating the safety and efficacy of their drug. When the patent term on that drug expires, generic firms can make copies of that drug. Rather than repeat the costly and difficult tasks needed to replicate the data that demonstrated the drug's safety and efficacy, the generic firm will simply use the first firm's data. After all, if H_2O was safe to consume when it was sold by Prescott Pharmaceuticals, it should be just as safe when sold by a different firm.

Research-based firms argue that the generic firm using their data is still free riding and that the research-based firm that produced the data owns and should have exclusive rights to it. The government granting the data exclusivity effectively lengthens patent times by forcing the generics firm to repeat the trials that created the data, making it more difficult for a generic to enter the market. Research firms base their arguments in favor of data exclusivity on the same incentives-promotion premises as their support for extensive patents.[9] Though there is some validity in drug firms' claims regarding IP regulations, one has to take their position with a grain of salt, given that it is in their financial interests to promote high IP regulations.

While they do create powerful incentives for innovation, high IP regulations are not without drawbacks. Monopolies, which are what patents effectively constitute, limit competition, thus raising prices for consumers. The very profits that incentivize innovation come from consumers, insurance companies, and governments. That incentive may have sparked innovation but is still expensive. In the United States, $374 billion were spent on prescription drugs in 2014.[10] There is a great deal of profit making in that. The 10 largest pharmaceutical firms had an average profit margin of 19.6 percent in 2013.[11]

One of the major drivers of these profits is that medicines are the epitome of inelastic goods. When the extent to which a good is purchased varies more than a change in price, that good is elastic. So if a good's price increases by 10 percent and its sales drop by 30 percent, that good is elastic. If that same 10 percent increase only leads to a 3 percent sales drop, that good is inelastic. Elastic goods are typically less necessary, have many substitutes, and can easily be postponed in purchase. Medications for serious diseases do not have any of those properties. The upshot of a good being inelastic is that the most sensible business strategy, from a purely revenue perspective, is to raise the price, since the revenue increase from the raised price will overwhelm the revenue loss from the few people who stop purchasing it. At a basic level, the source of drug firms' big profits is that they produce what might be the world's most inelastic goods. Inelasticity, not research costs, determines a drug's price.[12]

From a purely revenue perspective, it makes sense for pharmaceutical firms to charge as much as they can get for a product, but from a societal perspective, generating huge revenues for drug companies is not the point of IP regulation. The point is generating an incentive to innovate. Those opposed to higher IP regulations, such as access-to-medicine groups like Oxfam International, argue that it is not obvious that prices and profits must be totally unbounded to produce that incentive. Gilead made $10.3 billion on Sovaldi in 2014; would they really not have done research on hepatitis C if Sovaldi were only going to net $4 billion in revenue in 2014?[13] Must drug companies be allowed to charge whatever the market will bear for an adequate incentive to innovate to be present? Drug companies would say so, access advocates would say no, and both answers come from sources with clear, vested interests in giving them. The correct answer, like so many answers in social science, is probably a combination of "We do not know" and "It depends."

Opponents further contend that higher IP regulations slow innovation by preventing researchers from borrowing certain ideas or working on certain projects. Such regulations also restrict the flow of information, which, almost by definition, slows scientific progress. For that reason, opponents are particularly critical of data exclusivity provisions and efforts to limit Bolar exemptions.[14] Relatedly, they are major proponents of compulsory licenses, a mechanism by which a state gives a license to a generic firm to make copies of a patented drug without the permission of the inventing firm. Those licenses are, in effect, patent revocations and bring drug costs down. As will be discussed below, there have been extensive negotiations over the conditions under which states may issue compulsory licenses. Pharmaceutical firms want those conditions to be as constraining as possible, while access-to-medicine advocates want them as permissive as possible. Concern with costs is also why access advocates want tight rules on patentability, to prevent companies from profiting through "evergreening," which occurs when a firm extends a patent's life by making small changes to a drug and repatenting it, keeping the drug's cost high.[15]

In a nutshell, activists want shorter patent times, no data exclusivity, fewer curbs on Bolar exemptions, fewer strings on compulsory licensing, and tight rules on what qualifies as patentable. They also point out that drug firms' claims about huge costs in research and development are undermined by the fact that 9 out of 10 of the largest drug firms spend more on sales and advertising than they do on R&D.[16] They note that the U.S. government deploys NIH grants and tax credits to subsidize much of drug firms' R&D costs.[17] Because the financial risks of a failed drug have been socialized, the benefit from a successful drug should also be socialized. Entirely privatized profits only makes sense if the risks are entirely privatized. Most critically, opponents argue that higher IP regulations lead to drug prices so high that they make drugs unaffordable for poor people in developing countries.

Background to the Cases

Outside of Western developed countries, there have been few cultural traditions supporting stringent IP rights.[18] Knowledge has been considered a collective good, and imitation was considered appropriate, possibly even a form of flattery.[19] For the first two decades after World War II, the lack of patent protection in developing countries did not really concern Western pharmaceutical firms because their profits were much less dependent on patent protection than they are now.[20] Until the 1960s, most developed countries did not have extensive IP protections. Patents were often only on the process of producing a drug, not on the drug itself, so a significant amount of reciprocal reverse engineering helped those states build large pharmaceutical infrastructures and keep drug prices down.

Even once they became more concerned with patents, few firms in developing states, if any, had the capacity to copy drugs. IP was not considered a trade issue at that time. It had been left out of the GATT almost entirely, and the World Intellectual Property Organization (WIPO) did not exist until 1967.[21] Developments from the late 1960s to the early 1980s, however, created tensions between Western drug firms' commercial aims and developing countries' IP regulations.

During the 1960s, India had some of the world's highest drug prices, despite its poverty, so its government redesigned its IP legal system to reduce the costs of drugs. In 1970, India passed a new patent law that prohibited patents on drugs. It only allowed patents on the process by which a drug was made. Allowing process patents but not product patents meant that makers of generic drugs were incentivized to produce the same drugs as Western firms but more cheaply. That incentive led Indian firms to become highly skilled reverse engineers that excelled at producing drugs at very low cost. The resulting new IP regime resulted in much lower drug prices, and Indian firms became major exporters to other developing states. India's IP regulations were important not just because of their effect in the Indian market but also because India led developing states in attacking stringent IP regulations.

Pushing against an Open Door: The TRIPS Negotiation

As IP regulations in developing countries became more injurious to the interests of Western drug firms, the latter became much more highly motivated to reduce those regulatory trade barriers in IP. They were also able to effectively leverage competitiveness framings. Activists who might have fought against those firms' efforts were not yet significant participants in IP politics. With businesses promoting TRIPS and with activists largely silent, government officials in the United States and India faced one-sided incentives and gave businesses what they sought: significantly reduced regulatory trade barriers related to IP.

Business Efforts to Strengthen International IP Regulations

By the late 1970s, the less-stringent IP rules in developing countries, especially India, were starting to irritate Western drug firms.[22] Advances in technology and a lack of enforcement had made violating IP easier and increasingly rampant.[23] In drugs, technological advances had made reverse engineering patented drugs easier and cheaper. By the early 1980s, Western drug firms had also become more dependent on patents for their revenue.[24] At the same time, U.S. drug firms were honing their lobbying skills and forming political coalitions with each other as they collectively fought for changes in U.S. patent regulation.[25]

Reverse engineering was hurting sales across the developing world. Drug companies started to worry that the emergence of cheaper copies of drugs there might lead citizens of developed countries to wonder why they had to pay so much more for a drug than people in developing countries paid.[26] Western firms tended to view developing country arguments against stringent IP regulations as a smoke screen for their "real" motivation, giving an advantage to domestic firms.[27] If developing countries' IP regulations were going to hurt Western companies' competitiveness in new and established markets, something had to be done about them.

U.S. drug companies such as Pfizer, as well as other IP-intensive firms such as IBM, wanted an international IP-regime that had two characteristics. First, they wanted developing states' IP regulations to be raised to match U.S regulations:[28] patent terms should be extended; all classes of products, including drugs, should be patentable; and the means to break patents should be greatly circumscribed.[29] Second, they wanted the regime to have strong enforcement to prevent developing countries from backsliding or ignoring their own laws.[30]

At the time, the primary international organization for IP issues, the World Intellectual Property Organization, had no real means of enforcement and no mechanism for dispute settlement. Also, because WIPO only dealt with IP issues, it offered no possibility of cross-issue linkage. Even worse from the perspective of Western firms, WIPO had a one-country, one-vote structure, which meant it was dominated by developing states. Furthermore, given that developing countries were a majority in WIPO, the leadership of that organization had little ability to give in to U.S. demands to any significant degree and still retain leadership roles. Western businesses attempted to achieve their goals through WIPO at first but began looking for a new forum after being stymied.[31] The GATT and explicitly linking IP with trade enter the picture here. Recalling a meeting with Arpad Bogsch, the head of WIPO, Jim Enyart, Monsanto's point man on IP, explained how Western firms approached that organization.

> We said to him, "Look, Mr. Bogsch, we have found WIPO to be not constructive in the protection of IP and we are going to do something about it. You are either going to help out or we are going to go right around you." And he said, "Well you can't do that, we are the only authorized organization." And we said, "Well, we are going to do it. You've got your choice; you either get on board or get left in the dust." It turned out, when the negotiations started in GATT, Mr. Bogsch became very friendly and said that there was a great deal of expertise in WIPO and how there ought to be a huge role for WIPO in the TRIPS agreement. You will notice that the TRIPS Agreement has a reasonably weak consultative role for WIPO.[32]

IP-intensive firms, led by the drug companies, argued that the lower IP standards of developing states amounted to IP theft and piracy.[33] The firms successfully sold the causal story that IP rights lead to free trade and investment and thus promote economic growth.[34] The U.S. trade deficit had more than quadrupled from 1980 to 1985 (36.3 billion to 148.5 billion),[35] so by the mid-1980s, the perception of a loss of competitiveness was something of a policy crisis in the United States. Businesses successfully capitalized on that crisis by arguing that the best way to improve American competitiveness would be to force other states to cease and desist from IP theft.[36] The best place to do that, according to the firms, was in trade policy.

They argued that linking IP with trade had three advantages. First, through the Generalized System of Preferences, something could be exchanged for a country agreeing to higher IP regulations. Second, the single undertaking of the Uruguay Round meant that states could not pick and choose areas of the agreement to sign. It thus created cross-issue linkage, and states that never would have countenanced stringent IP rules in isolation could be bought off with concessions in other areas. Third, the GATT, unlike WIPO, had a dispute mechanism, albeit a relatively weak one (though it would get strengthened as part of the round).

The industry's lobbying to place IP regulations on the negotiating table in the Uruguay Round were considerable. According to one U.S. negotiator, Edmund Pratt and John Opel, the bosses of Pfizer and IBM, "basically engineered, pushed, and cajoled the government into including IP as one of the topics for the negotiation."[37] Pratt and other drug executives repeatedly beseeched officials to make increasing other states' IP regulations a centerpiece of U.S. trade policy.[38] To build an intellectual foundation for linking trade and IP, executives partnered with conservative think tanks like the Heritage Foundation, which President Reagan was known to respect.[39] To pressure their governments to take a stronger stand on IP regulations, business leaders formed alliances with European and Japanese executives.[40] To sustain momentum, they created organizations such as the Intellectual Property Committee, a coalition of representatives from IP-intensive industries.

NGOs Remain Silent; Government Listens to Business

In contrast to firms' concerted efforts, there was little to no pushback from activists against using trade policy to reduce differences in IP regulations. Prior to TRIPS, public health advocates really did not engage in IP at all; it was not part of their agenda, because it was not perceived to directly affect their goals.[41] NGOs were not part of most of the Uruguay Round negotiations on IP.[42] James Love, a prominent activist on medicine and IP, has admitted that even as late as 1994, much less in the 1980s, "there was virtually no awareness in the United States or European [NGO community] of the scope and importance of the trade effort to raise levels of patent protection on medicines."[43] Public health agencies also sat on the sidelines and had little understanding of what was being negotiated.[44] With activists not taking part in the Uruguay Round's IP negotiations, business was pushing against an open door.

U.S. government officials responded warmly to the arguments made by those vocal businesses. Competitiveness was a major concern at the time, and blaming America's loss of competitiveness on foreigners was a convenient argument to buy and did have at least some merit.[45] In 1984, the U.S. International Trade Commission estimated that American businesses lost between $6 billion and $8 billion due to other states' more relaxed IP regulations.[46] The language of piracy was highly effective at getting U.S. government officials to take a very hard line in favor of higher IP standards, as it made the standards a moral issue with many fewer shades of gray. U.S. trade representative Clayton Yuetter, who saw "no difference at all between stealing the patent for a product and stealing the product itself," as "thievery is thievery," argued that developing countries' lower IP regulations were "really an indefensible way to run a society. I don't see how any nation in the world can defend piracy."[47]

Even if they were not IP specialists (in almost all cases, they were not), congressmen could not help but notice that the businesses animated by a desire for higher IP regulations were some of the most significant businesses in their districts and America.[48] Additionally, once drug firms' focus was foreign rather than domestic IP laws, the issue of drug costs became much less important to legislators.[49] The pharmaceutical industry's status as one of the few industries that maintained a trade surplus augmented its political standing on Capitol Hill further.[50] Finally, the arcane character of IP meant that government officials often relied on business for guidance.[51]

The executive branch was also receptive to the businesses pushing for regulation. The Reagan and Bush administrations deeply respected property rights, so framing high IP regulations as defending intellectual property rights was highly effective with them.[52] The Reagan administration was a major proponent of trade liberalization and was eager to spearhead a new GATT round. U.S. trade representative Bill Brock also saw IP as a way of bolstering business support for trade liberalization.[53]

Since 1981, Edmund Pratt headed the Advisory Committee for Trade Negotiations, a key group charged with giving trade policy advice from businesses to the executive branch.[54] Changes in U.S. trade law in 1984 gave IP-intensive firms greater access to the Office of the United States Trade Representative. In 1985, Representative Yuetter created an assistant USTR position dedicated to promoting higher IP regulations globally.[55] IP-intensive firms began employing former USTR negotiators, which gave the firms special expertise in how the USTR operated and strongly signaled the rewards that doing the bidding of those firms might yield for USTR officials after they left their posts.[56] In that context, it is unsurprising that businesses' assessment of what IP-trade policy should be, published in *Basic Framework of GATT Provisions on Intellectual Property: Statement of Views of the European, Japanese, and the United States Business Communities*, became the foundation of the USTR's negotiating position in the Uruguay Round.[57]

As I discussed in chapter 3, the main drivers of government officials' stances on regulatory trade barriers are how much officials prioritize trade relative to regulatory independence, whether their staffing favors business or activists, and who officials identify as their core constituency. This part of the pharmaceutical case clearly demonstrates all of those dynamics. The Reagan administration cared more about promoting trade than about regulatory independence, its staff favored business, and its officials identified business as a core constituency.

Alternative Explanations

Some scholars, such as Peter Drahos and John Braithwaite, have criticized U.S. officials' willingness to act as lawyers for the businesses pushing for regulation, portraying the officials as part puppets, part bullies bent on strong-arming developing countries into an agreement that benefited corporate America, whatever the cost to public health.[58] But given the incentives and information around the officials, it would have been surprising for them not to have taken the actions they did. From an informational perspective, there were not yet any activists providing officials with framings based on preventing needless death, which would have countered the competitiveness claims of IP-intensive businesses. From an electoral perspective, backing the drug companies was a high-reward, low-cost strategy. The resistance from developing countries was also minimal. This case of was not a cabal or a conspiracy against poor, sick people. It is a lesson in what happens in the politics of regulation and trade when businesses show up for a policy fight while activists do not.

The trajectory of events in this case also undermines state-centric explanations of international trade politics. The U.S. government's stance was not independently designed. It only came about because businesses lobbied vigorously and successfully for it. Likewise, developing countries' willingness to yield in these negotiations had everything to do with the fact that domestic actors within their societies were not particularly animated by TRIPS.[59] One cannot explain those states' positions without first examining those societal actors.

How the U.S. Government Promoted Higher IP Regulations in the Uruguay Round

In 1984, the United States made IP regulations a major part of its bilateral trading relationships by turning to Section 301 of the 1974 Trade Act, which had authorized the executive branch to retaliate against trade policies implemented by other states if those policies violated international trade treaties, discriminated against American products, or posed an unreasonable restriction on U.S. commercial interests. Retaliation through 301 could be initiated by the executive branch or, more commonly, after a U.S. firm petitioned the executive branch to act on its behalf. The 301 provision thus gave U.S. businesses a powerful institutional mechanism with which to seek reductions in other countries' trade barriers.

The 1984 Trade Act amended Section 301 by explicitly defining inadequately high IP regulations as an unreasonable restriction on U.S. commercial interests. U.S. firms could thus demand that the executive branch retaliate against states that had insufficiently high IP regulations according to those firms. The 1984 Trade Act made having high IP regulations a key criterion for receiving benefits through the Generalized System of Preferences (GSP),[60] which were important to agriculture. That lost benefits could have serious social and political ramifications on many least-developed states with economies dependent on agriculture helps explain why 301 was so effective and powerful in the minds of developing country officials. The Reagan administration also floated the idea of trying to make IP regulations a criterion for assistance from the International Monetary Fund and the World Bank.[61]

These mechanisms were further strengthened in the Trade and Competitiveness Act of 1988.[62] That act erased the requirement that drug firms petitioning the government for 301 action show that foreign regulation actually hurt them.[63] It also created the Special 301 mechanism, which charged the USTR with monitoring other states' IP regulations and annually making the Special 301 Watch List, recording states whose IP regulations impeded U.S. firms by being lower than U.S. regulations.[64] The USTR was required to enter into negotiations to raise IP regulations in the states on that list. If a country did not raise its IP regulations, it could be put on the Priority Watch List. The USTR would then issue a set of actions it wanted that state to take. If that state did not carry out those actions, the USTR could downgrade that state to the most serious level, Priority Foreign Country (PFC). A PFC faces an imminent threat of retaliatory sanctions.

The U.S. government assertively used these measures in its bilateral relationships to get its trading partners, one by one, to raise their IP regulations.[65] First, the USTR used 301 to get South Korea to raise its IP regulations.[66] Then, it targeted Brazil over its lack of pharmaceutical patents; after retaliatory tariffs started to be imposed, that country too raised its IP regulations.[67] Negotiations using 301 got Argentina to do the same.[68] The United States used GSP to get developing countries like Thailand to raise their IP regulations as well.[69] This bilateral strategy had two benefits for the United States. First, direct benefits would accrue to U.S. IP-intensive firms doing business in those states. Second, the strategy indirectly helped the United States at the multilateral level because a state that had already raised its standard to what the United States wanted would not object to TRIPS.[70]

While deploying 301 at the bilateral level, the United States had also been pushing to include an agreement on higher IP regulations in the Uruguay Round. The same aspects of WIPO that Western firms found so frustrating—its lack of enforcement mechanism and its one-country, one-vote model—made it popular with developing countries. They saw no reason why IP should be handled by any institution other than WIPO.[71] U.S. officials insisted that IP be put on the agenda, threatening to scuttle the whole round if it were not included. Developing countries got agricultural liberalization added to the agenda in exchange.

Developing countries thought they had given away very little by agreeing to discuss IP in the Uruguay Round.[72] At this point, those countries, as well as public health activists, had no idea what TRIPS would become. There were general perceptions that any IP provisions added to the GATT would be relatively weak, that they would likely only focus on counterfeit goods, and that even if states violated the rules, the GATT's institutional structure would provide no mechanism to punish them.[73] IP was officially put on the agenda in 1986, and all three of those perceptions turned out to be very wrong.

Over the next several years, the United States worked with European states and Japan, in private, informal sessions, to arrive at common positions so that a united front could be presented to developing countries.[74] Developing states understood that much of the key negotiating was going on between developed states and that forums they were invited to were mere formalities. One negotiator from a developing state admitted, "We lost interest [in the TRIPS forums]."[75] Developing states later became highly engaged in IP politics regarding drugs, but they did not consider TRIPS a big deal at that early point. Unlike the United States, many developing states had no IP experts on their trade teams.[76] Many did not understand the details of what they were negotiating or the full measure of their concessions. Even if they had been more engaged on IP, developing states were far less organized under the GATT than under WIPO.[77] There was often little to no coordination between their trade teams in Geneva and national capitals.[78] Lodging negotiators in Geneva is not cheap, and many of these countries had tiny, poorly funded negotiation teams that would get overwhelmed in trade negotiations with the U.S. team.[79]

India was one of the only developing countries that had the technical expertise to resist American demands on IP, so many developing states looked to India for leadership.[80] It was the most resilient developing state in its opposition to TRIPS.[81] Its leadership on the issue was still quite spotty, though. Given the stakes, Indian drug companies did surprisingly little lobbying; like access-to-medicine advocates, they did not really get engaged with the issue until after TRIPS had been signed.[82] India did not often engage with other developing states on the issue and skipped what was supposed to be a key meeting allowing those states to coordinate their negotiating position on IP regulations.[83] When Indian representatives did engage in negotiations, U.S. negotiators were prepared to beat back any argument they made; Mike Hathaway, the lead U.S. negotiator on IP, recalled, "We certainly had fun . . . beating down arguments made by India."[84]

Even if India had wanted to oppose the United States more forcefully, many of its key allies, such as Argentina and Brazil, had been peeled away. South Korea, which was attempting to gain admission to the Organization for Economic Cooperation and Development, was more concerned with pleasing developed countries than with showing solidarity with Brazil and India.[85] Other developing states, such as the members of the Association of Southeast Asian Nations, badly wanted a deal for which they believed that giving the United States what it wanted on IP was the required price, so they had little appetite for a fight over IP.[86] Developing countries generally perceived liberalization of services to be the biggest threat and thought TRIPS to be a lesser issue, so they reserved their energy for fighting on services rather than IP.[87] India, like other developing countries, was attempting to liberalize its investment laws to attract foreign direct investment, and raising IP regulations seemed to be consistent with that.[88] The one area where India did fight hard was on compulsory licensing, where it was able to win more permissive language that would have major ramifications later.[89]

Developing countries were not going home empty-handed. In exchange for acquiescing to the United States on IP, they won concessions in two areas more important to them, textiles and agriculture.[90] An Argentinian negotiator said, "They didn't give a damn what was in the IP code as long as they got what they wanted in agriculture."[91] Leaders of developing countries perceived IP as part of broader bargain, in which they would get investment and benefits in market access in textiles and agriculture in exchange for increasing their IP regulations.[92]

Developing states inaccurately believed that TRIPS would curtail America's 301 unilateralism.[93] Also, because these states were to be given a grace period to implement the new IP regulations, they lowered the extent to which they prioritized the costs of higher IP; the costs were far down the road and not so salient.[94] Finally, the Uruguay Round came with many other agreements, of which TRIPS was only one. Collectively, the texts of the agreements ran over 1,000 pages, and most developing state legislatures had little discussion of the impact TRIPS would have; only later, when those impacts became more clear, did the legislatures take more interest.[95] In the United States, TRIPS was an afterthought for the public as well. Unlike NAFTA, the completion of the Uruguay Round, including TRIPS, was not particularly controversial.[96]

Developing states' decision to accept TRIPS was understandable, but the agreement, which came into force in 1995, represented a major reduction in regulatory differences by requiring all signatories to adopt the higher IP regulations wanted by developed countries. All signatories had to have patents that lasted 20 years. None were allowed to prohibit patents on drugs. The use of compulsory licenses was constrained.[97] All states were required to stringently enforce IP regulations. Failure on any stipulation could lead to a state being taken before the WTO, which had a dispute settlement mechanism that was much more robust than the GATT's had been.[98]

The California effect applies well here. To recap, the elements of the California effect are that businesses will support stricter regulations when those regulations make them more competitive; that richer states with higher standards force producers in other states to raise their standards in order to export to them, which raises foreign standards; and that trade agreements give richer states with higher standards leverage to pressure other states to raise their standards to the richer states' level. All three elements were present here. U.S. IP-intensive firms saw high IP regulations as a competitive advantage. The United States linked the access of producers in other states to the U.S. market and used the Uruguay Round to pressure other states to raise their IP standards. This case suggests that the California Effect may, at times, be applicable outside of the two regulatory areas that Vogel originally intended (consumer safety and the environment). It further suggests that IP regulations and the more traditional areas of regulatory trade barriers (e.g., health, safety, and environmental policies) may share more political similarities than may be immediately apparent.

TRIPS required little adjustment for the United States but came with large adjustment costs for many developing countries, such as India.[99] All WTO members were now required to adopt the exact kind of IP regulations demanded by the United States. In the words of one pharmaceutical lobbyist, "we got 95 percent of what we wanted."[100] It would not be that long, however, before the connection between IP regulations and trade became a white-hot international political issue.

The Doha Declaration: Access-to-Medicine Activists Show Up . . . and Win

In the second half of the 1990s, the AIDS epidemic grew into a public health nightmare, especially in sub-Saharan Africa. Given the relative newness of the disease, practically all effective HIV drugs were patented and expensive. Poor people were dying of a disease for which effective medicines existed but were far too expensive for them to afford. Public health advocates began to take a closer look at the connection between IP regulations and the cost of drugs and concluded that the high regulations mandated by TRIPS, the main drivers behind the expense of the medicines, were complicit in widespread death. Drug companies compounded this imagery when they sued South Africa over measures it had taken to stem the AIDS crisis. Even after they dropped the lawsuit, developing countries and access-to-medicine advocates wanted states to have more flexibility under TRIPS to institute different IP regulations. For a variety of reasons, the U.S. government, which normally would have been expected to oppose any increase in regulatory barriers in pharmaceuticals, relented and accepted the Doha Declaration, which strengthened developing states' ability to implement different IP regulations.

The HIV Crisis Gets Really Bad, but Drug Firms and the U.S. Government Hold Their Ground

In 1998, HIV/AIDS killed more than two million people in sub-Saharan Africa, and life expectancy there had fallen by 20 to 30 years.[101] By the late 1990s, 25 million Africans had HIV/AIDS.[102] Drug firms were reluctant to substantially lower their prices in developing countries because that would demonstrate just how low their marginal costs were and could lead government officials and citizens in wealthier states to ask why they should have to pay so much more for the drug than it cost to make.[103] In 1997, with HIV rates soaring and drug prices out of reach for most of its victims, the South African government passed a law permitting the parallel importing of generic drugs manufactured under compulsory licenses.[104] In effect, it said that the AIDS crisis justified ignoring drug companies' patents on antiretroviral drugs.[105]

Western firms stridently opposed the South African policy. They believed it amounted to "carte blanche for the wholesale abrogation of patent rights for all pharmaceuticals" in a $2.5 billion market.[106] They worried that the legislation would set a precedent that other states would follow and implement on other diseases, which could unravel TRIPS.[107] Not only were they opposed to weakening TRIPS, they had been wanting TRIPS strengthened through state-granted patents on biologics, more limits on compulsory licensing, greater enforcement, and tougher rules on data exclusivity.[108] So the drug companies filed a lawsuit in South Africa against the government's new policy. The suit was part of the pharmaceutical firms' overarching approach of taking a maximalist position on IP and trying to use the trade regime to uphold that position. They did not want to find a compromise. U.S. officials said that when they asked drug representatives whether they could accept some concessions to South Africa, the companies "said no, we really just want you to hold the line and continue to pressure South Africa to terminate this law altogether."[109]

Drug firms first attempted to intimidate the South African government into backing down. Merck threatened to leave the country and take millions of dollars and thousands of jobs with it.[110] Bristol-Myers Squibb, Pharmacia and Upjohn, and Eli Lilly all closed plants after the introduction of the bill.[111] The International Federation of Pharmaceutical Manufacturers said that the weakening of patents could lead to South Africa being denied access to any new HIV drugs that came on the market.[112] That threat was extremely serious and not at all veiled.

The same firms continued to hold a privileged position in U.S. trade policymaking. The 1984 Trade Act required the USTR to consult with a range of businesses through the Industrial Functional Advisory Committee for Intellectual Property (IFAC-3), a group of 40 industry representatives that plays a key role in preparing the USTR's annual Section 301 reports as well as reports on trade agreement that go to the executive branch and Congress.[113] IP-intensive businesses also continued to have the ear of Capitol Hill; 47 members of Congress signed a letter encouraging the USTR to fight the South African law.[114] Congress even reduced foreign aid to South Africa over the law.[115] Officials echoed the drug industry's precedent argument, with one official stating,

> If the Health Minister thought it was in the interest of public health that those $10,000 AIDS cocktails be cheaper, she could just rip off the patents and set up a factory in Cape Town to make them. . . . and if the Minister of Health says this is O.K., then the Minister of Education will be able to say, "Well, affordable computers are in the interest of public education, but Windows is just too darn expensive, so we're going to buy knockoff copies."[116]

The fight was not just about AIDS drugs. The way U.S. officials saw it, the South African law was a direct challenge to the new, higher IP regulations embodied in TRIPS. They had fought to reduce those regulatory barriers and were in no mood to see their work undone. U.S. government officials thus sallied forth in defense of the drug companies. In 1998, the USTR placed South Africa on the 301 Priority Watch List. IP regulations were the central issue at the August 1998 meetings of the U.S.-South Africa Binational Commission.[117] By the U.S. government's own admission, multiple agencies and branches of the government colluded to put extraordinary diplomatic pressure on South Africa to scrap the 1997 Medicines Act.[118]

The HIV Crisis Prompts Access-to-Medicine Advocates to Engage in IP Politics

Meanwhile, activists had gotten engaged in the politics of IP regulations in a way they never had during the TRIPS negotiation. The first big international meeting of NGOs on the relationship between IP and public health was in 1996, the year after TRIPS came into effect.[119] The second meeting was hosted by the Indian National Working Group on Patents and brought in government representatives and generic drug producers.[120] The U.S. attempt to coerce South Africa infuriated NGOs. As one NGO leader put it, "This whole debate in 1998 woke people up. It really got the attention of the public health community, which really started to get engaged at this point. It was what paved the way for the Doha Declaration—it was Doha before Doha."[121]

Activists' engagement in the politics surrounding trade and IP regulations highlights the limitations of the cleavage-based explanations of trade politics. The cleavage here was not between a sector of society that profited from trade and a sector that lost. It was between a sector (drug firms) that had an economic stake and a sector (access-to-medicine advocates) that wanted to prioritize noneconomic goals of public policy. By focusing exclusively on economic considerations, the cleavage-based explanations again miss how trade increasingly animates actors with normative concerns once regulations get added to the political equation.

In 1998, activists went to the World Health Organization (WHO) and were instrumental in that organization crafting its Revised Drug Strategy, which emphasized the need to prioritize public health over commercial interests and mandated that the WHO monitor trade agreements for their effect on public health.[122] U.S. negotiators were not happy that the WHO was now taking part in IP discussion, but the WHO's governing body has a rotating board exempting the United States every third year, and 1998 was one of those off years, allowing activists to sidestep the United States at the WHO.[123] The next year, Doctors Without Borders launched its Access to Essential Medicines Campaign and began closely collaborating with other NGOs, such as Health Action International, the Consumer Project on Technology, and Oxfam International.[124] Doctors Without Borders then won the Nobel Peace Prize for its efforts and used the prize money toward boosting its Access to Essential Medicines Campaign.[125]

Activists started to engage with key governments, including the United States.[126] The Indian Commerce Ministry set up a consultation process, beginning in 1996, that involved industry representatives and NGOs.[127] Activists lobbied the USTR to take more relaxed positions on IP regulations. Afterward, USTR and EU officials acknowledged that NGOs were crucial in bringing attention to the connection between IP and access to medicine.[128] In June 1999, they disrupted Al Gore's announcement that he was running for president.[129] They successfully lobbied key segments of the Democratic Party, such as the Congressional Black Caucus.[130] In May 2000, they convinced the Clinton administration to back off threatened trade sanctions against South Africa. Those events provide further evidence against the argument of disguised protectionism. The defenders of regulatory barriers throughout this period were not firms looking for protectionism; they were NGOs trying to maintain policy space. The same would continue to be true in the WTO stalemate and in India's use of flexibilities in response, examined in the next chapter.

As activists and developing countries fought to broaden that policy space by increasing IP regulatory differences while businesses and the U.S. government resisted, the relationship between the two sides grew more acrimonious. NGOs portrayed the drug companies as death merchants.[131] Nkosozana Zuma, the South African health minister and the leading force behind the South African law, said of her critics, "If they had their way, we would all die of AIDS."[132] Drug companies saw the South African law as a smoke screen for a WHO plot to eradicate patents, a move by Indian generics firms to increase market share, and an ideological crusade against Western businesses by the African National Congress.[133] They also argued that corruption and poor governance, rather than high IP regulations, were the real facilitators of the AIDS crisis.[134]

The standoff came to a head in March 2001. The case between the drug firms and the South African government had finally come before the South African High Court and was accompanied by a wave of anti-industry protests.[135] Access-to-medicine advocates kept up the pressure for the next several weeks, raising the salience of the issue and threatening to badly damage drug companies' image.[136] The WHO and the EU publicly sided with South Africa.[137] In April 2001, before the public relations damage could get any worse, the drug companies dropped their lawsuit and agreed to pay the South African government's legal costs.[138] Beyond the immediate costs on AIDS, drug firms worried about potentially disastrous implications for them if the issue spilled over into a broader discussion of drug pricing in developed states.[139] For the firms, it was better to concede defeat at that point than to continue fighting on terrain so disadvantageous.

The AIDS crisis was tailor-made for activist victory. As Keck and Sikkink point out, activism is more effective on "issues involving bodily harm to vulnerable individuals, especially when there is a short clear causal chain (or story) assigning responsibility."[140] The HIV crisis had all those requirements. AIDS is clearly bodily harm, poor Africans are among the most vulnerable people anywhere, and the story that activists told—that corporate greed was leading to needless death—provided a short clear causal chain assigning responsibility.

Activists Win a More Durable Victory at Doha

The dropping of the lawsuit by the drug firms did not settle the matter, though. Just because the firms had backed down this time did not mean developing states were free from worrying about being challenged in the future. What was or was not TRIPS-compliant needed to be clarified and was still a matter of debate because Articles 30 and 31 of TRIPS, which covered patent exceptions, were ambiguous on the conditions under which a compulsory license was allowed. The Bush administration had also been pushing for a new trade round. With respect to IP, the most important issue was under what circumstances compulsory licenses could be issued. Was AIDS sui generis and the sole permissible exception to strict patentability, or did all diseases merit such consideration? Would which diseases made the list be determined by each national government, the WTO, or the WHO? Or would the list be an independently negotiated text? The upcoming ministerial meeting seemed to be the arena at which these matters could get decided.

Several factors led developing states to punch harder and more effectively than they had during the original TRIPS negotiation. First, whereas they were in the dark in many ways about the connection between IP and access to medicine during the Uruguay Round, they were quite aware of that connection by 2000. The AIDS crisis and the pharmaceutical companies' suit against South Africa had ensured that awareness. In fact, starting in 1998, the developing countries comprising the Group of 77 in the United Nations issued an annual statement arguing for expanding TRIPS flexibilities.[141] Second, the year 2000 had been a deadline for many developing countries to become TRIPS compliant, so they were now becoming fully aware of how much policy adjustment TRIPS required.[142] Third, the benefits they were supposed to receive in exchange for TRIPS had been slow in coming. The concessions in textiles and agriculture were weaker and more delayed than anticipated.[143] Fourth, though it was implied that TRIPS would lead to a reduction of America's use of 301 and other unilateral measures, the United States had actually used them more after TRIPS than before it.[144] Access advocates were much more organized at this point than in the TRIPS negotiations and effectively augmented the developing states' efforts.[145] They worked with those countries' governments to strengthen their negotiating performance and encouraged them not to limit their demands to AIDS but to include public health more broadly.[146]

Developing states, led by India, had several demands. They wanted a new declaration stating that TRIPS "does not in any way undermine the legitimate rights of WTO Members to formulate their own public health policies."[147] They wanted a text focused on public health, a broader topic than just access to medicine. They wanted governments to have the right to decide what constituted a national emergency, because only under conditions of national emergency can a state issue compulsory licenses without prior consultation with the patent holder. They wanted a moratorium on disputes against access-to-medicine policies. They wanted developed countries (i.e., the United States) to be prohibited from basing unilateral trade preferences on IP (i.e., from using 301).[148] They wanted TRIPS flexibilities to cover as many diseases as possible, not just AIDS.[149]

Developed countries, led by the United States, had several concerns. First, they worried that developing countries would use compulsory licenses to promote industrial and economic concerns, instead of just access to medicine.[150] U.S. officials believed that India's involvement, in particular, was really just a smoke screen for allowing India to advance its generics industry.[151] Second, given that the declaration language that developing states wanted could cover practically any policy, it would have effectively eradicated TRIPS altogether.[152] Third, even if that language were narrowed, a moratorium on disputes and preference linkage would take the enforcement teeth out of TRIPS. Fourth, they wanted the list of diseases covered by flexibilities to be agreed on and narrowly tailored to HIV/AIDS and other epidemics, not whatever disease the government of a developing country decided constituted an emergency. Finally, they wanted developing countries to implement policies designed to prevent reimportation (i.e., people buying drugs cheaply in a developing country and then sneaking them into a developed country where prices were higher). Contra to state-centric explanations, the negotiating positions of both developed and developing states were based mainly on the demands being made by societal actors.

In November 2001, the negotiating states agreed to the Doha Declaration. It was largely based on developing states' proposals.[153] It reaffirmed states' rights to issue compulsory licenses under three conditions: (1) an attempt was made to obtain a voluntary license from the patent holder but was unsuccessful, a condition that could be bypassed in a national emergency; (2) the patent holder was adequately compensated; and (3) the license was predominately for the supply of the domestic market. The declaration also said that states could determine for themselves what constitutes a national emergency. Developing states now had a confirmed right to institute different IP regulations that could amount to a regulatory trade barrier. The Doha Declaration made it much more difficult, legally and politically, to challenge a developing country's use of a compulsory license. The side in favor of reducing regulatory barriers in IP by raising them to a high level, which seemed so dominant during the TRIPS negotiation, had backed down. In particular, the U.S. government had abandoned the maximalist position it once held.

Why the United States Backed Down

Several factors led to the U.S. climb down in the push for high IP standards. First, the relationship between the drug firms and the U.S. government had been damaged, albeit temporarily, by the South African episode. U.S. officials were greatly annoyed with drug representatives' refusal to recognize that high drug prices were at least partially exacerbating the AIDS crisis in South Africa.[154] Several Democratic congressmen were not pleased with those representatives either. After an amendment that would have prevented the United States from challenging access-to-medicine policies in sub-Saharan African countries was stripped from a trade bill, Dianne Feinstein and Russ Feingold threatened to filibuster that bill.[155]

Second, after anthrax was sent via mail shortly after 9/11, both Canada and the United States threatened Bayer with a compulsory license for the anthrax drug Cipro, to get Bayer to lower its price.[156] In other words, the United States had just threatened a company's IP based on public health considerations. How could U.S. negotiators at the Doha ministerial conference a few months later argue, with a straight face, that threatening IP to protect public health was unacceptable?

Third, after 9/11, the United States was determined to launch a new trade round at the Doha ministerial conference to demonstrate its global leadership, and it wanted to attain that goal so badly that it was willing to accept language that developing countries were demanding.[157] Conversely, developing states prioritized public health over the start of a new round, especially since they were not entirely sure that the Uruguay Round had been good for them given the painfully slow implementation of the agricultural and textile concessions that were supposed to benefit them. This case shows that considerations of market power, while important, can be overridden if the noneconomic policy goals prioritized by activists have enough salience. It also implicitly critiques the "bicycle theory" of trade, which argues that for trade liberalization to be maintained, there must constantly be forward momentum (i.e., a new round on the agenda); otherwise those actors opposed to trade can more easily promote protectionism.[158]

At this point, there was a new round on the agenda, but that still was not enough to counter the power of activists' lobbying.

Fourth, given the greater salience of the connection between IP and drug cost, a greater array of U.S. agencies had taken interest in the regulation issue, and they often had a different perspective than the USTR.[159] That situation is a reminder that as trade increasingly impacting regulation brings more societal actors into trade politics (especially actors with normative concerns related to those regulations), agencies primarily interested in those regulations take a greater interest in trade. If the agencies generally side with activists, the USTR and other agencies that frequently side with businesses may find their control over trade policymaking greatly diluted.

Several of the preceding factors, such as the U.S. eagerness to start negotiations for a trade round, had little to do with preventing needless death and were not directly related to business lobbying on competitiveness grounds. Still, activists' ability to frame upholding regulatory differences in IP as intimately tied to preventing needless death was crucial to their success in this case. If the TRIPS negotiation is a lesson in what happens when activists do not show up for a policy fight, the passage of the Doha Declaration is a lesson in the extent to which it is possible for a ragtag crew of activists to beat some of the world's most powerful corporations. In the next chapter, we see what happens when both sides are actively engaged.

SEVEN

Small Details, Enormous Consequences (Part 2)

Regulation and the Trade in Pharmaceuticals Post-Doha

By the conclusion of the Doha Declaration in 2001, drug companies and access-to-medicine advocates as well as government officials in developed and developing countries were well aware of and invested in the politics of intellectual property and pharmaceuticals. Each side had achieved a significant victory, and there were more battles to be fought. In the decisions of the World Trade Organization that pertained to IP and drugs, the two sides fought to a draw, so the international legal architecture on IP has largely remained the same. The Indian government has creatively found a number of policy means to relax their IP regulations but has been judicious in its use of these measures, employing them much less than they otherwise could have. Their implementation of IP law relating to the Agreement on Trade-Related Aspects of Intellectual Property Rights (TRIPS) has been something of a compromise between the policies that activists and drug firms would prefer. Developed countries, especially the United States, continued to build on TRIPS and demand reduction of IP regulatory barriers as part of free trade agreements. The negotiations between the United States and Brazil that were part of the push for the Free Trade Area of the Americas (FTAA) completely broke down, in large part due to disagreements on IP policy. Meanwhile, in the negotiations between the United States and Central American countries that were part of the Central American Free Trade Agreement, the opposite happened; the parties agreed to CAFTA and the TRIPS-plus provisions that came with it. This chapter explains that variation in outcomes.

Stalemate and Constructive Ambiguity at the WTO

The Doha Declaration was a big victory for access-to-medicine advocates and developing countries, but it did not settle three issues: (1) which diseases warranted issue of a compulsory license, (2) what exceptions to make for states that did not have production capacity, and (3) whether nonviolation complaints could move forward. On which diseases to cover, the language in Doha was never clarified to either side's benefit. For states without production capacity, the same flexibilities were granted to them as to other states. On nonviolation complaints, there has been a rolling temporary moratorium. In sum, the regulatory barriers on these issues remained static through a mix of constructive ambiguity and stalemate.

Three Outstanding Issues Left Over from Doha

While the Doha Declaration had affirmed developing states' right to institute IP regulations differing from developed states' preferences, several important details remained deeply contested and were the crux of political wrangling over the next few years. Those details were deeply legalistic and technical on one level and entirely political on another. They determined the extent to which less-stringent IP regulations could get used and thus the extent to which different states' use of these regulatory vehicles could constitute a barrier to trade. In other words, they involved a fight over a potential regulatory trade barrier that had the power to determine the relative prioritization of commercial interests and public health.

The first and second contested issues related to compulsory licenses. The definition of a national emergency facilitated the issuance of such licenses. Paragraph 5(c) of the Doha Declaration reads, "Each Member has the right to determine what constitutes a national emergency or other circumstances of extreme urgency, it being understood that public health crises, including those relating to HIV/AIDS, tuberculosis, malaria and other epidemics, can represent a national emergency."[1] The first clause seems to give states a great deal of leeway, but the second part implies that states cannot just label anything a national emergency; the declaration hints at criteria but does not specifically enumerate what is or is not an emergency.

The first vector of this wrangling concerned which diseases counted as a national emergency.[2] Activists wanted to cover as many diseases as possible. By contrast, a U.S. official criticized the NGOs stance, saying that they were "trying to break patent protections on every conceivable health product, even X-ray machines."[3] Developing countries held that the reference to AIDS in the Doha Declaration was not exhaustive; they wanted no limits on the diseases covered.[4]

Drug companies had politically lost on AIDS and wanted to limit their loss to just that disease.[5] AIDS was undoubtedly an enormous crisis, and drug companies could live with it being the only exception to TRIPS rules. At the very least, they had the public relations acumen not to again directly challenge a developing state's anti-AIDS policies as they had with South Africa. But a situation in which seemingly any disease could be labeled an emergency would quickly undermine drug companies' overseas profit. Letters from the U.S. Congress to the Office of the United States Trade Representative on this issue essentially repeated industry talking points.[6] The United States later somewhat expanded its list of acceptable diseases, even saying that it might consider all infectious diseases acceptable, but it still wanted a defined list.[7] That stipulation was not good enough for developing countries.[8] The EU tried to float a compromise, which was shot down by African states.[9] The two sides have never resolved this disagreement. The United States refused to countenance the position of developing countries but stated that it would forgo pursuing disputes against states that were attempting to combat AIDS or other epidemics.[10] The United States has never pursued a dispute against another state's IP regulations based on the target disease, so developing states have never had the opportunity to challenge such pursuit. A dispute could lead the issue to be clarified, but neither side can be sure it will not be clarified in ways that benefit the other side. Both seem to consider it better to have a murky disagreement than a clear loss.

The second vector of post-Doha wrangling involved states that did not possess the domestic capability to make drugs. The original TRIPS Agreement had conditioned a state's ability to issue a compulsory license on that license being primarily for the supply of the domestic market. Paragraph 6 of the Doha Declaration recognized the condition to mean that states without the domestic wherewithal to manufacture generic medicines would have difficulty using a compulsory license, as another state making those medicines for them would violate the condition.[11] For India, this meant that even though it would not get entangled by the condition when it was producing drugs for its own citizens, it would run into difficulties when other developing countries could not make the generic and turned for production to India, often called the pharmacy of the Third World.

The condition did not constitute much of a practical problem until January 2005, when India had to abide by the TRIPS Agreement. Until that date, India could supply generic drugs for states without domestic manufacturing capacity, but India would be in clear violation of the letter of the TRIPS Agreement if it continued supplying those drugs after that date. Developing countries wanted a resolution to the issue before that January 2005 deadline. Activists argued that developing countries without domestic manufacturing capacity should be allowed to issue compulsory licenses for a drug and then import that drug from another state, likely India. The Doha Declaration mandated that states find a negotiated solution over this issue in order to help disease-stricken developing countries.

Western pharmaceutical companies wanted to ensure that developing countries' use of compulsory licenses did not undermine patent protections in richer countries. They were especially wary of two problems. First, they were concerned that drugs made for developing countries would get diverted away from those countries and into richer states where, given their significantly lower costs, they would undermine drug companies' profits.[12] To reduce the chance of that happening, the United States wanted developing countries using the licensing system to make the drugs manufactured under compulsory license easily distinguishable by packaging and coloring. Given that special packaging and distribution could increase the cost of producing and distributing those drugs, developing countries initially did not want to comply.[13] Second, the pharmaceutical firms were worried that richer developing countries would also try to use the system even though they could better afford patent-protected medicines than the least-developed countries.[14]

The United States very much wanted to revive the flagging Doha Round of WTO negotiations at a ministerial meeting in Cancun scheduled for September 2003. The standoff over IP regulations and pharmaceuticals threatened to block that revival. As September 2003 got closer and closer, the United States became more and more willing to cut a deal, and developing countries perceived that now was their best opportunity to exert leverage. Just two weeks before that meeting was scheduled to begin, WTO members agreed on a compromise. Countries without domestic manufacturing capacity would be given a waiver to use compulsory licenses in much the same way as other developing countries, but to prevent diversion into richer countries, they had to implement "reasonable measures within their means proportionate to their administrative capacities."[15] The stipulation was another example of constructive ambiguity in that period. Additionally, 44 developed and richer developing states agreed to forgo their use of compulsory licensing or to limit it only to serious epidemics.[16]

The waiver was made official in 2005 and was renewed every two years, starting in 2007. In 2017, it was finally ratified by enough WTO members to become an official, permanent amendment.[17]

Interestingly, this case contradicts what the California effect would have predicted and suggests a possible caveat to it. The United States wanted higher standards but was unable to use a trade agreement to raise other countries' standards because it wanted an agreement more eagerly than its negotiating partners. It is often presumed that the smaller country benefits from increased access to the larger market more than the other way round, giving the country with the larger market the power to leverage increases in the other states' level of regulatory protection. But as we have seen in the case of compulsory licensing and the other cases analyzed in this book, market power is far from the only factor at play. If the other factors lead the larger market country to more desperately want the trade deal than the smaller market country does, the market leverage that the larger would normally enjoy evaporates. In those circumstances, the California effect is much more likely to break down.

The third area of post-Doha disagreement centered on nonviolation complaints, which argue that a state has denied another state market access even though its behavior is not outside the letter of the agreement. In October 2002, developing countries pushed for a prohibition on nonviolation disputes.[18] The United States did not want a permanent prohibition but was willing to agree to a moratorium on them. Thereafter, the moratorium was renewed every two years, with little disagreement, until 2014. In that year, after U.S. businesses complained about India's IP policies (discussed below), the United States began opposing extending the moratorium.[19] The WTO nevertheless extended the moratorium again in December 2017. Given that Switzerland is the only country that supports the U.S. position, extension of the moratorium is likely to continue for the foreseeable future.[20]

Another notable development occurred in 2015, when the Sustainable Development Goals, the UN's follow-on efforts to build on the Millennium Development Goals, affirmed states' right to use TRIPS flexibilities to promote access to medicines. Again, developed countries, led by the United States, and developing countries, led by India, have not been able to agree to specifics, so the language has been left vague. For all of the details in this period, the result of negotiations at the WTO level has been either an exercise in constructive ambiguity or a compromise. Once both sides knew the policy stakes and were eager to fight, it was difficult for either to gain the upper hand.

Legal Creativity: India's Interpretation and Use of TRIPS Flexibilities

Under the provisions of TRIPS, India had to implement TRIPS-compliant IP regulations beginning in 2005. India has creatively found a number of policy means to relax their IP regulations. They used a narrow set of patentability requirements and greater policy access for patent opponents, limiting which drugs could get patented. They also employed novel injunction policies and compulsory licenses to control drug prices. All of those measures made India's IP regulations differ significantly from the high IP standards that the United States wanted. All of the measures were also technically TRIPS-compliant. Still, India has been judicious in its use of those measures, employing them much less than they otherwise could have, to maintain amicable relations with U.S. drug firms and U.S. businesses more generally. As the following discussion will show, the Indian government took that compromise approach because its officials were mixed in terms of the three factors that drive government officials' behavior on regulation and trade: they wanted to promote trade and to protect regulatory autonomy, their institutional structure gave access to both activists and businesses, and they identified both activists and international pharmaceutical firms as important constituencies.

Flexibilities in India's 2005 Patent Act

The Indian government used administrative delays to lessen the early impact of TRIPS.[21] Still, by 2005, India would have to be TRIPS-compliant. The cost of patented drugs was a looming challenge, especially because drugs are a much larger share of health expenditures in India (44 percent) than in the United States (12 percent).[22] To make matters worse, the paucity of insurance in India means that drug costs are borne directly by the consumer in a highly salient manner. Seventy percent of expenses in health care are paid out of pocket in India, and even the tiny fraction of India's population that have health insurance must pay for drugs themselves because health insurance in India generally does not cover drugs.[23] India had not allowed patents on drugs since the 1970s and was able to issue compulsory licenses for drugs made and sold in India prior to 2005, when the Indian government revised its IP regulations to allow for drug patents as well as for 20-year patents and other TRIPS provisions. Concerns over drug cost remained ever present though, and TRIPS was not as airtight as its proponents believed. A number of the terms in TRIPS are quite vague; for example, the agreement says that governments should undertake "reasonable" efforts to work with patent holders but does not specify what counts as reasonable. Rather than reject TRIPS outright or seek an international dispute, India chose to interpret provisions in creative ways, primarily in three areas: patentability, injunctions, and compulsory licenses.

While TRIPS undeniably forced many states to strengthen their IP regulations, which was exactly the agreement's point, it left a number of patent-related matters firmly in the hands of national government officials. For applicants to receive patents, their inventions must be new, nonobvious, and useful; TRIPS gives national patent offices the power to define what those stipulations require and to determine what information must be disclosed in a patent application.[24]

During the debate over the 2005 Patent Act, activists like the Delhi Network of Positive People opposed the expansion of drug patents.[25] Doctors Without Borders opposed granting patents to new forms of known drugs and wanted extensive opportunities for opposition in the approval process.[26] Officials in the Indian Parliament cited these activists in their arguments in the debate over the bill.[27] The 2005 Patents Act reflected many of those activists' concerns.

Patentability

Since the passage of the 2005 Patents Act, the Indian government has implemented a number of limitations on what subject matter can and cannot be patented,[28] and India's definition of what counts as nonobvious is exceptionally high.[29] The biggest curtailment of patentable products is Section 3(d) of that law, which is aimed at preventing evergreening.[30] The section says that to receive a patent, new forms of known drugs must enhance the drug's efficacy, defined as healing effectiveness.[31]

Section 3(d) is in stark contrast to other states' IP regulations. In the United States, a new compound may receive a patent by being easier to store or more easily absorbed by the body,[32] more forgiving standards that are easier to prove. Proving therapeutic effectiveness is difficult and costly. Relatedly, India does not allow patenting combinations of known drugs.[33] In the United States, even if drug A and drug B are not patented, a combination of them, drug AB, can be patented; in India, that cannot be done. India also does not grant data exclusivity.[34] Those exceptions mean that India can subject a drug patented in other states to generic competition without needing to issue a compulsory license.[35] Importantly, none of these maneuvers to relax IP standards violate the letter of TRIPS.[36]

Not just the content of India's IP regulations limit patentability; the procedure by which patenting decisions get made helps activists and curtails drug firms. The opponents of a patent have three opportunities to make their case before the government: (1) at a pre-grant stage in front of patent officials, (2) at a post-grant proceeding at the patent office, or (3) through revocation proceedings before India's Intellectual Property Appellate Board.[37] That procedure gives them significant opportunities to present framings based on preventing needless death.

The pre-grant stage is particularly important. In that stage, the Indian patent office allows activist organizations and makers of generic drugs to review pending patent applications and decide which ones to oppose; at this stage, any individual or activist organization, not just rival companies, may oppose a patent being granted. Indeed, NGOs have filed many of the pre-grant oppositions.[38] Again, India's procedure stands in marked contrast to the situations in the United States and other high-IP states that have no mechanism for pre-grant opposition. Here as elsewhere in the pharmaceutical case, cleavage-based explanations do not fit well; the battle lines are not between businesses and other businesses but between businesses and activists.

Once the less-friendly IP regulations of the Patents Act were put in place, it did not take long for Western pharmaceutical companies to start to feel the bite. In 2006, despite protests from activists, Novartis filed for a patent in India on its new leukemia drug Glivec. Access-to-medicine activists immediately protested, pointing to Glivec as an example of evergreening.[39] The Indian government denied that patent application because Glivec was a modification of an earlier drug (imatinib); the only change was its salt format, which Novartis claimed made it a patentable improvement since the salt form can be absorbed by the body 30% more easily.[40] Novartis could not prove that Glivec had greater therapeutic efficacy and thus could not prove that it met the Indian patent office's definitions of "new" and "useful."

To the delight of access-to-medicine advocates, the Glivec decision set the precedent for using therapeutic efficacy as a key criterion for patentability. In 2012, the Indian Intellectual Property Appellate Board appeared to uphold this standard when it revoked patents on drugs made by Pfizer, Merck, and Roche because they were not sufficiently innovative over existing drugs.[41] The Glivec case went to the Indian Supreme Court, which upheld the decision to not grant the patent, further bolstering the precedent.[42] The Indian government cited similar grounds when rejecting a patent for Sovaldi, the hepatitis C cure that sold in the United States for

$84,000. Thus India has been able to keep the price of that drug at around $900, a discount of roughly 99 percent.[43]

Compulsory Licenses

The Indian government has also begun using compulsory licenses to lower drug prices. One advantage of a compulsory license is that it requires relatively few technical resources.[44] India issued its first compulsory license under TRIPs in March 2012, for Bayer's drug Nexavar, which is used to treat kidney and liver cancers. Bayer charged $5,500 per month for Nexavar; Natco, an Indian generics firm, sold a copy for $173 a month after the compulsory license was issued.[45] The Nexavar compulsory license opened the possibility for India to issue compulsory licenses for at least four other patented drugs.[46] There likely would have been more compulsory licenses issued, but some drug companies faced with imminent compulsory licensing decisions cut deals to allow local producers to make generic versions of their drugs.[47] Given the very high costs of many cancer medicines and given that the number of cancer cases in India is expected to double in the next two decades, it is possible that the Indian government will increase its use of compulsory licenses.[48]

Injunctions

In addition to tight patentability requirements, a patent-granting process open to activists, and compulsory licenses, the Indian government developed new policies on injunctions, an effort that ironically received a major boost from the U.S. Supreme Court. In the 1990s and early 2000s, more and more companies found themselves being sued for patent infringement by shell firms that filed patents but never did anything with them. Those companies, which came to be known as patent trolls, were basically waiting for someone else to infringe their patents so they could sue them and profit from settling out of court. In 2006, a case involving one of those trolls (MercExchange) and eBay came before the U.S. Supreme Court.[49]

When plaintiffs in cases prior to that one argued that their patent was being infringed, courts had generally issued injunctions, which forced the firm accused of infringing the patent to cease the activities involving the patent. In their decision on *eBay v. MercExchange*, the Supreme Court ruled automatic injunction unwarranted and argued for a more balanced approach.[50] According to the Supreme Court's decision, for an injunction to be granted, the plaintiff (i.e., the patent holder)—in this case, the patent troll MercExchange—must show that (1) it suffered irreparable injury, (2) it could not be fairly compensated, (3) the balance of hardship between the two parties merits an injunction, and (4) the public interest would not be disserved by injunction.[51] That unanimous decision constitutes a powerful change to how patent infringement should be handled by the courts and, by extension, to the regulatory standards that dictate how much protection IP should receive when that IP affects a tangible aspect of the public interest.

When Clarence Thomas was writing the opinion and the other eight justices were joining, they may or may not have been considering how it would affect India's treatment of drugs, but their decision nevertheless handed the Indian government a powerful new legal justification for refusing to force a maker of generic drugs to cease making copies of patented drugs. Shortly thereafter, the Indian Court cited the U.S. Supreme Court decision numerous times to defend its decision to not issue an injunction that would have forced Cipla (a generics firm) to stop making copies of a drug for which Hoffman-La Roche held the patent.[52] In other words, an Indian court cleverly based its decision against a foreign pharmaceutical firm on precedent in the U.S. Supreme Court. How could U.S. government officials in the Office of the U.S. Trade Representative and Congress insist that the Indian court's actions in denying injunctions were illegitimate and a denial of due process when those actions rested on legal foundations constructed by the U.S. Supreme Court? The U.S. Supreme Court has given the Indian government the legal means to grant patents but then selectively refuse to enforce those patents if they lead to higher prices, which is exactly what patents do. In fact, the nonuse of injunctions may be an even more robust check on drug firms' market exclusivity than compulsory licenses, because court decisions are less vulnerable to unilateral retaliation, given the political insulation that judges often enjoy.[53]

The pharmaceutical representatives and government officials that were the primary authors of TRIPS never anticipated this kind of attack on stringent IP regulations via new injunction standards. TRIPS says absolutely nothing about such measures. No one foresaw this series of events. India thus has a TRIPS-compliant means of indirectly invalidating any patent it issues. Article 44.1 of TRIPS only gives judiciaries the authority to issue injunction; it never says that they must. This loophole was not the only gap in TRIPS. While TRIPS seemed a blowout victory for drug firms, it was actually full of holes that India has been able to exploit. The holes were not intentional but the result of sloppiness and lack of legal imagination on the part of the officials that negotiated TRIPS. Emory Simon, then director for IP at the USTR, said, "The reality is that we do not spend a lot of time thinking about legal issues when we negotiate agreements in the GATT. . . . The concerns that we have are with the commercial results of what a negotiated agreement is, rather than with the legal niceties."[54] If anyone should have been obsessed with the legal niceties of TRIPS, it should have been the director of IP at the USTR. For whatever reason, Simon and his colleagues allowed the alluring nature of big commercial wins to make them forget that small details in international law can have enormous consequences.

In addition to the small but critical distinction that national judicial bodies could but did not have to issue injunctions, the TRIPS language on pharmaceuticals only covered small-molecule drugs and enabled countries to deny patents on biologics.[55] That the TRIPS Agreement never defines "inventive step" also gives India considerable leeway.[56] Moreover, states are allowed to employ patent exemptions for noncommercial use, such as second use, and Bolar exemptions.[57] India has taken advantage of both those exemptions.[58] Finally, the TRIPS procedure for dispute settlement does not allow for retroactive sanctions, so there is an incentive for developing countries to push the boundaries as far as they can.[59]

Checks on The Flexibilities

Despite what appear to be robust opportunities for India to implement IP regulations far lower than those envisioned by TRIPS, the Indian government has been temperate in its use of those flexibilities. As Indian commerce minister Shri Anand Sharma has pointed out, the Indian government has still been granting many patents to Western drug firms; the Glivec decision is not representative of most cases.[60] The Indian government has also been careful to issue compulsory licenses only when necessary to further public health and not when it might violate international rules.[61] There are a number of factors behind that policy temperance.

First, many Indian generics firms have developed increasingly tight connections with Western research-based firms.[62] Relatedly, TRIPS and the attendant reduction in IP regulatory barriers have led many of the largest Indian drug companies to make more of their money abroad than at home.[63] For many of them, licensing foreign IP, rather than copying it, is the more profitable route, but Western firms want effective IP protection before they agree to give a license to a firm based in a developing country.[64] Western firms such as AstraZeneca, GlaxoSmithKline, Eli Lilly, Pfizer, and Novartis have increasingly partnered with Indian firms to conduct clinical testing to achieve cost savings of 40–60 percent.[65] That Indian firms' competitiveness would suffer if India were to become perceived as a pariah on protecting IP incentivizes the Indian government to loosen IP regulations where it can but not go so far as to make foreign investors skittish. The disguised protectionism argument would fail to correctly explain the source of that regulatory difference. In this case, activists, not businesses, were clamoring for regulatory differences that could impede trade.

Second, rather than focusing on generics production, many Indian firms are increasingly involved in research and development, either on their own or in a partnership with foreign firms.[66] India has a significant talent pool in chemistry and chemical engineering, two building blocks of pharmaceutical research; 122,000 Indians annually graduate from Indian universities with degrees in those two areas, and they work for far lower wages than their Western counterparts.[67] With R&D costs one-eighth of those in Western countries, India is highly competitive in that subfield.[68] R&D requires IP protection, though. When Western companies believe that protection is not high enough, they pull their investments. After initiating new investments in rural India in 2008, Novartis announced in 2013, after the Indian Supreme Court's Glivec decision, that it would no longer make any R&D investments in India.[69]

Additionally, because the point of compulsory licensing is to bring down drug prices and because those licenses come with considerable scrutiny, many Indian firms increasingly perceive producing drugs under compulsory license as not very profitable. Thus Indian firms are much less enthusiastic about loose IP regulations than might first be assumed. India also has the world's largest film industry and a sizable software industry, both of which want strong copyright protection, which only adds to the volume of domestic voices calling for higher IP regulations.

Third, India does not want a WTO ruling against it and has been careful not to use the policy flexibilities to address a potentially disadvantageous case. For example, it rejected a compulsory license on AstraZeneca's drug Saxagliptin, a diabetes drug, because the ready availability of substitutes meant little potential cost savings given Saxagliptin's already low price.[70] The Indian government knows that stretching TRIPS to the point of clear violation would invite a dispute with the United States. A WTO ruling against India could constrain its space for policy flexibility. The United States may have lost a WTO dispute panel over Nexavar had such a dispute materialized, so the United States too is a bit gun-shy about starting WTO cases that could go against it and that could put India's IP regulations on firmer legal grounds. A WTO case involving the EU and

Canada defined IP trade discrimination as "differential treatment without a reasonable justification."[71] Had the WTO decided that bringing down the high cost of Nexavar was a reasonable justification, the United States would have lost that case, and the global use of compulsory licenses would have been augmented. As with the WTO stalemates discussed earlier, having a murky nonresolution is better for both sides than risking a clear loss.

Fourth, the United States has means of pressuring India to not go too far in its creativity. U.S. officials can employ the Special 301 mechanism, and under pressure from business, they came close to doing so after the Nexavar decision.[72] The U.S. drug market is the world's largest, so the Indian government views friendly cooperation with the United States and its Food and Drug Administration as crucial in protecting the competitiveness of India's pharmaceutical sector.[73] Indian patent authorities have relatively few resources for pushing back against that pressure, and their patent examiners generally receive their training in the West and rely on their Western counterparts for guidance.[74] As elsewhere in this analysis, where regulatory barriers are prevented from increasing, it is at least partly due to concerns about competitiveness.

Finally, the Modi-led government that assumed power in 2014 has been especially keen to attract foreign direct investment from multinational corporations and has been careful not to implement IP regulations that would make foreign firms wary of investing in India. Modi has even suggested that he would like to see India change its IP laws to more closely match other states' higher standards: "If we don't work towards bringing our intellectual property rights at par with global parameters, then the world will not keep relations with us. If we give confidence to the world on IPR, then we can become a destination globally for their creative work."[75] To the delight of international drug companies, Modi disbanded a subcommittee that was making compulsory licenses more likely to be approved.[76] He also set up a think tank to review India's IP regulations; of that group's six members, four were connected with large businesses that have an interest in raising India's level of IP protection, and none were access-to-medicine advocates or from academia.[77] As occurred in several parts of the beef case, Modi's position here suggests some of the difficulties of formally modeling government officials' stances. A different Indian prime minister, even one that was a Hindu nationalist like Modi, may have taken a very different stance on these issues.

In sum, then, the Indian position on IP regulations has been a compromise. India's patentability regulations are much more restrictive than developed countries, such as the United States, would prefer. India's procedures allow NGOs to challenge patents at multiple stages, its new policies related to injunctions are backed by the U.S. Supreme Court, and the Indian government has begun issuing compulsory licenses. All of these policies mean that India could have given an across-the-board victory to access-to-medicine advocates. Instead, it opted for a middle-ground approach, for several reasons. Indian drug firms often have close relationships with international drug companies and are increasingly involved in R&D. Also, Indian firms in other industries want IP protection. Additionally, India is wary of a WTO ruling against it and is pressured by the U.S. government. Finally, its prime minister has prioritized attracting foreign direct investment.

Still, even taking into account Modi's position and the other checks on India's creative use of TRIPS flexibilities, India's IP regulations stand as a model for other developing countries that want to maintain different regulations than those espoused by the states with high IP regulations. In 2008, the Philippines, for example, added a patentability provision to their patent law that is modeled after India's Section 3(d).[78] Argentina has also implemented IP regulations similar to 3(d), and other developing countries are considering doing the same.[79]

Negotiating with a Behemoth: Free Trade Agreements between the United States and Latin American Countries

Notwithstanding the outcome of the Doha Declaration negotiations, the U.S. government, particularly the USTR, maintained much closer connections to IP-intensive firms, especially pharmaceutical companies, than to access-to-medicine advocates. It continued to seek elevations in other states' IP regulations closer to those of the United States. At the same time, the government hoped to deepen the U.S. trade relationship with Latin America.

The Bush administration first sought to deepen that relationship by promoting the Free Trade Area of the Americas. In the FTAA talks, the main country negotiating with the United States was Brazil. It rejected raising its level of IP regulations, even though that rejection made the successful conclusion of the FTAA impossible. Access advocates in Brazil were able to depict those kinds of IP regulations as threatening Brazil's program of universal access to AIDS medicine and thus as creating needless death. Meanwhile, those Brazilian industries that could have made the most compelling competitiveness-based argument in favor of an FTAA could not do so because they were agribusiness firms. Granting them access to the U.S. market would have required the United States to reduce its agricultural subsidies, which it was not willing to do.

With the FTAA clearly going nowhere, the Bush administration turned its attention to Central American and Andean countries. Those countries did not have Brazil's universal access program, had much weaker access-to-medicine advocacy organizations, and contained businesses that, because of the industries they were in, could make much stronger competitiveness-based claims than their Brazilian counterparts. Their competitiveness led to those countries reducing their regulatory trade barriers in IP to secure free trade agreements with the United States.

The USTR and IP-Intensive Firms: A Cozy Relationship

As I mentioned in chapters 3 and 6, IP-intensive firms, especially drug companies, have generally enjoyed a very cozy relationship with the Office of the United States Trade Representative. The USTR hires much of its negotiating staff from drug companies, and those companies, in turn, hire USTR alumni. For example, both the two lead negotiators of the IP provisions in 2003 and 2004 (the key period, discussed below, in which free trade agreements with Central American countries were being negotiated) received senior positions with pharmaceutical companies within three months after the agreement was signed.[80]

Perhaps the best demonstration of this revolving door is Kira Alvarez,[81] the lead IP negotiator for the USTR in the United States–Chile Free Trade Agreement, the United States–Morocco Free Trade Agreement, and the Central America Free Trade Agreement. Alvarez next worked for the pharmaceutical company Eli Lilly, implementing their government affairs strategy on IP, after which she worked for Time Warner and, later, was the U.S. Chamber of Commerce's cochair on global IP. She then went back to the USTR, to be its chief negotiator on IP enforcement, before she went back to the pharmaceutical industry again, taking a job with AbbVie.

The policy access given to IP-intensive businesses reinforces such hiring practices. For example, during the negotiations for the Trans-Pacific Partnership, the attendees at an IP meeting held in Winder Room 305 of the USTR headquarters at 11:00 a.m. on February 1, 2011, included Shawn Brown, Matthew McGrath, Ralph Ives (via phone), Claude Burcky, Trevor Gunn, and Doug Nelson, all representatives of IP-intensive businesses, but did not include any representatives of access-to-medicine activists or public health organizations.[82] Through the Freedom of Information Act (FOIA), Knowledge Ecology International obtained 127 pages of emails (available online) between industry and USTR leaders.[83] Through a different FOIA request, IP Watch obtained an additional 379 pages of such emails.[84] From reading through those emails, one gets a consistent picture of a tight and very friendly relationship between representatives of IP-intensive firms and USTR officials, in which firms and the USTR make trade policy and make essentially no effort to include NGOs in the policymaking process.

For example, on January 12, 2010, John Nueffer, president of the Semiconductor Industry Association, set up a meeting with Barbara Weisel, lead USTR negotiator for the TPP. When she asked if there would be any press there, he responded, "No press at all and will make clear at the outset the discussion is only for company consumption. . . . should not be reading about it in Inside US Trade."[85] A high-ranking official in the USTR thus not only attended a meeting held by an IP-intensive firm at its K Street lobbying office (where policy strategies designed to benefit those firms were formulated) but also implicitly accepted that firm's rather pointed request that such meetings be kept secret. None of this maneuvering is illegal or undeniably corrupt in a direct way involving quid pro quo, and its overall ethicality is in the eye of the beholder, depending on how one views drug companies. At minimum, though, it smacks of cronyism and suggests the extent to which the USTR identifies its mission as advancing the interests of IP-intensive firms.

Given such close links between drug firms and the USTR as well as their other political assets discussed in chapter 6, it is not surprising that the United States wanted to further move their trading partners' IP standards closer to U.S. standards and reduce regulatory barriers. Those regulation increases above what TRIPS mandated became known as TRIPS-plus provisions and had four aspects. First, they placed greater limits on states' ability to use compulsory licenses. Second, they linked marketing approval to patent expiration. Third, they established tighter rules on data exclusivity. Fourth, they mandated patent extensions to offset regulatory delays. All of those aspects were anathema to access-to-medicine advocates.

Why Brazil Blocked the FTAA over Drugs

Access-to-medicine Advocates and the Universal Coverage Program in Brazil

In 1996, Brazil passed Law 9.313, which made access to AIDS medication a universal right and obligated the government to provide that medicine at no cost to the patient.[86] It also passed a new IP law to become compliant with TRIPS, with two articles of particular note in the present analysis. First, Article 71 had a robust compulsory licensing scheme. Second, Article 68 contained a local production requirement that drug firms would have to make their drugs in Brazil or face a compulsory license. Those articles were meant to support Brazil's universal treatment program. Without the threat of compulsory licensing and without a local production requirement that could give that threat real teeth, the high costs of patented AIDS drugs would have made Brazil's universal treatment program fiscally unsustainable.

The Free Trade Area of the Americas had first been proposed by President Bill Clinton in 1994. Within FTAA negotiations, IP was a consistent point of emphasis for the United States. Less than a week after Brazil had approved its new, TRIPS-compliant law that would protect drug patents, U.S. secretary of state Warren Christopher visited Brazil and urged its officials to help create a hemispheric free trade agreement.[87] The United States also pushed for the creation of special police units and courts to prosecute IP violations, but Brazil and Argentina objected to that measure.[88] As I discussed in chapter 6, after TRIPS came into force and once access advocates and developing countries came to realize what it entailed, the politics surrounding it grew more charged. That intensity occurred within the FTAA specifically. In one FTAA meeting in Colombia, the discussion of drugs got so heated that security had to be called in to protect U.S. officials.[89]

The intensity of FTAA negotiations and the opposition to TRIPS continued to build over the next few years. Negotiating the FTAA was a major priority of the Bush administration when it took office in January 2001. At the same time, the United States was suing Brazil before the WTO for Brazil's program to issue compulsory licenses for AIDS drugs in a way the United States believed violated TRIPS. The United States threatened to target Brazil under Special 301 (which it would threaten again in 2003), while Brazil threatened to issue compulsory licenses on drugs made by Merck and Hoffman-La Roche. U.S. diplomats responded to the Brazilian Ministry of Health that if Brazil used a compulsory license, the United States would reassess all partnerships with Brazil and even consider ending the training of Brazilian scientists in U.S. research centers.[90]

That wrangling between the United States and Brazil occurred during the height of the South African lawsuit. Access advocates strongly denounced the FTAA and generated significant attention to the FTAA's IP provisions in the lead-up to the Quebec ministerial meeting in April 2001. Business groups in favor of the FTAA acknowledged the strength of that opposition and the difficulty of responding effectively to their demands. Nancy Hughes Anthony, the president of the Canadian Chamber of Commerce, summarized, "We are competing with a circus that includes every activist in the country and even some members of Parliament preparing to demonstrate."[91]

Brazilian access-to-medicine advocates already had the requisite institutional structure to lobby effectively. Grupo de Apoio a Prevencao a AIDS was particularly important in spearheading early AIDS activism in Brazil.[92] By the mid-1990s, there were over 600 different activist organizations working on AIDS and public health under the aegis of the States Forum of AIDS NGOs.[93] Like other activists, they became much more aware of and engaged in the politics of IP as the consequences of TRIPS for public health became more salient. The forum's activists helped make the issue even more salient by organizing an effective attention-grabbing campaign of public demonstrations outside of U.S. consulates in Brazil.[94] Just two months later, in May 2001, all the major access-to-medicine and AIDS activist organizations from across Brazil came together for the first time, to strategize for pushing back against U.S. attempts to raise Brazil's IP regulations.[95]

Given the very high salience of the issue at that particular moment, given Brazil's universal access program, and given that the United States was clearly attempting to use trade agreements to raise other countries' IP standards in ways that could very plausibly threaten Brazil's program, access-to-medicine advocates in Brazil were able to make a strong case that an FTAA system requiring Brazil to adopt TRIPS-plus provisions would cause a significant amount of needless death. Again and again, advocacy groups went before Brazilian government officials to make the case that raising IP regulations would yield needless death.[96] There is considerable evidence that those officials found the advocates' arguments persuasive.[97] Activists also provided the Brazilian government with crucial technical assistance in its legal case against the United States.[98] Countering activists' arguments would have required very strong competitiveness-based arguments from businesses in Brazil, and those latter arguments were not forthcoming.

Agricultural Subsidies and Brazilian Competitiveness

Three main factors led to Brazil taking the toughest stance against the U.S. position of any country in the lead-up to the 2001 Doha summit. First, Brazil is an agricultural powerhouse. It has a fifth of the world's arable land, good rainfall, modern farming, and advantageous weather. It is the world's most efficient and leading producer of a range of agricultural products, including sugar, coffee, oranges, cotton, and a host of others. Agriculture is thus a huge part of the Brazilian economy. As of 2006, it accounted for 27 percent of the Brazilian gross domestic product, 25 percent of Brazil's employment, and 40 percent of its exports.[99] Second, Brazilian officials, like their counterparts in other developing countries, were frustrated with the outcomes of the Uruguay Round because it had forced considerable policy changes in their countries, while they believed that developed countries had dragged their feet on issues like textiles and agriculture that would have benefited Brazil. Third, the United States maintained significant subsidies and tariffs in precisely those products, such as sugar and orange juice, in which Brazil was most internationally competitive.[100] Those subsidies and tariffs effectively locked Brazilian producers out of the U.S. market. While raising Brazil's IP regulations was the top concern of American FTAA negotiators, Brazilian negotiators' top concern was reducing U.S. agricultural subsidies.

Brazilian officials said that they would agree to an FTAA only if it addressed agricultural commodities and especially subsidies and only if the United States revised its antidumping laws, which often targeted Brazil. The United States was highly reluctant to do so. U.S. officials stated that they would only consider reducing agricultural subsidies if doing so was part of a larger WTO deal that also reduced European and Japanese agricultural subsidies.[101] FTAA negotiations over agricultural subsidies were already going to be difficult, but the United States made it more so when it solidified its support for agricultural protection. The fast-track bill that allowed President Bush to attempt to negotiate the FTAA excluded about 300 items, most of which agricultural products and some of which were Brazil's most competitive goods.[102] Then the 2002 farm bill increased agricultural subsidies by 70 percent, to over $180 billion annually.[103] Brazilian producers wanted fewer U.S. agricultural subsidies, not more. Those producers could have been Brazil's biggest domestic proponents of the FTAA, if subsidy reduction had been on the table. Since it was not, no business arguments in favor could be made, so there was no countervailing political force against the pressure access-to-medicine advocates put on the Brazilian government not to agree to the FTAA.

As FTAA talks dragged in 2002 and 2003, IP and agricultural protection continued to be the main bones of contention between the United States and Brazil, and neither country showed any willingness to concede on the other's core demand. By November 2003 (though the final definitive collapse of the FTAA did not come until 2005), it was clear to all parties that finding some sort of agreement was unlikely, so both sides effectively gave up. At that point, the United States, which could not reduce regulatory barriers in pharmaceuticals (as it wanted to do) without reducing agricultural subsidies, began to look more seriously to other Latin American countries for potential partners in free trade agreements.[104]

Chile and Central America Make a Faustian Bargain

Chile and Central America had the exact opposite domestic political configuration as Brazil in terms of activists versus exporters. Exporters from the former regions actively engaged in domestic lobbying and were able to make strong arguments that a free trade agreement with the United States would make them more competitive in the world's largest economy. Conversely, Chilean and Central American access-to-medicine advocates were much weaker than their Brazilian counterparts, did not have an effective and popular program to defend, and thus were less effective in their lobbying.

Exporters Wanted Access to the U.S. Market and, Unlike Brazilian Exporters, Could Get It

As the Bush administration ramped up its efforts with Latin America, Chile was ready to agree to a deal. With plentiful sea connections and a long, mountainous land topography, Chile's geography lends itself to a pro-trade stance. It is often much easier for a Chilean business to sell to a foreign buyer than to ship products to the other end of Chile. After NAFTA, Chile was told that it was next in line for a free trade deal with the United States, and Chile had the most open economy in Latin America and had already signed bilateral deals with Mexico in 1991 and Canada in 1997.[105] A free trade deal could increase the competitiveness of producers in the primary products Chile exported to the United States (copper, fish, wine, and paper products).[106] Even some of the agricultural productions that Chile wanted to include, such as grapes and pears, presented the United States with relatively few problems in tariff reduction.[107]

A free trade agreement with the United States could also increase the competitiveness of Central American textiles (one of the region's most important export-oriented industries) in the U.S. market.[108] This would be especially helpful in that regard vis-à-vis Chinese competition, given that quotas on Chinese textiles had been lifted earlier that year as part of the abolition of the Multi-Fibre Arrangement.[109] Given the size of the U.S. market, virtually all exporters in Central American countries would benefit from a free trade deal. All those countries had very high levels of trade dependence on the United States.[110]

Chilean and Central American exporters were more capable than Brazil of making competitiveness-based arguments in favor of a free trade agreement regardless of the cost in terms of reducing regulatory trade barriers in pharmaceuticals. Competitiveness goals were why the trade and economic ministers of the five Central American countries signaled that they were willing to make whatever compromises were necessary to gain permanent, open access to the U.S. economy and attract foreign investment.[111]

Chilean and Central American Access-to-Medicine Advocates, Unlike Brazil's, Were Weak and Unengaged

A litany of obstacles stood in the way of Central American countries developing civil society opposition to U.S. demands for increased IP standards. Significant domestic strife in Guatemala, El Salvador, Honduras, and Nicaragua throughout the 1990s had greatly undermined civic engagement and had increased poverty, leaving huge swaths of those countries' populations too busy surviving to politically organize.[112] The few activist organizations in Guatemala were interested in postwar reconciliation and promoting indigenous rights.[113] In El Salvador, there was very little cooperation between generics firms and activists, who deeply mistrusted each other because they had been on different sides in the country's civil war.[114] Unlike Brazil, Central American countries had almost no access-to-medicine NGOs and had no domestic access-to-medicine program to defend. The few health advocates organized in Central American countries were more concerned with broader community health provision than were international NGOs, so the former sometimes prioritized IP considerations less than the latter did.[115] The IP provisions in the Central America Free Trade Agreement did not receive meaningful public attention anywhere outside of Guatemala, and even there, the main organization interested in the issue, the Alianza Civil por el Acceso e Medicamentos, had only formed in 2003.[116] Elsewhere in Central America, access-to-medicine advocates did not begin engaging on IP until 2003, after CAFTA was already being negotiated.[117]

Central American civil society organizations did not even mount serious efforts to monitor the impact of IP, and government officials made little effort to help.[118] Officials were also not eager to court disagreement with drug companies by issuing compulsory licenses. Even though such licensing might have reduced the price on particular drugs, government officials needed to maintain good relations with drug firms to get good pricing deals on other drugs.[119]

The obstacles to oppositional development meant that access advocates were in no position to effectively lobby against exporters eager to see CAFTA get completed. With exporters making compelling competitiveness claims and with access-to-medicine advocates unable to make effective claims about preventing needless death, Central American government officials were in a similar position as U.S. officials during the negotiation of TRIPS; they were hearing from only one side, so sought to reduce the IP regulatory barriers in pharmaceuticals. Ultimately, the IP regulations in the Dominican Republic–Central America Free Trade Agreement were significantly higher than those prescribed by TRIPS, which is why Rachel Cohen of Doctors Without Borders called the agreement "the worst case scenario."[120]

Bringing the Story Up to Today: Post-CAFTA Developments in the United States

The May 10th Agreement

U.S. Democrats' criticism of the U.S. trade-related stance on IP went back to the 2001 South African suit and had been especially disapproving of the IP provisions in CAFTA.[121] Though still largely supportive of pharmaceutical firms, Democrats wanted those provisions to leave greater policy space for developing countries. A combination of three factors that came together in early 2007 gave the Democrats the chance to accomplish that goal.

First, Democrats won back control of the U.S. Congress in the 2006 midterms, meaning their votes would be crucial to passing the implementing legislation on trade agreements.[122] Second, slowly but surely, more and more Republicans were becoming increasingly skeptical of international trade agreements. That skepticism reduced the Bush administration's already thin margin for error, which made attaining Democrats' approval effectively a requirement. Third, that the implementing legislation for free trade agreements signed with Peru, Panama, and Colombia still needed to be approved by Congress gave Democrats a point of leverage to push for their preferences.

On May 10, 2007, the Bush administration and congressional Democrats forged a compromise on labor and environmental issues and, most important for our purposes, IP in drugs. The IP provisions of the May 10th Agreement did not fundamentally challenge the negotiating position advocated by pharmaceutical companies, but the agreement rhetorically emphasized the need for developing countries to have greater policy flexibility and stipulated some small steps to promote that flexibility. For example, it clarified that data exclusivity should not last longer in the partner country than in the United States and that developing countries could make exceptions to data exclusivity rules and adopt a less rigid approach on patent linkages.

The Trans-Pacific Partnership

The Trans-Pacific Partnership was a proposed free trade deal between the United States and 11 other countries around the Pacific. It was eventually scuttled by the Trump administration and would have faced significant opposition to ratification even if Democratic presidential candidate Hillary Clinton had been elected. Among other issues, the TPP contained an IP chapter, with two major provisions that differed from previous trade deals struck by the United States.

The first difference involved data exclusivity for biologics. As I mentioned in chapter 6, biologics are a new class of drugs that represent some of the most cutting-edge research in the pharmaceutical industry and that can be hugely expensive to develop. Pharmaceutical companies wanted to use data exclusivity provisions in the TPP to ensure that their effective monopolies held for longer to ensure that they have time to recoup their investments. As I mentioned at the beginning of chapter 1, trade-related IP rules have generally only applied to synthetic chemical compounds, and the United States wanted to maximize the regulatory protections on biologics by granting 12 years of data exclusivity, while other states wanted 5 years or less. The final compromise in the TPP guaranteed a minimum of 5 years of data exclusivity but added another 3 years through regulatory procedures. The TPP required adjustments to patent terms so that if there was an "unreasonable delay" of a patent being granted in a country, that country's government would be required to extend the patent to make up for the delay.[123] That requirement would help the drug company extend its patent. The May 10th Agreement had said that such adjustments should remain optional; the TPP would have made them mandatory.

Many Democrats disliked the TPP's IP provisions, as they tightened flexibilities designed to help developing countries and agreed to in the May 10th Agreement.[124] Congressional Democrats asserted that the of IP flexibilities for developing countries in the May 10th Agreement should have been the minimum expected. Drug firms responded that biologics were just starting to become more important in 2007 and that new deals should take into account the high development costs of those new drugs and grant firms greater IP protection. For their part, many Republicans, such as Orrin Hatch (representing Utah), believed that the TPP did not go far enough in protecting IP. Their yardstick for adequacy was not the May 10th Agreement but U.S. law, which, as I said, grants 12 years of data exclusivity to biologics.[125]

In retrospect, how the TPP's IP provisions came about is clear. The USTR wanted to sign a deal but also needed to get it through Congress. Republicans were always going to give most of the votes in support of TPP, and many of them wanted as much protection for IP as possible. If the USTR had come back with too little IP protection, the TPP would have died in Congress for lack of Republican support. Developing countries, Australia, and some Democrats wanted as many IP flexibilities as possible. They were not going to sign on to a deal that gave U.S. Republicans and American IP-intensive firms everything they wanted. The USTR thus needed to thread a very fine needle for sewing up this deal. The negotiations over IP were so tricky and so contentious that data exclusivity was the very last issue settled in the TPP negotiations. The TPP was ultimately killed by the Trump administration, but even had Hillary Clinton become president, it is not a given that she would have pushed hard for the partnership, after having turned against it as a candidate and with much of the liberal base opposed to it. Even if she had promoted the TPP, Congress would likely not have ratified it, given that much of the support the agreement would have needed would have had to come from Republicans. Still, the terms that got negotiated in the deal itself before it was killed give a sense of the broader trajectory of IP regulations and trade agreements.

Conclusion: What We Know

IP regulation, especially as it pertains to pharmaceuticals, is often held up as an exemplar of big business getting its way politically, and the TRIPS agreement did largely reflect the wishes of IP-intensive firms. Yet, among the cases analyzed in this study, the TRIPS and CAFTA negotiations are the only ones in which businesses were able to secure their preferences, and those businesses were able to get their way because they were able to link their policy requests with broader concerns about competitiveness and because NGOs did not take the field. In the negotiation of the Doha Declaration, access-to-medicine advocates politically cornered pharmaceutical companies and won significant legal reinforcement for differing IP policies. In the WTO and Indian cases, businesses did not suffer resounding defeats, but because of the opposition of NGOs and officials from developing countries, businesses were also unable to fully achieve their policy preferences. Far from demonstrating the political power of business, the negotiations over IP regulations and trade show just how contingent and limited that power is.

Those negotiations also demonstrate how important not knowing the impact of trade regulation can be. Access-to-medicine activists did not get engaged in the TRIPS negotiation in the 1980s and early 1990s because they did not yet understand how significant IP regulations were to their overall goals. In the negotiation over the Doha Declaration in 2001, pharmaceutical companies walked into a policy fight they had no chance of winning, because they had no idea just how fierce the public relations backlash against them was going to be. India's creative use of TRIPS flexibilities only happened because the original authors of the TRIPS Agreement did not understand how important the legal details were and did not anticipate the extent to which clever, oppositional interpretations could exploit the holes they left behind. When it comes to regulatory trade barriers, what you do not know will hurt you.

We do know that people will continue to get sick. Cardiovascular disease killed an estimate 17.9 million people in 2016,[126] and 8.5 percent of all adults now have diabetes.[127] The biggest challenge of all is cancer, called the emperor of all maladies with good reason.[128] In 2018, it caused roughly one in six deaths globally.[129] The political fight over how best to help people dying from those diseases, as well as how to pay for that help, is just starting. Trade-related IP regulations, as dry and technical as they may sound, are at the very center of that fight.

EIGHT

Conclusion

Regulation and Trade Politics in the Twenty-First Century

The intersection of trade and national regulations has significant consequences for our contemporary world and is likely to continue to do so for the foreseeable future. In this chapter, I review the evidence I have provided in support of this book's major claims. I discuss other theoretical implications that the book has for scholarship on the international political economy, and I discuss how lessons from the industries examined here may apply to other industries as well. Finally, I offer political recommendations for the businesses, nongovernmental organizations, and government officials examined in this book.

Reviewing the Evidence in Support of This Book's Major Claims

This book has advanced a central thesis and three other major claims. The central thesis is that regulatory trade barriers are most likely to be reduced when businesses are able to link their desire for that reduction with societal concerns about economic competitiveness, while activists are likely to succeed at increasing or defending regulatory trade barriers when they can link their desire for maintaining or increasing that barrier with preventing needless death. The other major claims are that cleavage-based explanations are less effective once regulations become a core facet of trade politics, that disguised protectionism is the driver of regulatory trade barriers less often than is commonly presumed, and that activists have more agency and power in trade politics and that businesses are less dominant than is commonly presumed.

Competitiveness and Death Framings

In the auto case analyzed in this study, European automakers were able to use competitiveness framings from 1983 to 1988 to convince officials in the European Community to stymie intracontinental emissions-based regulatory trade barriers. After 1988, environmentalists were able to mount a stronger campaign for high emissions standards that required catalytic converters. Automakers still wanted a unified continental auto market, but small-car manufacturers no longer perceived those regulations to be a threat to their competitiveness, so European officials were able to find a compromise position: a unified, high emissions standard. In North America, automakers were able to use competitiveness-based claims to prevent regulatory barriers related to domestic content from being erected in the United States. They used those same framings to get such barriers reduced in Mexico and Canada respectively and then removed entirely between the three North American states as part of the North American Free Trade Agreement. When automakers began to explore trying to reduce the regulatory trade barriers between Europe and North America in relation to consumer safety, activists were able to portray those barriers as preventing needless death and thus were able to prevent their reduction. Throughout the auto case, government officials played an active but varying role, with their behavior being best explained by their relative prioritization of trade versus regulatory autonomy, their staffing, and who they considered their core constituencies.

In the beef case analyzed in this study, after the Japanese government badly mishandled the country's response to its first case of mad cow disease in 2001, it instituted the world's strictest countermeasures against bovine spongiform encephalopathy, regulations that applied to U.S. beef after the United States had its first BSE case in 2003. Those regulations amounted to regulatory trade barriers for U.S. beef producers, because it inhibited their market access or would have raised their production costs if they had wanted to maintain that access. So those producers lobbied U.S. officials to try to pressure Japanese officials to relax their regulatory approach. Japanese consumer groups were effective at defending the regulatory barriers throughout the 2000s because they could portray those barriers as preventing the spread of BSE and, by extension, variant Creutzfeldt-Jacob disease, a deadly, incurable illness. The competitiveness of Japanese businesses was unthreatened by the regulatory trade barriers of that period.

Once the United States signed a free trade agreement with South Korea, Japanese businesses feared that their competitiveness in the U.S. market would be undermined if Japan was not able to complete a free trade deal with the United States. That reducing the BSE-related regulatory trade barriers would be a key demand of the United States as the price of starting negotiations of such an agreement led those businesses to advocate for reducing the barriers in order to maintain their competitiveness. By this point, the overall number of global BSE cases had fallen significantly, so consumer groups were both less animated and less effective on the issue. As a result, Japanese officials were able to relax the regulatory standards that had presented such a problem for U.S. beef producers.

In the beef case as in the auto one, when regulatory trade barriers were reduced, businesses making competitiveness claims were a key driver of that reduction. When regulatory trade barriers were increased or maintained, activists making claims for preventing needless death were a key factor. Once again, government officials played a key role in the negotiations, with their stances being driven by the same factors as in the auto case.

Finally, in the pharmaceutical case, Western drug firms were able to successfully advocate for the Agreement on Trade-Related Aspects of Intellectual Property Rights, which reduced the differences between states' IP regulations by requiring that all members of the World Trade Organization adopt what were essentially U.S. standards on IP. The firms were able to do this because they were able to effectively tie that request to broader concerns about their and U.S. competitiveness. They were aided in their effort by the fact that access-to-medicine activists were not yet engaged on the issue.

In the negotiations surrounding the Doha Declaration, access-to-medicine activists were able to achieve a major victory and reinforce policy space allowing developing states to implement a greater range of IP regulations. Activists were able to do this by framing the stringent IP regulations in TRIPS as contributing to the AIDS crisis and thus causing needless death. After the declaration, three issues leftover from the negotiations engaged both drug companies and access activists, who fought to a draw. Meanwhile, India employed creative regulations that differ significantly from U.S. standards but are still TRIPS-compliant. They have not used those novel regulations as much as one might initially expect, however, because Indian officials have wanted to side with both access advocates and businesses.

In the negotiations for the Free Trade Area of the Americas, access advocates in Brazil were able to portray agreement to U.S. IP demands as a threat to Brazil's program of universal access to HIV medication. Meanwhile, because of U.S. intransigence on agricultural liberalization, the Brazilian businesses that might have been able to counter that framing with competitiveness-based claims were unable to do so. In Central American countries, the opposite happened, with respect to negotiations of the Central America Free Trade Agreement. Firms were able to make competitiveness claims, while activists there were much less effective.

In the pharmaceutical case as in the auto and beef cases, government officials sometimes sided primarily with firms, sometimes sided primarily with activists, and sometimes took up positions between them, based on factors outlined in chapter 3. The trajectory of all three cases undermines state-centric explanations. In all the cases, the stances the states take are not preordained; they are driven by the demands and lobbying of domestic societal actors. In short, throughout all three cases, regulatory trade barriers were reduced when firms could connect their desire for that reduction with concerns around competitiveness. Those barriers were maintained when consumer safety activists could connect their defense of those barriers with preventing needless death.

Questioning Cleavage-Based Explanations

As I discussed in chapter 2, the increasing extent to which international trade negotiations involve national domestic regulations has fundamentally altered the politics of trade by bringing in activists that previously were uninterested in trade negotiations. As I pointed out in all three case studies, the involvement of those actors and the importance of the stances that government officials take on regulatory trade barriers mean that the cleavage-based explanations of trade politics are no longer sufficient. In the case of European emissions standards, the division that occurred was not between economic winners and losers but between a sector (automakers) that had an economic stake and a sector (environmentalists) that wanted to prioritize noneconomic public policy goals. Such positions also characterized the negotiations around intercontinental regulatory trade barriers related to consumer safety. The same was true for the regulatory wrangling between Japanese consumer organizations and American beef producers. The negotiating faultline there was not between commercial winners and commercial losers from trade but between actors with material commercial motivations and actors with nonmaterial normative motivations. That division was continuously the major fault line in the pharmaceutical case as well. As regulatory barriers become more and more central to trade negotiations, we are likely to see that division with greater regularity. Indeed, Alasdair Young found that the division between activists and multinational businesses, rather than an economic cleavage-driven division, best described the negotiations over the Transatlantic Trade and Investment Partnership.[1]

Given the centrality of the cleavage-based explanations to understanding trade politics, their weakness in the cases examined in this study presents a major challenge but also a significant opportunity. It is a challenge because if those giant shoulders can no longer be stood upon, new theories of trade politics must be constructed. It is an opportunity because it allows future researchers to critically question many of the assumptions made in twentieth-century scholarship and ask whether they still hold today.

Rogowski divided society into three groups based on which factor of production they possessed: landowners, capital holders, and laborers. Hiscox sharpened Rogowski's work by adding another economic factor to the mix, asset specificity. Regulation brings whole new noneconomic factors into play in trade politics. Given their introduction, is division that is based solely on economic endowments still the most useful way to conceptualize groups in society? Economic factors certainly continue to have leverage, and I do not mean to suggest otherwise (owners of mobile capital still have quite different interests from relatively immobile laborers), but perhaps regulation requires us to rethink how we conceptually divide society. In this study, I have divided it in one particular way—between businesses, activists, and government officials. But that division is certainly not the only way to conceive of the actors in trade politics.

Disguised Protectionism Is Less Common Than Is Often Presumed

I found the dynamic of disguised protectionism most surprising over the course of this project. I began the research for this book with a background presumption that regulatory trade barriers are driven by disguised protectionism. That is an intuitive story, but as the evidence continually contradicted my prior beliefs, I became convinced that those beliefs were misguided.

Time and again in the case studies in this book, when regulatory trade barriers were increased or defended, those barriers were not simply disguised forms of protectionism. The regulatory barriers related to emissions that Denmark and the Netherlands tried to create were clearly not at the behest of a domestic automaker, since neither of those countries even had domestic automakers. In the United States, domestic automakers fought hard against regulatory barriers related to domestic content; when they did seek protection from Japanese automakers, the protectionism they asked for took the form of nonregulatory quota-based restraints. The environmental regulations in NAFTA were demanded not by automakers seeking protectionism but by activists seeking noneconomic policy goals. The same could be said of the safety-related regulatory barriers that continue to impede the transatlantic auto trade.

With regard to beef, the Japanese government repeatedly went out of its way to reduce the trade impact of its regulations. After the initial outbreak of BSE in Japan in 2001, the Japanese government exempted U.S. beef from the regulations it imposed on domestic firms. Even after the initial U.S. outbreak of BSE, Japanese officials did not require that U.S. suppliers implement the kind of traceability programs required in Japan. The Japanese government also allowed for an exception that allowed meat from cattle slaughtered before 30 months of age to be sold. In pharmaceuticals, the actors defending and promoting regulatory trade barriers were always access-to-medicine advocates, not drug companies.

None of the preceding evidence against disguised protectionism is dispositive by itself. Collectively, however, it suggests that the background presumption that disguised protectionism is the core driver of regulatory trade barriers needs to be questioned. In chapter 3, I explained why the disguised protectionism argument is a less effective explanation than may be apparent.

Activists' Political Power

This study underscores just how much political power activists actually have. Popular conceptions of lobbying often presume that business interests are the powerhouses and that activists are the underdogs. This book suggests that activists succeed in their opposition to business more often than that popular conception implies.

In the case of cars, environmentalists in the European Community were able to win increases in emissions standards. In North America, they won environmental improvements in Mexico via NAFTA. Consumer activists were successful at raising the safety standards of Mexican trucks and at blocking transatlantic regulatory barrier reductions. Japanese consumer advocates were able to promote strict anti-BSE policies and to defend them even against considerable U.S. pressure. That those regulatory barriers were only reduced when the consumer advocates were satisfied testifies to the strength of those activists. In pharmaceuticals, activists achieved a sweeping success in the Doha Declaration, which bolstered states' ability to use IP regulatory flexibilities, such as compulsory licenses, to promote public health. They have successfully resisted attempts by drug firms to limit which diseases count as national emergencies and to use nonviolation complaints. They efficiently promoted creative, TRIPS-compliant regulatory flexibilities that have effectively relaxed IP regulations in developing countries, such as India. Finally, they also played a vital role in the FTAA negotiations between the United States and Brazil.

In all 25 subcases analyzed in this book, businesses only dominated in the domestic content regulations for the North American auto industry and in the TRIPS and CAFTA negotiations regarding pharmaceuticals. Everywhere else, activists had a meaningful amount of political power and at least some success in advancing their goals. That material interests are important in the international political economy is beyond dispute, but I hope this book has shown that nonmaterial, noneconomic considerations matter a great deal too in the politics around regulation and trade. Activists' power points to the power and significance of nonmaterial interests and nonmaterial framings. Every instance in which activists had some success exemplifies the importance of nonmaterial framing.

Theoretical Implications for IPE Scholarship

This book has five other implications for IPE scholarship on trade. It qualifies the California effect. It highlights the growing importance of national courts in international trade politics. It helps explain the rise of regionalism. It clarifies the trade policy options that developing countries have. Finally, it points to emerging vectors in the U.S.-China relationship.

Qualifying the California Effect

The cases analyzed in this study suggest three conditions under which the California effect is more or less likely. First, the smaller state in the trade negotiation has to actually want the agreement more than the larger state. The key causal mechanism in the California effect is market size. The state with the larger market is able to use the potentially lucrative access to that market as leverage in the trade negotiation. Market size is not, however, the only potential political leverage that may exist. If the state with the smaller market is less eager to seal the agreement than the larger state, the smaller state has much more relative leverage. In the pharmaceutical case, developing countries were much less eager than the United States to revive the flagging Doha talks to negotiate issues leftover from the Doha Declaration. The United States was thus less able to use its market size as leverage to raise IP regulations, which short-circuited market power as a causal mechanism that can create a California effect.

Second, a California effect is less likely to happen if the firms whose market access is being impeded by regulatory barriers believe they can get the state with the higher standards to lower those regulations. If that is the case, they may choose to fight barriers rather than to accept them and then promote higher standards. Such a fight occurred in the beef case, when U.S. producers believed they could get the U.S. trade representative to pressure Japanese regulators to reduce anti-BSE regulations inhibiting U.S. exports.

Third, a California effect is less likely if access narratives override protection narratives. Calls for more-stringent regulation flow from a desire to protect consumers from risky products. But when consumers are more concerned with promoting access to a good, consumer advocates who would normally enthusiastically pursue higher regulations do not do so. Because narratives of access have predominated among Mexican car purchasers, there has not been a California effect bringing consumer safety regulations in Mexico to match U.S. safety standards. Narratives of access have also predominated IP discussions in developing countries, bolstering resistance to higher IP regulations there as well.

The Growing Importance of National Courts in International Trade Politics

Now that trade agreements involve national regulations, courts can have indirect but powerful effects on trade, by affecting those regulations. In the beef case, that Japanese consumers were less able than their American counterparts to seek redress and recompense through courts made them more eager for strict regulations. Their eagerness was the foundation of the resilience of the regulatory barriers that impeded imports of U.S. beef. In the auto case, the inability of the National Highway Transportation Safety Administration to use a type-approval system was rooted in the U.S. tradition of adversarial legalism and led to the NHTSA's recall system. The differences between the EU's type-approval system and the U.S. recall system is the foundation of many of the differences the two regions have on consumer safety in automobiles. In the pharmaceutical case, a U.S. Supreme Court case on patent injunctions bolstered India's policy space to implement less-stringent IP regulations. As long as trade politics involves regulations, it involves courts.

Courts may thus be required to increasingly think about how other states have adjudicated an issue and about the effect their rulings may have on foreign jurisdictions. Indeed, U.S. Supreme Court justice Stephen Breyer argues that jurists must now be constitutional diplomats, carefully weighing how international politics affect their decisions and how their decisions affect international politics.[2] In this endeavor, however, courts must be careful not to overinvolve themselves in international matters in ways that could both add to their already full dockets and invite heightened international tensions. They must also be wary of their potential to be perceived as illegitimate lawmakers. Citizens already do not like when judiciaries behave like activist judges; that would likely only grow worse if activist judges operated from a foreign court.

The Rise of Regionalism

Since the 1990s, regional trade agreements have proliferated at a remarkable rate. Economists have generally been skeptical of such agreements and have argued that the growth of regionalism is inferior to multilateral liberalization and undermines multilateralism.[3] As Greg Anderson points out, noneconomic reasons account for why regional trade liberalization is growing despite its inferiority to multilateralism in terms of efficiency.[4] Anderson lists motivations that drive states to liberalize trade regionally: geopolitical imperatives, the desire to solidify partner states' economic reforms, the desire to help developing countries, and the increasing difficulty of collective action problems as negotiating groups grow larger.[5] To that list, we can add the growing importance of regulatory trade barriers.

In principle, it is usually easier to reach agreement among a smaller group of states, but the inclusion of once-excluded domestic actors and greater sensitivity over regulations make agreement an even more acute obstacle than would otherwise be the case. Exhibit A on this is the Doha Round. As I explained in chapter 2, it has been clear since the mid-2000s that the round would not result in substantive trade liberalization in the regulatory barriers that developed states would like to target. Thus, developed states have pursued trade liberalization bilaterally and regionally. In other words, one of the central trends in international trade, the rise of regionalism, can be traced to the increasing importance of regulatory barriers and the politics that surround them.

This study also suggests that the trend toward regionalism, rather than multilateralism, is unlikely to reverse itself. As I argued throughout this book, businesses are at their most effective in seeking reduced regulatory trade barriers when they can connect their pursuit of that goal with broader concerns about competitiveness. That connection is more difficult to make at the multilateral level. The argument that a regional trade deal makes the states within that region more competitive vis-à-vis states outside the region has a certain intuitive appeal. It becomes much more difficult to make that argument if the deal is at the WTO level, as such an agreement would include nearly all countries. Everyone cannot simultaneously become more competitive.

Developing Countries' Options

In exchange for concessions on agriculture and textiles, developed countries would likely insist on greater regulatory constraints on developing countries. In the Doha Round, developed states asked for that basic exchange when they pushed for reductions of regulatory trade barriers in the Singapore issues (investment, competition, government procurement, and trade facilitation). Once they could not get barrier reductions in those areas, developed states refused to offer concessions on agriculture and textiles. Such exchange has also been the basic bargain in regional trade deals. In the Trans-Pacific Partnership, Malaysia and Vietnam would have gained greater access in Japanese and North American agriculture and textile markets in exchange for agreeing to greater regulatory constraints in IP, competition rules, investment, human rights enforcement, labor standards, environmental protection, and health and safety standards.

For developing countries to get more agricultural liberalization, they have three options. First, they can continue to push for it through the WTO and accept movement on the Singapore issues, but that option seems unlikely. The second option is to accept inclusion into regional trade deals involving developed states. The third option would be for developing countries to construct a new trade agreement among themselves. Tariffs remain much higher between developing countries than between developed and developing countries. As developing countries become more prosperous and more populous, the gains from trade between them is likely to continue increasing.[6] Reducing tariffs can promote economic growth in developing countries, especially in sub-Saharan Africa, by helping those countries engage in global supply chains and greater intra-industry trade.[7] A 2018 free trade deal in Africa holds out a lot of promise but can be taken much further.[8] Furthermore, a trade agreement focused on tariffs in the Global South would mean that developing countries could benefit from trade liberalization without having to undermine their regulatory flexibility. The second and third options are not mutually exclusive. Developing countries could continue to join regional trade agreements when and where they choose and, at the same time, work toward greater trade liberalization between their states.

The U.S.-China Relationship

The economic relationship between the United States and China is likely to be one of the most important dynamics in global politics for the foreseeable future. The scope and trajectory of that relationship could obviously occupy a whole series of books, and I will not try to encapsulate all facets of it here. The political negotiations over regulatory barriers in each of the three industries analyzed in this book point to a significant aspect of that relationship.

Cars

The auto industry highlights the potential rewards for successfully entering the Chinese market. The Chinese auto market is now the largest in the world.[9] From 2004 to 2014, the annual growth in the Chinese auto industry averaged 11.4 percent, versus growth in North America, Europe, and Japan of 0.9, 1.4, and –0.5 percent respectively.[10] The Chinese market is expected to grow another 20 percent, to 30 million cars sold annually, by 2020, which represents a significant portion of overall global growth.[11] The expansion opportunity for automakers is in China.

That opportunity comes with challenges, particularly in relation to differences in consumer tastes. Beyond obvious taste differences, such as Chinese buyers' greater preference for subcompact cars, are less obvious differences about which automakers should remain vigilant. For example, surveys have shown that Chinese consumers are much more particular than their American counterparts about what smell fabrics and other interior materials in a new car should have.[12] Significant differences in consumer tastes were one of the key factors that undermined automakers' desire to pursue regulatory convergence in safety standards between the United States and Europe. For that reason, automakers may want to consider not pursuing regulatory convergence with China on matters of taste.

Given the increasing number of cars on Chinese roads and the concomitant deterioration of air quality in Chinese cities, China's emission regulations are likely to become much tougher, very soon. In fact, Ford chief executive officer Mark Fields believes that China's environmental regulations on cars will be the strictest in the world at some point in the next five years.[13] Automakers would do well not to resist an increase in emissions standards but simply to ask for standards to be set in a high, uniform way. If and when China raises its emissions standards, that increase could be an excellent opportunity to promote a mega-sized California effect.

Similar rewards and challenges can be seen in other industries. The wealth and size of the Chinese middle class is continually expanding; there are now more people considered middle class in China than in the United States.[14] Urban Chinese consumers' disposable income was expected to grow from $4,000 to $8,000 dollars from 2010 to 2020.[15] The share of the middle class that lives in inland China was expected to triple from 13 to 39 percent from 2010 to 2020.[16] Middle-class consumers are a key market for firms selling everything from laptops to laundry softener. One of the major challenges for those companies is China's slough of regulatory barriers that sometimes impede companies' ability to reach the middle-class market.[17]

In other words, the single biggest commercial opportunity for countless firms is directly connected to regulatory trade barriers. As I have argued, linking a reduction of regulatory barriers with economic competitiveness has been the most effective means of seeking a reduction in those barriers. Joint ventures between multinational corporations and Chinese firms, as well as other means of more tightly intertwining the Chinese economy with the global economy, may best portray reductions of regulatory barriers as boosting Chinese competitiveness and convince Chinese leaders to reduce them.[18]

Beef

Trade in beef underscores how difficult it will be for the United States to impose its preferences on China. In December 2003, when the first case of BSE was discovered in the United States, China closed its market to imports of U.S. beef, just as Japan did. Whereas the Japanese market was gradually reopened to U.S. beef, the Chinese market was not. Well past the time when Japan had relaxed its opposition to U.S. beef, China was still refusing to allow imports of U.S. beef unless it put in place a traceability system, which we saw U.S. producers refuse to do in the Japan case.[19] In 2017, China announced that it would allow imports of beef from cattle less than 30 months, but it still required traceability.[20] Even by 2017, only 15 percent of U.S. beef producers could meet those traceability requirements, so that market reopening was greatly constrained.[21]

The reduction in mad cow cases and the relaxation of Japanese consumers was crucial to the reopening of the Japanese market, but another important factor was that Japanese businesses were concerned about losing competitiveness in the U.S. market relative to their Korean rivals. The United States was able to use that market power and the lure of the TPP to get those Japanese businesses to lobby for a reduction in the regulatory barriers in beef.

The United States does not have that kind of leverage over the Chinese government. To the contrary, China's rapidly increasing demand for beef gives it market leverage over U.S. beef producers. As a result of that market leverage in many consumer markets, not just beef, China has a much greater ability to set regulatory standards that differ from other states and still get businesses to comply. Australian beef producers, for instance, have been happy to abide by Chinese regulations in order to gain access to such a large and lucrative market.[22] That trend can be seen in other sectors as well.[23] Traditionally, the United States and the European Union have been the global powerhouses in regulation and trade. China has become a third pole.

Drugs

The pharmaceutical trade and the general IP issue point to the tension created by the competition and shared interests between the United States and China. In June 2012, the Chinese government amended their country's IP regulations to facilitate a greater use of compulsory licenses in cases of epidemics like SARS and Ebola, though, at least through 2019, it had not actually issued a compulsory license.[24] China is determined to become a global leader in pharmaceutical research; from 2004 to 2012, its annual spending on research and development in pharmaceuticals increased tenfold, to $1.1 billion.[25] That spending is still small by Western standards, and the Chinese pharmaceutical industry still mostly specializes in drug ingredients rather than new medicines, but China's investments in pharmaceutical R&D is likely to grow even more, and its companies are set to become more oriented toward advanced research and patented drugs. As that happens, Chinese firms not only will be the direct competitors of Western firms but will want IP protected, so China's stance on IP is likely to increasingly complement, rather than contradict, America's IP preferences.

IP is not the only area in which China is trying to catch up to the United States. In 2012, a group of Chinese nationals employed by agricultural companies in China was arrested for trying to smuggle cutting-edge genetically modified corn seeds, being developed by Monsanto and DuPont, out of the United States.[26] The group was attempting to steal those companies' IP, with the complicity of the Chinese government, so that China could increase its corn production without having to either compensate the American companies for the use of their technology or invest millions in research the way those companies had.[27] On the one hand, China and the United States both have an interest in the use of these hybrid seeds increasing, so that China and other countries can more efficiently feed their growing populations. On the other hand, the smuggling attempt was blatant corporate espionage.

In many instances, Chinese companies have attempted to steal American companies' branding. Nike, Apple, and many other firms have had their branding copied by Chinese imitators.[28] The copycats are in direct competition with the Western firms that want their IP rights upheld. That kind of competitive clash is occurring in the automotive sector. Via Tesla and BYD, the United States and China are locked in fierce competition to establish an edge in the fast-growing and potentially revolutionary market in electric vehicles.[29] Across many areas, businesses in China and the United States—and, by extension, the two countries—are in direct competition.

Despite that competition, China and the United States often have more in common in terms of IP than is usually assumed. Not long ago, China was a capital-poor country that specialized in making cheap imitations of other countries' innovations. That image becomes less accurate by the day; China is increasingly a hotbed of technological innovation in its own right.[30] China's innovative growth not only increases the quality of Chinese goods exported to other countries but also encourages entrepreneurs, programmers, and engineers to work in China.[31] As China becomes more innovation-centric rather than imitation-centric, its desire to protect IP will become more aligned with the IP preferences of the United States. China and the United States are likely to be the two most economically and politically powerful states in the twenty-first century. They may never be close allies, and their relationship could be in for some rocky moments, but they both have an interest in a stable Middle East, a prosperous Africa, calm financial markets, and alleviating climate change, to name just a few areas. How they handle IP regulations and trade may be a good bellwether of how well they can handle other issue areas in which their interests overlap somewhat though not entirely.

Examining Cases Not Covered in This Book

There are, of course, other cases of negotiations over regulatory barriers. The findings from the cases examined in this book may help explain the outcomes in those negotiations too. One of the first high-profile negotiations over a regulatory barrier concerned hormones in beef. The controversy started when Italian officials linked developmental abnormalities in babies to hormones given to livestock.[32] That link would later be discredited, but European consumers at that time believed that banning hormones in beef would protect children. Such a ban would not have made European beef more competitive, because Europe already had a surplus of beef.[33]

Genetically modified organisms have been banned in the EU but allowed in the United States. Activists pushed for that regulatory barrier because it came on the heels of a number of food safety crises, including dioxin in Belgian meat and chocolate, contaminated soda (again in Belgium), and, most seriously, the peak of the mad cow crisis.[34] As I mentioned in chapter 2, that crisis discredited the idea that combining regulatory harmonization with trade liberalization would improve Europeans' quality of life. EU consumers believed that the deaths that resulted from the mad cow crisis were preventable and that a new expansion of trade in an agricultural product suspicious to them was another disaster waiting to happen; David Vogel points out, "Although there was no link between GMOs and the BSE crisis, European consumers connected the two."[35]

The business most interested in trading in GMOs, Monsanto, was an American company and could not make a competitiveness-based argument. Furthermore, if GMOs raised productivity, the subsidies given to farmers under the EU's Common Agricultural Policy would also have increased; EU officials did not want that.[36] Interestingly and not coincidentally, the three areas where EU authorities made exceptions to their anti-GMO stance involved three industries in which European companies are internationally competitive and wanted to use genetically modified enzymes: cheese, wine, and beer.[37] In shipping, firms in states with high standards were able to raise international shipping standards by arguing to government officials in those states that raised, uniform standards would create a balanced playing field in which their competitiveness would not be undermined by more unscrupulous shippers.[38] Businesses have used similar arguments to reduce regulatory barriers in telecommunications.[39]

Applying the Lessons from This Study to a Different Industry: The Case of Toys

The dynamics surrounding the political negotiations over regulatory barriers discussed in this book hold lessons for other industries too, including, but not limited to, chemicals, textiles, coffee, diamonds, cocoa, minerals, gold, wood, cosmetics, electronics, and toys. Rather than discuss how this study applies to all those industries, I will focus on just the last. The toy industry depends on economies of scale and product differentiation and is hampered by regulatory trade barriers that impede toymakers' market access or raise their production costs.

LEGO's CEO has spoken of his firm as "operating globally, on a vertical integration from basic manufacturing to global distribution," and as wanting "to see the world in three vertical regions: the Americas, Europe/the Middle East/Africa, and then obviously Asia so we're looking to have a manufacturing hub in each of the three regions."[40] He is not alone in that desire. The U.S. Toy Industry Association was eager to pursue reduction in regulatory trade barriers in the Transatlantic Trade and Investment Partnership and will likely be so again if TTIP negotiations restart.[41] If toymakers want to reduce regulatory barriers, they must engage their respective trade representatives to negotiate those reductions, and the most effective rhetorical strategy that they are likely to have is that foreign regulatory barriers make them uncompetitive.

Toymakers should take care, though, to ensure that the reductions they call for will not be seen to endanger children. Greenpeace was able to increase regulatory stringency in Europe on phthalates (chemicals that make plastics softer), which, in turn, created regulatory barriers between the United States and Europe by emphasizing the risks phthalates in toys posed to children.[42] Given the sensitivity parents have regarding the safety of their kids, it must be indisputable that the toy industry's efforts to reduce regulatory trade barriers will have no negative consequences on children's safety. Such indisputability is likely to be especially important for firms, such as Mattel, that conduct much of their production in countries, such as China, that have spotty records in safety standards.[43]

It seems unlikely that government officials would marginalize consumer groups in toys to the extent that North American officials ignored labor unions in the case involving the auto industry. Therefore, if toymakers want to reduce regulatory barriers, they must accommodate consumer groups in the manner that automakers in Europe and North America accommodated environmentalists. Accommodating consumers was also critical in the beef case, where regulatory barriers were reduced only after Japanese consumer groups were satisfied with the safety of U.S. beef. One lesson for consumer advocates is that they should not refuse to participate in negotiations. Such refusal did Canadian labor groups no favors in NAFTA. Advocates should also remain uncommitted to a trade deal rather than implacably opposed. Being uncommitted helped American environmentalists get what they wanted in NAFTA. Being resolutely opposed contributed to labor getting ignored.

Recommendations to Businesses, Activists, and Government Officials

The political recommendations that this section offers to businesses, activists, and government officials in the automotive, beef, and pharmaceutical industries are based on this book's analyses of cases in those industries.

Cars

Automakers

Automakers had perhaps the most unalloyed victory reported in this book when they convinced North American government officials to reduce regulatory trade barriers related to domestic content. Manufacturers did so by connecting their interests to broader concerns about competitiveness. That connection is their strongest rhetorical tool. There are other policy areas where states' differing regulations could be portrayed as unfairly harming U.S. automakers' and, by extension, U.S. competitiveness.

As the American Automotive Policy Council has pointed out, Japan has historically maintained an array of investment and distribution regulations that have made it the most closed auto market in the Organization for Economic Cooperation and Development.[44] Portraying those investment and distribution regulations as curbs on competitiveness can be an especially effective way to argue for regulation reduction. Those regulations cannot easily be portrayed as saving lives and protecting consumers. Japanese activists are unlikely to consider distribution and investment issues salient and are thus unlikely to fight U.S. automakers' attempts at reducing the regulatory barriers concerned with those issues.

Automakers should beware challenging Japan's safety regulations as nontariff measures, however. It would be very easy for a Japanese consumer group to portray those regulations as preventing needless death. As this book's beef chapter demonstrated, Japanese consumer safety advocates can be highly effective at defending regulatory barriers in such scenarios. That defense would put U.S. automakers in a difficult position, forcing them to preemptively prove that the regulatory changes they seek will not harm anyone, which would be difficult to definitively prove at the outset. Of all of the regulatory barriers hampering their access to the Japanese market, automakers should challenge those linked to preventing needless death last, if at all.

Consumer Safety Advocates

Consumer safety advocates who want to defend such regulatory trade barriers as those existing between the United States and the European Union must emphasize sovereignty concerns and the extent to which those regulatory differences save lives. For a few auto parts, such as seat belt anchors, in which equivalent effectiveness between U.S.-regulated parts and EU-regulated parts has been proven, there is no safety cost associated with mutual recognition or regulatory harmonization. However, for many other parts, there is not sufficient evidence to prove equivalency. In fact, tests done by a team of research centers based in the United States and the EU have shown that European-regulated vehicles are safer in side and front collisions while U.S.-regulated vehicles are safer in rollovers.[45] It would not be difficult for European consumer groups to argue that reducing transatlantic regulatory barriers would endanger European drivers in collisions, while American consumer groups could as easily argue that reducing those barriers would endanger Americans in rollover crashes.[46] Moreover, given the diminishing marginal returns to scale, the difficulty of implementing just-in-time inventory systems intercontinentally, and the diverging consumer preferences between regions (discussed in chapter 4), reducing those production differences through regulation would not be a boon to automakers' competitiveness anyway.

Environmentalists

When environmentalists advocate raising some regulatory standard to promote environmental protection, they present automakers with a trade-off pitting compliance costs against company reputation. If that new regulatory standard comes with high compliance costs and if environmentalists cannot convince automakers that opposing a new standard will significantly hurt the automakers' reputations, as happened with emissions regulations in Europe from 1983 to 1988, the automakers oppose it. If compliance is cheap and the reputational consequences severe, as they were in 1989 and 1990 in the European case, the automakers accept the new standard and abide by it.

Environmentalists should not focus solely on reputation. Naming and shaming has been an effective strategy in many policy areas, but it is not the only effective strategy. As I mentioned in chapter 3, environmentalists have been able to engage in a wide variety of strategic interplay with firms, and there is significant evidence that when they have designed standards for which compliance is cheaper, they have been more effective at eliciting cooperation from business and thus protecting the environment.[47]

Environmentalists can work not only to undermine some firms' arguments that compliance with environmental regulations makes them uncompetitive but also to appropriate the competitiveness frame altogether. Michael Porter has argued that firms and the states they are based in can become more competitive if those firms are pressured to innovate.[48] Environmental regulations apply such pressure. By pushing firms to innovate to meet higher standards, environmental regulations can make those companies more internationally competitive, not less. Environmental rules can create more wealth than compliance of them costs. For example, by preventing millions of lost work and school days, by preventing premature deaths, and by reducing health care spending, the Clean Air Act is estimated to have created $12 trillion in net economic benefits from 1990 to 2020.[49]

Labor Unions

This study's first recommendation for unions regards rhetorical strategy. The most politically powerful argument in defense of regulatory barriers, that their reduction would lead to needless death, is not available to unions. Therefore, unions' best strategy is a defensive one: undermine the competitiveness arguments made by firms seeking to reduce regulatory barriers. To reduce domestic content regulation that unions prized, automakers successfully linked reduction with societal concerns about competitiveness. To protect their interests, unions must dispel competitiveness arguments by emphasizing the strong evidence that worker involvement in decision-making through unions and work councils boosts productivity and enhances the competitiveness of a plant and company.[50]

This study's second implication for labor unions is that personnel is policy. Which officials are involved in trade negotiations has a big impact on those negotiations. For navigating that impact, labor unions could learn from this book's beef chapter. In 2004–5, the resilience of Japan's position on BSE regulations was reinforced by the fact that the universal testing policy was overseen by Japan's Food Safety Commission (an independent, politically insulated panel of experts) rather than by that country's Ministry of Agriculture or the Ministry of Health, both of which could more easily have been pressured to relent to U.S. demands. One of the factors that promoted a later reduction in the BSE-related regulatory barriers was that negotiations over those barriers became linked to other trade issues, so that the Ministry of Industry and Trade, which is pro-liberalization, was in charge of the trade negotiations, rather than the Ministry of Agriculture, which is more protectionist.

Labor unions can apply the lesson learned from the beef case by being strategically creative in terms of promoting differing jurisdictional understandings, specifically by getting the U.S. Department of Labor involved in trade negotiations. Such a maneuver would not be totally unprecedented. A recent decision by the Department of Labor suggests a possible route that labor unions might take. For decades, financial advisers were not required to put their clients' interests first when giving them financial advice and could guide clients toward products that gave incentives to advisers, such as bonuses and trips. Consumer advocates pushed for a rule, known as the fiduciary standard, requiring financial advisers to give advice based on what is best for the client. The financial industry opposed that rule, and the Securities and Exchange Commission, which traditionally has had a close relationship with the financial industry, refused to move forward. The Department of Labor, which does not have that kind of cozy relationship with the financial industry and asserted that it too had jurisdiction on the issue, instituted the fiduciary standard.[51] Labor unions, which are usually protectionist, typically have not found a favorable hearing before the Office of the U.S. Trade Representative (USTR), as it is pro-trade. If labor unions can convince the Department of Labor to insert itself into trade negotiations, based on the idea that trade involves that department's jurisdictional prerogatives, then perhaps labor unions will have an ally in those trade negotiations.

Government Officials in the NHTSA and Europe

For regulators on both sides of the Atlantic, this book suggests that automakers will likely continue to request greater regulatory cooperation but that mutual recognition or regulatory harmonization will be a tough sell, given the concerns of consumer safety advocates and the power of the rhetoric surrounding preventing needless death. The major implication of the situation is that part-by-part negotiations seem the best way forward. The current collaboration over the two part types where equivalency has been proven, seat belt anchors and visibility equipment, provide a model for the painstaking way in which regulatory cooperation should proceed.[52]

Beef

Activists Concerned about Food

The biggest implication of this study for activists in food pertains to focus. In short, they should concentrate less on GMOs and more on heart disease and climate change. As yet, there is no definitive scientific evidence that GMOs are harmful to humans.[53] Relatedly, it is difficult to show a tangible, direct way in which GMOs have hurt anyone. The reason that preventing unnecessary death is such a powerful rhetorical tool is that death is highly tangible and motivates risk aversion. The alleged risks associated with GMOs remain hypothetical.

A more favorable opportunity for the food consumer movement to push for better regulation is in the connection between meat, especially beef, and public health. Meat consumption is directly connected with heart disease, the leading killer globally.[54] The causal chain between using regulations to reduce meat consumption and preventing needless death is clear and direct.

Consumer advocates should focus on the connection between meat and climate change. Livestock are responsible for 15 percent of greenhouse gas emissions, equivalent to the emissions of all vehicles.[55] Beef is particularly carbon-intensive.[56] Environmentalists are wary that appearing to dictate people's consumption might elicit backlash, but poll respondents appear less reluctant to address climate change if businesses appear to be the entities bearing the costs.[57] Pushing for regulations that require meat producers to minimize their carbon footprint could be not only good policy but good politics.

The USDA

The USDA should adopt a more flexible position toward firms, such as Creekstone, that want to institute standards that exceed federal requirements. That department should also adopt a more consumer-centric perspective. Its stance on carbon monoxide in beef packaging is a good example of a policy that needs to change. For years, U.S. meat producers were losing sales because consumers were bypassing meat that, though still safe to eat, had lost the bright red color that people associate with freshness.[58] One way to alleviate that problem was to inject the meat with carbon monoxide. In 2002, the USDA approved the use of carbon monoxide in beef for that purpose.[59] There are no requirements that packages of meat be labeled as treated with carbon monoxide.[60] The treatment does not preserve the meat's freshness, only its color; in fact, carbon monoxide may accelerate bacteria growth if the meat is stored improperly.[61]

Carbon monoxide helps beef keep its bright red color for much longer than it otherwise could.[62] Ingesting meat treated with carbon monoxide is not harmful in the way the gas can be when inhaled; the treatment itself does not make the consumer ill.[63] But because the carbon monoxide keeps the meat appearing fresh even after it has spoiled, consumer groups fear that it may lead some buyers to eat spoiled beef, which can make them very ill.[64] Producers have responded that consumers will abide by sell-by dates and thus not inadvertently eat spoiled meat even if it is red and that consumers do not care if the meat they purchase is treated with carbon monoxide.[65]

Even if that use of carbon monoxide does not contribute to making people sick (an open question), it is a deceptive business practice. It fools consumers into thinking meat is fresh when it may not be. For this reason, some retailers (e.g., Wegmans, Publix, and Meijer) refuse to sell meat treated with carbon monoxide.[66] That abstention, though, is not nearly as extensive as a USDA prohibition on the use of carbon monoxide in beef would entail. That use creates an unnecessary regulatory difference between the United States, Japan, and the European Union. Japan and the EU ban the practice because it deceives consumers, while the United States allows the practice because it protects industry profits.[67] The U.S. government can, in one stroke, adopt a more consumer-friendly position and reduce a regulatory trade barrier.

Drugs

Pharmaceutical Companies

This study suggests how drug companies can more effectively defend high IP regulations to the general public. Drug firms did not have to gain the reputation they did. Cigarette firms profit from products that kill people. Drug companies provide products that save lives. There was no preordained reason why drug manufacturers had to gain a negative image. To reverse it, the pharmaceutical industry should shift how it justifies high IP regulations, emphasize the high-paying jobs the industry creates, highlight the cost savings it delivers, and police itself more thoroughly.

First, drug companies should justify their preference for high IP regulations through personal stories rather than through statistics and abstract logic regarding incentives to innovate. The argument for preventing needless death works because it makes an issue clear and salient. That argument was used by access-to-medicine advocates to fight for lower IP regulations, but it can also be used by drug companies to defend higher regulations. Stories sell. Access-to-medicine advocates were able to paint drug companies as villainous because they were able to tell a story of company greed costing lives. To reverse that image, drug companies need to tell the story of how their actions save lives. Drug companies have, on many occasions in their advertising, featured real people who could have died without that company's drug; they could double-down on that strategy and be more explicit in asserting that they would not have been able to invent the life-saving drug without stringent IP regulations. The newest wave of hepatitis C drugs, such as Sovaldi and Harvoni, are perfectly tailored for such campaigns. Gilead Sciences should be making a compelling story out of people they have cured of hepatitis C.

Second, the pharmaceutical industry should emphasize the number of high-paying jobs and foreign direct investment that the industry brings to states. The competitiveness argument is so effective because it comes with an implied promise of jobs and prosperity. No government officials in the United States, India, or Europe want to be held responsible for costing their constituencies lucrative jobs. All officials want to be able to brag about bringing in those jobs. In the pharmaceutical case analyzed in this study, the competitiveness argument was key to drug firms' ability to advance their interest, and that salience is likely to remain. In 2008, the CEO of Pfizer encapsulated that kind of sales pitch to Washington in three short sentences: "The protection of intellectual property equals innovation. Innovation equals competitiveness. Competitiveness equals jobs."[68] Based on the cases studied in this book, that message works and is one that it is in the best interests of the pharmaceutical companies to keep repeating.

Third, drug firms should emphasize the money they save the health care industry and the overall economy. Prescription drugs account for 9 percent of all health care spending in the United States,[69] while hospital care accounts for 32 percent.[70] By preventing more expensive procedures, such as transplants and extended hospital stays, drug companies save the overall system a great deal of money. Relatedly, the drug industry should emphasize that it, not NGOs, created the portfolio of miraculous drugs now available. One observer reckons that at today's cheap generic-level prices, a person can buy a set of drugs that have more medical utility than all drugs, patented or generic, that existed in 1995.[71] Of course, drug companies' profit-driven motives contributed to today's market, but perhaps no industry demonstrates better than pharmaceuticals how effective capitalism can be at harnessing greed for social good.[72]

Fourth, the pharmaceutical industry needs to police itself much more robustly. When executives like Martin Shkreli radically increase the price of a monopoly-controlled generic drug like Daraprim, such greed makes the entire industry look bad. He is only the most visible example. Questcor Pharmaceuticals raised the price of a drug for multiple sclerosis from $40 to $28,000, an increase of 70,000 percent.[73] Other medicines, such insulin and EpiPens, have seen significant price increases due to anticompetitive practices, despite being off-patent. Drug firms' adoption of such anticompetitive strategies as pay-for-delay schemes also hurts the industry's image. When firms engage in such behaviors, they undermine public confidence in the high IP regulations that are the source of the firms' profit. As Pfizer CEO Ian Read put it in 2014, "Unless we're respected by society, unless we're seen as good stewards of our resources, then we run the risk of losing both patents and losing the ability to price our medications."[74]

To curtail anticompetitive behaviors, the drug industry needs to create a mechanism to enforce good practices among all manufacturers. On such a goal, drug firms could learn from the legal profession. Lawyers who violate what the bar association says is acceptable practice can lose their ability to practice. That mechanism benefits the entire profession. Drug companies could form a pharmaceutical bar association and, with the help of government, compel all firms to abide by a set of good practices, including, though not limited to, no pay-for-delay schemes, no sudden price spikes for generic drugs that have no substitute, and low prices for off-patent medicines such as insulin.

If the pharmaceutical industry does not police itself better, it will find that it loses even more esteem in the eyes of the public. That esteem can only fall so far before the public stops believing that IP regulations enabling profits for the drug industry are good for society, rather than just a handout to a well-connected but morally bankrupt industry. Should that shift in public esteem happen, pharmaceutical companies may find that their ability to set prices becomes as constrained in the United States as it is in other developed countries.

Access-to-Medicine Advocates

If access-to-medicine advocates want to reduce the stringency of IP regulations, they must be able to demonstrate that new breakthrough medicines can be developed and guided through the approval process without the patent system on which the pharmaceutical industry is built. Through whatever means they choose (perhaps university-funded basic research followed by prize pools for applied research followed by NGO leadership through the approval process), advocates must be able to show that a system not based on patents can promote just as much innovation as the current system. Until they can do that, they will consistently run into the concern that reducing IP regulations, as the activists want to do, will slow medical innovation and ultimately cost lives.

Access advocates who can drive a wedge between other businesses and drug companies on costs may be successful in promoting a reduction of IP regulations on drugs.[75] In the United States, the average annual contribution a business made to a family health plan through employee insurance in 2015 was $12,591.[76] Access-to-medicine advocates who can convince businesses that the high cost of health insurance is partly due to the high cost of patented medicines may gain powerful allies. They are likely to have even more success if they can paint those costs as undermining the international competitiveness of U.S. businesses. Drug companies' most powerful rhetorical tool is the narrative that high IP regulations on drugs make American business more competitive. Access-to-medicine advocates are more likely to win if they can weaken or appropriate the power of that narrative.

Officials in the USTR

The USTR should make its processes more transparent and more inclusive, by having a more diverse set of cleared advisers and making negotiating texts public during negotiations. As I discussed in chapter 3, cleared advisers are allowed to view confidential negotiating texts. Firms have had many representatives named cleared advisers; however, when asked about cleared advisers from nonbusiness groups, a USTR spokesperson could not name a single cleared adviser from a public interest group or activist NGO.[77] Even to someone who accepts the need for strong IP protection, the current revolving door between IP-intensive firms and the USTR reeks of cronyism.

The concern limiting necessary change is that allowing activists to see negotiation texts would jeopardize talks because those activists would leak the documents. Choosing cleared advisers from more moderate NGOs, such as the Natural Resources Defense Council, can alleviate that concern. On the IP issue, Doctors Without Borders is fairly moderate and accepts the need for patents to incentivize innovation. Excluding such groups from negotiations makes enemies unnecessarily. Bringing them into the process could win them over and dilute opposition to trade deals, as happened with environmentalists in NAFTA. Allowing environmentalists access resulted in stricter provisions but won the support of moderate environmental NGOs, which gave Democrats political cover to vote for NAFTA.[78]

Bringing in activists might help the reputation of the USTR by showing that the office often takes a balanced approach. For example, during the TPP negotiations, the USTR took the most pro-environment stance of any negotiating team.[79] The reason that there are not more environmental provisions in the TPP is not because the USTR betrayed environmentalists but because developing countries, such as Vietnam and Malaysia, opposed those provisions.[80]

The secrecy and exclusivity currently surrounding negotiations are not helping. They have led many observers, including congressmen, to believe that the secrecy of trade negotiations is meant to shroud nefarious intent.[81] If the TPP really was as good as the USTR said it was, people may ask, why did so much secrecy surround it? The public now expects much more transparency than it once did. The days of secrecy being tolerated are over. The USTR should make negotiating texts publicly available during trade negotiations. There is no clear evidence that secrecy strengthens one's negotiating position.[82] In fact, transparency might be used to credibly signal that a government cannot abandon a position due to domestic pressure.

There are some examples of transparency upgrades in other trade institutions. The World Intellectual Property Organization conducts its negotiations on public webcasts and has given a wide variety of stakeholders access.[83] The EU published drafts of its negotiating positions in the TTIP. Negotiating transparently would be different from the way things have traditionally been done but not impossible. Even if a given trade agreement does have benefits, the USTR should only push for that agreement if it has broad societal buy-in and accompanying legitimacy. Including activists in trade talks and making those negotiations more accessible might make trade deals more difficult to conclude but would make them more likely to be ratified.

Concluding Remarks

As states' economies grow more interconnected, regulatory trade barriers cannot help but grow in importance. The political negotiations that surround them affect the safety and cost of the products consumers buy. They affect how much a state can export and, thus, the number of export-oriented jobs in that state. They affect the extent to which trade helps or hurts the environment. They affect how workers get treated. All of these issues are hugely consequential and are greatly affected by the politics of regulatory barriers.

At the beginning of this book, I mentioned the regulatory trade barriers that influence airbags, the U.S.-China pork trade, and PD-1 inhibitors. Those barriers affect the health outcome of car crashes in the United States and Europe, the affordability and quality of the meat a Chinese family puts on its table, and, globally, how quickly new medicines can be created and how costly they are. Those regulatory barriers may affect whether you personally survive a car crash or cancer. Regulatory trade barriers are everywhere around us, and once they stop being abstract and technical, once the central role they play in the global economy and in everyone's daily life becomes clear, their significance becomes inescapable.

Notes

CHAPTER 1

1. "Why Cars from Europe and the US Just Can't Get Along," *Planet Money*, episode 533, National Public Radio, April 18, 2014.

2. Ibid.

3. "Empire of the Pig," *Economist*, December 20, 2014.

4. "Pork Facts," National Pork Producers' Council, accessed May 1, 2016, http://www.nppc.org/pork-facts/

5. Arlene Weintraub, "UPDATED: Merck's Melanoma 'Game-Changer' Keytruda Likely to Bolster Drug Pricing Debate," *FiercePharma*, September 5, 2014, http://www.fiercepharma.com/pharma/updated-merck-s-melanoma-game-changer-keytruda-likely-to-bolster-drug-pricing-debate

6. Nick Stockton, "How Prescription Drugs Get So Wildly Expensive," *Wired*, September 23, 2015; Carolyn Johnson and Brady Dennis, "How an $84,000 Drug Got Its Price: 'Let's Hold Our Position Whatever the Headlines,'" *Washington Post*, December 1, 2015.

7. "U.S., TPP Countries Mull Compromise on Biologics Data Exclusivity," *Inside U.S. Trade*, August 7, 2015.

8. "U.S., Australia Float Joint Biologics Text to Other Countries for Vetting," *Inside U.S. Trade*, October 4, 2015.

9. World Trade Organization, *World Trade Report 2012: Trade and Public Policies; A Closer Look at Non-tariff Measures in the 21st Century*, Geneva (2012) 3.

10. Ronald Rogowski, *Commerce and Coalitions: How Trade Affects Domestic Political Alignments* (Princeton: Princeton University Press, 1989); Michael Hiscox, *International Trade and Political Conflict: Commerce, Coalitions, and Mobility* (Princeton: Princeton University Press, 2002).

11. The present study does not focus on land, labor, and capital. I bring Rogowski's work up here as an exemplar of the kind of trade politics analysis that centers on the cleavages between economic winners and losers.

12. Peter Gourevitch, *Politics in Hard Times: Comparative Responses to International Economic Crises* (Ithaca: Cornell University Press, 1986); Paul Midford, "International Trade and Domestic Politics," *International Organization* 47, no. 4 (1993): 535–64.

13. For the first camp, see Dani Rodrik, *The Globalization Paradox: Democracy and the Future of the World Economy* (New York: W. W. Norton, 2011); Joseph Stiglitz, *Making Globalization Work: The Next Steps to Global Justice* (London: Penguin, 2006); Eric Helleiner and Andreas Pickel, eds., *Economic Nationalism in a Globalizing World* (Ithaca: Cornell University Press, 2005); David Vogel and Robert Kagan, eds., *Dynamics of Regulatory Change: How Globalization Affects National Regulatory Policies* (Berkeley: University of California Press, 2004). For the second camp, see Miles Kahler and David Lake, eds., *Governance in a Global Economy: Political Authority in Transition* (Princeton: Princeton University Press, 2003); Daniel Drezner, "Globalization and Policy Convergence," *International Studies Review* 3, no. 1 (2003): 55, 65–75.

14. Daniel Drezner, *All Politics Is Global: Explaining International Regulatory Regimes* (Princeton: Princeton University Press, 2007), 25–26. On case studies, see Alexander George and Andrew Bennett, *Case Studies and Theory Development in the Social Sciences* (Cambridge, MA: MIT Press 2005); Stephen Van Evera, *Guide to Methods for Students of Political Science* (Ithaca: Cornell University Press, 1997), 49–88.

15. James Shoch, *Trading Blows: Party Competition and U.S. Trade Policy in a Globalizing Era* (Chapel Hill: University of North Carolina Press, 2001), 44–46; Margaret Keck and Kathryn Sikkink, *Activists beyond Borders: Advocacy Networks in International Politics* (Ithaca: Cornell University Press, 1998), 5–6.

16. Drezner, *All Politics Is Global*; Tim Büthe and Walter Mattli, *The New Global Rulers: The Privatization of Regulation in the World Economy* (Princeton: Princeton University Press, 2011); Shoch, *Trading Blows*; Susan Aaronson, *Trade and the American Dream: A Social History of Postwar Trade Policy* (Lexington: University of Kentucky Press, 1996); Aaronson, *Taking Trade to the Streets: The Lost History of Public Efforts to Shape Globalization* (Ann Arbor: University of Michigan Press, 2001).

17. Yannick Lung and Rob van Tulder, "Introduction: In Search of a Viable Automobile Space," in *Cars, Carriers of Regionalism?*, ed. Jorge Carrillo, Yannick Lung, and Rob van Tulder (New York: Palgrave Macmillan, 2004), 10.

18. On hormones, see William Kerr and Jill Hobbs, "The North American–European Union Dispute over Beef Produced Using Growth Hormones: A Major Test for the New International Trade Regime," *World Economy* 25, no. 2 (2002): 283–96; David Vogel, *The Politics of Precaution: Regulating Health, Safety, and Environmental Risks in Europe and the United States* (Princeton: Princeton University Press, 2012), 54–62. On GMOs, see Mark Pollack and Gregory Shaffer, *When Cooperation Fails: The International Law and Politics of Genetically Modified Foods* (Oxford: Oxford University Press, 2009); Grant Isaac and William Kerr, "Genetically Modified Organisms at the World Trade Organization: A Harvest of Trouble," *Journal of World Trade* 37, no. 6 (2003): 1083–95.

19. The data reported is for 2017 and drawn from World Trade Organization, Statistics Database, Merchandise Trade by Commodity, accessed May 1, 2019. https://timeseries.wto.org/

20. "Restrictions on U.S. Beef to Be Eased," *Yomiuri Shimbun*, September 6, 2012.

21. The "California Effect" is David Vogel's argument on how, rather than creating a race to the bottom, trade can encourage states to raise their environmental and consumer safety standards. The effect is discussed in more detail in chapter 3.

CHAPTER 2

* This chapter is based on Gary Winslett, "How Regulations Became the Crux of Trade Politics," *Journal of World Trade* 50, no. 1 (2016): 47–70.

1. Steven Vogel, "Why Freer Markets Need More Rules," in *Creating Competitive Markets: The Politics of Regulatory Reform*, ed. Marc Landy, Martin Levin, and Martin Shapiro (Washington, DC: Brookings Institution, 2007), 25–42.

2. Dani Rodrik, "Why Do More Open Economies Have Bigger Governments?," *Journal of Political Economy* 106, no. 5 (1998): 997–1032.

3. This paragraph draws on Charan Devereaux, Robert Lawrence, and Michael Watkins, *Case Studies in U.S. Trade Negotiations, vol. 2, Resolving Disputes* (Washington, DC: Institute for International Economics, 2006), 6–7.

4. On intra-industry trade, see Mary Anne Madeira, "The New Politics of the New Trade: The Political Economy of Intra-Industry Trade," in *Handbook of the International Political Economy of Trade*, ed. David Deese (Northampton, MA: Edward Elgar, 2014), 113–34; Howard Marvel and Edward Ray, "Intraindustry Trade: Sources and Effects on Protection," *Journal of Political Economy* 95, no. 6 (1987): 1278–91.

5. "Why Cars from Europe and the US Just Can't Get Along," *Planet Money*, episode 533, National Public Radio, April 18, 2014.

6. David Vogel, *Trading Up: Consumer and Environmental Regulation in a Global Economy* (Cambridge, MA: Harvard University Press, 1995), 27–28.

7. Ibid., 28–29.

8. This paragraph draws on ibid., 30–35.

9. Helen Milner, *Resisting Protectionism: Global Industries and the Politics of International Trade* (Princeton: Princeton University Press, 1988).

10. Susan Aaronson, *Taking Trade to the Streets: The Lost History of Public Efforts to Shape Globalization* (Ann Arbor: University of Michigan Press, 2001), 101–6.

11. James Shoch, *Trading Blows: Party Competition and U.S. Trade Policy in a Globalizing Era* (Chapel Hill: University of North Carolina Press, 2001), 81–83, 98–107; I. M. Destler, *American Trade Politics*, 4th ed. (Washington, DC: Institute for International Economics, 2005), 81–83.

12. David Vogel, "Consumer Protection and Protectionism in Japan," *Journal of Japanese Studies* 18, no. 1 (1992): 119–54.

13. Clyde Haberman, "Japanese are Special Types, They Explain," *New York Times*, March 6, 1988.

14. Peter Edelman, "Japanese Product Standards as Non-tariff Barriers: When Regulatory Policy Becomes a Trade Issue," *Stanford Journal of International Law* (1987–88): 391–92.

15. Charan Devereaux, Robert Lawrence, and Michael Watkins, *Case Studies in U.S. Trade Negotiations, vol. 1, Making the Rules* (Washington, DC: Institute for International Economics, 2006), 48.

16. Ibid.

17. Ibid., 49–58.

18. Susan Sell, *Private Power, Public Law: The Globalization of Intellectual Property Rights* (Cambridge: Cambridge University Press, 2003), 94–108.

19. Staiger and Sykes, who make the point that the WTO's TBT and SPS agreements do a good job of constraining regulatory discrimination, argue that these agreements do not do much to constrain what they consider "excessive nondiscriminatory regulation." Robert Staiger and Alan Sykes, "International Trade, National Treatment, and Domestic Regulation," *Journal of Legal Studies* 40, no. 1 (2011): 149–203. In many ways, that lack in constraint is precisely the point. The TBT and SPS do not hold economic efficiency as their only goal; they also aim for policy autonomy. Moreover, activists would likely defend the higher regulations that are protected by this policy autonomy as not excessive at all. In earlier work, Bagwell and Staiger noted that the further the WTO wades into at-the-border measures, the more potential it has to constrain national sovereignty. Kyle Bagwell and Robert Staiger, "National Sovereignty in an Interdependent World" (working paper 10249, National Bureau of Economic Research, Cambridge, MA, 2004). Again though, with regard to regulation, the TBT and SPS are attempts at avoiding such constraint.

20. D. Vogel, *Trading Up*, 196.

21. Destler, *American Trade Politics*, 257. The 1980s also saw a linkage between labor standards and trade in certain commodities, such as tin (1981), cocoa (1986), sugar (1987), and rubber (1987). John Braithwaite and Peter Drahos, *Global Business Regulation* (Cambridge: Cambridge University Press, 2000), 234.

22. Of course, this was not the first time that there was a link between trade and human rights.

23. Lizabeth Cohen, *A Consumer's Republic: The Politics of Mass Consumption in Postwar America* (New York: Vintage Books, 2003), 345–87.

24. Matthew Hilton, *Consumerism in Twentieth-Century Britain* (Cambridge: Cambridge University Press, 2003), 241, 279–97; Gunnar Trumbull, "Consumer Policy: Business and the Politics of Consumption," in *The Oxford Handbook of Business and Government*, ed. David Coen, Wyn Grant, and Graham Wilson (Oxford: Oxford University Press, 2010), 631–37.

25. Steven Vogel, "When Interests Are Not Preferences: The Cautionary Tale of Japanese Consumers," *Comparative Politics* 31, no. 2 (1999): 190; Patricia Maclachlan, *Consumer Politics in Postwar Japan: The Institutional Boundaries of Citizen Activism* (New York: Columbia University Press, 2002), 111–40, 175–200.

26. David Vogel, *The Politics of Precaution: Regulating Health, Safety, and Environmental Risks in Europe and the United States* (Princeton: Princeton University Press, 2012), 54–62.

27. Ibid., 238.

28. D. Vogel, *Trading Up*, 60–63.

29. D. Vogel, *Trading Up*, 112–17. For the advertisement showing "GATTzilla" crushing a dolphin, see Daniel Esty, *Greening the GATT: Trade, Environment, and the Future* (Washington, DC: Institute for International Economics, 1994), 34, or the cover of Aaronson's *Trade and the American Dream* (1996). The Tuna-Dolphin case was one of the major reasons U.S. environmentalists were highly engaged in the

politics surrounding NAFTA even though they had not been particularly engaged in the Canada-U.S. Free Trade Agreement.

30. For a review of the weak empirical support for the race to the bottom, see Daniel Drezner, *All Politics Is Global: Explaining International Regulatory Regimes* (Princeton: Princeton University Press, 2007), 14–17.

31. Aaronson, *Taking Trade to the Streets*, 139.

32. Ibid., 177.

33. Frederick Mayer, *Interpreting NAFTA: The Science and Art of Political Analysis* (New York: Columbia University Press, 1998), 165–204.

34. Sheila Jasanoff, "Civilization and Madness: The Great BSE Scare of 1996," *Public Understanding of Science* 6, no. 3 (1997): 221–32.

35. Alberto Alemanno, "Food Safety and the Single European Market," in *What's the Beef? The Contested Governance of European Food Safety*, ed. Christopher Ansell and David Vogel (Cambridge, MA: MIT Press, 2006), 243.

36. D. Vogel, *Politics of Precaution*, 72, 76; Mark Pollack and Gregory Shaffer, *When Cooperation Fails: The International Law and Politics of Genetically Modified Foods* (Oxford: Oxford University Press, 2009), 64–68.

37. Gunnar Trumbull, *Strength in Numbers: The Political Power of Weak Interests* (Cambridge, MA: Harvard University Press, 2012), 151–52.

38. For example, when U.S. citizens were asked what percentage of Chinese imports they believed violate American safety standards, the mean guess was 45 percent. Gallup Poll, August 2007, retrieved August 17, 2015, from iPOLL Databank, Roper Center for Public Opinion Research, University of Connecticut.

39. Michael Trebilcock and Robert Howse, *The Regulation of International Trade, 3rd ed.* (New York: Routledge 2005), 203.

40. Democracy Corps / Campaign for America's Future Poll, November 2008, retrieved November 24, 2014, from iPOLL Databank, Roper Center for Public Opinion Research, University of Connecticut, Storrs.

41. Susan Aaronson and Jamie Zimmerman, *Trade Imbalance: The Struggle to Weigh Human Rights Concerns in Trade Policymaking* (Cambridge: Cambridge University Press, 2007), 151–52, 162–63.

42. Evgeny Postnikov, "The Design of Social Standards in EU and US Preferential Trade Agreements," in Deese, *Handbook of the International Political Economy of Trade*, 531–49.

43. "Support in Principle for U.S.-E.U. Trade Pact: But Some Americans and Germans Wary of TTIP Details," Pew Research Center, April 9, 2014.

44. Andrew Moravcsik, *The Choice for Europe* (Ithaca: Cornell University Press, 1998), 314–78.

45. This mechanism is weaker at reducing regulatory barriers where the science is contested.

46. Braithwaite and Drahos, *Global Business Regulations*, 407–8.

47. Aaronson, *Taking Trade to the Streets*, 110–15; Michael Hart, Bill Dymond, and Colin Robertson, eds., *Decision at Midnight: Inside the Canada-US Free-Trade Negotiation* (Vancouver: University of British Columbia Press, 1994).

48. D. Vogel, *Trading Up*. For a review of a number of other works that also demonstrate the rarity of businesses fleeing to jurisdictions with more lax standards, see Drezner, *All Politics Is Global*, 14–17.

49. Jayson Myers, president of Canadian Manufacturers and Exporters, quoted in Barrie McKenna, "In Cross-Border Trade Rules, a Whiff of Pointlessness," *Globe and Mail*, February 14, 2011.

50. Christina Davis, *Food Fights over Free Trade: How International Institutions Promote Agricultural Trade Liberalization* (Princeton: Princeton University Press, 2005), 1–13.

51. Trebilcock and Howse, *Regulation of International Trade*, 472. Pietra Rivoli, *The Travels of a T-Shirt in the Global Economy*, 2nd ed. (Hoboken: John Wiley, 2009), 170.

52. Jane Kelsey, "The Trans-Pacific Partnership Agreement: A Gold-Plated Gift to the Global Tobacco Industry?" *American Journal of Law and Medicine* 39 (2013): 237–64.

53. Winslett, Gary. "How Regulations Became the Crux of Trade Politics." *Journal of World Trade*, 50, no. 1, 68.

54. James Hookway, "U.S. Trade Aspirations Could Spark Backlash in Malaysia," *Wall Street Journal*, April 26, 2014.

55. "The Trans-Pacific Partnership: Undermining Food Safety," Public Citizen, accessed May 1, 2016, https://www.citizen.org/article/undermining-food-safety/

56. Consumers Union, "Letter to the U.S. Trade Representative," April 30, 2014; Sean Flynn, Brook Baker, Margot Kaminski, and Jimmy Koo, "The U.S. Proposal for an Intellectual Property Chapter in the Trans-Pacific Partnership Agreement," *American University International Law Review* 28, no. 1 (2012): 105–202.

57. "Why TPP Matters." U.S. Business Coalition for the TPP, May 1, 2016.

58. "Trans-Atlantic Trade and Investment Partnership," United States Chamber of Commerce, Accessed May 1, 2016. https://www.uschamber.com/issue-brief/trans-atlantic-trade-and-investment-partnership

59. Winslett, Gary. "How Regulations Became the Crux of Trade Politics." *Journal of World Trade*, 50, no. 1, 69.

60. "Consumers at the Heart of the Transatlantic Trade and Investment Partnership" (position paper, BEUC: The European Consumer Organisation, Brussels, May 21, 2014); "Letter to USTR and European Commission: EU and US Consumer Groups Initial Reaction to the Announcement of a Transatlantic Trade and Investment Partnership," *Transatlantic Consumer Dialogue*, March 5, 2013.

CHAPTER 3

1. John Braithwaite and Peter Drahos, *Global Business Regulation* (Cambridge: Cambridge University Press, 2000), 401, 407–8.

2. Shujen Wang, "Recontextualizing Copyright: Piracy, Hollywood, the State, and Globalization," *Cinema Journal* 43, no. 1 (2003): 25–43.

3. John Braithwaite and Peter Drahos, *Information Feudalism: Who Owns the Knowledge Economy* (New York: New Press, 2002), 68–71.

4. Michael Conroy, *Branded! How the "Certification Revolution" Is Transforming Global Corporations* (Gabriola Island, BC: New Society Publishers, 2007), 63–79.

5. Wyn Grant, "Government Environmental Policy and the Chemical Industry," in *The Global Chemical Industry in the Age of the Petrochemical Revolution*, ed.

Louis Galambos, Takashi Hikino, and Vera Zamagni (Cambridge: Cambridge University Press, 2007), 114–37.

6. Since this project is concerned with the approach of businesses to regulatory trade barriers, it largely bypasses the voluminous literature on corporate political activity more broadly, except where it specifically relates to regulatory barriers. For a useful review of the literature on corporate political activity, see Amy Hillman, Gerald Keim, and Douglas Schuler, "Corporate Political Activity: A Review and Research Agenda," *Journal of Management* 30, no. 6 (2004): 837–57.

7. On NTT, see Paul Krugman, "Scale Economies, Product Differentiation, and the Pattern of Trade," *American Economic Review* 70, no. 5 (1980): 950–59; James Markusen and Anthony Venables, "Multinational Firms and the New Trade Theory," *Journal of International Economics* 46 (1998): 183–203; Paul Krugman, "Increasing Returns and Economic Geography," *Journal of Political Economy* 99, no. 3 (1991): 483–99; James Tybout, "Plant and Firm-Level Evidence on 'New' Trade Theories" (working paper 8418, National Bureau of Economic Research, Cambridge, MA, 2001).

8. David Hanson, *Limits to Free Trade: Non-tariff Barriers in the European Union, Japan, and the United States* (Northampton, MA: Edward Elgar, 2010), 3–4.

9. OECD, WTO, and World Bank, "Global Value Chains: Challenges, Opportunities, and Implications for Policy," joint report prepared for the G20 Summit, July 19, 2014; Gary Gereffi, John Humphrey, and Timothy Sturgeon, "The Governance of Global Value Chains," *Review of International Political Economy* 12, no. 1 (2005): 78–104; Ranier Lanz and Sebastien Miroudot, "Intra-Firm Trade: Patterns, Determinants, and Policy Implications" (OECD Trade Policy Papers 114, OECD Publishing, Paris, 2011).

10. Mary Anne Madeira, "New Trade, New Politics: Intra-Industry Trade and Domestic Political Coalitions," *Review of International Political Economy* 23, no. 4 (2016): 677–711; Mark Manger, "Vertical Trade Specialization and the Formation of North-South PTAs," *World Politics* 64, no. 4 (2012): 622–58; Michael Gilligan, "Lobbying as a Private Good with Intra-Industry Trade," *International Studies Quarterly* 41, no. 3 (1997): 455–74.

11. Helen Milner and David Yoffie, "Between Free Trade and Protectionism: Strategic Trade Policy and a Theory of Corporate Trade Demands," *International Organization* 43, no. 2 (1989): 240–41, 245–46; Dale Murphy, *The Structure of Regulatory Competition: Corporations and Public Policies in a Global Economy* (Oxford: Oxford University Press, 2004), 18–19.

12. David Bach and Abraham Newman, "Governing Lipitor and Lipstick: Capacity, Sequencing, and Power in Pharmaceutical and Cosmetics Regulation," *Review of International Political Economy* 17, no. 4, (2010): 675.

13. Jack Ewing, "Carmakers Are Central Voice in U.S.-Europe Trade Talks," *New York Times*, July 14, 2014.

14. Helen Milner, *Resisting Protectionism: Global Industries and the Politics of International Trade* (Princeton: Princeton University Press, 1988).

15. Charan Devereaux, Robert Lawrence, and Michael Watkins, *Case Studies in U.S. Trade Negotiations, Vol. 1, Making the Rules* (Washington, DC: Institute for International Economics, 2006), 48.

16. Andrew Cortell, "Centralization, Access, and Influence: The Reagan Administration and the Semiconductor Industry's Trade Complaints," *Governance: An International Journal of Policy, Administration, and Institutions* 10, no. 3 (1997): 261–85.

17. J. Lawrence Broz and Seth Werfel, "Exchange Rates and Industry Demands for Trade Protection," *International Organization* 68, no. 2 (2014): 393–416. The findings of Broda, Limao, and Weinsteinon nontariff barriers also focus on non-regulatory NTBs, such as antidumping duties. Christian Broda, Nuno Limao, and David Weinstein, "Optimal Tariffs and Market Power: The Evidence," *American Economic Review* 98, no. 5 (2008): 2032–65.

18. Moonhawk Kim, "Disguised Protectionism and Linkages to the GATT/WTO," *World Politics* 64, no. 3 (2012): 426–75.

19. Daniel Kono, "Optimal Obfuscation: Democracy and Trade Policy Transparency." *American Political Science Review* 100, no. 3 (2006): 369–84.

20. On NNTT, see Marc Melitz, "The Impact of Trade on Industry Reallocations and Aggregate Industry Productivity," *Econometrica* 71, no. 6. (2003): 1695–1725; Andrew Bernard, Jonathan Eaton, Bradford Jensen, and Samuel Kortum, "Plants and Productivity in International Trade," *American Economic Review* 93, no. 4 (2003): 1268–90; Pol Antras and Elhanan Helpman, "Global Sourcing," *Journal of Political Economy* 112, no. 3 (2004): 552–80; Gianmarco Ottoviano, "'New' New Economic Geography: Firm Heterogeneity and Agglomeration Economies," *Journal of Economic Geography* 11 (2011): 231–40; Elhanan Helpman, Marc Melitz, and Stephen Yeaple, "Export versus FDI with Heterogeneous Firms," *American Economic Review* 94, no. 1 (2004): 300–316; Dan Ciuriak et al., "New-New Trade Policy" (working paper 1263, Economics Department, Queen's University, Kingston, Ontario, 2011).

21. On firm heterogeneity and trade, see especially Iain Osgood, "The Breakdown of Industrial Opposition to Trade: Firms, Product Variety, and Reciprocal Liberalization," *World Politics* 69, no. 1 (2017): 184–231.

22. Leonardo Baccini, Pablo Pinto, and Stephen Weymouth, "The Distributional Consequences of Preferential Trade Liberalization," *International Organization* 71, no. 2 (2017): 373–95; Mahmut Yaşar, "Political Influence of Export and Import-Competing Firms: Evidence from Eastern European and Central American Countries," *World Development* 51 (2013): 154–68.

23. J. Bradford Jensen, Dennis Quinn, and Stephen Weymouth, "The Influence of Firm Global Supply Chains and Foreign Currency Undervaluations on U.S. Trade Disputes," *International Organization* 69, no. 4 (2015): 913–47.

24. In Song Kim, "Political Cleavages within Industry: Firm-Level Lobbying for Trade Liberalization," *American Political Science Review* 111, no. 1 (2017): 1–20.

25. Alasdair Young, "Not Your Parents' Trade Politics: The Transatlantic Trade and Investment Partnership Negotiations," *Review of International Political Economy* 23, no. 3 (2016): 345–78; Ferdi De Ville and Gabriel Siles-Brügge, *TTIP: The Truth about the Transatlantic Trade and Investment Partnership* (Cambridge: Polity, 2016), 93–127.

26. Lyndsey Layton and Annys Shin, "Toymakers Assail Cost of New Law," *Washington Post*, December 21, 2008.

27. John Braithwaite and Peter Drahos, *Global Business Regulation* (Cambridge: Cambridge University Press, 2000), 265–66.

28. Murphy, *Structure of Regulatory Competition*, 45–71.

29. Osgood, "Breakdown of Industrial Opposition," 186.

30. Cornelia Woll and Alvaro Artigas, "When Trade Liberalization Turns into Regulatory Reform: The Impact on Business-Government Relations in International Trade Politics," *Regulation and Governance* 1 (2007): 126.

31. On intra-firm disagreements, see Brian Shaffer and Amy Hillman, "The Development of Business-Government Strategies by Diversified Firms," *Strategic Management Journal* 21, no. 2 (2000): 175–90; Woll and Artigas, "When Trade Liberalization Turns," 126–28.

32. Andrew Tucker, "Trade Associations as Industry Reputation Agents: A Model of Reputational Trust," *Business and Politics* 10, no. 1 (2008): 1–26.

33. Henry Farrell, "Constructing the International Foundations of E-Commerce: The EU-U.S. Safe Harbor Arrangement," *International Organization* 57, no. 2 (2003): 277–306.

34. "Nanomaterials, Sunscreens, and Cosmetics: Small Ingredients, Big Risks," Friends of the Earth, 2006; "Out of the Laboratories and on to Our Plates: Nanotechnology in Food and Agriculture," Friends of the Earth, 2008.

35. Greg Shaffer, "How the World Trade Organization Shapes Regulatory Governance," *Regulation and Governance* 9, no. 1 (2015): 1–15; Peter Van den Bosche, "NGO Involvement in the WTO: A Comparative Perspective," *Journal of International Economic Law* 11, no. 4 (2008): 717–49.

36. See, for example, Amy Quark, "Ratcheting Up Protective Regulations in the Shadow of the WTO: NGO Strategy and Food Safety Standard-Setting in India," *Review of International Political Economy* 23, no. 5 (2016): 872–98. In the EU, the officials may also be EU-level, given that many regulations are promulgated at that level.

37. Margaret Keck and Kathryn Sikkink, *Activists beyond Borders: Advocacy Networks in International Politics* (Ithaca: Cornell University Press, 1998), 12–13. There are, of course, some exceptions.

38. Keck and Sikkink, *Activists beyond Borders*, 150–64.

39. Sarah Stroup, *Borders among Activists: International NGOs in the United States, Britain, and France* (Ithaca: Cornell University Press, 2012), 3.

40. Goods that consumer seek out based on ethical characteristics are credence goods. On the interplay between activists and firms in credence goods, see Timothy Feddersen and Thomas Gilligan, "Saints and Markets: Activists and the Supply of Credence Goods," *Journal of Economic and Management Strategy* 10, no. 1 (2001): 149–71.

41. Susan Hadden, "Regulating Product Risks through Consumer Information," *Journal of Social Issues* 47, no. 1 (1991): 93–105.

42. Deborah Doane, "The Myth of CSR: The Problem with Assuming That Companies Can Do Well While Also Doing Good Is That Markets Don't Really Work That Way," *Stanford Social Innovation Review*, Fall 2005: 23-29.

43. David Vogel, "Private Regulation of Global Corporate Conduct," in *The Politics of Global Regulation*, ed. Walter Mattli and Ngaire Woods (Princeton: Princeton University Press, 2009).

44. Brayden King, "A Political Mediation Model of Corporate Response to Social Movement Activism," *Administrative Science Quarterly* 53, no. 3 (2008): 395–421.

45. Andrew Walter, "NGOs, Business, and International Investment: The Multilateral Agreement on Investment, Seattle, and Beyond," *Global Governance* 7, no. 1 (2001): 51–73.

46. Peter Newell, "Environmental NGOs, TNCs, and the Question of Governance," in *The International Political Economy of the Environment: Critical Perspectives*, ed. Dimitris Stevis and Valerie Assetto (Boulder: Lynn Reinner, 2001), 95–99.

47. Susan Sell and Aseem Prakash, "Using Ideas Strategically: The Contest between Business and NGO Networks in Intellectual Property Rights," *International Studies Quarterly* 48, no. 1 (2004): 163; "TPP Trade Deal Moves toward Completion, Threatening Access to Medicine for Millions," Doctors Without Borders, June 12, 2015.

48. David Vogel, *Trading Up: Consumer and Environmental Regulation in a Global Economy* (Cambridge, MA: Harvard University Press, 1995), 196–97.

49. Oklahoma State University, Department of Agricultural Economics, *Food Demand Survey*, vol. 2, no. 9, January 16, 2015, 4; John Deike, "Europe Installs Raw Milk Vending Machines While U.S. Rules Unpasteurized Dairy Illegal," EcoWatch, March 11, 2014.

50. "Support in Principle for U.S.-E.U. Trade Pact: But Some Americans and Germans Wary of TTIP Details," Pew Research Center, April 9, 2014.

51. Democracy Corps National–Public Citizen Poll, June 23–28, 2016. https://www.citizen.org/wp-content/uploads/greenberg-polling-memo-july-2016.pdf

52. Gallup / *USA Today* Poll, July 2007, and Gallup Poll, August 2007, both retrieved August 17, 2015, from iPOLL Databank, Roper Center for Public Opinion Research, University of Connecticut, Storrs.

53. Jonathan Watts, "Made in China: Tainted Food, Fake Drugs, and Dodgy Paint," *Guardian*, July 5, 2007.

54. James Van Alstine and Eric Neumayer, "The Environmental Kuznets Curve," in *Handbook on Trade and the Environment*, ed. Kevin Gallagher (Northampton, MA: Edward Elgar 2008), 49–59; Brian Copeland, "The Pollution Haven Hypothesis," in *Handbook on Trade and the Environment*, ed. Kevin Gallagher (Northampton, MA: Edward Elgar 2008), 60–70.

55. Daniel Esty, *Greening the GATT: Trade, Environment, and the Future* (Washington, DC: Institute for International Economics, 1994), 137–54; Michael Trebilcock and Robert Howse, *The Regulation of International Trade, 3rd ed.* (New York: Routledge 2005), 507–11; D. Vogel, *Trading Up*, 125–36; David Vogel, *The Politics of Precaution: Regulating Health, Safety, and Environmental Risks in Europe and the United States* (Princeton: Princeton University Press, 2012), 120–28.

56. D. Vogel, *Trading Up*, 110, 127, 139.

57. Der-Chin Horng, "The Human Rights Clause in the European Union's External Trade and Development Agreements," *European Law Journal* 9, no. 5 (2003): 677–701.

58. Philip Alston, "Labor Rights Provisions in U.S. Trade Law: Aggressive Unilateralism?," in *Human Rights, Labor Rights, and International Trade*, ed. Lance Compa and Stephen Diamond (Philadelphia: University of Pennsylvania Press, 2003), 71–95.

59. Gunnar Trumbull, *Strength in Numbers: The Political Power of Weak Interests* (Cambridge, MA: Harvard University Press, 2012), 26–29, 124–50.

60. Matthew Hilton, *Prosperity for All: Consumer Activism in an Era of Globalization* (Ithaca: Cornell University Press, 2009), 21–50; Lizabeth Cohen, *A Consumer's Republic: The Politics of Mass Consumption in Postwar America* (New York: Vintage Books, 2003), 345–87.

61. Bob Burgdorfer, "Heat's on COOL; U.S. Food Labeling Law Shakes Up All Producers," *National Post's Financial Post and FP Investing* (Canada), April 9, 2009; Susan Salisbury, "Where'd the Beef Come From? Gaps Cloud New Food-Labeling Law," *Palm Beach Post*, October 4, 2008.

62. D. Vogel, *Politics of Precaution*, 203–7.

63. Office of the United States Trade Representative, *2015 National Trade Estimate Report on Foreign Trade Barriers*, March 2015, 121–22.

64. Anthony Downs, "The Public Interest: Its Meaning in a Democracy," *Social Research* 29, no. 1 (1962): 12.

65. David Baron, "Private Politics, Corporate Social Responsibility, and Integrated Strategy," *Journal of Economics and Management Strategy* 10, no. 1 (2001): 7.

66. Samuel Barrows, "Racing to the Top . . . at Last: The Regulation of Safety in Shipping," in Mattli and Woods, *Politics of Global Regulation*, 200–202.

67. On issue framing in trade, see, among others, Matthew Eagleton-Pierce, "The Competing Kings of Cotton: (Re)framing the WTO African Cotton Initiative," *New Political Economy* 17, no. 3 (2012): 313–37; Quark, "Ratcheting Up Protective Regulations"; Michael Hiscox, "Through a Glass and Darkly: Attitudes toward International Trade and the Curious Effects of Issue Framing," *International Organization* 60, no. 3 (2006): 755–80; Edward Mansfield and Diana Mutz, "Support for Free Trade: Self-Interest, Sociotropic Politics, and Out-Group Anxiety," *International Organization* 63, no. 3 (2009): 425–57.

68. James Perry and Andreas Nolke, "The Political Economy of International Accounting Standards," *Review of International Political Economy* 13, no. 4 (2006): 559–86.

69. Walter Mattli and Ngaire Woods, "In Whose Benefit? Explaining Regulatory Change in Global Politics," in *Politics of Global Regulation*, 18; Tim Büthe and Nathaniel Harris, "Codex Alimentarius Commission," in *Handbook of Transnational Governance: New Institutions and Innovations*, ed. Thomas Hale and David Held (Cambridge: Polity, 2011), 219–28.

70. Kristen Hopewell, "Multilateral Trade Governance as Social Field: Global Civil Society and the WTO," *Review of International Political Economy* 22, no. 6 (2015): 1128–58.

71. Mary Douglas and Aaron Wildavsky, *Risk and Culture: An Essay on the Selection of Technological and Environmental Dangers* (Berkeley: University of California Press, 1983).

72. John Audley, *Green Politics and Global Trade: NAFTA and the Future of Environmental Politics* (Washington, DC: Georgetown University Press, 1997), 35.

73. On business attempts to win credibility through voluntary regulation, see Oren Perez, "Between Soft Law and Greenwash: The Compliance Dynamic of Civil Forms of Environmental Regulation," in *Handbook on the Politics of Regulation*, ed. David Levi-Faur (New York: Edward Elgar, 2011), 347–59.

74. David Baron, "The Industrial Organization of Private Politics," *Quarterly Journal of Political Science* 7, no. 2 (2012): 135–74.

75. Mary-Hunter McDonnell, Brayden King, and Sarah Soule, "A Dynamic Process Model of Private Politics: Activist Targeting and Corporate Receptivity to Social Challenges," *American Sociological Review* 80, no. 3 (2015): 654–78.

76. Tim Bartley, "Certifying Forests and Factories: States, Social Movements, and the Rise of Private Regulation in the Apparel and Forest Products Fields," *Politics and Society* 31, no. 3 (2003): 433–64; Philipp Pattberg, "What Role for Private Rule-Making in Global Environmental Governance? Analysing the Forestry Stewardship Council," *International Environmental Agreements* 5 (2005): 175–89.

77. Aseem Prakash and Matthew Potoski, *The Voluntary Environmentalists: Green Clubs, ISO 14004, and Voluntary Environmental Regulation* (Cambridge: Cambridge University Press, 2006); Philip Pattberg, "The Institutionalization of Private Governance: How Business and Nonprofit Organizations Agree on Transnational Rules," *Governance* 4 (2005): 589–610; Dennis Rondinelli and Ted London, "How Corporations and Environmental Groups Cooperate: Assessing Cross-Sector Alliances and Collaborations," *Academy of Management Executive* 17, no. 1 (2003): 61–76.

78. Newell, "Environmental NGOs," 91–94; Pattberg, "Institutionalization of Private Governance," 589–610.

79. On private regulations, see A. Claire Cutler, Virginia Haufler, and Tony Porter, eds., *Private Authority and International Affairs* (New York: State University of New York Press, 1999); David Vogel, "Private Global Business Regulation," *Annual Review of Political Science* 11 (2008): 261–82; Harm Schepel, *The Constitution of Private Governance: Standards in the Regulation of Integrating Markets* (Oxford: Hart, 2005); Jessica Green, *Rethinking Private Authority: Agents and Entrepreneurs in Global Environmental Governance* (Princeton: Princeton University Press, 2013).

80. Kenneth Abbott and Duncan Snidal, "The Governance Triangle: Regulatory Standards Institutions and the Shadow of the State," in Mattli and Woods, *Politics of Global Regulation*, 44, 52–54.

81. Ibid., 50–51.

82. David Baron and Daniel Diermeier, "Strategic Activism and Nonmarket Strategy," *Journal of Economics and Management Strategy* 16, no. 3 (2007): 599–634.

83. "Corporate Responsibility: Private Initiatives and Public Goals," OECD, 2001, 47–71.

84. On self-regulation, see Virginia Haufler, *A Public Role for the Private Sector: Industry Self-Regulation in a Global Economy* (Washington, DC: Carnegie Endowment, 2001).

85. David Baron, "Self-Regulation in Public and Private Politics," *Quarterly Journal of Political Science* 9, no. 2 (2014): 231–67.

86. Andrew King and Michael Lenox, "Regulation without Sanctions: The Chemical Industry's Responsible Care Program," *Academy of Management Journal* 43, no. 4 (2000): 698–716.

87. Abbott and Snidal, "Governance Triangle," 76–77.

88. Andreas Scherer and Guido Palazzo, "The New Political Role of Business in a Globalized World: A Review of a New Perspective on CSR and Its Implications for the Firm, Governance, and Democracy," *Journal of Management Studies* 48, no. 4 (2011): 901. On CSR more broadly, see David Vogel, *The Market for Virtue: The Potential and Limits of Corporate Social Responsibility* (Washington, DC: Brookings, 2005).

89. Julia Rotter, Peppi-Emilia Airike, and Cecilia Mark-Herbert, "Exploring Political Corporate Social Responsibility in Global Supply Chains," *Journal of Business Ethics* 125 (2014): 581–99; Jonathan Doh and Terrence Guay, "Globalization and Corporate Social Responsibility: How Non-governmental Organizations Influence Labor and Environment Codes of Conduct," *Management International Review* 44: 7–29; Axel Marx, "Limits to Non-state Market Regulation: A Qualitative Comparative Analysis of the International Sport Footwear Industry and the Fair Labor Association," *Regulation and Governance* 2 (2008): 253–73.

90. Rotter and Mark-Herbert, "Exploring Political Corporate Social Responsibility," 587–90.

91. Jose Miguel Abito, David Besanko, and Daniel Diermeier, "Corporate Reputational Dynamics, Private Regulation, and Activist Pressure," in *Strategy beyond Markets*, edited by Jose Miguel Abito, David Besanko, and Daniel Diermeier (Bingley: Emerald Group, 2016), 235–99.

92. J. Andrew Grant and Ian Taylor, "Global Governance and Conflict Diamonds: The Kimberley Process and the Quest for Clean Gems," *Round Table: Commonwealth Journal of International Affairs* 93, no. 375 (2004): 385–401.

93. Carola Kantz, "The Power of Socialization: Engaging the Diamond Industry in the Kimberley Process," *Business and Politics* 9, no. 3 (2007): 13–15.

94. Deborah Spar and Lane LaMure, "The Power of Activism: Assessing the Impact of NGOs on Global Business," *California Management Review* 45, no. 3 (2003): 78.

95. Tim Bartley, "Certification as a Mode of Social Regulation," in Levi-Faur, *Handbook on the Politics of Regulation*, 441–52; Conroy, *Branded.*

96. Conroy, *Branded*, 6–10.

97. Elliot Schrage and Anthony Ewing, "The Cocoa Industry and Child Labour," *Journal of Corporate Citizenship* 18 (2005): 99–112.

98. Conroy, *Branded*, 53–55, 242.

99. Ibid., 19–20.

100. David Singer, "Capital Rules: The Domestic Politics of International Regulatory Harmonization," *International Organization* 58, no. 3 (2004): 545–49.

101. Kathryn Sikkink, "Codes of Conduct for Transnational Corporations: The Case of the WHO/UNICEF Code," *International Organization* 40, no. 4 (1986): 815–40; Keck and Sikkink, *Activists beyond Borders*, 29.

102. David Coen, Wyn Grant, and Graham Wilson, "Political Science: Perspectives on Business and Government," in *The Oxford Handbook of Business and Government*, ed. David Coen, Wyn Grant, and Graham Wilson (Oxford: Oxford University Press, 2010), 10–11.

103. This paragraph draws on Mattli and Woods, "In Whose Benefit?," especially 15–16.

104. Miles Kahler and David Lake, "Economic Integration and Global Governance: Why So Little Supranationalism," in Mattli and Woods, *Politics of Global Regulation*, 268–73.

105. Martin Shapiro, "Administrative Law Unbounded: Reflections on Government and Governance," *Indiana Journal of Global Legal Studies* 8 (2001): 369–77.

106. Gene Grossman and Elhanan Helpman, "A Protectionist Bias in Majoritarian Politics," *Quarterly Journal of Economics* 120, no. 4 (2005): 1239–82; Susanne

Lohmann and Sharyn O'Halloran, "Divided Government and U.S. Trade Policy: Theory and Evidence," *International Organization* 48, no. 4 (1994): 595–632; Wendy Schiller, "Trade Politics in the American Congress: A Study of the Interaction of Political Geography and Interest Group Behavior," *Political Geography* 18, no. 7 (1999): 769–89; Daniel Nielson, "Supplying Trade Reform: Political Institutions and Liberalization in Middle-Income Presidential Democracies," *American Journal of Political Science* 47, no. 3 (2003): 470–91. For studies that disagree, see Ronald Rogowski and Mark Kayser, "Majoritarian Electoral Systems and Consumer Power: Price-Level Evidence from the OECD Countries," *American Journal of Political Science* 46, no. 3 (2002): 526–40; David Karol, "Does Constituency Size Affect Elected Officials' Trade Policy Preferences?," *Journal of Politics* 69, no. 2 (2007): 483–94.

107. Fiona McGillivray, "Party Discipline as a Determinant of the Endogenous Formation of Tariffs," *American Journal of Political Science* 41, no. 2 (1997): 584–607.

108. Tim Büthe and Walter Mattli, *The New Global Rulers: The Privatization of Regulation in the World Economy* (Princeton: Princeton University Press, 2011), 42–59.

109. Bach and Newman, "Governing Lipitor and Lipstick."

110. Susan Aaronson and Jamie Zimmerman. *Trade Imbalance: The Struggle to Weigh Human Rights Concerns in Trade Policymaking* (Cambridge: Cambridge University Press: Cambridge, 2007), 78–84.

111. Michael Moran has referred to these two impulses as the American government's smiling and snarling faces toward business. Michael Moran, "The Rise of the Regulatory State," in Coen, Grant, and Wilson, *Oxford Handbook of Business and Government*, 385–91. European Union government officials have their own set of competing impulses. Ibid., 395–97.

112. Steven Vogel, *Freer Markets, More Rules: Regulatory Reform in Advanced Industrial Countries* (Ithaca: Cornell University Press, 1996); David Levi-Faur, "The Global Diffusion of Regulatory Capitalism," *Annual of the American Academy of Political and Social Sciences* 598 (2005): 12–32.

113. James Q. Wilson, *Bureaucracy: What Government Agencies Do and Why They Do It* (New York: Basic Books, 1989), 63–64.

114. Timothy Lee, "Here's Why Obama's Trade Negotiators Push the Interests of Hollywood and Drug Companies," *Washington Post*, November 26, 2013.

115. Timothy Lee, "Emails Show Cozy Relationship between Obama Trade Negotiators and Industry," *Washington Post*, November 29, 2013.

116. Woll and Artigas, "When Trade Liberalization Turns," 129–31.

117. On variance in officials' prioritization of general welfare versus particular interests in their trade policymaking, see Kishore Gawande, Pravin Krishna, and Marcelo Olarreaga, "What Governments Maximize and Why: A View From Trade," *International Organization* 63, no. 3. (2009): 491–532.

118. Wilson, *Bureaucracy*, 295–96.

119. Ibid., 108–9.

120. Mattli and Woods, "In Whose Benefit?," 31.

121. Steve Dryden, *Trade Warriors: USTR and the American Crusade for Free Trade* (Oxford: Oxford University Press, 1995).

122. Pierre-Hugues Verdier, "Transnational Regulatory Networks and Their Limits," *Yale Journal of International Law* 34 (2009): 113–72; David Bach and Abra-

ham Newman, "Transgovernmental Networks and Domestic Policy Convergence: Evidence from Insider Trading Regulation," *International Organization* 64, no. 3 (2010): 505–28; Pamela Camerra-Rowe and Michelle Egan, "International Regulators and Network Governance," in Coen, Wyn, and Wilson, *Oxford Handbook of Business and Government*, 404–21.

123. Thomas Eimer, "Decoding Divergence in Software Regulation: Paradigms, Power Structures, and Institutions in the United States and the European Union," *Governance: An International Journal of Policy, Administration, and Institutions* 21, no. 2 (2008): 275–96.

124. Mansfield and Mutz, "Support for Free Trade," Richard Herrmann, Philip Tetlock, and Matthew Diascro, "How Americans Think about Trade: Reconciling Conflicts among Money, Power, and Principles," *International Studies Quarterly* 45, no. 2 (2001): 191–218, especially 202.

125. Judith Goldstein, *Ideas, Interests, and American Trade Policy* (Ithaca: Cornell University Press, 1993), 13.

126. Joseph Stiglitz, *Making Globalization Work: The Next Steps to Global Justice* (London: Penguin, 2006); Stiglitz, *Globalization and Its Discontents* (New York: W. W. Norton, 2002); John Braithwaite and Peter Drahos, *Global Business Regulation* (Cambridge: Cambridge University Press, 2000), 27 (Braithwaite and Drahos do not reductively suggest that businesses are the only actors that have influence, but they generally argue that businesses are the most powerful actors in shaping regulations); David Korten, *When Corporations Rule The World*, 2nd ed. (New York: Kumarian Press, 2001); Lori Wallach and Michelle Sforza, *The WTO: Five Years of Reasons to Resist Corporate Globalization* (New York: Seven Stories, 1999); Sharon Beder, *Suiting Themselves: How Corporations Drive the Global Agenda* (London: Routledge, 2006), 109–72.

127. E. E. Schattschneider, *Politics, Pressures, and the Tariff* (Englewood Cliffs, NJ: Prentice Hall, 1935).

128. Charan Devereaux, Robert Lawrence, and Michael Watkins, *Case Studies in U.S. Trade Negotiations*, 1:135–82.

129. Young, "Not Your Parent's Trade Politics," 345–78; Andreas Dur and Gemma Mateo, "Public Opinion and Interest Group Influence: How Citizen Groups Derailed the Anti-counterfeiting Trade Agreement," *Journal of European Public Policy* 21, no. 8 (2014): 1199–1217.

130. That idea was perhaps most famously summarized by George Stigler's widely cited argument that "as a rule, regulation is acquired by industry and is designed and operated primarily for its benefit." George Stigler, "The Theory of Economic Regulation," *Bell Journal of Economic and Management Science* 2, no. 1 (1971): 3.

131. M. Kim, "Disguised Protectionism," 426–75; Alan Sykes, "Regulatory Protectionism and the Law of International Trade," *University of Chicago Law Review* 66, no. 1 (1999): 1–46; C. Ford Runge, "Trade Protectionism and Environmental Regulations: The New Nontariff Barriers," *Northwestern Journal of International Law and Business* 11, no. 1 (1990): 47–61; Richard Baldwin, "Regulatory Protectionism, Developing Nations, and a Two-Tier World Trade System" (discussion paper 2574, Centre for Economic Policy Research, London, 2000); Simon Evenett and John Whalley, "Resist Green Protectionism—or Pay the Price at Copenhagen," in

The Collapse of Global Trade, Murky Protectionism, and the Crisis: Recommendations for the G20, ed. Richard Baldwin and Simon Evenett (London: Centre for Economic Policy Research, 2009), 93–98.

132. D. Vogel, *Trading Up*, 153.

133. Ibid., 229–31.

134. Braithwaite and Drahos, *Global Business Regulation*, 453.

135. D. Vogel, *Trading Up*. The race to the bottom has been thoroughly discredited elsewhere. For me to use the race to the bottom as an alternative explanation would amount to building a straw man, as it has been thoroughly discredited elsewhere: Claudio Radaelli, "The Puzzle of Regulatory Competition," *Journal of Public Policy* 24, no. 1 (2004): 3; Geoffrey Garrett, *Partisan Politics in the Global Economy* (Cambridge: Cambridge University Press, 1998); A. Dreher, "The Influence of Globalization on Taxes and Social Policy: An Empirical Analysis for OECD Countries," *European Journal of Political Economy* 22, no. 1 (2007): 179–201. Daniel Drezner reviews a number of other works that undermine the race to the bottom argument, in *All Politics Is Global: Explaining International Regulatory Regimes* (Princeton: Princeton University Press, 2007), 14–17. See also Kyle Bagwell and Robert Staiger, "The WTO as a Mechanism for Securing Market Access Property Rights: Implications for Global Labor and Environmental Perspectives," *Journal of Economic Perspectives* 15, no. 3 (2001): 69–88.

136. D. Vogel, *Trading Up*, 95, 259.

137. These three elements are covered in D. Vogel, *Trading Up*, 259–68.

138. Vogel's California effect is not the only explanation of trade politics that relies on power and leverage to do much of its analytical lifting. Simmons has argued, for example, that market power gives some states a dominant position from which to promulgate regulatory innovations to which other states must respond, allowing dominant states to graft their regulatory preferences onto smaller states. Beth Simmons, "The International Politics of Harmonization: The Case of Capital Market Regulation," *International Organization* 55, no. 3 (2001): 589–620.

139. Stephen Krasner, "Global Communication and National Power: Life on the Pareto Frontier," *World Politics* 43, no. 3 (1991): 336–66; Joseph Grieco, *Europe, America, and Non-tariff Barriers to Trade* (Ithaca: Cornell University Press, 1990).

140. Amy Quark, *Global Rivalries: Standards Wars and the Transnational Cotton Trade* (Chicago: University of Chicago Press, 2013); John Stopford and Susan Strange, *Rival States, Rival Firms: Competition for World Market Shares* (Cambridge: Cambridge University Press, 1991).

141. Drezner, *All Politics Is Global*, 72.

142. Ibid., xii–xiii.

143. Abbott and Snidal, "Governance Triangle," 50–51.

144. On the political negotiations surrounding the choice between these different means of promoting regulatory cooperation, see Gary Winslett, "Choosing among Options for Regulatory Cooperation," *Global Governance* 25, no. 1 (2019): 100–122.

CHAPTER 4

1. Levi Tilleman, *The Great Race: The Global Quest for the Car of the Future* (New York: Simon and Schuster, 2015), 2.

2. “Automotive Industry: Employment, Earnings, and Hours,” Bureau of Labor Statistics, U.S. Department of Labor, accessed May 1, 2019. https://www.bls.gov/iag/tgs/iagauto.htm

3. World Trade Organization, Statistics on Merchandise Trade, 2017, accessed May 1, 2019. https://www.wto.org/english/res_e/statis_e/merch_trade_stat_e.htm

4. Roland Stephen, *Vehicle of Influence: Building a European Car Market* (Ann Arbor: University of Michigan Press, 2000), 7.

5. Jean-Bernard Layan and Yannick Lung, “The Dynamics of Regional Integration in the European Car Industry,” in *Cars, Carriers of Regionalism?*, ed. Jorge Carrillo, Yannick Lung, and Rob van Tulder (New York: Palgrave MacMillan, 2004), 66.

6. On the political drive to create a common market and how regulations played into that situation, see Michelle Egan, *Constructing a European Market: Standards, Regulation, and Governance* (Oxford: Oxford University Press, 2001). On this trajectory in the 1970s, see ibid., 61–82.

7. Council Directive (EC) 1970/156, February 6, 1970, [1970] O.J. L. 42/1.

8. Directive (EC) 1970/220, March 20, 1970, [1970] O.J. L. 76/1. In a type-approval system like the EU’s, automakers submit plans for a given design, which are rejected or approved. In the U.S. system, automakers self-certify that they have met government standards, and the government requires them to recall vehicles found to be noncompliant.

9. Council Regulation (EC) 1972/306, August 2, 1972, [1972] O.J. L. 190/1.

10. Directive (EC) 1978/611, June 29, 1978, [1978] O.J. L. 197/19.

11. Isabel Studer-Noguez, *Ford and the Global Strategies of Multinationals: The North American Auto Industry* (New York: Routledge, 2002), 100. On scale economies and minimum efficient size pushing European firms to promote regional integration, see Kerry Chase, *Trading Blocs: States, Firms, and Regions in the World Economy* (Ann Arbor: University of Michigan Press 2005), 146–54.

12. James Rubenstein, *Making and Selling Cars: Innovation and Change in the U.S. Automotive Industry* (Baltimore: Johns Hopkins University Press), 89, 98.

13. Chase, *Trading Blocs*, 159.

14. “Atmospheric Pollution—Motor Vehicle Emissions, Background Note on Environmental Directives,” note to the commissioner for Jean-Francois Verstrynge, Commission of the European Communities, January 19, 1985, Historical Archives of the European Union, European University Institute (hereinafter EUI), Florence. Copies of all documents from the Historical Archive of the European Union cited in this chapter are available from the author by request.

15. “Octane Level Set for Lead-Free Petrol,” *European Community Newsletter* (Dublin), October 17, 1984, Historical Archive of the European Union, EUI; James Markham, “In a ‘Dying’ Forest, the German Soul Withers Too,” *New York Times*, May 25, 1984; Markham, “Angst on the Autobahn: Would Slowdown Aid Trees?” *New York Times*, October 31, 1984.

16. William Drozdiak, “Push for Speed Limits Divides West Germans,” *Washington Post*, October 19, 1984.

17. Rupert Cornwell, “Bonn Faces Tough Fight over Car Pollution Plan,” *Financial Times*, September 21, 1984.

18. Ibid.

19. Catherine Day, "Atmospheric Pollution—New Developments," note to Commissioner Sutherland, January 22, 1985, Historical Archive of the European Union, EUI; Anna Tomforde, "Bonn Flouts EEC with Early Date for Exhaust Control," *Guardian*, September 19, 1984.

20. David Vogel, *Trading Up: Consumer and Environmental Regulation in a Global Economy* (Cambridge, MA: Harvard University Press, 1995), 70.

21. Ibid.

22. Stephen, *Vehicle of Influence*, 90.

23. Jørgen Andersen, "Denmark: Environmental Conflict and the 'Greening' of the Labour Movement," *Scandinavian Political Studies* 13, no. 2 (1990): 191.

24. Stephen, *Vehicle of Influence*, 90.

25. "Atmospheric Pollution—Motor Vehicle Emissions."

26. John Tagliabue, "Germany Fights for Car Pollution Limits," *New York Times*, March 18, 1985.

27. Ibid.; D. Vogel, *Trading Up*, 68.

28. D. Vogel, *Trading Up*, 68.

29. Eberhard von Kuenheim, statement of the spokesman of the European Automobile Industry (CCMC) at a meeting of the environment ministers of the EC, December 6, 1984, Historical Archive of the European Union, EUI.

30. D. Vogel, *Trading Up*, 69.

31. "Note for the File, Subject: Meeting between Messers. Sutherland, Narjes and Mme. Cresson Minister for External Trade and Industry," February 5, 1985, Historical Archive of the European Union, EUI. The UK government also opposed it for similar reasons. EC Commission, "Motor Vehicle Issues concerning the UK," February 13, 1985, Historical Archive of the European Union, EUI.

32. Jan Candies, letter from the director of European affairs at Ford of Europe to the European Economic Commission, with accompanying paper, February 1, 1985, Historical Archive of the European Union, EUI.

33. D. Vogel, *Trading Up*, 67.

34. Kenneth Gooding, "Europe's Chance to Clear the Air; Car Exhaust Controls," *Financial Times*, December 5, 1984.

35. Wayne Sandholtz and John Zysman, "1992: Recasting the European Bargain," *World Politics* 62, no. 1 (1989): 107–14.

36. Geoffrey Garrett and Barry Weingast, "Ideas, Interests, and Institutions: Constructing the European Community's Internal Market," in *Ideas and Foreign Policy: Beliefs, Institutions, and Political Change*, ed. Judith Goldstein and Robert Keohane (Ithaca: Cornell University Press, 1993), 187.

37. Garrett and Weingast, "Ideas, Interests, and Institutions," 188.

38. Geoffrey Garrett and Peter Lange, "Political Responses to Interdependence: What's Left of the Left?" *International Organization* 45, no. 4 (1991): 539–64.

39. EC Council, "Outcome of Proceedings of Permanent Representatives Committee," February 20, 1985, Historical Archive of the European Union, EUI; D. Vogel, *Trading Up*, 71.

40. Paul Cheeseright, "Bonn Relaxes Insistence on Strict Exhaust Rules," *Financial Times*, June 28, 1985.

41. Hilary Barnes and Quentin Peel, "Denmark Poses Threat to EEC Reforms," *Financial Times*, November 30, 1985.

42. John Ardill, "Exhaust Pact Doubts / Danish Government Refuses to Withdraw Calls for Tougher Anti-Pollution Measures," *Guardian*, September 23, 1986.

43. Jacques Neher, "EC Emissions Plan in Jeopardy, Danes Press for More Rapid Solution to Question of Small Cars," *Journal of Commerce*, November 6, 1986; Kenneth Gooding, "EEC Rows over Timetable for Cars," *Financial Times*, March 6, 1987.

44. On the importance of business interests in promoting the single market, see Maria Cowles, "Setting the Agenda for a New Europe: the ERT and EC 1992," *Journal of Common Market Studies* 33, no. 4 (1995), 501–26.

45. William Dawkins and John Griffiths, "EC Agrees Car Exhaust Plan," *Financial Times*, July 7, 1987.

46. William Dawkins, "EC Agrees Measures to Cut Car Pollution," *Financial Times*, December 4, 1987.

47. "Exhaust Plan Delayed," *Globe and Mail*, January 22, 1988.

48. Paul Betts, "Greens Make Peugeot Car Chief See Red," *Financial Times*, July 14, 1988.

49. Paul Betts, "France Withdraws Backing for EC Proposals on Car Pollution," *Financial Times*, July 22, 1988.

50. Hilary Barnes, "A Danish Passion for Cleanliness," *Financial Times*, August 19, 1988.

51. Karen DeYoung, "Sweden's Greens Add Only Dash of Color to Dull Election Campaign," *Washington Post*, September 18, 1988.

52. Laura Raun, "Dutch Defy Brussels on 'Clean Car' Measure," *Financial Times*, October 14, 1988.

53. John Wyles, "Tardy Government Catches Up with Green Mood in Italy," *Financial Times*, October 5, 1988; Bruce Clark, "Older Parties Covet the Green Family's Clothes," *Financial Times*, April 24, 1989; Ken Cooper, "Taking Up the Green Issue," *Financial Times*, November 3, 1988.

54. Derek Brown, "Lead-Free Petrol to Be Adopted by EEC in 1989," *Guardian*, December 7, 1984; "Octane Level Set for Lead-Free Petrol."

55. John Griffiths, "EC Closer to Full Commitment," *Financial Times*, June 15, 1988.

56. John Griffiths, "VW Says Lean-Burn Engines Cannot Match Catalysts," *Financial Times*, January 12, 1989.

57. Stephen, *Vehicle of Influence*, 104.

58. Della Bradshaw, "Bumpy Ride on the Road to Conversion," *Financial Times*, March 15, 1989.

59. Philip Ross, "Ford's Catalytic Converter Eliminates Use of Platinum," *New York Times*, December 16, 1988.

60. D. Vogel, *Trading Up*, 74.

61. Ibid.

62. Tim Dickson, "Europe at the Crossroads on Car Pollution," *Financial Times*, March 10, 1989.

63. Tim Dickson, "Brussels Calls for Stricter Car Pollution Standards," *Financial Times*, March 9, 1989; William Dawkins, "Strict EC Car Exhaust Limits Proposed," *Financial Times*, April 6, 1989.

64. Tim Dickson, "Green Issues on Centre Stage," *Financial Times*, April 21, 1989.

65. D. Vogel, *Trading Up*, 73.

66. William Dawkins, "Strict EC Car Exhaust Limits Proposed," *Financial Times*, April 6, 1989.

67. Tim Dickson, "UK Reverses Position on Car Emission Standards," *Financial Times*, May 24, 1989; Dickson, "EC Curbs on Car Pollution Agreed," *Financial Times*, June 10, 1989.

68. William Dawkins and Kevin Done, "Plan for Compulsory EC Standards," *Financial Times*, June 23, 1989; Peter Guilford, "EC Moves to Single Approval for Cars," *Financial Times*, March 14, 1990.

69. Rob van Tulder and Denis Audet, "The Faster Lane of Regionalism," in Carillo, Lung, and van Tulder, *Cars, Carriers of Regionalism?*, 34.

70. James Womack, Daniel Jones, and Daniel Roos, *The Machine That Changed the World: The Story of Lean Production* (New York: Free Press, 1990), 75–97.

71. Rubenstein, *Making and Selling Cars*, 232; Jonathan Mantle, *Car Wars: Fifty Years of Greed, Treachery, and Skulduggery in the Global Marketplace* (New York: Arcade, 1995), 136.

72. John Tuman, *Reshaping the North American Automobile Industry: Restructuring, Corporatism, and Union Democracy in Mexico* (New York: Continuum, 2003), 27; Leslie Hiraoka, *Global Alliances in the Motor Vehicle Industry* (London: Quorum Books, 2000), 4, 121.

73. John Conybeare, *Merging Traffic: The Consolidation of the International Automobile Industry* (Lanham, MD: Rowman and Littlefield, 2004), 28.

74. Dana Frank, *Buy American: The Untold Story of Economic Nationalism* (Boston: Beacon, 1999), 161.

75. Ibid., 162–71.

76. Warren Brown and Stuart Auerbach, "Domestic Content Bill Takes Aim at Japan," *Washington Post*, December 9, 1982.

77. James. Shoch, *Trading Blows: Party Competition and U.S. Trade Policy in a Globalizing Era* (Chapel Hill: University of North Carolina Press, 2001), 80–84.

78. Frank, *Buy American*, 172.

79. Paul Ingrassia, *Crash Course: The American Automobile Industry's Road from Glory to Disaster* (New York: Random House, 2010), 80.

80. Ibid., 9.

81. Ibid., 94.

82. Clyde Farnsworth, "Vote Due on U.S. Auto Content Bill," *New York Times*, December 8, 1982.

83. Kenneth Gilpin, "Local Content: Global Practice," *New York Times*, June 23, 1983.

84. "It Will Come Back to Haunt Us," *New York Times*, July 25, 1982; "The Job-Killer Bill," *New York Times*, December 14, 1982.

85. Shoch, *Trading Blows*, 79; Clyde Farnsworth, "Auto Talks with Japan: A Drama of Euphemisms," *New York Times*, March 26, 1981; Peter Behr, "President's Dilemma," *Washington Post*, March 22, 1981.

86. Shoch, *Trading Blows*, 79.

87. Stewart Fleming, "The Great American Debate," *Financial Times*, December 7, 1983.

88. I. M. Destler, *American Trade Politics*, 4th ed. (Washington, DC: Institute for International Economics, 2005), 79.

89. Michel Freyssenet and Yannick Lung, "Multinational Carmakers' Regional Strategies," in Carrillo, Lung, and van Tulder, *Cars, Carriers of Regionalism?*, 45.

90. Roberto Newell and Luis Rubio, *Mexico's Dilemma: The Political Origins of the Economic Crisis* (Boulder: Westview, 1984), 127–28; Michael Lusztig, *The Limits of Protectionism: Building Coalitions for Free Trade* (Pittsburgh: University of Pittsburgh Press, 2004), 95.

91. Richard Meislin, "Mexico Set to Revamp Troubled Auto Industry," *New York Times*, September 15, 1983.

92. Lusztig, *Limits of Protectionism*, 88–89.

93. William Orme, "Brazilian Automakers Forge Deal; U.S. Automakers' Mexican Units Steering Cars North," *Journal of Commerce*, April 9, 1987.

94. Hiraoka, *Global Alliances in the Motor Vehicle Industry*, 124.

95. William Orme, "Ford Motor Will Build New Plant in Mexico," *Washington Post*, January 11, 1984.

96. Manuel Pastor and Carol Wise, "The Origins and Sustainability of Mexico's Free Trade Policy," *International Organization* 48, no. 3 (1994): 479.

97. Dale Story, "Trade Politics in the Third World: A Case Study of the Mexican GATT Decision," *International Organization* 36, no. 4 (1982): 784–86.

98. Strom Thacker, *Big Business, the State, and Free Trade: Constructing Coalitions in Mexico* (Cambridge: Cambridge University Press, 2000), 103.

99. Strom Thacker, "Private Sector Trade Politics in Mexico," *Business and Politics* 2, no. 2 (2000): 172.

100. Ibid., 179.

101. Dale Story, *Industry, the State, and Public Policy in Mexico* (Austin: University of Texas Press, 1986), 200.

102. Pastor and Wise, "Origins and Sustainability of Mexico's Free Trade Policy," 479; Miguel Centeno and Sylvia Maxfield, "The Marriage of Finance and Order: Changes in the Mexican Political Elite," *Journal of Latin American Studies* 24 (1992): 57–85. That stacking is another example, similar to the one presented in the discussion of U.S. domestic content rules earlier in this chapter, where the predilections of government officials mattered a great deal but would be difficult to formally model.

103. Thacker, *Big Business, the State, and Free Trade*, 109–10; Centeno and Maxfield, "Marriage of Finance and Order."

104. William Chislett, "Ford Motor Kills Two Birds with One Stone in Mexican Outlay," *Financial Times*, January 18, 1984.

105. The percentages are based on data in Jorge Carrillo, "NAFTA: The Process of Regional Integration of Motor Vehicle Production," in Carillo, Lung, and van Tulder, *Cars, Carriers of Regionalism*, 110.

106. Studer-Noguez, *Ford and the Global Strategies of Multinationals*, 164–65, 175.

107. Ibid., 205.

108. Ibid., 173–74, 178.

109. Ibid., 183–84.
110. Lusztig, *Limits of Protectionism*, 104.
111. Ibid., 113; Michael Hart, *Bill Dymond, and Colin Robertson. Decision at Midnight: Inside the Canada-US Free Trade Negotiations* (Vancouver: University of British Columbia Press, 1994), 16.
112. Glen Williams, *Not for Export: The International Competitiveness of Canadian Manufacturing*, 3rd ed. (Toronto: McClelland and Stewart, 1994), 148; Gordon Ritchie, *Wrestling with the Elephant: The Inside Story of the Canada-U.S. Trade Wars* (Toronto: McFarlane, Walter, and Ross, 1997), 45.
113. David Langille, "The Business Council on National Issues and the Canadian State," *Studies in Political Economy* 24 (1987): 64–66; Lusztig, *Limits of Protectionism*, 104.
114. John King, "Business Council Recommends Canada-U.S. Free Trade Pact," *Globe and Mail*, April 19, 1983; Hart, *Decision at Midnight*, 15–16; Langille, "Business Council on National Issues," 64–66.
115. Langille, "Business Council on National Issues."
116. Lusztig, *Limits of Protectionism*, 108.
117. On Canadian trade policy during the 1960s and 1970s, see Michael Hart, *A Trading Nation: Canadian Trade Policy from Colonialism to Globalization* (Vancouver: University of British Columbia Press, 2002), 233–338.
118. Hart, *Decision at Midnight*, 16; Lusztig, *Limits of Protectionism*, 115.
119. Gregory Inwood, *Continentalizing Canada: The Politics and Legacy of the Macdonald Royal Commission* (Toronto: University of Toronto Press, 2005), 36.
120. Hart, *Decision at Midnight*, 17–20.
121. Ibid., 21.
122. Inwood, *Continentalizing Canada*, 36, 67–68.
123. Imtiaz Hussain and Roberto Dominguez, *North American Regionalism and Global Spread* (New York: Palgrave Macmillan, 2015), 3.
124. Inwood, *Continentalizing Canada*, 91–96.
125. Hart, *Decision at Midnight*, 35.
126. Canada is the leading export market for 36 of the 50 states and is in the top three exporters in all but 4 states. Hussain and Dominguez, *North American Regionalism*, 21.
127. Fred Blaser, "Auto Pact's Been Irrelevant for Years," *Financial Post*, July 6, 1987; John Ferguson, "Trade Negotiators Said Ready for Deal to Replace Auto Pact," *Toronto Star*, September 22, 1987.
128. "Auto Pact Won't Be Hurt by Trade Deal, Envoy Says," *Toronto Star*, January 14, 1987; Ferguson, "Trade Negotiators Said Ready for Deal."
129. Charlotte Yates, "Public Policy and Canadian and American Autoworkers: Divergent Fortunes," in *Driving Continentally: National Policies and the North American Auto Industry*, ed. Maureen Molot (Don Mills: Carleton University Press, 1993), 223; Bob White, "The Deal Undermines Canada's Auto Industry," *Toronto Star*, October 19, 1987 (Bob White was the president of the Canadian Auto Workers' union).
130. R. Jack Richardson, "Free Trade: Why Did It Happen?," *Canadian Review of Sociology and Anthropology* 29, no. 3 (1992): 318–19; Langille, "Business Council on National Issues," 72. The neoliberal zeitgeist at the time added to these trends.

131. Hart, *Decision at Midnight*, 130.

132. Lusztig, *Limits of Protectionism*, 93–94.

133. Guy Poitras and Raymond Robinson, "The Politics of NAFTA in Mexico," *Journal of Interamerican Studies and World Affairs* 36 (1994): 14–15; Lusztig, *Limits of Protectionism*, 93–95.

134. Lusztig, *Limits of Protectionism*, 92; Poitras and Robinson, "The Politics of NAFTA in Mexico," 19.

135. Thacker, *Big Business, the State, and Free Trade*, 126.

136. Poitras and Robinson, "Politics of NAFTA in Mexico," 17; Lusztig, *Limits of Protectionism*, 100; Thacker, *Big Business, the State, and Free Trade*, 142–53.

137. Remonda Kleinberg, "Strategic Alliances: State-Business Relations in Mexico under Neo-Liberalism and Crisis," *Bulletin of Latin American Research* 18, no. 1 (1999): 78.

138. Ibid., 78–80.

139. Maxwell Cameron and Brian Tomlin, *The Making of NAFTA: How the Deal Was Done* (Ithaca: Cornell University Press, 2000), 134.

140. Maria Murillo, *Labor Unions, Partisan Coalitions, and Market Reforms in Latin America* (New Haven: Yale University Press, 2001), 100.

141. Poitras and Robinson, "Politics of NAFTA in Mexico," 23.

142. Ibid., 8, 23–24.

143. Frederick Mayer, *Interpreting NAFTA: The Science and Art of Political Analysis* (New York: Columbia University Press, 1998), 120–21.

144. Leo Ryan, "Auto Leader Wants Canada to Withdraw from North America Talks," *Journal of Commerce*, April 8, 1992.

145. Mayer, *Interpreting NAFTA*, 136.

146. Cameron and Tomlin, *Making of NAFTA*, 34–35.

147. Even when companies could not meet those content requirements, they were not excluded from the market in the way that automakers had been under earlier rules. They were simply subjected to fairly low tariffs of 2.5 percent on cars. Thus, automakers' defense of regionalized content was simply a way of maintaining those tariffs.

148. D. Vogel, *Trading Up*, 106–8.

149. Charlotte Grimes, "Borderline: Many in U.S. Oppose Trade Pact with Mexico," *St. Louis Dispatch*, April 7, 1991; D. Vogel, *Trading Up*, 235.

150. Stewart Baker, "Playing the Environmental Card," *Journal of Commerce*, February 11, 1992; D. Vogel, *Trading Up*, 235.

151. Nancy Dunne and Damian Fraser, "Environmentalists Starting to Call Tune in U.S," *Financial Times*, May 3, 1991; D. Vogel, *Trading Up*, 236.

152. D. Vogel, *Trading Up*, 236.

153. John Kirton, "The Impact of Environmental Regulation on the North American Auto Industry since NAFTA," in *The North American Auto Industry under NAFTA*, ed. Sidney Weintraub and Christopher Sands (Washington, DC: Center for Strategic and International Studies, 1998), 187, 199.

154. On business strategies over NAFTA's environmental rules, see Alan Rugman, John Kirton, and Jule Soloway, *Environmental Regulations and Corporate Strategy: A NAFTA Perspective* (New York: Oxford University Press, 1999), 23–37. On least trade-restrictiveness, see Bradly Condon, "NAFTA and the Environment: A

Trade-Friendly Approach," *Northwestern Journal of International Law and Business* 14, no. 3 (1993–94): 537–38.

155. John Maggs, "US Yields on 'Green' Language in Proposed N. America Trade Pact," *Journal of Commerce*, June 18, 1992.

156. John Audley, *Green Politics and Global Trade: NAFTA and the Future of Environmental Politics* (Washington, DC: Georgetown University Press, 1997), 53.

157. John Maggs, "Environmental Advisors on Trade Issues Named," *Journal of Commerce*, August 20, 1991.

158. D. Vogel, *Trading Up*, 239.

159. Mark Aspinwall, "The NAFTA Side Agreements and Governance in Mexico," in *Leveling the Playing Field: Transnational Regulatory Integration and Development*, ed. Laszlo Brust and Gerald McDermott (Oxford: Oxford University Press, 2014), 105–7.

160. Kirton, "Impact of Environmental Regulation," 190.

161. D. Vogel, *Trading Up*, 237.

162. Ibid., 245.

163. William Dietrich, "Harmonization of Automobile Emission Standards under International Trade Agreements: Lessons from the European Union Applied to the WTO and the NAFTA," *William and Mary Environmental Law and Policy Review* 20 (1995–96): 212–13.

164. Audley, *Green Politics and Global Trade*, 76; D. Vogel, *Trading Up*, 244.

165. Though it did not mandate harmonization of the content of regulations in the three countries, the environmental side agreement did encourage Mexico to improve its environmental performance. Beginning in 1994, as a result of NAFTA, Mexico raised its air quality regulations to bring them closer to U.S. regulations, began cooperating with U.S. authorities on air quality to a greater extent, and significantly increased maquiladoras' compliance with environmental regulations. Kirton, "Impact of Environmental Regulation," 198, 202.

166. Canadian regulations are generally aligned with U.S. regulations.

167. Adriana Gomez Licon, "Mexico's Car Industry Booms While Selling Unsafe Cars," *Seattle Times*, November 28, 2013.

168. See chapter 3 for an explanation of the California effect.

169. "Regulations Matter: Just Look at Mexico," *Santa Fe New Mexican*, December 9, 2013.

170. Licon, "Mexico's Car Industry Booms."

171. See chapter 3 for an explanation of Trumbull's narratives argument.

172. Licon, "Mexico's Car Industry Booms."

173. NAFTA, "In the Matter of Cross-Border Trucking Services," final panel report, February 6, 2001, 17.

174. David Sanger, "Dilemma for Clinton on NAFTA Truck Rule," *New York Times*, December 17, 1995.

175. NAFTA, "Matter of Cross-Border Trucking Services, 16.

176. Sanger, "Dilemma for Clinton."

177. David Sanger, "U.S. and Mexico Postpone NAFTA on Truck Crossings," *New York Times*, December 18, 1995.

178. NAFTA, "Matter of Cross-Border Trucking Services," 14–16.

179. Robert Carbaugh, "NAFTA and the U.S. Mexican Trucking Dispute," *Journal of International and Global Economic Studies* 4, no. 1 (2011): 6–7.

180. Ibid., 5–6.

181. Ibid., 7.

182. Gerard Bordenave and Yannick Lung, "The Twin Internationalization Strategies of US Automakers: GM and Ford," in *Globalization or Regionalization of the American and Asian Car Industry?* ed. Michel Freyssenet, Koichi Shimuzi, and Giuseppe Volpato (New York: Palgrave Macmillan, 2003), 57; Studer-Noguez, *Ford and the Global Strategies*, 118.

183. Bill Canis and Richard Lattanzio, "U.S. and EU Motor Vehicle Standards: Issues for Transatlantic Trade Negotiations," Congressional Research Service, February 18, 2014, 9; John Braithwaite and Peter Drahos, *Global Business Regulation* (Cambridge: Cambridge University Press, 2000), 438–39.

184. Braithwaite and Drahos, *Global Business Regulation*, 439–41.

185. On the politics of European standards bodies, see Egan, *Constructing a European Market*, 133–65.

186. Ibid., 439.

187. Jerry Mashaw and David Harfst, "Regulation and Legal Culture: The Case of Motor Vehicle Safety," *Yale Journal of Regulation* 4 (1987): 273–74.

188. Ibid.

189. Justin Berkowitz, "Free-Trade Cars: Why a U.S.-Europe Free-Trade Agreement Is a Good Idea," *Car and Driver*, June 28, 2013.

190. Alex Trotman, the CEO of Ford, was the co-chair of the TABD in 1996. Michael Lelyveld, "Panel Aims to Abolish Non-tariff Barriers; Business Forum on Mission to Harmonize Standards, Spur Trans-Atlantic Talks," *Journal of Commerce*, May 21, 1997.

191. Dave Gullford, "Regulations Creating Obstacles," *Crain's Detroit Business*, June 17, 1996.

192. "Text: TABD Final Recommendations," *Inside U.S. Trade*, November 17, 1995.

193. "TABD Suggests Harmonization of Auto Safety, Environmental Rules," *Inside U.S. Trade*, April 16, 1996.

194. Canis and Lattanzio, "U.S. and EU Motor Vehicle Standards," 20–21; Vann Wilber and Paul Eichbrecht, "Transatlantic Trade, the Automotive Sector: The Role of Regulation in a Global Industry, Where We Have Been and Where We Need to Go, How Far Can EU-US Cooperation Go toward Achieving Regulatory Harmonization" (paper presented at the GMF Academic Policy Research Conference "Systemic Implications of Transatlantic Regulation Cooperation and Competition," University of Michigan, 2008), 13–14.

195. Canis and Lattanzio, "U.S. and EU Motor Vehicle Standards," 20–21; Wilber and Eichbrecht, "Transatlantic Trade, the Automotive Sector," 13–14.

196. Jeff Gerth, "Where Business Rules; Forging Global Regulations That Put Industry First," *New York Times*, January 9, 1998.

197. Ibid.

198. Ibid.

199. Ibid.

200. Braithwaite and Drahos, *Global Business Regulation*, 447.

201. James Q. Wilson, *Bureaucracy: What Government Agencies Do and Why They Do It* (New York: Basic Books, 1989), 62.

202. Berkowitz, "Free-Trade Cars."

203. "Why Cars From Europe and the US Just Can't Get Along," *Planet Money*, episode 533, National Public Radio, April 18, 2014.

204. Conybeare, *Merging Traffic*, 24–25.

205. Rubenstein, *Making and Selling Cars*, 94, 322.

206. Ulrich Jürgens, "Characteristics of the European Automotive System: Is There a Distinctive European Approach" (discussion paper SP III 2003–301, Leibniz Information Centre for Economics, Berlin, 2003), 12–13.

207. Ibid.

208. Studer-Noguez, *Ford and the Global Strategies*, 133; Bordenave, "Twin Internationalization Strategies," 58.

209. "EU Sets Most Ambitious Goals in Auto Sector Regulations in TTIP Talks," *Inside U.S. Trade*, July 12, 2013; "U.S., EU Officials Say Auto Regulators Making Headway in TTIP Talks." *Inside U.S. Trade*, July 18, 2014.

210. "Automobile Industry Welcomes the Opening of EU-US Trade Talks," European Automobile Manufacturers Association (ACEA), press release, June 17, 2013.

211. "Support in Principle for U.S.-E.U. Trade Pact: But Some Americans and Germans Wary of TTIP Details," Pew Research Center, April 9, 2014.

212. Anthony Faiola, "Free Trade with U.S.? Europe Balks at Chlorine Chicken, Hormone Beef," *Washington Post*, December 4, 2014; Renee Johnson, "U.S.-EU Poultry Dispute on the Use of Pathogen Reduction Treatments (PRTs)," Congressional Research Service, January 15, 2015.

213. "Letter to USTR and European Commission: EU and US Consumer Groups Initial Reaction to the Announcement of a Transatlantic Trade and Investment Partnership," *Transatlantic Consumer Dialogue*, March 5, 2013.

214. Chelsea Abbott, "European Standards versus American Standards: Car Seat Edition," *Magic Beans*, June 30, 2013, http://mbeans.com/spillingthebeans/baby/car-seats/european-standards-vs-american-standards-car-seat-edition/

CHAPTER 5

1. United States Department of Agriculture, Economic Research Service, Statistics and Information, accessed April 30, 2016, http://www.ers.usda.gov/topics/animal-products/cattle-beef/statistics-information.aspx

2. Ibid.

3. On this stereotype, see Steven Vogel, "When Interests Are Not Preferences: The Cautionary Tale of Japanese Consumers," *Comparative Politics* 31, no. 2 (1999): 189; Patricia Maclachlan, *Consumer Politics in Postwar Japan: The Institutional Boundaries of Citizen Activism* (New York: Columbia University Press, 2002), 1–3.

4. Alexander Prasol, *Modern Japan, Origins of the Mind: Japanese Traditions and Approaches to Contemporary Life* (New York: World Scientific, 2010), 113–16, 141–42.

5. Gunnar Trumbull, *Strength in Numbers: The Political Power of Weak Interests* (Cambridge, MA: Harvard University Press, 2012), 47, 50.

6. Ibid., 50.

7. Machlachlan, *Consumer Politics in Postwar Japan*, 178, 236; Trumbull, *Strength in Numbers*, 51–52.

8. David Vogel, "Consumer Protection and Protectionism in Japan," *Journal of Japanese Studies* 18, no. 1 (1992): 141.

9. Machlachlan, *Consumer Politics in Postwar Japan*, 175; D. Vogel, "Consumer Protection and Protectionism in Japan," 124, 128, 134.

10. D. Vogel, "Consumer Protection and Protectionism in Japan," 124, 128, 131–32; Machlachlan, *Consumer Politics in Postwar Japan*, 181, 188–190.

11. Machlachlan, *Consumer Politics in Postwar Japan*, 196.

12. Susan Chira, "Diffuse Goals Set by Naders of Japan," *New York Times*, July 14, 1986.

13. David and Karen Martin, "Western Ideology, Japanese Product Safety Regulation and International Trade," *University of British Columbia Law Review* 19, no. 2 (1985): 363; S. Vogel, "When Interests Are Not Preferences," 194.

14. D. Vogel, "Consumer Protection and Protectionism in Japan," 140.

15. Machlachlan, *Consumer Politics in Postwar Japan*, 234, 243–46.

16. S. Vogel, "When Interests Are Not Preferences," 192.

17. D. Vogel, "Consumer Protection and Protectionism in Japan," 148.

18. S. Vogel, "When Interests Are Not Preferences," 192; Trumbull, *Strength in Numbers*, 63–64.

19. Michael Conlon, "The History of U.S. Beef and Pork Exports to Japan," USDA Foreign Agricultural Service, Global Agriculture Information Network, April 24, 2009, 3, 8–9.

20. Conlon, "History of U.S. Beef and Pork Exports," 13. John Dyck, "U.S.-Japan Agreements on Beef Imports," United States Department of Agriculture, Economic Research Service, 1998., 99-107.

21. Katarzyna Cwiertka, *Modern Japanese Cuisine: Food, Power and National Identity* (London: Reaktion, 2006), 172–73.

22. Center for Disease Control and Prevention, U.S. Department of Health and Human Services, "vCJD: Variant Creutzfeldt-Jakob Disease," accessed March 8, 2016, https://www.cdc.gov/prions/vcjd/resources.html

23. Kathryn Tolbert, "Japan to Test 1 Million Cattle for 'Mad Cow'; Concerns Grow after First Case Botched," *Washington Post*, September 20, 2001.

24. Ibid.

25. Ibid.

26. "Mad-Cow Disease Plagues Beef Industry," *Nikkei Weekly*, October 1, 2001. As this article reports, by the time the MAFF banned the practice after the first BSE case was discovered, over 2,000 cows had consumed the infected bone meal that had been imported from Europe.

27. "Full Disclosure on BSE Needed," *Yomiuri Shimbun*, October 14, 2001. I do not read Japanese and have used English translations of *Yomiuri Shimbun* from the LexisNexis database, where the publication is referred to as *Japan News*.

28. "Mad-Cow Disease Plagues Beef Industry."

29. Tolbert, "Japan to Test 1 Million Cattle."

30. James Brooke, "In Japan, Beef Business Sinks in a Sea of Skepticism," *New York Times*, November 4, 2001.

31. "Snow Brand Lied about Beef's Origin," *Yomiuri Shimbun*, January 24, 2002; "Beef Scandal Exposes Fault," *Yomiuri Shimbun*, January 25, 2002; "Snow Brand Foods Sold Old Meat to Government," *Yomiuri Shimbun*, February 11, 2002.

32. "9 Tons of U.S. Beef Labeled Domestic," *Yomiuri Shimbun*, February 16, 2002; "Starzen Admits Mislabeling Meat," *Yomiuri Shimbun*, March 1, 2002.

33. Akiko Kashiwagi, "Scandals Cause Japanese to Lose Their Appetite; Once Revered Local Food in Doubt," March 25, 2002.

34. "Where's the Beef From?," *Yomiuri Shimbun*, February 16, 2002; "Government Must Toughen Product Label Laws," *Yomiuri Shimbun*, March 12, 2002.

35. "Tracking Systems Try to Tackle Food Safety," *Japan Times*, May 1, 2002; Roxanne Clemens, "Meat Traceability and Consumer Assurance in Japan" (briefing paper 03-MBP 5, Midwest Agribusiness Trade Research and Information Center, Ames, IA, September 2003), 7–8. This kind of traceability system is not possible for U.S. beef. Whereas a package of Japanese beef might contain meat from up to three to five cows, a single hamburger made from U.S. beef contains meat from hundreds or thousands of cows. Clemens, "Meat Traceability"; interview with Dr. Robert Tauxe (chief of foodborne diseases at the CDC), *Frontline*, PBS, 2002, accessed March 8, 2016, http://www.pbs.org/wgbh/pages/frontline/shows/meat/interviews/tauxe.html

36. Akiko Kashiwagi, "Scandals Cause Japanese to Lose Their Appetite; Once Revered Local Food In Doubt," *The Washington Post*, March 25, 2002. The MAFF continued to make this claim in later years as well. "Tariff Hikes on Beef Lack Justification," *Nikkei Weekly*, August 4, 2003.

37. "Government Must Toughen Product Label Laws," *Yomiuri Shimbun*, March 12, 2002.

38. "Government to Ban Beef on the Bone to Prevent BSE Transmission," *Yomiuri Shimbun*, September 14, 2003.

39. Conlon, "History of U.S. Beef and Pork Exports," 15–16; James Brooke, "Scandals Tainting Japan's Pride in Its Food," *New York Times*, June 1, 2002.

40. James Brooke, "Mad Cow Disease Sets Off a Scare in Japan," *New York Times*, September 27, 2001; "Veneman Out to Demonstrate There's No Beef with U.S. Cattle," *Yomiuri Shimbun*, July 26, 2002.

41. "Trust Not a Given after Mad Cow Debacle," *Japan Times*, May 29, 2003.

42. "BSE, Food Additives," dedicated issue, *Food Safety Citizen's Watch Newsletter* 1 (July 2005).

43. Justin McCurry and Suzanne Goldenberg, "BSE-Infected Beef Spreads to Eight US States: Officials Lobby Japanese to Accept That Meat Is Safe," *Guardian*, December 29, 2003; Lynette Clemetson, "U.S. Officials Say Suspect Beef Went to Wider Region," *New York Times*, December 29, 2003.

44. In contrast to the fallout in Japan in 2001–2, the effect that the BSE discovery in the United States had on Americans' purchasing decisions was tiny and lasted less than two weeks. Fred Kuchler and Abebayehu Tegene, "Did BSE Announcements Reduce Beef Purchases?" (Economic Research Report 34, United States Department of Agriculture, Economic Research Service, 2006).

45. "Beef Shortages a Possibility," *Yomiuri Shimbun*, December 26, 2003.

46. Diane Farsetta, "The Cows Have Come Home," CorpWatch, September 1, 2005.

47. Jeff Nesmith, "New Rules Aim to Protect U.S. from Mad Cow," *Atlanta Journal-Constitution*, December 31, 2003. In 2008, the Humane Society released footage of downer cows being shocked and blasted with water hoses to force them to stand long enough to be certified for slaughter, which suggests that these regulations have not always been enforced. "U.S. Beef Inspections Don't Inspire Much Confidence," *International Herald Tribune*, June 12, 2008.

48. Farsetta, "Cows Have Come Home."

49. James Q. Wilson, *The Politics of Regulation* (New York: Basic Books, 1980), 370; Wilson, *Bureaucracy: What Government Agencies Do and Why They Do It* (New York: Basic Books, 1989), 77.

50. "Resist U.S. Pressure to Lift Beef Ban," *Yomiuri Shimbun*, January 23, 2004.

51. "Koizumi: US Must Match Japan," *Yomiuri Shimbun*, January 23, 2004.

52. "Review of Blanket Testing for BSE Timely," *Yomiuri Shimbun*, September 7, 2004.

53. Kakuyu Obara, Michael McConnell, and John Dyck, "Japan's Beef Market," LDP-M-194-01, United States Department of Agriculture, Economic Research Service, August 2010, 18.

54. Ibid.

55. Ben Scott, "Beef Safety on Stock Show Menu; Cattle Tracking, Testing Discussed," *Denver Post*, January 14, 2004.

56. D. Vogel, *Trading Up*, 261–63.

57. "Kansas Beef Firm Setting Up BSE Lab," *Yomiuri Shimbun*, March 6, 2004; Charles Hanrahan and Geoffrey Becker, "Mad Cow Disease and U.S. Beef Trade," Congressional Research Service, June 4, 2008, 5; Donald McNeil, "Barred from Testing for Mad Cow, Niche Meatpacker Loses Clients," *New York Times*, April 18, 2004.

58. Eric Schlosser, "The Cow Jumped over the USDA," *New York Times*, January 2, 2004.

59. Steve Johnson, "The Politics of Meat." *Frontline*, PBS, accessed March 8, 2016, http://www.pbs.org/wgbh/pages/frontline/shows/meat/politics/

60. Ibid.

61. Jan Lyons, "U.S. Beef Is Well Tested, Safe," *USA Today*, March 25, 2004; "USDA Weighs Packer Request to BSE-Test All Cattle," *Reuters*, March 15, 2004.

62. For example, the National Cattlemen's Beef Association stated that Japan's universal testing made as much sense as "testing kindergartner's for Alzheimer's." McNeil, "Barred from Testing for Mad Cow."

63. Center for Responsive Politics, Livestock: Summary and Top Recipients, 2014, accessed March 8, 2016, http://www.opensecrets.org/industries/indus.php?Ind=A06 and http://www.opensecrets.org/industries/recips.php?ind=A06++

64. Charles Craypo, "Meatpacking: Industry Restructuring and Union Decline," in *Contemporary Collective Bargaining in the Private Sector*, ed. Paula Voos (Madison, WI: Industrial Relations Research Association, 1994), 63–96; Human Rights Watch, *Blood, Sweat, and Fear: Workers' Rights in U.S. Meat and Poultry Plants* (New York, 2004), 75–100.

65. On the structure of the beef industry, see "Modern Meat," *Frontline*, PBS, April 18, 2002.

66. Brendan Pearson, "Pressure Builds on Japan to Lift U.S. Beef Import Ban," *Australian Financial Review*, March 19, 2004; Kanako Takahara, "Beef Talks to Resume, Cheney Says," *Japan Times*, April 14, 2004.

67. "Koizumi Sticks to His Guns on SDF," *Nikkei Weekly*, June 14, 2004.

68. Asahi Shimbun, "U.S. Presses Japan," *Edmonton Journal*, October 4, 2004.

69. On the USTR, see Steve Dryden, *Trade Warriors: USTR and the American Crusade For Free Trade* (New York: Oxford University Press, 1995).

70. "Japan May Resume U.S. Beef Imports," *Yomiuri Shimbun*, September 8, 2004.

71. Both MAFF and the HLW had called the 20-month rule "absolutely non-negotiable." "Washington Unhappy with Japan's Beef Plan," *Yomiuri Shimbun*, September 12, 2004.

72. Kanako Takahara, "Japan-U.S. Beef Talks to Continue," *Japan Times*, October 23, 2004; Todd Zaun, "Agreement to Ease Ban on U.S. Beef," *New York Times*, October 24, 2004.

73. Ibid.

74. Anthony Faiola, "Japan Warns of Delays for U.S. Beef; Despite Agreement, Imports Await Rules," *Washington Post*, October 27, 2004.

75. Kanako Takahara, "Tentative Accord Reached on U.S. Beef," *Japan Times*, October 24, 2004; Zaun, "Agreement to Ease Ban on U.S. Beef."

76. Faiola, "Japan Warns of Delays for U.S. Beef."

77. "Government Ready to Lift U.S. Beef Ban," *Nikkei Weekly*, February 14, 2005.

78. "Panel: Ease Blanket Testing for BSE," *Yomiuri Shimbun*, March 12, 2005; "A Cow Walk toward a Crisis," *Japan Times*, March 21, 2005.

79. Glenn Kessler, "Bush Presses Koizumi on Japan's Beef Ban," *Washington Post*, March 10, 2005.

80. "U.S. Turning Up Pressure as Japan Continues Beef Ban," *Nikkei Weekly*, March 7, 2005.

81. Kessler, "Bush Presses Koizumi on Japan's Beef Ban."

82. Kanako Takahara, "Let Consumers Decide for Themselves: Eatery Lobbyist," *Japan Times*, March 19, 2005.

83. James Brooke, "Japan Still Bans U.S. Beef, Chafing American Officials," *New York Times*, April 21, 2005.

84. "U.S. Turning Up Pressure as Japan Continues Beef Ban; "U.S. Senate Mulls Japan Sanctions," *Yomiuri Shimbun*, March 16, 2005.

85. "BSE, Food Additives," dedicated issue, *Food Safety Citizen's Watch Newsletter* 1, July 2005; Anthony Faiola, "Japan Says Man Died of Mad Cow Disease," *Washington Post*, February 5, 2005; Ryuichi Sonada and Tadashi Isozumi, "Stakes Run High in Resuming U.S. Beef Imports," *Yomiuri Shimbun*, October 24, 2005.

86. "Failure to Solve Beef Row May Threaten Japan-U.S. Ties," *Yomiuri Shimbun*, March 21, 2005.

87. "Trust and the Food Safety Commission," *Japan Times*, April 22, 2006.

88. Mayumi Megishi, "Onus on Japan to Ensure U.S. Beef Safety, Report Says," *Japan Times*, November 1, 2005; "Beef-Safety Report Being Misused: Panelist," *Japan Times*, December 9, 2005.

89. "Koizumi Sticks to His Guns on SDF"; Anthony Faiola, "Japan Plans to Press U.S. on Troops," *Washington Post*, October 6, 2004; "Wag the Cow," *Washington Post*, March 11, 2005.

90. "Beef Upstaged Security, Nukes in Talks with Rice," *Nikkei Weekly*, April 4, 2005.

91. "Japanese, U.S. Foreign Ministers Meet to Discuss North Korea, Iran," *BBC Monitoring Asia Pacific*, May 3, 2006.

92. Martin Fackler, "Japan Partly Lifts Ban on Imports of U.S. Beef, Easing Trade Dispute," *New York Times*, December 12, 2005.

93. "Opposition Statement: 'We Oppose the Decision to Reopen the Japanese Market to Beef Imports from the United States and Canada,'" dedicated issue, *Food Safety Citizen's Watch Newsletter* 5, December 2005.

94. *Audit Report: Animal and Plant Health Inspection Service Bovine Spongiform Encephalopathy (BSE) Surveillance Program*, report 50601-10-KC, United States Department of Agriculture, Office of Inspector General, January 2006, 71–72. An earlier version of the audit had been reported in Japanese media. Mayumi Negishi, "Easing Beef Ban Seen as Missing Chance to Let Consumers Rule," *Japan Times*, November 15, 2005; "Perception of Safe Beef," *Japan Times*, December 22, 2005.

95. "U.S. Shipments of Risky Beef Part Outrage Japanese Consumers," Kyodo News, BBC Monitoring Asia Pacific, January 21, 2006.

96. Nobuhiko Harada and Ryuichi Sonada, "Consumer Trust Shattered," *Yomiuri Shimbun*, January 22, 2006; "Japan Stops U.S. Beef Shipments Again," *CNN Money*, January 20, 2006.

97. "U.S. Should Have Been More Careful," *Aberdeen American News*, January 24, 2006.

98. Andrew Martin, "U.S. Beef Banned in Japan—Again," *Chicago Tribune*, January 21, 2006.

99. Kohei Murayama, "U.S. Beef Industry Says Mad Cow Mishap a 'Technical Error,'" Kyodo News, BBC Monitoring Asia Pacific, January 21, 2006.

100. "Penn's BSE Comment Raises Eyebrows," *Yomiuri Shimbun*, January 26, 2006.

101. "In Beef Dispute, U.S. Should Cater to Japan," *Denver Post*, January 24, 2006.

102. "Demands with Regards to the Problem of American Beef Imports," dedicated issue, *Food Safety Citizen's Watch Newsletter* 7, January 2006.

103. Harada and Sonada, "Consumer Trust Shattered."

104. "Japan Says USDA Report on Beef Highlights Additional Violations," *Inside U.S. Trade*, February 24, 2006.

105. Takashi Oda, "Ban on U.S. Beef about More Than Just Meat," *Yomiuri Shimbun*, January 25, 2006.

106. "Beef Safety Audit Passes Muster," *Japan Times*, May 20, 2006.

107. Trumbull, *Strength in Numbers*, 26–29, 124–50.

108. "U.S. Shipments of Risky Beef Part Outrage Japanese Consumers."

109. Deborah Cameron, "Japan's Beef with US a Plus for Australia," *Sydney Morning Herald*, January 27, 2006.

110. Ibid.

111. Stephen Cooke, "Latest Japanese Ban Lifts Export Hopes," *Weekly Times* (Australia), January 25, 2006.

112. "Decision on U.S. Beef Ban Likely before End of June," *Nikkei Weekly*, May 8, 2006.

113. Tatsuya Watanabeand, and Toru Takahashi, "Beef Ban Dropped to Avoid Political Stew," *Yomiuri Shimbun*, May 21, 2006.

114. "Pressure Grows to Lift U.S. Beef Ban," *Yomiuri Shimbun*, May 7, 2006; Paul Wiseman, "Trade War Looms over Beef Dispute; Japan's Ban Stands amid Mad Cow Fears," *USA Today*, April 20, 2006; "Beef Safety Audit Passes Muster."

115. "U.S. Beef Exporters Must Not Slip Up Again," *Yomiuri Shimbun*, May 21, 2006; "Text: U.S.-Japan Statement on Beef," *Inside U.S. Trade*, June 23, 2006.

116. "Japan Set to Lift U.S. Beef Ban," *Japan Times*, June 21, 2006.

117. "Japanese Minister Rejects U.S. Call for Talks to Expand Beef Exports," Kyodo News, BBC Monitoring Asia Pacific, August 1, 2006; Yumi Wijers-Hasagawa, "Japan Receives First Batch of U.S. Beef," *Japan Times*, August 8, 2006; "Japan Opens to Limited U.S. Beef Trade amid Calls for Broader Openings," *Inside U.S. Trade*, July 28, 2006.

118. "Japan Turns Down US Request for Beef Talks," Kyodo News, BBC Monitoring Asia Pacific, January 25, 2007.

119. Tom McGhee, "Swift Moves to Ease Japanese Beef Fears," *Denver Post*, November 10, 2006; "Japan Suspends Beef Imports from One U.S. Facility," Kyodo News, BBC Monitoring Asia Pacific, February 16, 2007; "Japan Suspends Beef Imports from U.S. Meatpacking Facility," Kyodo News, BBC Monitoring Asia Pacific, April 6, 2007; "Japan's PM Wants Current US Beef Inspection System Reassessed," Kyodo News, BBC Monitoring Asia Pacific, April 25, 2008.

120. Tom McGhee, "Swift Moves to Ease Japanese Beef Fears," *Denver Post*, November 10, 2006. "Japan Suspends Beef Imports from One U.S. Facility"; "Japan Suspends Beef Imports from U.S. Meatpacking Facility."

121. "U.S. Allows Japan Beef Audits: Japan Eases Inspections," *Inside U.S. Trade*, April 27, 2007.

122. Hiryuki Nakamura and Toshihiko Yada, "OIE OK's U.S. Beef Exports from Older Cows," *Yomiuri Shimbun*, May 24, 2007.

123. "Government Eyes Relaxing U.S. Beef Rules," *Yomiuri Shimbun*, August 4, 2007; "Japan Fails to Move on Full Beef Access, Drug Prices," *Inside U.S. Trade*, December 2007.

124. Anthony Bowe, "Meaty Comeback," *Denver Post*, February 27, 2009.

125. "USDA Asks Japan to Accept All U.S. Beef in Wake of OIE Finding," *Inside U.S. Trade*, June 1, 2007.

126. Nakamura and Yada, "OIE OK's U.S. Beef Exports."

127. "Japan Fails to Move on Full Beef Market Access."

128. "USDA Unveils Long-Awaited BSE Rule, Says It Will Help Open Foreign Markets," *Inside U.S. Trade*, March 16, 2012.

129. Rod Walton, "Animal Risk Status: Much Improved; U.S. Mad Cow 'Controlled,'" *Tulsa (OK) World*, May 23, 2007; Nakamura and Yada, "OIE OK's U.S. Beef Exports."

130. "Japan-US Beef Talks Hit Snag amid Farm Ministry Row," Kyodo News, BBC Monitoring Asia Pacific, September 7, 2007.

131. "Bush Asks Japanese PM to Fully Open Market to US Beef," Kyodo News, BBC Monitoring Asia Pacific, July 6, 2008.

132. Larry Rohter, "When a Populist Meets a Complex Issue," *New York Times*, June 15, 2008.

133. Ibid.

134. "U.S. Critiques Japan on Familiar Issues at WTO Trade Policy Review," *Inside U.S. Trade*, February 20, 2009.

135. "Beef Industry Groups Press for Incremental Beef Export Policy," *Inside U.S. Trade*, May 29, 2009.

136. "U.S. Critiques Japan on Familiar Issues"; "U.S. Trade Diplomat Hits Japan's Control on U.S. Beef Imports," Kyodo News, BBC Monitoring Asia Pacific, May 23, 2009.

137. "Ways and Means Republicans Call on USTR to Enhance Beef Access," *Inside U.S. Trade*, July 31, 2009.

138. "Japanese Ministerial Visit Brings Little Trade Action due to Elections," *Inside U.S. Trade*, May 8, 2009.

139. "Failure to Solve Beef Row May Threaten Japan-U.S. Ties"; "Opposition Jerry Rigs United Front," *Yomiuri Shimbun*, June 26, 2006.

140. "New Japanese Government Divided on Trade Policy Despite Rhetoric," *Inside U.S. Trade*, September 4, 2009.

141. Satoshi Ogawa and Toshimitsu Miyai, "Election 2009—Battle for Power; U.S. Keeps Close Eye on DPJ Manifesto," *Yomiuri Shimbun*, August 11, 2009.

142. Peter Alford and Rick Wallace, "Japan PM Quits for Party's Sake," *Australian*, June 3, 2010.

143. "Easing Beef Rules Faces Japanese Political Hurdles, May Take Years," *Inside U.S. Trade*, April 30, 2010.

144. Rick Wallace, "Japan Hardliner Hits FTA Hopes," *Australian*, June 9, 2010.

145. Hidetaka Yoshimatsu, "Japanese Economic Policy toward Asia: International Pressure and Domestic Politics," *Electronic Journal of Japanese Studies* 12, no. 2 (2013); "Japan's New Cabinet to Be Formed as DPJ Gear Up for Upper House Election," Xinhua News, June 8, 2010.

146. Rick Wallace, "Japan Raises Hopes of FTA Action," *Australian*, October 14, 2010.

147. William Cooper and Mark Manyin, "Japan Joins the Trans-Pacific Partnership: What Are the Implications?," Congressional Research Service, August 13, 2013, 8.

148. "Japan Queries U.S. on BSE, Risk Assessment May Lead to Beef Access," *Inside U.S. Trade*, October 22, 2010.

149. On Australian beef filling this market vacuum, see "U.S. Beef Hard Sell: As Concern Lingers, Aussies Fill Void," *Japan Times*, October 5, 2006.

150. Mayumi Negishi, "Oddly, Japan Keeps Tariffs Intact as It Gropes for Beef," *Japan Times*, January 29, 2004.

151. "U.S. Official Urges Japan to Open Up, Sign FTA," *Japan Times*, December 7, 2007; "Farm Protection Stands in the Way of Aussie Trade Pact," *Nikkei Weekly*, June 23, 2008.

152. Hiroko Tabuchi, "Fear of Free Trade," *New York Times*, November 12, 2010.

153. "U.S.-Seoul FTA Deal May Keep Japan Exporters at Bay," *Yomiuri Shimbun*, December 6, 2010.

154. Brock Williams, "Trans-Pacific Partnership Countries: Comparative Trade and Economic Analysis," Congressional Research Service, June 10, 2013, 7.

155. "U.S.-Seoul FTA Deal May Keep Japan Exporters at Bay."

156. Dustin Klinger, "Comparing Apples to Oranges: Lessons from the Failure of US Apple Exports to Japan," *Pacific Rim Law and Policy Journal* 8 (1999): 144–45.

157. "Beef Import Limits Must Conform to Global Standards," *Yomiuri Shimbun*, October 22, 2011.

158. "Easing Restrictions on U.S. Beef Justifiable," *Yomiuri Shimbun*, November 4, 2012.

159. "Restrictions on U.S. Beef to Be Eased," *Yomiuri Shimbun*, September 6, 2012.

160. "Johanns: Japan Beef Progress Should Be Prerequisite for TPP Inclusion," *Inside U.S. Trade*, February 25, 2011.

161. "Japan Takes Step toward Relaxing BSE Restrictions on U.S. Beef Imports," *Inside U.S. Trade*, October 28, 2011.

162. The data in this paragraph and figure 2 are based on statistics from the U.S. Meat Export Federation "U.S. Beef Exports to Japan" accessed April 28, 2016, https://www.usmef.org/news-statistics/statistics/

163. This figure was arrived at by subtracting actual monthly exports from the monthly average of $118.2 million for January through November 2003 and then summing those differences.

164. "Marantis Visits Tokyo; Outlines U.S. Priorities on Autos, Beef, and Japan Post," *Inside U.S. Trade*, November 25, 2011.

165. "Chamber Stresses Need for Japan to Follow 'Words' with 'Action' on TPP," *Inside U.S. Trade*, December 9, 2011. Besides beef access, the other two confidence-building measures related to the state-owned Japan Post and greater access to the Japanese car market. "USTR Continues TPP Consultations with Japanese Officials in Tokyo," *Inside U.S. Trade*, May 11, 2012.

166. "TPP Partners Invite Mexico and Canada to Join TPP Talks, but Not Japan," *Inside U.S. Trade*, June 22, 2012.

167. "NCBA Wants Movement on Beef Access before Japan Joins TPP Talks," *Inside U.S. Trade*, January 20, 2012.

168. "Japan Moves Closer to Raising 20-Month Age Limit for Beef Imports," *Inside U.S. Trade*, September 7, 2012.

169. "Japan, U.S. to Start Talks on Beef Imports Protocol Needed to Expand Access," *Inside U.S. Trade*, November 23, 2012.

170. Reiji Yoshida, "Abe to Meet Obama with Hands Tied," *Japan Times*, February 6, 2013.

171. "Agriculture, Food Coalition Urges Quick Decision on Japan's TPP Entry," *Inside U.S. Trade*, March 29, 2013.

CHAPTER 6

1. World Trade Organization, Statistics Database, Merchandise Trade by Commodity, accessed May 16, 2019.

2. William Mauldin, "U.S., Australia Agree on Complicated Compromise on Biologic Drugs," *Wall Street Journal*, October 4, 2015; "U.S., Australia Float Joint Biologics Text to Other Countries for Vetting," *Inside U.S. Trade*, October 4, 2015.

3. On how upward harmonization of IP improves trade and investment and

how different IP regulations constitute regulatory trade barriers, see Keith Maskus, *Intellectual Property Rights in the Global Economy* (Washington, DC: Institute for International Economics, 2000), 112–18, 186–94.

4. I am defining high regulations as those that increase the scope of IP protection. Thus a 20-year patent and 12 years of data exclusivity are considered higher regulations than 15-year patents and 5 years of data exclusivity.

5. For an example of the argument that businesses dominate in this policy space, see Peter Drahos and John Braithwaite, *Information Feudalism: Who Owns the Knowledge Economy?* (New York: , 2002); Susan Sell, *Private Power, Public Law: The Globalization of Intellectual Property Rights* (Cambridge: Cambridge University Press, 2003).

6. As will be explained in chapter 7, different states' patent regulations define and apply these terms in different ways, which has significant implications for which drugs receive patents and which do not.

7. "Intellectual Property," Pharmaceutical Research and Manufacturers of America, accessed February 11, 2016, https://www.phrma.org/en/Advocacy/Intellectual-Property

8. It is important to consider cost per dose versus cost per cure. In 2010, hepatitis C drugs cost $50,000 and cured a little over one-third of patients, so the cost per cure was about $140,000. Sovaldi is $85,000 but cures 95 percent of patients, so the cost per cure is about $50,000 less than previous treatments. Jack Scannell, "Four Reasons Drugs Are Expensive, of Which Two Are False," *Forbes*, October 13, 2015.

9. "Intellectual Property," Pharmaceutical Research and Manufacturers of America, accessed February 11, 2016, https://www.phrma.org/en/Advocacy/Intellectual-Property

10. Stuart Pfeifer, "Prescription Drug Spending Jumps 13% to Record $374 Billion in 2014," *Los Angeles Times*, April 14, 2015.

11. Richard Anderson, "Pharmaceutical Industry Gets High on Fat Profits," BBC News, November 6, 2014.

12. Nick Stockton, "How Prescription Drugs Get So Wildly Expensive," *Wired*, September 23, 2015.

13. Andrew Pollack, "Sales of Sovaldi, New Gilead Hepatitis C Drug, Soar to 10.3 Billion Dollars," *New York Times*, February 3, 2015.

14. Bolar exemptions allow a generic firm to use a patented product for testing while it is still under patent.

15. Unni Karunakara, "Removing Barriers to Access for a More Equitable, Healthy World," *Doctors Without Borders*, November 21, 2012. Drug companies argue that these changes are real improvements and thus patentable. GlaxoSmithKline, "GSK Public Policy Positions: Evergreening," August 2011; European Federation of Pharmaceutical Industries and Associations, "The Degree to Which Patenting, and in Particular Secondary Patenting, Protect Pharmaceutical Products during Their Lifecycle Is Often Misconstrued," November 28, 2012. For a balanced discussion, see Roger Collier, "Drug Patents: The Evergreening Problem," *Canadian Medical Association Journal* 185, no. 9 (2013): 385–86.

16. Those firms spent approximately 44 percent more on marketing than on research. Ana Swanson, "Big Pharmaceutical Companies Are Spending Far More

on Marketing Than Research," *Washington Post*, February 11, 2015; John Oliver, "Marketing to Doctors," *Last Week Tonight*, February 8, 2015.

17. Miriam Mazzucato, "How Taxpayers Prop Up Big Pharma, and How to Cap That," *Los Angeles Times*, October 27, 2015; Carolyn Johnson, "Taxpayers Helped Fund This $129,000 Cancer Drug; Should the Government Help Cut the Price?" *Washington Post*, January 14, 2016.

18. Carolyn Deere, *The Implementation Game: The TRIPS Agreement and the Global Politics of Intellectual Property Reform in Developing Countries* (New York: Oxford University Press, 2009), 34–35.

19. Drahos and Braithwaite, *Information Feudalism*, 20.

20. U.S. IP law had historically prioritized the public interest over the rights of profit-seeking private entities. Donald Harris, "TRIPS' Rebound: An Historical Analysis of How the TRIPS Agreement Can Ricochet back against the United States," *Northwestern Journal of International Law and Business* 25, no. 1. (2004–5): 122–28.

21. Michael Trebilcock and Robert Howse, *The Regulation of International Trade*, 3rd ed. (New York: Routledge), 402, 405.

22. Christopher Harrison, *The Politics of the International Pricing of Prescription Drugs* (New York: Praeger, 2004), 80.

23. Susan Sell and Aseem Prakash, "Using Ideas Strategically: The Contest between Business and NGO Networks in Intellectual Property Rights," *International Studies Quarterly* 48, no. 1 (2004): 154.

24. Iain Cockburn, "The Changing Structure of the Pharmaceutical Industry," *Health Affairs* 23, no. 1 (2004): 13–15.

25. David Tyfield, "Enabling TRIPs: The Pharma-Biotech-University Patent Coalition," *Review of International Political Economy* 15, no. 4 (2008): 535–66.

26. Drahos and Braithewaite, *Information Feudalism*, 67–68.

27. Duncan Matthews, *Globalising Intellectual Property Rights: The TRIPS Agreement* (London: Routledge, 2002), 11.

28. Charan Devereaux, Robert Lawrence, and Michael Watkins, *Case Studies in U.S. Trade Negotiations, vol. 1, Making the Rules* (Washington, DC: Institute for International Economics, 2006), 47; Drahos and Braithewaite, *Information Feudalism*, 59–69.

29. Drahos and Braithewaite, *Information Feudalism*, 144.

30. Ibid., 111.

31. Deere, *Implementation Game*, 48; Drahos and Braithewaite, *Information Feudalism*, 71.

32. Devereaux, Lawrence, and Watkins, *Case Studies in U.S. Trade Negotiations*, 1:56.

33. Drahos and Braithewaite, *Information Feudalism*, 61–63, 71.

34. Sell and Prakash, "Using Ideas Strategically," 145.

35. Ibid., 154.

36. Drahos and Braithewaite, *Information Feudalism*, 63–64; Sell, *Private Power, Public Law*, 75; Deere, *Implementation Game*, 46; Sell and Prakash, "Using Ideas Strategically," 145, 154, 159.

37. Devereaux, Lawrence, and Watkins, *Case Studies in U.S. Trade Negotiations*, 1:53.

38. Drahos and Braithewaite, *Information Feudalism*, 69–71; Devereaux, Lawrence, and Watkins, *Case Studies in U.S. Trade Negotiations*, 1:53–56.

39. Drahos and Braithewaite, *Information Feudalism*, 70.

40. Ibid., 91, 118; Devereaux, Lawrence, and Watkins, *Case Studies in U.S. Trade Negotiations*, 1:54–56. Sell and Prakash, "Using Ideas Strategically," 157.

41. Amy Kapczynski, "Harmonization and Its Discontents: A Case Study of TRIPS Implementation in India's Pharmaceutical Sector," *California Law Review* 97, no. 6 (2009): 1576.

42. Deere, *Implementation Game*, 134; Sell and Prakash, "Using Ideas Strategically," 161.

43. Devereaux, Lawrence, and Watkins, *Case Studies in U.S. Trade Negotiations*, 1:77.

44. Drahos and Braithewaite, *Information Feudalism*, 193.

45. Alfonse D'Amato, "Enough Pirating of U.S. Goods," *New York Times*, January 23, 1986.

46. D. Harris, "TRIPS' Rebound," 139.

47. Harrison, *Politics of the International Pricing of Prescription Drugs*, 81.

48. Drahos and Braithewaite, *Information Feudalism*, 86.

49. Harrison, *Politics of the International Pricing of Prescription Drugs*, 76.

50. Ibid., 82.

51. Sell and Prakash, "Using Ideas Strategically," 153.

52. Ibid., 157.

53. Steve Dryden, *Trade Warriors: USTR and the American Crusade for Free Trade* (New York: Oxford University Press, 1995), 312.

54. Sell and Prakash, "Using Ideas Strategically," 156.

55. The first person to occupy this position was Harvey Bale, who would later work as a pharmaceutical lobbyist.

56. Drahos and Braithewaite, *Information Feudalism*, 96.

57. Ibid., 123–26.

58. Drahos and Braithewaite, *Information Feudalism*; Sell, *Private Power, Public Law*.

59. Domestic NGOs and domestic firms lack of engagement on these issues is discussed in the following section.

60. The GSP is an American trade program dating back to 1974 that grants developing countries additional tariff reductions on items they export to the United States in order to promote poverty reduction.

61. Sell and Prakash, "Using Ideas Strategically," 156; Clyde Farnsworth, "U.S. Plans to Defend Its Patents," *New York Times*, April 7, 1986.

62. Judith Bello and Alan Holmer, "The Heart of the 1988 Trade Act: A History of Legislative Amendments to Section 301," *Stanford Journal of International Law* 25, no. 1 (1988): 1–44.

63. Harrison, *Politics of the International Pricing of Prescription Drugs*, 86.

64. On the standard simply being anything below U.S. rules, see Trebilcock and Howse, *Regulation of International Trade*, 407.

65. Even though 301 was almost certainly a violation of GATT rules, the GATT's weak enforcement rules meant that there was no real mechanism to punish the United States for using it. Trebilcock and Howse, *Regulation of International Trade*, 407.

66. Drahos and Braithewaite, *Information Feudalism*, 102–4.

67. Ibid., 105.

68. Ibid.

69. Stuart Auerbach, "Reagan Orders Sanctions against Thailand; Duty-Free Status Removed from $165 Million in Thai Imports," *Washington Post*, January 21, 1989; P. T. Bangsberg, "Thai Businesses Seek Patent Safeguards to Blunt US Moves," *Journal of Commerce*, April 14, 1989.

70. One U.S. trade official said that "each bilateral brought that country much closer to [the] TRIPS agreement, so accepting TRIPS was no big deal." Drahos and Braithewaite, *Information Feudalism*, 105.On this general strategy, see also Deere, *Implementation Game*, 55.

71. Trebilcock and Howse, *Regulation of International Trade*, 405; Drahos and Braithewaite, *Information Feudalism*, 114.

72. Drahos and Braithewaite, *Information Feudalism*, 119–20.

73. Devereaux, Lawrence, and Watkins, *Case Studies in U.S. Trade Negotiations*, 1:59.

74. Drahos and Braithewaite, *Information Feudalism*, 138–39.

75. Ibid.

76. Devereaux, Lawrence, and Watkins, *Case Studies in U.S. Trade Negotiations*, 1:59; Drahos and Braithewaite, *Information Feudalism*, 141.

77. Deere, *Implementation Game*, 51.

78. Ibid., 55.

79. Ibid., 120.

80. Ibid., 54.

81. Ibid., 55.

82. Drahos and Braithewaite, *Information Feudalism*, 141.

83. Ibid., 135.

84. Devereaux, Lawrence, and Watkins, *Case Studies in U.S. Trade Negotiations*, 1:60.

85. Drahos and Braithewaite, *Information Feudalism*, 140.

86. Devereaux, Lawrence, and Watkins, *Case Studies in U.S. Trade Negotiations*, 63.

87. Ibid., 57.

88. William Duperon and E. Mine Cinar, "Global Competition versus Regional Interests: FDI and Pharmaceuticals in India," *Journal of International Commercial Law and Technology* 5, no. 4 (2010): 187. Devereaux, Lawrence, and Watkins, *Case Studies in U.S. Trade Negotiations*, 1:64.

89. Drahos and Braithewaite, *Information Feudalism*, 145.

90. Sylvia Ostry, "The Uruguay Round North-South Grand Bargain: Implications for Future Generations" (Political Economy of International Trade Law, University of Minnesota, Minneapolis, September 2000); Amrita Narlikar, "Developing Countries and the WTO," in *Trade Politics*, ed. Brian Hocking and Steven McGuire, 2nd ed. (New York: Routledge, 2004), 135–36; Devereaux, Lawrence, and Watkins, *Case Studies in U.S. Trade Negotiations*, 1:64; Deere, *Implementation Game*, 56.

91. Jim Enyart recalled this quote afterward. Devereaux, Lawrence, and Watkins, *Case Studies in U.S. Trade Negotiations*, 1:63.

92. Deere, *Implementation Game*, 19–20.

93. C. M. Correa, *Intellectual Property Rights, the WTO, and Developing Countries: The TRIPs Agreement and Policy Options* (London: Zed Books / Third World Network, 2000), 11; Devereaux, Lawrence, and Watkins, *Case Studies in U.S. Trade Negotiations*, 1:64; Harrison, *Politics of the International Pricing of Prescription Drugs*, 157–58; Drahos and Braithewaite, *Information Feudalism*, 194.

94. Drahos and Braithewaite, *Information Feudalism*, 193.

95. Deere, *Implementation Game*, 205.

96. I. M. Destler, *American Trade Politics*, 4th ed. (Washington, DC: Institute for International Economics, 2005), 210.

97. TRIPS requirements for a state to use a compulsory license are (1) that state must have attempted to obtain use on "reasonable commercial terms"; (2) the license must be nonexclusive; (3) the license must primarily be for the domestic market, not exports; and (4) adequate compensation must be given.

98. In contrast to the GATT system, the WTO dispute settlement mechanism cannot be blocked by the accused, proceeds more expeditiously, possesses a greater ability to enforce its decision by sanctioning retaliation, and has more formalized panel proceedings. Trebilcock and Howse, *Regulation of International Trade*, 112–47.

99. In 2002, the World Bank estimated that implementing TRIPS would generate $900 million in net losses for India. World Bank, "Global Economic Prospects and the Developing Countries," table 5.1 (Washington, DC, 2002), 10.

100. Sell and Prakash, "Using Ideas Strategically," 160.

101. Ibid., 179.

102. Daniel Drezner, *All Politics Is Global: Explaining International Regulatory Regimes* (Princeton: Princeton University Press, 2007), 179.

103. Trebilcock and Howse, *Regulation of International Trade*, 430.

104. Devereaux, Lawrence, and Watkins, *Case Studies in U.S. Trade Negotiations*, 78–79.

105. Though the act was signed in December 1997, its implementation was repeatedly held up by legal challenges, the last of which was the pharmaceutical companies' suit in March 2000.

106. Paula Green, "Companies Say Bill Guts Patent Protection Law," *Journal of Commerce*, September 2, 1997.

107. Deere, *Implementation Game*, 114–15. With some activists calling for TRIPS to be gutted, precedent was not an entirely idle concern.

108. "U.S. Firms to Push for More IPR Protection in WTO, FTAA Talks," *Inside U.S. Trade*, August 28, 1998.

109. Barton Gellman, "A Conflict of Health and Profit: Gore at Center of Trade Policy Reversal on AIDS Drugs to South Africa," *Washington Post*, May 21, 2000; Devereaux, Lawrence, and Watkins, *Case Studies in U.S. Trade Negotiations*, 1:83. They continued to resist all compromise well into 1999. Gellman, "Conflict of Health."

110. Mary Braid, "Drug Giants Flex Muscles as SA Tries to Cut Health Bill," *Independent*, October 8, 1997.

111. Donald McNeil, "South Africa's Bitter Pill for World's Drugmakers," *New York Times*, March 29, 1998.

112. Braid, "Drug Giants Flex Muscles."

113. Deere, *Implementation Game*, 115.

114. McNeil, "South Africa's Bitter Pill for World's Drugmakers."

115. Gellman, "Conflict of Health and Profit."

116. McNeil, "South Africa's Bitter Pill for World's Drugmakers."

117. Drahos and Braithwaite, *Information Feudalism*, 7.

118. "US Government Efforts to Negotiate the Repeal, Termination, or Withdrawal of Article 15(c) of the South African Medicines and Related Substances Act," U.S. Department of State, February 5, 1999.

119. Devereaux, Lawrence, and Watkins, *Case Studies in U.S. Trade Negotiations*, 1:78–79.

120. Ibid., 78.

121. Ibid., 81.

122. Ibid., 80–81.

123. Ibid.; Sell and Prakash, "Using Ideas Strategically," 163. The World Health Assembly, the governing body of the WHO, has budgetary powers, and being on that board would have given the United States significant leverage to prevent the WHO from taking an active role in discussions surrounding IP protection.

124. Devereaux, Lawrence, and Watkins, *Case Studies in U.S. Trade Negotiations*, 1:85.

125. Ibid., 88.

126. Deere, *Implementation Game*, 118.

127. Ibid., 213.

128. Anna Lanoszka, "The Global Politics of Intellectual Property Rights and Pharmaceutical Drug Policies in Developing Countries," *International Political Science Review* 24, no. 2 (2003): 181–97; Gellman, "Conflict of Health and Profit."

129. Gellman, "Conflict of Health and Profit."

130. NGOs argued that patents made drugs "unaffordable to most South Africans and only the affluent (predominately white) could afford them. Thus, the policy of compulsory licenses that the USTR was opposing was, in part, a challenge to medical apartheid. Such arguments resonated well with the U.S. Congressional Black Caucus, a key pillar of support for President Clinton." Sell and Prakash, "Using Ideas Strategically," 165.

131. Ibid., 163.

132. McNeil, "South Africa's Bitter Pill for World's Drugmakers."

133. Ibid.

134. Sell and Prakash, "Using Ideas Strategically," 145, 165.

135. Henri Cauvin, "Trial in AIDS Drug Lawsuit Opens in Pretoria," *New York Times*, March 6, 2001; "Dying for Drugs, Protests, Global Day of Action," *Guardian*, March 5, 2001; "Thousands Protest Cost of AIDS Drugs," *Toronto Star*, March 6, 2001; Huntly Collins, "AIDS Activists Target a Disparity of Care," *Philadelphia Enquirer*, March 5, 2001.

136. Sheryl Stolberg, "AIDS Groups Revive a Fight, and Themselves," *New York Times*, March 18, 2001.

137. Rachel Swarns, "Drugmakers Drop South Africa Suit over AIDS Medicine," *New York Times*, April 20, 2001.

138. Ibid.

139. Drahos and Braithwaite, *Information Feudalism*, 8.

140. Margaret Keck and Kathryn Sikkink, *Activists beyond Borders: Advocacy Networks in International Politics* (Ithaca: Cornell University Press, 1998), 27.

141. Deere, *Implementation Game*, 119.

142. Ibid.

143. J. Michael Finger and Philip Schuler, "Implementation of Uruguay Round Commitments: The Development Challenge," *World Economy* 23, no. 4 (2000): 511–25; Deere, *Implementation Game*, 118; Peter Yu, "TRIPS and Its Discontents," *Marquette Intellectual Property Review* 369 (2006): 379.

144. Trebilcock and Howse, *Regulation of International Trade*, 434.

145. Devereaux, Lawrence, and Watkins, *Case Studies in U.S. Trade Negotiations*, 1:101; Geoff Winestock and Helene Cooper, "How Activists Outmaneuvered Drug Makers in WTO Deal," *Wall Street Journal*, November 15, 2001.

146. Deere, *Implementation Game*, 135; Devereaux, Lawrence, and Watkins, *Case Studies in U.S. Trade Negotiations*, 1:100.

147. "Developing Countries Push For TRIPS to Allow Cheaper Medicines," *Inside U.S. Trade*, June 22, 2001.

148. "TRIPS–Public Health Declaration Splits Developing, Developed Nations," *Inside U.S. Trade*, September 28, 2001.

149. "Countries Still Split in WTO Drug Patent Talks, Close In on Scope," *Inside U.S. Trade*, September 27, 2002. "Developing Countries Push for Broad Leeway under Drug Patent Rules," *Inside U.S. Trade*, October 25, 2002.

150. "Developing Countries Push for TRIPS to Allow Cheaper Medicines."

151. "U.S. Hopeful Africans Coming on Board in TRIPS/Health Dispute," *Inside U.S. Trade*, November 2, 2001.

152. Ibid.; Devereaux, Lawrence, and Watkins, *Case Studies in U.S. Trade Negotiations*, 1:100.

153. Bruce Moon, "From Seattle and Doha to Cancun: The Trade Agenda in the New Millennium," in Hocking and McGuire, *Trade Politics*, 30.

154. Devereaux, Lawrence, and Watkins, *Case Studies in U.S. Trade Negotiations*, 1:87.

155. Ibid., 89.

156. Ibid., 98.

157. Drezner, *All Politics Is Global*, 192.

158. Destler, *American Trade Politics*, 18.

159. A point made in a *Washington Post* article (Gellman, "Conflict of Health and Profit") is insightful on this perspective: "Inertia led trade regulators to treat generic AIDS medicine on the model they use for pirated music discs and computer games—as a threat to the profits of copyright-holders, to be suppressed. 'You mean the U.S. Trade Representative doesn't know the difference between Barbie dolls, tennis rackets and AIDS drugs?' one senior health official recalls asking incredulously during the interagency fight. 'Well, the problem is, they didn't.'"

CHAPTER 7

1. Doha Declaration on TRIPS and Public Health, WT/MIN(01)/DEC/2, adopted November 14, 2001.

2. On the negotiations over these issues, see Frederick Abbott, "The WTO

Medicines Decision: World Pharmaceutical Trade and the Protection of Public Health," *American Journal of International Law* 99, no. 2 (2005): 317–58.

3. Charan Devereaux, Robert Lawrence, and Michael Watkins, *Case Studies in U.S. Trade Negotiations, vol. 1, Making the Rules* (Washington, DC: Institute for International Economics, 2006), 105.

4. "Countries Still Split in WTO Drug Patent Talks, Close In on Scope," *Inside U.S. Trade*, September 27, 2002. "Developing Countries Push for Broad Leeway under Drug Patent Rules," *Inside U.S. Trade*, October 25, 2002.

5. "PHRMA Looks to Limit Countries, Diseases Subject to New TRIPS Flexibility," *Inside U.S. Trade*, October 18, 2002; "Drug Companies Push for Limits on Disease Coverage in Drug Patent Deal," *Inside U.S. Trade*, November 22, 2002.

6. "WTO Fails to Bridge Gaps on TRIPS and Health Deal, Sets New Deadline," *Inside U.S. Trade*, December 13, 2002.

7. The U.S. list included yellow fever, HIV, malaria, plague, cholera, hepatitis, typhoid, typhus, measles, and other epidemics. "WTO Awaits U.S. on Disease Limits on TRIPS, Fail to Get Deal on S&D," *Inside U.S. Trade*, December 20, 2002; F. Abbott, "WTO Medicines Decision," 329.

8. "Consensus on TRIPS Unravels as U.S. Blocks Deal on Scope of Diseases," *Inside U.S. Trade*, January 3, 2003.

9. "EU, Japan Compromise Efforts for WTO Medicines Deal Fall Short," *Inside U.S. Trade*, February 7, 2003.

10. Duncan Matthews, "WTO Decision on Implementation of Paragraph 6 of the Doha Declaration on the TRIPS Agreement and Public Health: A Solution to the Access to Essential Medicines Problem?," *Journal of International Economic Law* 7, no. 1 (2004): 84–85.

11. On the politics surrounding Paragraph 6 in the Doha Declaration, see Brook Baker, "Arthritic Flexibilities for Accessing Medicines: Analysis of WTO Action regarding Paragraph 6 of the Doha Declaration on the TRIPS Agreement and Public Health," *Indiana International and Comparative Law Review* 14, no. 3 (2004): 613–715.

12. "Larson Expects Little Further Debate on TRIPS and Health in WTO," *Inside U.S. Trade*, November 30, 2001.

13. "EU Floats Compromise Drug Patent Plan before Senior Officials Meeting," *Inside U.S. Trade*, November 1, 2002.

14. "PhRMA Looks to Limit Countries, Diseases Subject to New TRIPS Flexibility," *Inside U.S. Trade*, October 18, 2002.

15. "Implementation of Paragraph Six of the Doha Declaration on the TRIPS Agreement and Public Health," Decision of the General Council, Paragraph Four, WT/L/540 and Corr.1, September 1, 2003.

16. "TRIPS and Pharmaceutical Patents: Obligations and Exceptions," World Trade Organization, accessed February 16, 2016, https://www.wto.org/english/tratop_e/trips_e/factsheet_pharm02_e.htm#importing

17. William New, "It's Official: TRIPS Health Amendment in Effect, First Ever to a WTO Agreement," *Intellectual Property Watch*, January 23, 2017.

18. "Non-violation and Situation Nullification or Impairment under the TRIPS Agreement," IP/C/W/385, World Trade Organization, October 30, 2002.

19. "Non-violation Complaints under the TRIPS Agreement: A Communica-

tion from the United States," IP/C/W/599, World Trade Organization, June 10, 2013; "U.S. Steps Up Fight against Moratorium on TRIPS Non-violation Cases," *Inside U.S. Trade*, July 3, 2014.

20. "U.S. Steps Up Fight against Moratorium."

21. Carolyn Deere, *The Implementation Game: The TRIPS Agreement and the Global Politics of Intellectual Property Reform in Developing Countries* (New York: Oxford University Press, 2009), 159.

22. "The New Drug War: Hard Pills to Swallow," *Economist*, January 4, 2014.

23. Ibid.

24. Deere, *Implementation Game*, 80.

25. Amy Kapczynski, "Harmonization and Its Discontents: A Case Study of TRIPS Implementation in India's Pharmaceutical Sector," *California Law Review* 97, no. 6 (2009): 1586.

26. "Will the Lifeline of Affordable Medicines for Poor Countries Be Cut?," Doctors Without Borders, February 2005. Kapczynski, "Harmonization and Its Discontents," 1587.

27. Ibid.

28. Ibid., 1590.

29. Ibid., 1593.

30. On Section 3(d), see Jodie Liu, "Compulsory Licensing and Anti-Evergreening: Interpreting the TRIPS Flexibilities in Sections 84 and 3(d) of the Indian Patents Act," *Harvard International Law Journal* 56, no. 1 (2015): 207–27.

31. Kapczynski, "Harmonization and Its Discontents," 1593; Janice Mueller, "Taking TRIPS to India—Novartis, Patent Law, and Access to Medicines," *New England Journal of Medicine*. 356 (2007): 543.

32. Kapczynski, "Harmonization and Its Discontents," 1591.

33. Ibid., 1594.

34. Narayanan Lalitha, "Access to Indian Generic Drugs: Emerging Issues," in *Intellectual Property, Pharmaceuticals and Public Health: Access to Drugs in Developing Countries*, ed. Kenneth Shadlen, Samira Guennif, Alenka Guzman, and Narayanan Lalitha (Cheltenham: Edward Elgar, 2013), 244–45.

35. Kapczynski, "Harmonization and Its Discontents." 1594.

36. Ibid., 1595.

37. Lalitha, "Access to Indian Generic Drugs," 237; Kapczynski, "Harmonization and Its Discontents," 1598–1600.

38. Kapczynski, "Harmonization and Its Discontents," 1599–1600.

39. Mueller, "Taking TRIPS to India," 541.

40. "Taking Pains," *Economist*, September 8, 2012.

41. "Drug Companies Face Mounting Hurdles in India due to Patent Revocation," *Inside U.S. Trade*, December 20, 2012.

42. Subodh Varma, "SC Rules for Cheap Cancer Drug," *Times of India*, April 2, 2013.

43. "Indian Generic at 1/100th the Cost, Saves Aussie's Life," *Times of India* (Jaipur edition), August 21, 2015.

44. Kapczynski, "Harmonization and Its Discontents," 1633.

45. Andrew Ward and Amy Kazmin, "Bayer Loses Bid to Block Cheap Version of Cancer Drug in India," *Financial Times*, December 12, 2014.

46. "U.S. Business Steps Up Fight against Indian Trade Barriers Ahead of Election," *Inside U.S. Trade*, June 14, 2013.

47. Amy Kazmin, "Roche Drops Patent for Herceptin in India," *Financial Times*, August 16, 2013; Gardiner Harris, "India's Efforts to Aid Poor Worry Drug Makers," *New York Times*, December 30, 2013.

48. Hari Pulakkat, "Number of Cancer Cases in India Predicted to Double in Next 20 Years," *Economic Times*, April 18, 2014.

49. On the decision in that case, see Yixin Tang, "The Future of Patent Enforcement after *eBay v. MercExchange*," *Harvard Journal of Law and Technology* 20, no. 1 (2006): 236–52; Jeremiah Helm, "Why Pharmaceutical Firms Support Patent Trolls: The Disparate Impact of *eBay v. MercExchange* on Innovation," *Michigan Telecommunications and Technology Law Review* 13, no. 1 (2006): 331–43; David Conrad, "Mining the Patent Thicket: The Supreme Court's Rejection of the Automatic Injunction Rule in *eBay v. MercExchange*," *Review of Litigation* 26, no. 1 (2007): 119–54.

50. eBay v. MercExchange, 05–130, Supreme Court of the United States, May 15, 2006.

51. Ibid.

52. Kapczynski, "Harmonization and Its Discontents," 1606.

53. Ibid., 1632.

54. Drahos and Braithwaite, *Information Feudalism*, 139.

55. Deere, *Implementation Game*, 77.

56. Kapczynski, "Harmonization and Its Discontents," 1598.

57. Deere, *Implementation Game*, 80–81.

58. Ibid., 79.

59. Kapczynski, "Harmonization and Its Discontents," 1595.

60. "Indian Minister Touts Local Content Policy Change, Rebuts IPR Criticism," *Inside U.S. Trade*, July 15, 2013.

61. "India Again on US IPR Priority Watch List; Govt Disappointed, But Not Worried," *Business Line*, May 1, 2015.

62. Sudip Chaudhuri, "The Pharmaceutical Industry in India after TRIPS," in *New Political Economy of Pharmaceuticals: Production, Innovation, and TRIPS in the Global South*, ed. Hans Lofgren and Owain Williams (Gordonsville, VA: Palgrave MacMillan, 2013), 113–15.

63. Kapczynski, "Harmonization and Its Discontents," 1583.

64. Deere, *Implementation Game*, 103.

65. Sonia Baldia, "Knowledge Process Outsourcing to India: Important Considerations for U.S. Companies," in *Doing Business in India: Critical Legal Issues for U.S. Companies*, ed. Asish Prasad and Mark Schwartz (New York: Practicing Institute, 2007), 171–209.

66. Chaudhuri, "Pharmaceutical Industry in India," 125–26; "Good Chemistry," *Economist*, February 2, 2006.

67. Chaudhuri, "Pharmaceutical Industry in India," 127; "Good Chemistry."

68. "Good Chemistry."

69. "Racing down the Pyramid," *Economist*, November 13, 2008; "Novartis Order May Force Pharma MNCs to Change," *Times of India*, April 3, 2013.

70. "India Rejects Lee Pharma's Compulsory License Plea," *Economic Times*,

August 18, 2015; Balaji Subramanian, "Examining the Rejection of Lee's Saxagliptin CL Application," *Spicy IP*, January 22, 2016.

71. WTO Panel Report on EC Complaint concerning Canada—Patent Protection of Pharmaceutical Products, WT/DS114/R, March 17, 2000.

72. "Business Coalition Seeks PFC Designation for India in Special 301 Report," *Inside U.S. Trade*, February 14, 2014; "Special 301 Report Stops Short of Naming India PFC; Watch Lists Largely Unchanged," *Inside U.S. Trade*, May 1, 2014.

73. "Leavitt Says Placing FDA Inspectors in India Is a 'High Priority' for U.S.," *Inside U.S. Trade*, March 21, 2008.

74. Kapczynski, "Harmonization and Its Discontents," 1617–27.

75. Swaraj Barooah, "Modi Shames India, Calls Patent Laws Under-Developed," *Spicy IP*, April 30, 2015.

76. "U.S. Businesses Back Down from Targeting India as PFC under Special 301," *Inside U.S. Trade*, February 12, 2015.

77. Rema Gagarajan, "Panel to Draft Intellectual Property Policy Riddle with Conflict of Interest," *Times of India*, December 2, 2014.

78. Kapczynski, "Harmonization and Its Discontents," 1641.

79. Patralekha Chatterjee, "Novartis Loses Patent Bid: Lessons from India's 3(d) Experience," *Intellectual Property Watch*, April 1, 2013.

80. John Garnaut and Marian Wilkinson, "Plum Jobs for US Trade Deal Advisers," *Sydney Morning Herald*, July 27, 2004.

81. The information given on Kira Alvarez can be found in her LinkedIn profile, accessed May 3, 2016.

82. The list of attendees was emailed to the email accounts of meeting participants from Trevor Gunn's gphaonline.org email account on Saturday, January 22, 2011, at 6:43 PM. That email was released under a FOIA request made by IPWatch.

83. Knowledge Ecology International, "USTR FOIA, 127 Pages of Emails between Industry and USTR TPP negotiators," November 27, 2013. https://www.keionline.org/22342

84. William New, "Confidential USTR Emails Show Close Industry Involvement in TPP Negotiations," May 6, 2015, http://www.ip-watch.org/2015/06/05/confidential-ustr-emails-show-close-industry-involvement-in-tpp-negotiations/

85. See Knowledge Ecology International, "USTR FOIA, 127 Pages of Emails," 2–3.

86. Matthew Flynn, *Pharmaceutical Autonomy and Public Health in Latin America: State, Society, and Industry in Brazil's AIDS Program* (New York: Routledge, 2015), 88.

87. "Pushing Brazil, Christopher Urges Trade Zone by 2005," *New York Times*, March 4, 1996.

88. Kevin Hall, "Talks Get Down to Business; Prickliest Issue Still Intellectual Property Rights," *Journal of Commerce*, May 16, 1997.

89. Ibid.

90. M. Flynn, *Pharmaceutical Autonomy and Public Health*, 141.

91. Kate Jaimet, "Two Sides Spar over Free Trade: At Issue Is Proposed All-Americas Deal," *Ottawa Citizen*, April 12, 2001.

92. Duncan Matthews, *Intellectual Property, Human Rights, and Development: The Role of NGOs and Social Movements* (Northampton, MA: Edward Elgar, 2011), 126.

93. Ibid., 126.

94. Duncan Matthews, "NGOs, Intellectual Property Rights, and Multilateral Institutions," IP-NGOs Research Project, 2006, 20.

95. Matthews, *Intellectual Property, Human Rights, and Development*, 135.

96. "U.S. Action at WTO Threatens Brazil's Successful AIDS Programme," Doctors Without Borders, February 1, 2001; Tina Roseberg, "Look at Brazil," *New York Times*, January 28, 2001; Susan Sell, "TRIPS and the Access to Medicines Campaign," *Wisconsin International Law Journal* 20, no. 3 (2002): 495–96, 520.

97. Sell, "TRIPS and the Access to Medicines Campaign," 513; Jose Marcos Nogueira Viana, "The Global AIDS Crisis: Intellectual Property Rights, the World Trade Organization and Public Health; The Brazilian Perspective," *Connecticut Journal of International Law* 17 (2002): 311.

98. Matthews, *Intellectual Property, Human Rights, and Development*, 137.

99. Marcos Jank, "Agricultural Protectionism: FTAA Seed of Discord," Foreign Trade Information System, 2006.

100. Of America's 130 tariff lines, 100 (over 35 percent) were in agriculture and were clustered in products in which Brazil was most competitive. Ibid.

101. The United States was so adamant about including the EU and Japan because the agricultural subsidies in those countries were even more egregious than the American ones. In 2002, the U.S. subsidized agriculture at a value of 18 percent of total production, compared to 37 percent in the EU and 59 percent in Japan. David Hauck, "Subsidies Are a Focus of WTO Discontent," *Christian Science Monitor*, September 16, 2003. Those figures do not include programs like crop insurance and arguably understate the level of subsidization.

102. Larry Rohter and Jennifer Rich. "Brazil Takes a Stand and Offers a Warning to U.S," *New York Times*, December 19, 2001.

103. Daniel Altman, "Global Trade Looking Glass: Can the U.S. Have It Both Ways," *New York Times*, November 9, 2002; "Senate to Consider New Farm Bill Heavy on Subsidies," Institute for Agriculture and Trade Policy, May 8, 2002, http://iatp.org/news/senate-to-consider-new-farm-bill-heavy-on-subsidies

104. Simon Romero, "Frustrated, U.S. Will Seek Bilateral Trade Pacts," *New York Times*, November 19, 2003.

105. Elizabeth Becker and Larry Rohter, "U.S. and Chile Reach Free Trade Accord," *New York Times*, December 12, 2002.

106. Neil King, "U.S., Chile Open Trade," *Globe and Mail*, December 12, 2002.

107. Ibid.

108. Ann Saccomano, "Sewing Up a Deal," *Journal of Commerce*, April 21, 2003.

109. Richard Lapper, "Central American Leaders Lobby Bush on Trade," *Financial Times*, May 12, 2005.

110. Kevin Gallagher, "Trading Away the Ladder? Trade Politics and Economic Development in the Americas," *New Political Economy* 13, no. 1 (2008): 50.

111. Elizabeth Becker, "U.S. Begins Talks for Trade Pact with Central Americans," *New York Times*, January 9, 2003.

112. Angelina Godoy, *Of Medicines and Markets: Intellectual Property and Human Rights in the Free Trade Era* (Palo Alto: Stanford University Press, 2013).

113. Ibid., 2.
114. Ibid., 95–97.
115. Ibid., 80, 85, 99–100.
116. Ibid., 87–88.
117. Ibid., 59.
118. Ibid., 76.
119. Ibid., 95.
120. Elizabeth Becker, "A Pact on Central America Trade Zone, Minus One," *New York Times*, December 18, 2003.
121. They also wanted stronger labor and environmental stances. In a broader sense, they remained unconvinced that President Bush's approach to trade actually made the United States more economically competitive. Elizabeth Becker, "A Push for a Central American Trade Pact," *New York Times*, May 13, 2005.
122. The Democrats held 233 seats to the Republicans' 202 seats.
123. "Unreasonable delay" is defined as 5 years from the filing of a patent.
124. "House Dems Question TPP's Drug Provisions, 'May 10' Consistency," *Inside U.S. Trade*, December 11, 2015.
125. "Hatch Doubts TPP Vote in 2016, Says GOP Would Get Better Deal on Biologics," *Inside U.S. Trade*, November 13, 2015.
126. "Cardiovascular Disease," World Health Organization, fact sheet, updated May 17, 2017.
127. "Diabetes," World Health Organization, fact sheet, updated October 30, 2018.
128. Siddhartha Mukherjee, *The Emperor of All Maladies: A Biography of Cancer* (New York: Scribner, 2010).
129. "Cancer," World Health Organization, fact sheet, updated September 12, 2018.

CHAPTER 8

1. Alasdair Young, "Not Your Parents' Trade Politics: The Transatlantic Trade and Investment Partnership Negotiations," *Review of International Political Economy* 23, no. 3 (2016): 345–78.
2. Stephen Breyer, *The Court and the World: American Law and the New Global Realities* (New York: Knopf, 2015).
3. Arvind Panagariya, "The Regionalism Debate: An Overview," *World Economy* 22, no. 4 (1999): 477–511.
4. Greg Anderson, "Regionalism's Past, Present, and Future," in *Handbook of the International Political Economy of Trade*, ed. David Deese (Northampton, MA: Edward Elgar, 2014), 227–49.
5. Ibid., 232–34.
6. The United Nations estimates that by 2050, more than twice as many people will live in Africa as in Europe and North America combined (2.5 billion versus 1.1 billion). "World Population Prospects: 2015 Revision," United Nations, Department of Economic and Social Affairs, Population Division, 2015.
7. Bernard Hoekman, "Multilateral Institutions and African Economic Integration," in Deese, *Handbook of the International Political Economy of Trade*, 299–300.

8. On this trade deal, see John Campbell, "Africa's Free Trade Deal Signed in Kigali," *Council on Foreign Relations*, March 27, 2018; "African Countries Are Building a Giant Free Trade Area," *Economist*, December 7, 2017.

9. In 2015, 21.1 million cars were sold in China compared to 17.5 million in the United States. Rose Yu, "China Cars Sales Growth Slows Further," *Wall Street Journal*, January 12, 2016; Mike Spector, Jeff Bennett, and John Stoll, "U.S. Car Sales Set Record in 2015," *Wall Street Journal*, January 5, 2016.

10. Paul Gao, Russell Hensley, and Andreas Zielke, "A Road Map to the Future for the Auto Industry," *McKinsey Quarterly*, October 2014.

11. Ibid.

12. Keith Bradsher, "A Risky Expansion in China," *New York Times*, March 29, 2016.

13. "Ford Says Regulatory Scrutiny on Automakers Is Rising Globally," Bloomberg News, April 23, 2016.

14. Credit Suisse Research Institute, *Global Wealth Report*, Zurich, Switzerland, 2015, 31. In that report, "middle class" is defined as those adults possessing wealth of between $50,000 and $500,000.

15. Yuval Atsmon and Max Magni, "Meet the Chinese Consumer of 2020," *McKinsey Quarterly*, March 2012.

16. Barton Dominic, Yougang Chen, and Amy Jin. "Mapping China's Middle Class," *McKinsey Quarterly*, June 2013.

17. Laurie Burkitt, "American Companies Say Doing Business in China Is Getting Tougher," *Wall Street Journal*, January 19, 2016. An overview of many of these regulatory barriers can be found in "2015 Investment Climate Statement—China," United States Department of State, Bureau of Economic Affairs,, May 2015.

18. An example of a joint venture is Shanghai GM, a venture between GM and China's SAIC Motor Corporation.

19. "China Signals It Will Speed Review of Biotech Traits, Continue Beef Talks," *Inside U.S. Trade*, November 27, 2015.

20. Joel Greene, "U.S. Beef: It's What's for China," Congressional Research Service, Insight, June 22, 2017.

21. Simon Lester and Huan Zhu, "Where's the Beef? Finding a Better Way to Resolve U.S.-China Trade Conflicts" (Free Trade Bulletin 71, CATO Institute, Washington, DC, November 8, 2017), 6.

22. Australia's dominance of China's beef market is likely to further increase as a result of a recently signed free trade agreement between the two states. "China Signals It Will Speed Review of Biotech Traits, Continue Beef Talks," *Inside U.S. Trade*, November 27, 2015.

23. For the trend in cotton, for example, see Amy Quark, *Global Rivalries: Standards Wars and the Transnational Cotton Trade* (Chicago: University of Chicago Press, 2013).

24. Zhang Yu, "Pricey Pills," *Global Times* (China), January 8, 2015.

25. Yanzhong Huang, "Chinese Pharma: A Global Health Game Changer," Council on Foreign Relations, March 31, 2015.

26. Ted Genoways, "Corn Wars," *New Republic*, August 16, 2015.

27. Ibid.

28. Becky Sullivan, "The Trademark Woes of Michael Jordan (and Many Oth-

ers) in China," National Public Radio, August 16, 2015; Yimou Lee, "China's 'Fake' Apple Stores Thrive Ahead of New iPhone Launch," *Reuters*, September 23, 2015.

29. Levi Tilleman, *The Great Race: The Global Quest for the Car of the Future* (New York: Simon and Schuster, 2015), 237–51; "Tesla's Success Sparks China's e-Car Race," *China Daily*, April 26, 2016.

30. Clive Thompson, "How a Nation of Tech Copycats Became a Hub for Innovation," *Wired*, December 29, 2015.

31. Ibid.

32. David Vogel, *Trading Up: Consumer and Environmental Regulation in a Global Economy* (Cambridge, MA: Harvard University Press, 1995), 154.

33. Ibid., 156.

34. David Vogel, *The Politics of Precaution: Health, Safety, and Environmental Risks in Europe and the United States* (Princeton: Princeton University Press, 2012), 65, 76.

35. D. Vogel, *Politics of Precaution*, 75; Mark Pollack and Gregory Shaffer, *When Cooperation Fails: The International Law and Politics of Genetically Modified Foods* (Oxford: Oxford University Press, 2009) 65.

36. Daniel Drezner, *All Politics Is Global: Explaining International Regulatory Regimes* (Princeton: Princeton University Press, 2007), 155.

37. "GM Food and Trade: More Trouble," *Economist*, July 3, 2003.

38. Elizabeth DeSombre, *Domestic Sources of International Environmental Policy: Industry, Environmentalists, and U.S. Power* (Cambridge, MA: MIT Press, 2000).

39. John Braithwaite and Peter Drahos, *Global Business Regulation* (Cambridge: Cambridge University Press, 2000), 350.

40. "Brick by Brick: Inside LEGO," video documentary, Bloomberg News, accessed May 1, 2016, https://www.youtube.com/watch?v=SnI56MU6H_0

41. Toy Industry Association, "U.S.-EU Free Trade Agreement: Tipping over the Regulatory Barriers," statement to the House Subcommittee on Commerce, Manufacturing, and Trade, July 23, 2013.

42. D. Vogel, *Politics of Precaution*, 203–7.

43. David Barboza and Louise Story, "Toymaking in China, Mattel's Way," *New York Times*, July 26, 2007.

44. "How Japan Has Maintained the Most Protected and Closed Auto Market in the Industrialized World," American Automotive Policy Council, accessed May 23, 2019, http://www.americanautocouncil.org/sites/aapc2016/files/Japans%2BProtected%2BAuto%2BMarket.pdf

45. Carol Flannagan et al., "Comparing Motor Vehicle Crash Risks of EU and US Vehicles," University of Michigan Transportation Research Institute (US), CEESAR (France), and the Transport Research Laboratory (UK), May 2015.

46. This paragraph draws on "U.S., EU Auto Regulators to Cooperate on Seat Belt Anchors, Visibility," *Inside U.S. Trade*, March 18, 2016.

47. Aseem Prakash and Matthew Potoski, *The Voluntary Environmentalists: Green Clubs, ISO 14004, and Voluntary Environmental Regulation* (Cambridge: Cambridge University Press, 2006); Philip Pattberg, "The Institutionalization of Private Governance: How Business and Nonprofit Organizations Agree on Transnational Rules," *Governance* 4 (2005): 589–610; Dennis Rondinelli and Ted London, "How Corporations and Environmental Groups Cooperate: Assessing Cross-Sector Alli-

ances and Collaborations," *Academy of Management Executive* 17, no. 1 (2003): 61–76.

48. Michael Porter, *The Competitive Advantage of Nations* (New York: Free Press, 1998).

49. "The Benefits and Costs of the Clean Air Act from 1990 to 2020," U.S. Environmental Protection Agency, Office of Air and Radiation, final report, April 2011, 3.

50. Inge Lippert, Tony Huzzard, Ulrich Jurgens, and William Lazonik, *Corporate Governance, Employee Voice, and Worker Organization: Sustaining High Road Jobs in the Automotive Supply Industry* (Oxford: Oxford University Press, 2014).

51. This paragraph draws from Chris Arnold and Marilyn Geewax, "White House to Financial Advisers: Put Savers' Interest First," National Public Radio, April 6, 2016. See also Dave Michaels, "A Split over Protecting Investors: The Labor Department Is Moving Ahead of the SEC on Broker Rules," Bloomberg News, March 12, 2015; Mark Schoeff, "SEC Commissioner: DOL Fiduciary Rule Would Create 'a Mess,'" *Investment News*, August 4, 2015.

52. "U.S., EU Auto Regulators to Cooperate on Seat Belt Anchors."

53. American Association for the Advancement of Science, "Statement of the AAAS Board of Directors on Labeling of Genetically Modified Foods," October 20, 2012. The definitive EU-funded metastudy of GMOs determined that "the main conclusion to be drawn from the efforts of more than 130 research projects, covering a period of more than 25 years of research, and involving more than 500 independent research groups, is that biotechnology, and in particular GMOs, are not per se more risky than e.g. conventional plant breeding technologies." "A Decade of EU-Funded GMO Research, 2001–2010," European Commission, Directorate E- Food, Agriculture, Fisheries, and Biotechnology, 2010, 16.

54. "Cardiovascular Disease," World Health Organization, fact sheet, updated January 2015.

55. Laura Wellesley, Anthony Froggatt, and Catherine Happerl, "Changing Climate, Changing Diet: Pathways to Lower Meat Consumption," Chatham House, November 24, 2015, vii.

56. John Sutter, "Why Beef Is the New SUV?" CNN, November 24, 2015.

57. Rob Bailey, Anthony Froggatt, and Laura Wellesley, "Livestock—Climate Change's Forgotten Sector: Global Public Opinion on Meat and Dairy Consumption," Chatham House, December 3, 2014, 15; "Global Warming: What Should Be Done?" *New York Times*, January 29, 2015.

58. Chris Calkins, *Packaging and Product Effects on Sensory, Shelf-Life and Color of Beef: Project Summary*, (National Cattlemen's Beef Association, Center for Research and Knowledge Management, Centennial CO, 2003), 3.

59. Rick Weiss, "FDA Is Urged to Ban Carbon-Monoxide Treated Beef," *Washington Post*, February 20, 2006. The FDA and the USDA share jurisdiction in meat labeling.

60. Daren Cornforth and Melvin Hunt, "Low Oxygen Packaging of Fresh Meat with Carbon Monoxide: Meat Quality, Microbiology, and Safety" (white paper 2, American Meat Science Association, 2008), 7.

61. Marian Burros, "Which Cut Is Older? It's a Trick Question," *New York Times*, February 21, 2006.

62. Julie Schmit, "Carbon Monoxide Keeps Meat Red Longer; Is That Good?" *USA Today*, October 30, 2007.

63. Food and Water Watch, "Carbon Monoxide: Masking the Truth about Meat," 2008, 2.

64. Consumer Federation of America, Consumer Union, Food and Water Watch, Safe Tables Our Priority, Government Accountability Project, and National Consumer's League, Letter to the Department of Health and Human Services and the Department of Agriculture, June 2, 2008.

65. Weiss, "FDA Is Urged to Ban Carbon-Monoxide Treated Beef"; Consumer Federation of America, "Leading Supermarket Chains Refuse to Sell Carbon-Monoxide-Treated Beef," April 5, 2006.

66. "Leading Supermarket Chains Refuse to Sell Carbon-Monoxide-Treated Beef."

67. "Proof in the Pink: Meat Treated to Give It Fresh Look," ABC News, November 14, 2007; Standing Committee on the Food Chain and Animal Health, Section on Toxicological Safety of the Food Chain, summary record of a meeting under chairperson Patricia Brunko, April 7, 2003; T. Ohtsuki et al., "Improvement of Carbon Monoxide Analysis in Fish Meat," *Shokuhin Eiseigaku Zasshi* 52, no. 2 (2011): 130–34, English abstract available at http://www.ncbi.nlm.nih.gov/pubmed/21515968

68. Susan Sell, "TRIPS Was Never Enough: Vertical Forum Shifting, FTAs, ACTA, and TPP," *Journal of Intellectual Property Law* 18 (2011): 462.

69. Robert Zirkelbach, "The Reality of Prescription Medication Costs in Three Charts," Pharmaceutical Research and Manufacturers Association, May 27, 2014. Accessed May 1, 2016. https://www.phrma.org/catalyst/the-reality-of-prescription-medicine-costs-in-three-charts

70. Ibid.

71. Jack Scannell, "Four Reasons Drugs Are Expensive, of Which Two Are False," *Forbes*, October 13, 2015.

72. The pharmaceutical case also demonstrates the limits of that model. For example, the drug industry is much better at delivering innovation for diseases that afflict people in developed countries than for diseases that primarily afflict poor people in developing countries.

73. Matthew Herper, "My Lunch with Shkreli: What We Should Learn from Pharma's Latest Monster," *Forbes*, September 24, 2015.

74. "The New Drug War: Hard Pills to Swallow," *Economist*, January 4, 2014.

75. Indeed, there is already a brewing conflict between drug firms and insurance companies over high drug costs. Carolyn Johnson, "Secret Rebates, Coupons, and Exclusions: How the Battle over High Drug Prices Is Really Being Fought," *Washington Post*, May 12, 2016.

76. "Employer Health Benefits, 2015 Annual Survey," Kaiser Family Foundation and Health Research and Education Trust, 2015, 1. Businesses spend an average of $5,179 for individual plans. Ibid., 2.

77. Timothy Lee, "Emails Show Cozy Relationship between Obama Trade Negotiators and Industry," *Washington Post*, November 29, 2013.

78. Frederick Mayer, *Interpreting NAFTA: The Science and Art of Political Analysis* (New York: Columbia University Press, 1998), 186–89; John Audley, *Green Politics*

and Global Trade: NAFTA and the Future of Environmental Politics (Washington, DC: Georgetown University Press, 1997), 72–78.

79. "Leaked TPP Text Underscores U.S. Isolation in Environment Chapter Talks," *Inside U.S. Trade*, January 17, 2014.

80. "TPP Enviro Talks Get Bogged Down over MEAs, Conservation, and Biodiversity," *Inside U.S. Trade*, January 17, 2014.

81. Edward-Isaac Dovere, "Extreme Secrecy Eroding Support for Obama's Trade Pact," *Politico*, May 4, 2015.

82. Lydia DePillis, "The Catch-22 of Trade Deals Done in Secret," *Washington Post*, May 15, 2015.

83. Sean Flynn, "WIPO Treaty for the Blind Shows That Transparency Can Work (and Is Necessary)," *Infojustice*, June 26, 2013, http://infojustice.org/archives/30027

Bibliography

Aaronson, Susan. *Taking Trade to the Streets: The Lost History of Public Efforts to Shape Globalization*. Ann Arbor: University of Michigan Press, 2001.

Aaronson, Susan. *Trade and the American Dream: A Social History of Postwar Trade Policy*. Lexington: University of Kentucky Press, 1996.

Aaronson, Susan, and Jamie Zimmerman. *Trade Imbalance: The Struggle to Weigh Human Rights Concerns in Trade Policymaking*. Cambridge: Cambridge University Press, 2007.

Abbott, Chelsea. "European Standards versus American Standards: Car Seat Edition." *Magic Beans*, June 30, 2013. http://mbeans.com/spillingthebeans/baby/car-seats/european-standards-vs-american-standards-car-seat-edition/

Abbott, Frederick. "The WTO Medicines Decision: World Pharmaceutical Trade and the Protection of Public Health." *American Journal of International Law* 99, no. 2 (2005): 317–58.

Abbott, Kenneth, and Duncan Snidal. "The Governance Triangle: Regulatory Standards Institutions and the Shadow of the State." In *The Politics of Global Regulation*, edited by Walter Mattli and Ngaire Woods. Princeton: Princeton University Press, 2009.

Abito, Jose Miguel, David Besanko, and Daniel Diermeier. "Corporate Reputational Dynamics, Private Regulation, and Activist Pressure." In *Strategy beyond Markets*, edited by Jose Abito, David Besanko, and Daniel Diermeier. Bingley: Emerald Group, 2016.

"African Countries Are Building a Giant Free Trade Area." *Economist*, December 7, 2017.

"Agriculture, Food Coalition Urges Quick Decision on Japan's TPP Entry." *Inside U.S. Trade*, March 29, 2013.

Alemanno, Alberto. "Food Safety and the Single European Market." In *What's the*

Beef? The Contested Governance of European Food Safety, edited by Christopher Ansell and David Vogel. Cambridge, MA: MIT Press, 2006.

Alford, Peter, and Rick Wallace. "Japan PM Quits for Party's Sake." *Australian*, June 3, 2010.

Alston, Philip. "Labor Rights Provisions in U.S. Trade Law: Aggressive Unilateralism?" In *Human Rights, Labor Rights, and International Trade*, edited by Lance Compa and Stephen Diamond. Philadelphia: University of Pennsylvania Press, 2003.

Altman, Daniel. "Global Trade Looking Glass: Can the U.S. Have It Both Ways" *New York Times*, November 9, 2002.

Alvarez, Kira. Profile. LinkedIn. Accessed May 3, 2016. https://www.linkedin.com/in/kira-alvarez-trade/

American Association for the Advancement of Science. "Statement by the AAAS Board of Directors on Labeling of Genetically Modified Foods." October 20, 2012.

American Automotive Policy Council. "How Japan Has Maintained the Most Protected and Closed Auto Market in the Industrialized World." Accessed May 23, 2019. http://www.americanautocouncil.org/sites/aapc2016/files/Japans%2BProtected%2BAuto%2BMarket.pdf

Andersen, Jørgen. "Denmark: Environmental Conflict and the 'Greening' of the Labour Movement." *Scandinavian Political Studies* 13, no. 2 (1990): 185–210.

Anderson, Greg. "Regionalism's Past, Present, and Future." In *Handbook of the International Political Economy of Trade*, edited by David Deese. Northampton, MA: Edward Elgar, 2014.

Anderson, Richard. "Pharmaceutical Industry Gets High on Fat Profits." BBC News, November 6, 2014.

Antras, Pol, and Elhanan Helpman. "Global Sourcing." *Journal of Political Economy* 112, no. 3 (2004): 552–80.

Ardill, John. "Exhaust Pact Doubts / Danish Government Refuses to Withdraw Calls for Tougher Anti-Pollution Measures." *Guardian*, September 23, 1986.

Arnold, Chris, and Marilyn Geewax. "White House to Financial Advisers: Put Savers' Interest First." National Public Radio, April 6, 2016.

Aspinwall, Mark. "The NAFTA Side Agreements and Governance in Mexico." In *Leveling the Playing Field: Transnational Regulatory Integration and Development*, edited by Laszlo Brust and Gerald McDermott. Oxford: Oxford University Press, 2014.

"Atmospheric Pollution—Motor Vehicle Emissions, Background Note on Environmental Directives." Note to the commissioner for Jean-Francois Verstrynge, Commission of the European Communities, January 19, 1985. Historical Archives of the European Union, European University Institute, Florence.

Atsmon, Yuval, and Max Magni. "Meet the Chinese Consumer of 2020." *McKinsey Quarterly*, March 2012.

Audley, John. *Green Politics and Global Trade: NAFTA and the Future of Environmental Politics*. Washington, DC: Georgetown University Press, 1997.

Auerbach, Stuart. "Reagan Orders Sanctions against Thailand; Duty-Free Status Removed from $165 Million in Thai Imports." *Washington Post*, January 21, 1989.

"Auto Pact Won't Be Hurt by Trade Deal, Envoy Says." *Toronto Star*, January 14, 1987.

Baccini, Leonardo, Pablo Pinto, and Stephen Weymouth. "The Distributional Consequences of Preferential Trade Liberalization." *International Organization* 71, no. 2 (2017): 373–95.

Bach, David, and Abraham Newman. "Governing Lipitor and Lipstick: Capacity, Sequencing, and Power in Pharmaceutical and Cosmetics Regulation." *Review of International Political Economy* 17, no. 4 (2010): 675.

Bach, David, and Abraham Newman. "Transgovernmental Networks and Domestic Policy Convergence: Evidence from Insider Trading Regulation." *International Organization* 64, no. 3 (2010): 505–28.

Bagwell, Kyle, and Robert Staiger. "National Sovereignty in an Interdependent World." Working paper 10249, National Bureau of Economic Research, Cambridge, MA, 2004.

Bagwell, Kyle, and Robert Staiger. "The WTO as a Mechanism for Securing Market Access Property Rights: Implications for Global Labor and Environmental Perspectives." *Journal of Economic Perspectives* 15, no. 3 (2001): 69–88.

Bailey, Rob, Anthony Froggatt, and Laura Wellesley. "Livestock—Climate Change's Forgotten Sector: Global Public Opinion on Meat and Dairy Consumption." Chatham House, December 3, 2014.

Baker, Brook. "Arthritic Flexibilities for Accessing Medicines: Analysis of WTO Action Regarding Paragraph 6 of the Doha Declaration on the TRIPS Agreement and Public Health." *Indiana International and Comparative Law Review* 14, no. 3 (2004): 613–715.

Baker, Stewart. "Playing the Environmental Card." *Journal of Commerce*, February 11, 1992.

Baldia, Sonia. "Knowledge Process Outsourcing to India: Important Considerations for U.S. Companies." In *Doing Business in India: Critical Legal Issues for U.S. Companies*. New York: Practicing Institute, 2007.

Baldwin, Richard. "Regulatory Protectionism, Developing Nations, and a Two-Tier World Trade System." Discussion paper 2574, Centre for Economic Policy Research, London, 2000.

Bangsberg, P. T. "Thai Businesses Seek Patent Safeguards to Blunt US Moves." *Journal of Commerce*, April 14, 1989.

Barboza, David, and Louise Story. "Toymaking in China, Mattel's Way." *New York Times*, July 26, 2007.

Barnes, Hilary. "A Danish Passion for Cleanliness." *Financial Times*, August 19, 1988.

Barnes, Hilary and Quentin Peel. "Denmark Poses Threat to EEC Reforms." *Financial Times*, November 30, 1985.

Baron, David. "Private Politics, Corporate Social Responsibility, and Integrated Strategy." *Journal of Economics and Management Strategy* 10, no. 1 (2001): 7–45.

Baron, David. "Self-Regulation in Public and Private Politics." *Quarterly Journal of Political Science* 9, no. 2 (2014): 231–67.

Baron, David, and Daniel Diermeier. "Strategic Activism and Nonmarket Strategy." *Journal of Economics and Management Strategy* 16, no. 3 (2007): 599–634.

Barooah, Swaraj. "Modi Shames India, Calls Patent Laws Under-Developed." *Spicy IP*, April 30, 2015.

Barrows, Samuel. "Racing to the Top . . . at Last: The Regulation of Safety in Shipping," In *The Politics of Global Regulation*, edited by Walter Mattli and Ngaire Woods. Princeton: Princeton University Press, 2009.

Bartley, Tim. "Certification as a Mode of Social Regulation." In *Handbook on the Politics of Regulation*, edited by David Levi-Faur. New York: Edward Elgar, 2011.

Bartley, Tim. "Certifying Forests and Factories: States, Social Movements, and the Rise of Private Regulation in the Apparel and Forest Products Fields." *Politics and Society* 31, no. 3 (2003): 433–64.

Barton, Dominic, Yougang Chen, and Amy Jin. "Mapping China's Middle Class." *McKinsey Quarterly*, June 2013.

Beder, Sharon. *Suiting Themselves: How Corporations Drive the Global Agenda*. London: Routledge, 2006.

Becker, Elizabeth. "A Pact on Central America Trade Zone, Minus One." *New York Times*, December 18, 2003.

Becker, Elizabeth. "A Push for a Central American Trade Pact." *New York Times*, May 13, 2005.

Becker, Elizabeth. "U.S. Begins Talks for Trade Pact with Central Americans." *New York Times*, January 9, 2003.

Becker, Elizabeth, and Larry Rohter. "U.S. and Chile Reach Free Trade Accord." *New York Times*, December 12, 2002.

"Beef Import Limits Must Conform to Global Standards." *Yomiuri Shimbun*, October 22, 2011.

"Beef Industry Groups Press for Incremental Beef Export Policy." *Inside U.S. Trade*, May 29, 2009.

"Beef Safety Audit Passes Muster." *Japan Times*, May 20, 2006.

"Beef-Safety Report Being Misused: Panelist." *Japan Times*, December 9, 2005.

"Beef Scandal Exposes Fault." *Yomiuri Shimbun*, January 25, 2002.

"Beef Shortages a Possibility." *Yomiuri Shimbun*, December 26, 2003.

"Beef Upstaged Security, Nukes in Talks with Rice." *Nikkei Weekly*, April 4, 2005.

Behr, Peter. "President's Dilemma." *Washington Post*, March 22, 1981.

Bello, Judith, and Alan Holmer. "The Heart of the 1988 Trade Act: A History of Legislative Amendments to Section 301." *Stanford Journal of International Law* 25, no. 1 (1988): 1–44.

Berkowitz, Justin. "Free-Trade Cars: Why a U.S.-Europe Free-Trade Agreement Is a Good Idea." *Car and Driver*, June 28, 2013.

Bernard, Andrew, Jonathan Eaton, Bradford Jensen, and Samuel Kortum. "Plants and Productivity in International Trade." *American Economic Review* 93, no. 4 (2003): 1268–90.

Betts, Paul. "France Withdraws Backing for EC Proposals on Car Pollution." *Financial Times*, July 22, 1988.

Betts, Paul. "Greens Make Peugeot Car Chief See Red." *Financial Times*, July 14, 1988.

BEUC: The European Consumer Organisation. "Consumers at the Heart of the Transatlantic Trade and Investment Partnership." Position paper, Brussels, May 21, 2014.

Blaser, Fred. "Auto Pact's Been Irrelevant for Years." *Financial Post*, July 6, 1987.

Bloomberg News. "Brick by Brick: Inside LEGO." Video documentary. Accessed May 1, 2016. https://www.youtube.com/watch?v=SnI56MU6H_0

Bloomberg News. "Ford Says Regulatory Scrutiny on Automakers Is Rising Globally." April 23, 2016.

Bordenave, Gerard, and Yannick Lung. "The Twin Internationalization Strategies of US Automakers: GM and Ford." In *Globalization or Regionalization of the American and Asian Car Industry?*, edited by Michel Freyssenet, Koichi Shimuzi, and Giuseppe Volpato. New York: Palgrave Macmillan, 2003.

Bowe, Anthony. "Meaty Comeback." *Denver Post*, February 27, 2009.

Bradshaw, Della. "Bumpy Ride on the Road to Conversion." *Financial Times*, March 15, 1989.

Bradsher, Keith. "A Risky Expansion in China." *New York Times*, March 29, 2016.

Braid, Mary. "Drug Giants Flex Muscles as SA Tries to Cut Health Bill." *Independent*, October 8, 1997.

Braithwaite, John, and Peter Drahos. *Global Business Regulation*. Cambridge: Cambridge University Press, 2000.

Braithwaite, John, and Peter Drahos. *Information Feudalism: Who Owns the Knowledge Economy*. New York: New Press, 2002.

Breyer, Stephen. *The Court and the World: American Law and the New Global Realities*. New York: Knopf, 2015.

Broda, Christian, Nuno Limao, and David Weinstein. "Optimal Tariffs and Market Power: The Evidence." *American Economic Review* 98, no. 5 (2008): 2032–65.

Brooke, James. "In Japan, Beef Business Sinks in a Sea of Skepticism." *New York Times*, November 4, 2001.

Brooke, James. "Japan Still Bans U.S. Beef, Chafing American Officials." *New York Times*, April 21, 2005.

Brooke, James. "Mad Cow Disease Sets Off a Scare in Japan." *New York Times*, September 27, 2001.

Brooke, James. "Scandals Tainting Japan's Pride in Its Food." *New York Times*, June 1, 2002.

Brown, Derek. "Lead-Free Petrol to Be Adopted by EEC in 1989." *Guardian*, December 7, 1984.

Brown, Warren, and Stuart Auerbach. "Domestic Content Bill Takes Aim at Japan." *Washington Post*, December 9, 1982.

Broz, J. Lawrence, and Seth Werfel. "Exchange Rates and Industry Demands for Trade Protection." *International Organization* 68, no. 2 (2014): 393–416.

"BSE, Food Additives." Dedicated issue, *Food Safety Citizen's Watch Newsletter* 1 (July 2005).

Burgdorfer, Bob. "Heat's on COOL; U.S. Food Labeling Law Shakes Up All Producers." *National Post's Financial Post and FP Investing* (Canada), April 9, 2009.

Burkitt, Laurie. "American Companies Say Doing Business in China Is Getting Tougher." *Wall Street Journal*, January 19, 2016.

Burros, Marian. "Which Cut Is Older? It's a Trick Question." *New York Times*, February 21, 2006.

"Bush Asks Japanese PM to Fully Open Market to US Beef." Kyodo News, BBC Monitoring Asia Pacific, July 6, 2008.

"Business Coalition Seeks PFC Designation for India in Special 301 Report." *Inside U.S. Trade*, February 14, 2014.

Büthe, Tim, and Nathaniel Harris. "Codex Alimentarius Commission." In *Handbook of Transnational Governance: New Institutions and Innovations*, edited by Thomas Hale and David Held. Cambridge: Polity, 2011.

Büthe, Tim, and Walter Mattli. *The New Global Rulers: The Privatization of Regulation in the World Economy*. Princeton: Princeton University Press, 2011.

Calkins, Chris. *Packaging and Product Effects on Sensory, Shelf-Life and Color of Beef, Project Summary*. National Cattlemen's Beef Association, Center for Research and Knowledge Management, Centennial, CO, 2003.

Cameron, Deborah. "Japan's Beef with US a Plus for Australia." *Sydney Morning Herald*, January 27, 2006.

Cameron, Maxwell, and Brian Tomlin. *The Making of NAFTA: How the Deal Was Done*. Ithaca: Cornell University Press, 2000.

Camerra-Rowe, Pamela, and Michelle Egan. "International Regulators and Network Governance." In *Oxford Handbook of Business and Government*, edited by David Coen, Wyn Grant, and Graham Wilson. New York: Oxford University Press, 2010.

Campbell, John. "Africa's Free Trade Deal Signed in Kigali." Council on Foreign Relations, March 27, 2018.

Candies, Jan. Letter from the director of European affairs at Ford of Europe to the European Economic Commission, with accompanying paper. February 1, 1985. Historical Archive of the European Union, European University Institute, Florence.

Canis, Bill, and Richard Lattanzio. "U.S. and EU Motor Vehicle Standards: Issues for Transatlantic Trade Negotiations." Congressional Research Service, February 18, 2014.

Carbaugh, Robert. "NAFTA and the U.S. Mexican Trucking Dispute." *Journal of International and Global Economic Studies* 4, no. 1 (2011) 1–10.

Carrillo, Jorge. "NAFTA: The Process of Regional Integration of Motor Vehicle Production." In *Cars, Carriers of Regionalism?*, edited by Jorge Carrillo, Yannick Lung, and Rob van Tulder. New York: Palgrave Macmillan, 2004.

Cauvin, Henri. "Trial in AIDS Drug Lawsuit Opens in Pretoria." *New York Times*, March 6, 2001.

Centeno, Miguel, and Sylvia Maxfield. "The Marriage of Finance and Order: Changes in the Mexican Political Elite." *Journal of Latin American Studies* 24 (1992): 57–85.

"Chamber Stresses Need for Japan to Follow 'Words' with 'Action' on TPP." *Inside U.S. Trade*, December 9, 2011.

Chase, Kerry. *Trading Blocs: States, Firms, and Regions in the World Economy*. Ann Arbor: University of Michigan Press, 2005.

Chatterjee, Patralekha. "Novartis Loses Patent Bid: Lessons from India's 3(d) Experience." *Intellectual Property Watch*, April 1, 2013.

Chaudhuri, Sudip. "The Pharmaceutical Industry in India after TRIPS." In *New Political Economy of Pharmaceuticals: Production, Innovation, and TRIPS in the Global South*, edited by Hans Lofgren and Owain Williams. Gordonsville, VA: Palgrave MacMillan, 2013.

Cheeseright, Paul. "Bonn Relaxes Insistence on Strict Exhaust Rules." *Financial Times*, June 28, 1985.

"China Signals It Will Speed Review of Biotech Traits, Continue Beef Talks." *Inside U.S. Trade*, November 27, 2015.

Chira, Susan. "Diffuse Goals Set by Naders of Japan." *New York Times*, July 14, 1986.

Chislett, William. "Ford Motor Kills Two Birds with One Stone in Mexican Outlay." *Financial Times*, January 18, 1984.

Ciuriak, Dan, Beverly Lapham, Robert Wolfe, Terry Collins-Williams, and John Curtis. "New-New Trade Policy." Working paper 1263, Economics Department, Queen's University, Kingston, Ontario, 2011.

Clark, Bruce. "Older Parties Covet the Green Family's Clothes." *Financial Times*, April 24, 1989.

Clemens, Roxanne. "Meat Traceability and Consumer Assurance in Japan." Briefing paper 03-MBP 5, Midwest Agribusiness Trade Research and Information Center, Ames IA, September 2003.

Clemetson, Lynette. "U.S. Officials Say Suspect Beef Went to Wider Region." *New York Times*, December 29, 2003.

Cockburn, Iain. "The Changing Structure of the Pharmaceutical Industry." *Health Affairs* 23, no. 1 (2004): 10-22.

Coen, David, Wyn Grant, and Graham Wilson. "Political Science: Perspectives on Business and Government." In *The Oxford Handbook of Business and Government*, edited by David Coen, Wyn Grant, and Graham Wilson. New York: Oxford University Press, 2010.

Cohen, Lizabeth. *A Consumer's Republic: The Politics of Mass Consumption in Postwar America*. New York: Vintage Books, 2003.

Collier, Roger. "Drug Patents: The Evergreening Problem." *Canadian Medical Association Journal* 185, no. 9 (2013) E385–E386.

Collins, Huntly. "AIDS Activists Target a Disparity of Care." *Philadelphia Enquirer*, March 5, 2001.

Condon, Bradly. "NAFTA and the Environment: A Trade-Friendly Approach." *Northwestern Journal of International Law and Business* 14, no. 3 (1993–94) 528–48.

Conlon, Michael. "The History of U.S. Beef and Pork Exports to Japan." USDA Foreign Agricultural Service, Global Agriculture Information Network, April 24, 2009.

Conrad, David. "Mining the Patent Thicket: The Supreme Court's Rejection of the Automatic Injunction Rule in *eBay v. MercExchange*." *Review of Litigation* 26, no. 1: 119–54.

Conroy, Michael. *Branded! How the "Certification Revolution" Is Transforming Global Corporations*. Gabriola Island, BC: New Society Publishers, 2007.

"Consensus on TRIPS Unravels as U.S. Blocks Deal on Scope of Diseases." *Inside U.S. Trade*, January 3, 2003.

Consumer Federation of America. "Leading Supermarket Chains Refuse to Sell Carbon-Monoxide-Treated Beef." April 5, 2006.

Consumer Federation of America, Consumer Union, Food and Water Watch, Safe Tables Our Priority, Government Accountability Project, and National Consumer's League. Letter to the Department of Health and Human Services and the Department of Agriculture. June 2, 2008.

Conybeare, John. *Merging Traffic: The Consolidation of the International Automobile Industry*. Lanham, MD: Rowman and Littlefield, 2004.

Cooke, Stephen. "Latest Japanese Ban Lifts Export Hopes." *Weekly Times* (Australia), January 25, 2006.

Cooper, Ken. "Taking Up the Green Issue." *Financial Times*, November 3, 1988.

Cooper, William, and Mark Manyin. "Japan Joins the Trans-Pacific Partnership: What Are the Implications?" Congressional Research Service, August 13, 2013.

Copeland, Brian. "The Pollution Haven Hypothesis." In *Handbook on Trade and the Environment*, edited by Kevin Gallagher. New York: Edward Elgar, 2008.

Cornforth, Daren, and Melvin Hunt. "Low Oxygen Packaging of Fresh Meat with Carbon Monoxide: Meat Quality, Microbiology, and Safety." White paper 2, American Meat Science Association, 2008.

Cornwell, Rupert. "Bonn Faces Tough Fight over Car Pollution Plan." *Financial Times*, September 21, 1984.

Correa, C. M. *Intellectual Property Rights, the WTO, and Developing Countries: The TRIPs Agreement and Policy Options*. London: Zed Books / Third World Network, 2000.

Cortell, Andrew. "Centralization, Access, and Influence: The Reagan Administration and the Semiconductor Industry's Trade Complaints." *Governance: An*

International Journal of Policy, Administration, and Institutions 10, no. 3 (1997): 261–85.

"Countries Still Split in WTO Drug Patent Talks, Close In on Scope." *Inside U.S. Trade*, September 27, 2002.

Cowles, Maria. "Setting the Agenda for a New Europe: The ERT and EC 1992." *Journal of Common Market Studies* 33, no. 4 (1995): 501–26.

"A Cow Walk toward a Crisis." *Japan Times*, March 21, 2005.

Craypo, Charles. "Meatpacking: Industry Restructuring and Union Decline." In *Contemporary Collective Bargaining in the Private Sector*, edited by Paula Voos. Madison, WI: Industrial Relations Research Association, 1994.

Credit Suisse Research Institute. *Global Wealth Report*. Zurich, Switzerland, 2015.

Cutler, A. Claire, Virginia Haufler, and Tony Porter, eds. *Private Authority and International Affairs*. New York: State University of New York Press, 1999.

Cwiertka, Katarzyna. *Modern Japanese Cuisine: Food, Power and National Identity*. London: Reaktion, 2006.

D'Amato, Alfonse. "Enough Pirating of U.S. Goods." *New York Times*, January 23, 1986.

Davis, Christina. *Food Fights over Free Trade: How International Institutions Promote Agricultural Trade Liberalization*. Princeton: Princeton University Press, 2005.

Dawkins, William. "EC Agrees Measures to Cut Car Pollution." *Financial Times*, December 4, 1987.

Dawkins, William. "Strict EC Car Exhaust Limits Proposed." *Financial Times*, April 6, 1989.

Dawkins, William, and Kevin Done. "Plan for Compulsory EC Standards." *Financial Times*, June 23, 1989.

Dawkins, William, and John Griffiths. "EC Agrees Car Exhaust Plan." *Financial Times*, July 7, 1987.

Day, Catherine. "Atmospheric Pollution—New Developments." Note to Commissioner Sutherland, January 22, 1985. Historical Archive of the European Union, European University Institute, Florence.

"Decision on U.S. Beef Ban Likely before End of June." *Nikkei Weekly*, May 8, 2006.

Deere, Carolyn. *The Implementation Game: The TRIPS Agreement and the Global Politics of Intellectual Property Reform in Developing Countries*. New York: Oxford University Press, 2009.

Deike, John. "Europe Installs Raw Milk Vending Machines While U.S. Rules Unpasteurized Dairy Illegal." EcoWatch, March 11, 2014.

"Demands with Regards to the Problem of American Beef Imports." Dedicated issue, *Food Safety Citizen's Watch Newsletter* 7, January 2006.

Democracy Corps/Campaign for America's Future Poll, November 2008. Retrieved November 24, 2014, from iPOLL Databank, Roper Center for Public Opinion Research, University of Connecticut, Storrs.

Democracy Corps National–Public Citizen Poll. June 23–28, 2016. https://www.citizen.org/wp-content/uploads/greenberg-polling-memo-july-2016.pdf

DePillis, Lydia. "The Catch-22 of Trade Deals Done in Secret." *Washington Post*, May 15, 2015.

DeSombre, Elizabeth. 2000. *Domestic Sources of International Environmental Policy: Industry, Environmentalists, and U.S. Power*. Cambridge, MA: MIT Press.

Destler, I. M. *American Trade Politics*. 4th ed. Washington, DC: Institute for International Economics, 2005.

"Developing Countries Push for Broad Leeway under Drug Patent Rules." *Inside U.S. Trade*, October 25, 2002.

"Developing Countries Push for TRIPS to Allow Cheaper Medicines." *Inside U.S. Trade*, June 22, 2001.

Devereaux, Charan, Robert Lawrence, and Michael Watkins. *Case Studies in U.S. Trade Negotiations. Vol. 1, Making the Rules.* Washington, DC: Institute for International Economics, 2006.

Devereaux, Charan, Robert Lawrence, and Michael Watkins. *Case Studies in U.S. Trade Negotiations. Vol. 2, Resolving Disputes.* Washington, DC: Institute for International Economics, 2006.

De Ville, Ferdi, and Gabriel Siles-Brügge, *TTIP: The Truth about the Transatlantic Trade and Investment Partnership*. Cambridge: Polity, 2016.

DeYoung, Karen. "Sweden's Greens Add Only Dash of Color to Dull Election Campaign." *Washington Post*, September 18, 1988.

Dickson, Tim. "Brussels Calls for Stricter Car Pollution Standards." *Financial Times*, March 9, 1989.

Dickson, Tim. "EC Curbs on Car Pollution Agreed." *Financial Times*, June 10, 1989.

Dickson, Tim. "Europe at the Crossroads on Car Pollution." *Financial Times*, March 10, 1989.

Dickson, Tim. "Green Issues on Centre Stage." *Financial Times*, April 21, 1989.

Dickson, Tim. "UK Reverses Position on Car Emission Standards." *Financial Times*, May 24, 1989.

Dietrich, William. "Harmonization of Automobile Emission Standards under International Trade Agreements: Lessons from the European Union Applied to the WTO and the NAFTA." *William and Mary Environmental Law and Policy Review* 20 (1995–96): 175–221.

Doane, Deborah. "The Myth of CSR: The Problem with Assuming That Companies Can Do Well While Also Doing Good Is That Markets Don't Really Work That Way." *Stanford Social Innovation Review*, Fall 2005: 23–29.

Doctors Without Borders. "TPP Trade Deal Moves toward Completion, Threatening Access to Medicine for Millions." June 12, 2015.

Doctors Without Borders. "U.S. Action at WTO Threatens Brazil's Successful AIDS Programme." February 1, 2001.

Doctors Without Borders. "Will the Lifeline of Affordable Medicines for Poor Countries Be Cut?" February 2005.

Doh, Jonathan, and Terrence Guay. "Globalization and Corporate Social Responsibility: How Non-governmental Organizations Influence Labor and Environment Codes of Conduct." *Management International Review* 44 (2004): 7–29.

Doha Declaration on TRIPS and Public Health. WT/MIN(01)/DEC/2. Adopted November 14, 2001.

Douglas, Mary, and Aaron Wildavsky. *Risk and Culture: An Essay on the Selection of Technological and Environmental Dangers*. Berkeley: University of California Press, 1983.

Dovere, Edward-Isaac. "Extreme Secrecy Eroding Support for Obama's Trade Pact." *Politico*, May 4, 2015.

Downs, Anthony. "The Public Interest: Its Meaning in a Democracy." *Social Research* 29, no. 1 (1962): 12.

Drahos, Peter, and John Braithwaite. *Information Feudalism: Who Owns the Knowledge Economy?* New York: New Press, 2002.

Dreher, A. "The Influence of Globalization on Taxes and Social Policy: An Empirical Analysis for OECD Countries." *European Journal of Political Economy* 22, no. 1 (2007): 179–201.

Drezner, Daniel. *All Politics Is Global: Explaining International Regulatory Regimes*. Princeton: Princeton University Press, 2007.

Drezner, Daniel. "Globalization and Policy Convergence." *International Studies Review* 3, no. 1 (2001): 55, 65–75.

Drozdiak, William. "Push for Speed Limits Divides West Germans." *Washington Post*, October 19, 1984.

"Drug Companies Face Mounting Hurdles in India due to Patent Revocation." *Inside U.S. Trade*, December 20, 2012.

"Drug Companies Push for Limits on Disease Coverage in Drug Patent Deal." *Inside U.S. Trade*, November 22, 2002.

Dryden, Steve. *Trade Warriors: USTR and the American Crusade for Free Trade*. New York: Oxford University Press, 1995.

Dunne, Nancy, and Damian Fraser. "Environmentalists Starting to Call Tune in U.S." *Financial Times*, May 3, 1991.

Duperon, William, and E. Mine Cinar. "Global Competition versus Regional Interests: FDI and Pharmaceuticals in India." *Journal of International Commercial Law and Technology* 5, no. 4 (2010): 181-200.

Dur, Andreas, and Gemma Mateo. "Public Opinion and Interest Group Influence: How Citizen Groups Derailed the Anti-counterfeiting Trade Agreement." *Journal of European Public Policy* 21, no. 8 (2014): 1199–1217.

Dyck, John. "U.S.-Japan Agreements on Beef Imports." United States Department of Agriculture, Economic Research Service, 1998.

"Dying for Drugs, Protests, Global Day of Action." *Guardian*, March 5, 2001.

Eagleton-Pierce, Matthew. "The Competing Kings of Cotton: (Re)framing the WTO African Cotton Initiative." *New Political Economy* 17, no. 3 (2012): 313–37.

"Easing Beef Rules Faces Japanese Political Hurdles, May Take Years." *Inside U.S. Trade*, April 30, 2010.

"Easing Restrictions on U.S. Beef Justifiable." *Yomiuri Shimbun*, November 4, 2012.

eBay v. MercExchange. 05–130, Supreme Court of the United States, May 15, 2006.

European Commission. "Motor Vehicle Issues concerning the UK." February 13,

1985. Historical Archive of the European Union, European University Institute, Florence.

European Council. "Outcome of Proceedings of Permanent Representatives Committee." February 20, 1985. Historical Archive of the European Union, European University Institute, Florence.

Edelman, Peter. "Japanese Product Standards as Non-tariff Barriers: When Regulatory Policy Becomes a Trade Issue." *Stanford Journal of International Law* Vol. 389 (1987–88): 391–92.

Egan, Michelle. *Constructing a European Market: Standards, Regulation, and Governance*. New York: Oxford University Press, 2001.

Eimer, Thomas. "Decoding Divergence in Software Regulation: Paradigms, Power Structures, and Institutions in the United States and the European Union." *Governance: An International Journal of Policy, Administration, and Institutions* 21, no. 2 (2008): 275–96.

"Empire of the Pig." *Economist*, December 20, 2014.

Esty, Daniel. *Greening the GATT: Trade, Environment, and the Future*. Washington, DC: Institute for International Economics, 1994.

"E.U. Floats Compromise Drug Patent Plan before Senior Officials Meeting." *Inside U.S. Trade*, November 1, 2002.

"E.U., Japan Compromise Efforts for WTO Medicines Deal Fall Short." *Inside U.S. Trade*, February 7, 2003.

"E.U. Sets Most Ambitious Goals in Auto Sector Regulations in TTIP Talks." *Inside U.S. Trade*, July 12, 2013.

European Automobile Manufacturers Association (ACEA). "Automobile Industry Welcomes the Opening of EU-US Trade Talks." Press release, June 17, 2013.

European Commission. "A Decade of EU-Funded GMO Research, 2001–2010." Directorate E- Food, Agriculture, Fisheries, and Biotechnology, 2010.

European Community, Official Journal. Council Directive (EC) 1970/156. February 6, 1970. [1970] O.J. L. 42/1.

European Community, Official Journal. Council Regulation (EC) 1972/306. August 2, 1972. [1972] O.J. L. 190/1.

European Community, Official Journal. Council Directive (EC) 1970/220. March 20, 1970. [1970] O.J. L. 76/1.

European Community, Official Journal. Council Directive (EC) 1978/611. June 29, 1978. [1978] O.J. L. 197/19.

European Federation of Pharmaceutical Industries and Associations. "The Degree to Which Patenting, and in Particular Secondary Patenting, Protect Pharmaceutical Products during Their Lifecycle Is Often Misconstrued." November 28, 2012.

Evenett, Simon, and John Whalley. "Resist Green Protectionism—or Pay the Price at Copenhagen." In *The Collapse of Global Trade, Murky Protectionism, and the Crisis: Recommendations for the G20*, edited by Richard Baldwin and Simon Evenett. London: Centre for Economic Policy Research, 2009.

Ewing, Jack. "Carmakers Are Central Voice in U.S.-Europe Trade Talks." *New York Times*, July 14, 2014.

"Exhaust Plan Delayed." *Globe and Mail*, January 22, 1988.

Fackler, Martin. "Japan Partly Lifts Ban on Imports of U.S. Beef, Easing Trade Dispute." *New York Times*, December 12, 2005.

"Failure to Solve Beef Row May Threaten Japan-U.S. Ties." *Yomiuri Shimbun*, March 21, 2005.

Faiola, Anthony. "Free Trade with U.S.? Europe Balks at Chlorine Chicken, Hormone Beef." *Washington Post*, December 4, 2014.

Faiola, Anthony. "Japan Plans to Press U.S. on Troops." *Washington Post*, October 6, 2004.

Faiola, Anthony. "Japan Says Man Died of Mad Cow Disease." *Washington Post*, February 5, 2005.

Faiola, Anthony. "Japan Warns of Delays for U.S. Beef; Despite Agreement, Imports Await Rules." *Washington Post*, October 27, 2004.

"Farm Protection Stands in the Way of Aussie Trade Pact." *Nikkei Weekly*, June 23, 2008.

Farnsworth, Clyde. "Auto Talks with Japan: A Drama of Euphemisms." *New York Times*, March 26, 1981.

Farnsworth, Clyde. "U.S. Plans to Defend Its Patents." *New York Times*, April 7, 1986.

Farnsworth, Clyde. "Vote Due on U.S. Auto Content Bill." *New York Times*, December 8, 1982.

Farrell, Henry. "Constructing the International Foundations of E-Commerce: The EU-U.S. Safe Harbor Arrangement." *International Organization* 57, no. 2 (2003): 277–306.

Farsetta, Diane. "The Cows Have Come Home." CorpWatch, September 1, 2005.

Feddersen, Timothy, and Thomas Gilligan. "Saints and Markets: Activists and the Supply of Credence Goods." *Journal of Economic and Management Strategy* 10, no. 1 (2001): 149–71.

Ferguson, John. "Trade Negotiators Said Ready for Deal to Replace Auto Pact." *Toronto Star*, September 22, 1987.

Finger, J. Michael, and Philip Schuler. "Implementation of Uruguay Round Commitments: The Development Challenge." *World Economy* 23, no. 4 (2000): 511–25.

Flannagan, Carol, Andras Balint, Kathleen Klinich, Ulrich Sander, Miriam Manary, Sophie Cuny, Michael McCarthy, et al. "Comparing Motor Vehicle Crash Risks of EU and US Vehicles." University of Michigan Transportation Research Institute (US), CEESAR (France), and the Transport Research Laboratory (UK), May 2015.

Fleming, Stewart. "The Great American Debate." *Financial Times*, December 7, 1983.

Flynn, Matthew. *Pharmaceutical Autonomy and Public Health in Latin America: State, Society, and Industry in Brazil's AIDS Program*. New York: Routledge, 2015.

Flynn, Sean. "WIPO Treaty for the Blind Shows That Transparency Can Work (and Is Necessary)." *Infojustice*, June 26, 2013. http://infojustice.org/archives/30027

Flynn, Sean, Brook Baker, Margot Kaminski, and Jimmy Koo. "The U.S. Proposal for an Intellectual Property Chapter in the Trans-Pacific Partnership Agreement." *American University International Law Review* 28, no. 1 (2012): 105–202.

Food and Water Watch. "Carbon Monoxide: Masking the Truth about Meat." 2008.

Frank, Dana. *Buy American: The Untold Story of Economic Nationalism*. Boston: Beacon, 1999.

Freyssenet, Michel, and Yannick Lung. "Multinational Carmakers' Regional Strategies." In *Cars, Carriers of Regionalism?*, edited by Jorge Carrillo, Yannick Lung, and Rob van Tulder. New York: Palgrave MacMillan, 2004.

Friends of the Earth. "Nanomaterials, Sunscreens, and Cosmetics: Small Ingredients, Big Risks." 2006.

Friends of the Earth. "Out of the Laboratories and on to Our Plates: Nanotechnology in Food and Agriculture." 2008.

"Full Disclosure on BSE Needed." *Yomiuri Shimbun*, October 14, 2001.

Gagarajan, Rema. "Panel to Draft Intellectual Property Policy Riddle with Conflict of Interest." *Times of India*, December 2, 2014.

Gallagher, Kevin. "Trading Away the Ladder? Trade Politics and Economic Development in the Americas." *New Political Economy* 13, no. 1 (2008) 37–59.

Gallup Poll, August 2007. Retrieved August 17, 2015, from iPOLL Databank, Roper Center for Public Opinion Research, University of Connecticut, Storrs.

Gallup / *USA Today* Poll, July 2007. Retrieved August 17, 2015, from iPOLL Databank, Roper Center for Public Opinion Research, University of Connecticut, Storrs.

Gao, Paul, Russell Hensley, and Andreas Zielke. "A Road Map to the Future for the Auto Industry." *McKinsey Quarterly*, October 2014.

Garnaut, John, and Marian Wilkinson. "Plum Jobs for US Trade Deal Advisers." *Sydney Morning Herald*, July 27, 2004.

Garrett, Geoffrey. *Partisan Politics in the Global Economy*. Cambridge: Cambridge University Press, 1998.

Garrett, Geoffrey, and Peter Lange. "Political Responses to Interdependence: What's Left of the Left?" *International Organization* 45, no. 4 (1991): 539–64.

Garrett, Geoffrey, and Barry Weingast. "Ideas, Interests, and Institutions: Constructing the European Community's Internal Market." In *Ideas and Foreign Policy: Beliefs, Institutions, and Political Change*, edited by Judith Goldstein and Robert Keohane. Ithaca: Cornell University Press, 1993.

Gawande, Kishore, Pravin Krishna, and Marcelo Olarreaga, "What Governments Maximize and Why: A View From Trade," *International Organization* 63, no. 3 (2009): 491–532.

Gellman, Barton. "A Conflict of Health and Profit: Gore at Center of Trade Policy Reversal on AIDS Drugs to South Africa." *Washington Post*, May 21, 2000.

Genoways, Ted. "Corn Wars." *New Republic*, August 16, 2015.

George, Alexander, and Andrew Bennett. *Case Studies and Theory Development in the Social Sciences*. Cambridge, MA: MIT Press, 2005.

Gereffi, Gary, John Humphrey, and Timothy Sturgeon. "The Governance of Global Value Chains." *Review of International Political Economy* 12, no. 1 (2005): 78–104.

Gerth, Jeff. "Where Business Rules; Forging Global Regulations That Put Industry First." *New York Times*, January 9, 1998.

Gilligan, Michael. "Lobbying as a Private Good with Intra-Industry Trade." *International Studies Quarterly* 41, no. 3 (1997): 455–74.

Gilpin, Kenneth. "Local Content: Global Practice." *New York Times*, June 23, 1983.

GlaxoSmithKline. "GSK Public Policy Positions: Evergreening." August 2011.

"Global Warming: What Should Be Done?" *New York Times*, January 29, 2015.

"GM Food and Trade: More Trouble." *Economist*, July 3, 2003.

Godoy, Angelina. *Of Medicines and Markets: Intellectual Property and Human Rights in the Free Trade Era*. Palo Alto: Stanford University Press, 2013.

Goldstein, Judith. *Ideas, Interests, and American Trade Policy*. (Ithaca: Cornell University Press, 1993),

"Good Chemistry." *Economist*, February 2, 2006.

Gooding, Kenneth. "EEC Rows over Timetable for Cars." *Financial Times*, March 6, 1987.

Gooding, Kenneth. "Europe's Chance to Clear the Air; Car Exhaust Controls." *Financial Times*, December 5, 1984.

Gourevitch, Peter. *Politics in Hard Times: Comparative Responses to International Economic Crises*. Ithaca: Cornell University Press, 1986.

"Government Eyes Relaxing U.S. Beef Rules." *Yomiuri Shimbun*, August 4, 2007.

"Government Must Toughen Product Label Laws." *Yomiuri Shimbun*, March 12, 2002.

"Government Ready to Lift U.S. Beef Ban." *Nikkei Weekly*, February 14, 2005.

"Government to Ban Beef on the Bone to Prevent BSE Transmission." *Yomiuri Shimbun*, September 14, 2003.

Grant, J. Andrew, and Ian Taylor. "Global Governance and Conflict Diamonds: The Kimberley Process and the Quest for Clean Gems." *Round Table: Commonwealth Journal of International Affairs* 93, no. 375 (2004): 385–401.

Grant, Wyn. "Government Environmental Policy and the Chemical Industry." In *The Global Chemical Industry in the Age of the Petrochemical Revolution*, edited by Louis Galambos, Takashi Hikino, and Vera Zamagni. Cambridge: Cambridge University Press, 2007.

Green, Jessica. *Rethinking Private Authority: Agents and Entrepreneurs in Global Environmental Governance*. Princeton: Princeton University Press, 2013.

Green, Paula. "Companies Say Bill Guts Patent Protection Law." *Journal of Commerce*, September 2, 1997.

Greene, Joel. "U.S. Beef: It's What's for China." Congressional Research Service Insight, June 22, 2017.

Grieco, Joseph. *Europe, America, and Non-tariff Barriers to Trade*. Ithaca: Cornell University Press, 1990.

Griffiths, John. "EC Closer to Full Commitment." *Financial Times*, June 15, 1988.

Griffiths, John. "VW Says Lean-Burn Engines Cannot Match Catalysts." *Financial Times*, January 12, 1989.

Grimes, Charlotte. "Borderline: Many in U.S. Oppose Trade Pact with Mexico." *St. Louis Dispatch*, April 7, 1991.

Grossman, Gene, and Elhanan Helpman. "A Protectionist Bias in Majoritarian Politics." *Quarterly Journal of Economics* 120, no. 4 (2005): 1239–82.

Guilford, Dave. "Regulations Creating Obstacles." *Crain's Detroit Business*, June 17, 1996.

Guilford, Peter. "EC Moves To Single Approval For Cars." *Financial Times*, March 14, 1990.

Haberman, Clyde. "Japanese are Special Types, They Explain." *New York Times*, March 6, 1988.

Hadden, Susan. "Regulating Product Risks through Consumer Information." *Journal of Social Issues* 47, no. 1 (1991): 93–105.

Hall, Kevin. "Talks Get Down to Business; Prickliest Issue Still Intellectual Property Rights." *Journal of Commerce*, May 16, 1997.

Hanrahan, Charles, and Geoffrey Becker. "Mad Cow Disease and U.S. Beef Trade." Congressional Research Service, June 4, 2008.

Hanson, David. *Limits to Free Trade: Non-tariff Barriers in the European Union, Japan, and the United States*. Northampton, MA: Edward Elgar, 2010.

Harada, Nobuhiko, and Ryuichi Sonada. "Consumer Trust Shattered." *Yomiuri Shimbun*, January 22, 2006.

Harris, Donald. "TRIPS' Rebound: An Historical Analysis of How the TRIPS Agreement Can Ricochet Back against the United States." *Northwestern Journal of International Law and Business* 25, no. 1 (2004–5): 99–164.

Harris, Gardiner. "India's Efforts to Aid Poor Worry Drug Makers." *New York Times*, December 30, 2013.

Harrison, Christopher. *The Politics of the International Pricing of Prescription Drugs*. New York: Praeger, 2004.

Hart, Michael. *A Trading Nation: Canadian Trade Policy from Colonialism to Globalization*. Vancouver: University of British Columbia Press, 2002.

Hart, Michael, Bill Dymond, and Colin Robertson. *Decision at Midnight: Inside the Canada-US Free Trade Negotiations*. Vancouver: University of British Columbia Press, 1994.

Hart, Michael, Bill Dymond, and Colin Robertson, eds. *Decision at Midnight: Inside the Canada-US Free-Trade Negotiation*. Vancouver: University of British Columbia Press, 1994.

"Hatch Doubts TPP Vote in 2016, Says GOP Would Get Better Deal on Biologics." *Inside U.S. Trade*, November 13, 2015.

Hauck, David. "Subsidies Are a Focus of WTO Discontent." *Christian Science Monitor*, September 16, 2003.

Haufler, Virginia. *A Public Role for the Private Sector: Industry Self-Regulation in a Global Economy*. Washington, DC: Carnegie Endowment for International Peace, 2001.

Helleiner, Eric and Andreas Pickel, eds., *Economic Nationalism in a Globalizing World.* Ithaca: Cornell University Press, 2005.

Helm, Jeremiah. "Why Pharmaceutical Firms Support Patent Trolls: The Disparate Impact of *eBay v. MercExchange* on Innovation." *Michigan Telecommunications and Technology Law Review* 13, no. 1 (2006): 331–43.

Helpman, Elhanan, Marc Melitz, and Stephen Yeaple. "Export versus FDI with Heterogeneous Firms." *American Economic Review* 94, no. 1 (2004): 300–316.

Herper, Matthew. "My Lunch with Shkreli: What We Should Learn from Pharma's Latest Monster." *Forbes*, September 24, 2015.

Herrmann, Richard, Philip Tetlock, and Matthew Diascro. "How Americans Think about Trade: Reconciling Conflicts among Money, Power, and Principles." *International Studies Quarterly* 45, no. 2 (2001): 191–218.

Hillman, Amy, Gerald Keim, and Douglas Schuler. "Corporate Political Activity: A Review and Research Agenda." *Journal of Management* 30, no. 6 (2004): 837–57.

Hilton, Matthew. *Consumerism in Twentieth-Century Britain*. Cambridge: Cambridge University Press, 2003.

Hiraoka, Leslie. *Global Alliances in the Motor Vehicle Industry*. London: Quorum Books, 2000.

Hiscox, Michael. *International Trade and Political Conflict: Commerce, Coalitions, and Mobility*. Princeton: Princeton University Press, 2002.

Hiscox, Michael. "Through a Glass and Darkly: Attitudes toward International Trade and the Curious Effects of Issue Framing." *International Organization* 60, no. 3 (2006): 755–80.

Hoekman, Bernard. "Multilateral Institutions and African Economic Integration." In *Handbook of the International Political Economy of Trade*, edited by David Deese. Northampton, MA: Edward Elgar, 2014.

Hookway, James. "U.S. Trade Aspirations Could Spark Backlash in Malaysia." *Wall Street Journal*, April 26, 2014.

Hopewell, Kristen. "Multilateral Trade Governance as Social Field: Global Civil Society and the WTO." *Review of International Political Economy* 22, no. 6 (2015): 1128–58.

Horng, Der-Chin. "The Human Rights Clause in the European Union's External Trade and Development Agreements." *European Law Journal* 9, no. 5 (2003): 677–701.

"House Dems Question TPP's Drug Provisions, 'May 10' Consistency." *Inside U.S. Trade*, December 11, 2015.

Huang, Yanzhong. "Chinese Pharma: A Global Health Game Changer." Council on Foreign Relations, March 31, 2015.

Human Rights Watch. *Blood, Sweat, and Fear: Workers' Rights in U.S. Meat and Poultry Plants*. New York, 2004.

Hussain, Imtiaz, and Roberto Dominguez. *North American Regionalism and Global Spread*. New York: Palgrave Macmillan, 2015.

"Implementation of Paragraph Six of the Doha Declaration on the TRIPS Agreement and Public Health." Decision of the General Council, Paragraph Four, WT/L/540 and Corr.1, September 1, 2003.

"In Beef Dispute, U.S. Should Cater to Japan." *Denver Post*, January 24, 2006.

"India Again on US IPR Priority Watch List; Govt Disappointed, But Not Worried." *Business Line*, May 1, 2015.

"Indian Generic at 1/100th the Cost, Saves Aussie's Life." *Times of India* (Jaipur edition), August 21, 2015.

"Indian Minister Touts Local Content Policy Change, Rebuts IPR Criticism." *Inside U.S. Trade*, July 15, 2013.

"India Rejects Lee Pharma's Compulsory License Plea." *Economic Times*, August 18, 2015.

Ingrassia, Paul. *Crash Course: The American Automobile Industry's Road from Glory to Disaster*. New York: Random House, 2010.

Institute for Agriculture and Trade Policy. "Senate to Consider New Farm Bill Heavy on Subsidies." May 8, 2002. http://iatp.org/news/senate-to-consider-new-farm-bill-heavy-on-subsidies

Interview with Dr. Robert Tauxe. *Frontline*, PBS, 2002. Accessed March 8, 2016. http://www.pbs.org/wgbh/pages/frontline/shows/meat/interviews/tauxe.html

Inwood, Gregory. *Continentalizing Canada: The Politics and Legacy of the Macdonald Royal Commission*. Toronto: University of Toronto Press, 2005.

Isaac, Grant, and William Kerr, "Genetically Modified Organisms at the World Trade Organization: A Harvest of Trouble." *Journal of World Trade* 37, no. 6 (2003): 1083–95.

"It Will Come Back to Haunt Us." *New York Times*, July 25, 1982.

Jaimet, Kate. "Two Sides Spar over Free Trade: At Issue Is Proposed All-Americas Deal." *Ottawa Citizen*, April 12, 2001.

"Japan, U.S. to Start Talks on Beef Imports Protocol Needed to Expand Access." *Inside U.S. Trade*, November 23, 2012.

"Japanese Minister Rejects U.S. Call for Talks to Expand Beef Exports." Kyodo News, BBC Monitoring Asia Pacific, August 1, 2006.

"Japanese Ministerial Visit Brings Little Trade Action due to Elections." *Inside U.S. Trade*, May 8, 2009.

"Japanese, U.S. Foreign Ministers Meet to Discuss North Korea, Iran." Kyodo News, BBC Monitoring Asia Pacific, May 3, 2006. September 7, 2012.

"Japan Fails to Move on Full Beef Market Access, Drug Prices." *Inside U.S. Trade*, December 14, 2007.

"Japan May Resume U.S. Beef Imports." *Yomiuri Shimbun*, September 8, 2004.

"Japan Moves Closer to Raising 20-Month Age Limit for Beef Imports." *Inside U.S. Trade*, September 7, 2012.

"Japan Opens to Limited U.S. Beef Trade amid Calls for Broader Openings." *Inside U.S. Trade*, July 28, 2006.

"Japan Queries U.S. on BSE, Risk Assessment May Lead to Beef Access." *Inside U.S. Trade*, October 22, 2010.

"Japan Says USDA Report on Beef Highlights Additional Violations." *Inside U.S. Trade*, February 24, 2006.

"Japan's New Cabinet to Be Formed as DPJ Gear Up for Upper House Election." Xinhua News, June 8, 2010.

"Japan's PM Wants Current US Beef Inspection System Reassessed." Kyodo News, BBC Monitoring Asia Pacific, April 25, 2008.

"Japan Stops U.S. Beef Shipments Again." *CNN Money*, January 20, 2006.

"Japan Suspends Beef Imports from One U.S. Facility." Kyodo News, BBC Monitoring Asia Pacific, February 16, 2007.

"Japan Suspends Beef Imports from U.S. Meatpacking Facility." Kyodo News, BBC Monitoring Asia Pacific, April 6, 2007.

"Japan Takes Step toward Relaxing BSE Restrictions on U.S. Beef Imports." *Inside U.S. Trade*, October 28, 2011.

"Japan Turns Down US Request for Beef Talks." Kyodo News, BBC Monitoring Asia Pacific, January 25, 2007.

"Japan-US Beef Talks Hit Snag amid Farm Ministry Row." Kyodo News, BBC Monitoring Asia Pacific, September 7, 2007.

Jasanoff, Sheila. "Civilization and Madness: The Great BSE Scare of 1996." *Public Understanding of Science* 6, no. 3 (1997): 221–32.

Jensen, J. Bradford, Dennis Quinn, and Stephen Weymouth. "The Influence of Firm Global Supply Chains and Foreign Currency Undervaluations on U.S. Trade Disputes." *International Organization* 69, no. 4 (2015): 913–47.

"The Job-Killer Bill." *New York Times*, December 14, 1982.

"Johanns: Japan Beef Progress Should Be Prerequisite for TPP Inclusion." *Inside U.S. Trade*, February 25, 2011.

Johnson, Carolyn. "Secret Rebates, Coupons, and Exclusions: How the Battle over High Drug Prices Is Really Being Fought." *Washington Post*, May 12, 2016.

Johnson, Carolyn. "Taxpayers Helped Fund This $129,000 Cancer Drug; Should the Government Help Cut the Price?" *Washington Post*, January 14, 2016.

Johnson, Carolyn, and Brady Dennis. "How an $84,000 Drug Got Its Price: 'Let's Hold Our Position Whatever the Headlines.'" *Washington Post*, December 1, 2015.

Johnson, Renee. "U.S.-EU Poultry Dispute on the Use of Pathogen Reduction Treatments (PRTs)." Congressional Research Service, January 15, 2015.

Johnson, Steve. "The Politics of Meat." *Frontline*, PBS (2002). Accessed March 8, 2016. http://www.pbs.org/wgbh/pages/frontline/shows/meat/politics/

Jürgens, Ulrich. "Characteristics of the European Automotive System: Is There a Distinctive European Approach." Discussion paper SP III 2003–301, Leibniz Information Centre for Economics, Berlin, 2003.

Kahler, Miles, and David Lake. "Economic Integration and Global Governance: Why So Little Supranationalism." In *The Politics of Global Regulation*, edited by Walter Mattli and Ngaire Woods. Princeton: Princeton University Press, 2009.

Kahler, Miles, and David Lake, eds. *Governance in a Global Economy: Political Authority in Transition*. Princeton: Princeton University Press, 2003.

Kaiser Family Foundation and Health Research and Education Trust. "Employer Health Benefits, 2015 Annual Survey." 2015.

"Kansas Beef Firm Setting Up BSE Lab." *Yomiuri Shimbun*, March 6, 2004.

Kantz, Carola. "The Power of Socialization: Engaging the Diamond Industry in the Kimberley Process." *Business and Politics* 9, no. 3 (2007): 13–15.

Kapczynski, Amy. "Harmonization and Its Discontents: A Case Study of TRIPS Implementation in India's Pharmaceutical Sector." *California Law Review* 97, no. 6 (2009): 1571–1650.

Karol, David. "Does Constituency Size Affect Elected Officials' Trade Policy Preferences?" *Journal of Politics* 69, no. 2 (2007): 483–94.

Karunakara, Unni. "Removing Barriers to Access for a More Equitable, Healthy World." *Doctors Without Borders*, November 21, 2012.

Kashiwagi, Akiko. "Scandals Cause Japanese to Lose Their Appetite; Once Revered Local Food in Doubt." *The Washington Post*. March 25, 2002.

Kazmin, Amy. "Roche Drops Patent for Herceptin in India." *Financial Times*, August 16, 2013.

Keck, Margaret, and Kathryn Sikkink. *Activists beyond Borders: Advocacy Networks in International Politics*. Ithaca: Cornell University Press, 1998.

Kelsey, Jane. "The Trans-Pacific Partnership Agreement: A Gold-Plated Gift to the Global Tobacco Industry?" *American Journal of Law and Medicine* 39 (2013): 237–64.

Kerr, William, and Jill Hobbs, "The North American–European Union Dispute over Beef Produced Using Growth Hormones: A Major Test for the New International Trade Regime." *The World Economy* 25, no. 2 (2002): 283–96.

Kessler, Glenn. "Bush Presses Koizumi on Japan's Beef Ban." *Washington Post*, March 10, 2005.

Kim, In Song. "Political Cleavages within Industry: Firm-Level Lobbying for Trade Liberalization." *American Political Science Review* 111, no. 1 (2017): 1–20.

Kim, Moonhawk. "Disguised Protectionism and Linkages to the GATT/WTO." *World Politics* 64, no. 3 (2012): 426–75.

King, Andrew, and Michael Lenox. "Regulation without Sanctions: The Chemical Industry's Responsible Care Program." *Academy of Management Journal* 43, no. 4 (2000): 698–716.

King, Brayden. "A Political Mediation Model of Corporate Response to Social Movement Activism." *Administrative Science Quarterly* 53, no. 3 (2008): 395–421.

King, John. "Business Council Recommends Canada-U.S. Free Trade Pact." *Globe and Mail*, April 19, 1983.

King, Neil. "U.S., Chile Open Trade." *Globe and Mail*, December 12, 2002.

Kirton, John. "The Impact of Environmental Regulation on the North American Auto Industry since NAFTA." In *The North American Auto Industry under NAFTA*, edited by Sidney Weintraub and Christopher Sands. Washington, DC: Center for Strategic and International Studies, 1998.

Kleinberg, Remonda. "Strategic Alliances: State-Business Relations in Mexico under Neo-Liberalism and Crisis." *Bulletin of Latin American Research* 18, no. 1 (1999): 71–87.

Klinger, Dustin. "Comparing Apples to Oranges: Lessons from the Failure of US Apple Exports to Japan." *Pacific Rim Law and Policy Journal* 8 (1999): 131–60.

Knowledge Ecology International. "USTR FOIA, 127 Pages of Emails between Industry and USTR TPP negotiators." November 27, 2013. https://www.keionline.org/22342

"Koizumi Sticks to His Guns on SDF." *Nikkei Weekly*, June 14, 2004.

"Koizumi: US Must Match Japan." *Yomiuri Shimbun*, January 23, 2004.

Kono, Daniel. "Optimal Obfuscation: Democracy and Trade Policy Transparency." *American Political Science Review* 100, no. 3 (2006): 369–84.

Korten, David. *When Corporations Rule the World*. 2nd ed. New York: Kumarian Press, 2001.

Krasner, Stephen. "Global Communication and National Power: Life on the Pareto Frontier." *World Politics* 43, no. 3 (1991): 336–66.

Krugman, Paul. "Increasing Returns and Economic Geography." *Journal of Political Economy* 99, no. 3 (1991): 483–99.

Krugman, Paul. "Scale Economies, Product Differentiation, and the Pattern of Trade." *American Economic Review* 70, no. 5 (1980): 950–59.

Kuchler, Fred, and Abebayehu Tegene. "Did BSE Announcements Reduce Beef Purchases?" Economic Research Report 34. United States Department of Agriculture, Economic Research Service, 2006.

Kuenheim, Eberhard von. Statement of the spokesman of the European Automobile Industry (CCMC) at a meeting of the environment ministers of the EC, December 6, 1984. Historical Archive of the European Union, European University Institute, Florence.

Lalitha, Narayanan. "Access to Indian Generic Drugs: Emerging Issues," in *Intellectual Property, Pharmaceuticals and Public Health: Access to Drugs in Developing Countries*, Kenneth Shadlen, Samira Guennif, Alenka Guzman, and Narayanan Lalitha, eds., Cheltenham: Edward Elgar (2013).

Langille, David. "The Business Council on National Issues and the Canadian State." *Studies in Political Economy* 24 (1987): 64–66.

Lanoszka, Anna. "The Global Politics of Intellectual Property Rights and Pharmaceutical Drug Policies in Developing Countries." *International Political Science Review* 24, no. 2 (2003): 181–97.

Lanz, Ranier, and Sebastien Miroudot. "Intra-Firm Trade: Patterns, Determinants, and Policy Implications." OECD Trade Policy Papers 114, OECD Publishing, Paris, 2011.

Lapper, Richard. "Central American Leaders Lobby Bush on Trade." *Financial Times*, May 12, 2005.

"Larson Expects Little Further Debate on TRIPS and Health in WTO." *Inside U.S. Trade*, November 30, 2001.

Layan, Jean-Bernard, and Yannick Lung. "The Dynamics of Regional Integration in the European Car Industry." In *Cars, Carriers of Regionalism?*, edited by Jorge Carrillo, Yannick Lung, and Rob van Tulder. New York: Palgrave MacMillan, 2004.

Layton, Lyndsey, and Annys Shin. "Toymakers Assail Cost of New Law." *Washington Post*, December 21, 2008.

"Leaked TPP Text Underscores U.S. Isolation in Environment Chapter Talks." *Inside U.S. Trade*, January 17, 2014.

"Leavitt Says Placing FDA Inspectors in India Is a 'High Priority' for U.S." *Inside U.S. Trade*, March 21, 2008.

Lee, Timothy. "Emails Show Cozy Relationship between Obama Trade Negotiators and Industry." *Washington Post*, November 29, 2013.

Lee, Timothy. "Here's Why Obama's Trade Negotiators Push the Interests of Hollywood and Drug Companies." *Washington Post*, November 26, 2013.

Lee, Yimou. "China's 'Fake' Apple Stores Thrive Ahead of New iPhone Launch." *Reuters*, September 23, 2015.

Legrain, Phillipe. *Open World: The Truth about Globalization*. London: Abacus (2003).

Lelyveld, Michael. "Panel Aims to Abolish Non-tariff Barriers; Business Forum on Mission to Harmonize Standards, Spur Trans-Atlantic Talks." *Journal of Commerce*, May 21, 1997.

Lester, Simon, and Huan Zhu. "Where's the Beef? Finding a Better Way to Resolve U.S.-China Trade Conflicts." Free Trade Bulletin 71, CATO Institute, Washington, DC, November 8, 2017.

"Letter to the U.S. Trade Representative." Consumers Union, April 30, 2014.

"Letter to USTR and European Commission: EU and US Consumer Groups Initial Reaction to the Announcement of a Transatlantic Trade and Investment Partnership." *Transatlantic Consumer Dialogue*, March 5, 2013.

Levi-Faur, David. "The Global Diffusion of Regulatory Capitalism." *Annual of the American Academy of Political and Social Sciences* 598 (2005): 12–32.

Licon, Adriana Gomez. "Mexico's Car Industry Booms While Selling Unsafe Cars." *Seattle Times*, November 28, 2013.

Lippert, Inge, Tony Huzzard, Ulrich Jurgens, and William Lazonik. *Corporate Governance, Employee Voice, and Worker Organization: Sustaining High Road Jobs in the Automotive Supply Industry*. Oxford: Oxford University Press, 2014.

Liu, Jodie. "Compulsory Licensing and Anti-Evergreening: Interpreting the TRIPS Flexibilities in Sections 84 and 3(d) of the Indian Patents Act." *Harvard International Law Journal* 56, no. 1 (2015): 207–27.

Livestock: Summary. Center for Responsive Politics. Accessed March 8, 2016. http://www.opensecrets.org/industries/indus.php?Ind=A06

Livestock: Top Recipients, 2014. Center for Responsive Politics. Accessed March 8, 2016. http://www.opensecrets.org/industries/recips.php?ind=A06++

Lohmann, Susanne, and Sharyn O'Halloran. "Divided Government and U.S. Trade Policy: Theory and Evidence." *International Organization* 48, no. 4 (1994): 595–632.

Lung, Yannick, and Rob van Tulder. "Introduction: In Search of a Viable Automobile Space." In *Cars, Carriers of Regionalism?*, edited by Jorge Carrillo, Yannick Lung, and Rob van Tulder. New York: Palgrave Macmillan, 2004.

Lusztig, Michael. *The Limits of Protectionism: Building Coalitions for Free Trade*. Pittsburgh: University of Pittsburgh Press, 2004.

Lyons, Jan. "U.S. Beef Is Well Tested, Safe." *USA Today*, March 25, 2004.

Maclachlan, Patricia. *Consumer Politics in Postwar Japan: The Institutional Boundaries of Citizen Activism*. New York: Columbia University Press, 2002.

"Mad-Cow Disease Plagues Beef Industry." *Nikkei Weekly*, October 1, 2001.

Madeira, Mary Anne. "New Trade, New Politics: Intra-Industry Trade and Domestic Political Coalitions." *Review of International Political Economy* 23, no. 4 (2016): 677–711.

Madeira, Mary Anne. "The New Politics of the New Trade: The Political Economy of Intra-Industry Trade." In *Handbook of the International Political Economy of Trade*, edited by David Deese. Northampton, MA: Edward Elgar, 2014.

Maggs, John. "Environmental Advisors on Trade Issues Named." *Journal of Commerce*, August 20, 1991.

Maggs, John. "US Yields on 'Green' Language in Proposed N. America Trade Pact." *Journal of Commerce*, June 18, 1992.

Manger, Mark. "Vertical Trade Specialization and the Formation of North-South PTAs." *World Politics* 64, no. 4 (2012): 622–58.

Mansfield, Edward, and Diana Mutz. "Support for Free Trade: Self-Interest, Sociotropic Politics, and Out-Group Anxiety." *International Organization* 63, no. 3 (2009): 425–57.

Mantle, Jonathan. *Car Wars: Fifty Years of Greed, Treachery, and Skulduggery in the Global Marketplace*. New York: Arcade, 1995.

"Marantis Visits Tokyo; Outlines U.S. Priorities on Autos, Beef, and Japan Post." *Inside U.S. Trade*, November 25, 2011.

Marcos Jank. "Agricultural Protectionism: FTAA Seed of Discord." Foreign Trade Information System, 2006.

Markham, James. "Angst on the Autobahn: Would Slowdown Aid Trees?" *New York Times*, October 31, 1984.

Markham, James. "In a 'Dying' Forest, the German Soul Withers Too." *New York Times*, May 25, 1984.

Markusen, James, and Anthony Venables. "Multinational Firms and the New Trade Theory." *Journal of International Economics* 46 (1998): 183–203.

Martin, Andrew. "U.S. Beef Banned in Japan—Again." *Chicago Tribune*, January 21, 2006.

Martin, David. and Karen Martin. "Western Ideology, Japanese Product Safety Regulation and International Trade." *University of British Columbia Law Review* 19, no. 2 (1985): 315–74.

Marvel, Howard, and Edward Ray. "Intraindustry Trade: Sources and Effects on Protection." *Journal of Political Economy* 95, no. 6 (1987): 1278–91.

Marx, Axel. "Limits to Non-state Market Regulation: A Qualitative Comparative Analysis of the International Sport Footwear Industry and the Fair Labor Association." *Regulation and Governance* 2, no. 2 (2008): 253–73.

Mashaw, Jerry, and David Harfst. "Regulation and Legal Culture: The Case of Motor Vehicle Safety." *Yale Journal of Regulation* 4 (1987) 257–316.

Maskus, Keith. *Intellectual Property Rights in the Global Economy*. Washington, DC: Institute for International Economics, 2000.

Matthews, Duncan. *Globalising Intellectual Property Rights: The TRIPS Agreement*. London: Routledge, 2002.

Matthews, Duncan. *Intellectual Property, Human Rights, and Development: The Role of NGOs and Social Movements*. Northampton, MA: Edward Elgar, 2011.

Matthews, Duncan. "NGOs, Intellectual Property Rights, and Multilateral Institutions." IP-NGOs Research Project, 2006.

Matthews, Duncan. "WTO Decision on Implementation of Paragraph 6 of the Doha Declaration on the TRIPS Agreement and Public Health: A Solution to the Access to Essential Medicines Problem?" *Journal of International Economic Law* 7, no. 1 (2004) 73–107.

Mattli, Walter, and Ngaire Woods. "In Whose Benefit? Explaining Regulatory Change in Global Politics." In *The Politics of Global Regulation*, edited by Mattli and Woods. Princeton: Princeton University Press, 2009.

Mauldin, William. "U.S., Australia Agree on Complicated Compromise on Biologic Drugs." *Wall Street Journal*, October 4, 2015.

Mayer, Frederick. *Interpreting NAFTA: The Science and Art of Political Analysis*. New York: Columbia University Press, 1998.

Mazzucato, Miriam. "How Taxpayers Prop Up Big Pharma, and How to Cap That." *Los Angeles Times*, October 27, 2015.

McCurry, Justin, and Suzanne Goldenberg. "BSE-Infected Beef Spreads to Eight US States: Officials Lobby Japanese to Accept That Meat Is Safe." *Guardian*, December 29, 2003.

McDonnell, Mary-Hunter, Brayden King, and Sarah Soule. "A Dynamic Process Model of Private Politics: Activist Targeting and Corporate Receptivity to Social Challenges." *American Sociological Review* 80, no. 3 (2015): 654–78.

McGhee, Tom. "Swift Moves to Ease Japanese Beef Fears." *Denver Post*, November 10, 2006.

McGillivray, Fiona. "Party Discipline as a Determinant of the Endogenous Formation of Tariffs," *American Journal of Political Science* 41, no. 2 (1997): 584–607.

McKenna, Barrie. "In Cross-Border Trade Rules, a Whiff of Pointlessness." *Globe and Mail*, February 14, 2011.

McNeil, Donald. "Barred from Testing for Mad Cow, Niche Meatpacker Loses Clients." *New York Times*, April 18, 2004.

McNeil, Donald. "South Africa's Bitter Pill for World's Drugmakers." *New York Times*, March 29, 1998.

Megishi, Mayumi. "Onus on Japan to Ensure U.S. Beef Safety, Report Says." *Japan Times*, November 1, 2005.

Meislin, Richard. "Mexico Set to Revamp Troubled Auto Industry." *New York Times*, September 15, 1983.

Melitz, Marc. "The Impact of Trade on Industry Reallocations and Aggregate Industry Productivity." *Econometrica* 71, no. 6 (2003): 1695–1725.

Midford, Paul. "International Trade and Domestic Politics." *International Organization* 47, no. 4 (1993): 535–64.

Michaels, Dave. "A Split over Protecting Investors: The Labor Department Is Moving Ahead of the SEC on Broker Rules." Bloomberg News, March 12, 2015.

Milner, Helen. *Resisting Protectionism: Global Industries and the Politics of International Trade*. Princeton: Princeton University Press, 1988.

Milner, Helen, and David Yoffie. "Between Free Trade and Protectionism: Strategic Trade Policy and a Theory of Corporate Trade Demands." *International Organization* 43, no. 2 (1989): 239–72.

"Modern Meat." *Frontline*, PBS, April 18, 2002.

Moon, Bruce. "From Seattle and Doha to Cancun: The Trade Agenda in the New Millennium." In *Trade Politics*, edited by Brian Hocking and Steven McGuire. 2nd ed. New York: Routledge, 2004.

Moran, Michael. "The Rise of the Regulatory State." In *The Oxford Handbook of Business and Government*, edited by David Coen, Wyn Grant, and Graham Wilson. New York: Oxford University Press, 2010.

Moravcsik, Andrew. *The Choice for Europe*. Ithaca: Cornell University Press, 1998.

Mueller, Janice. "Taking TRIPS to India—Novartis, Patent Law, and Access to Medicines." *New England Journal of Medicine* 356 (2007): 541–43.

Mukherjee, Siddhartha. *The Emperor of All Maladies: A Biography of Cancer*. New York: Scribner, 2010.

Murayama, Kohei. "U.S. Beef Industry Says Mad Cow Mishap a 'Technical Error.'" Kyodo News, BBC Monitoring Asia Pacific, January 21, 2006.

Murillo, Maria. *Labor Unions, Partisan Coalitions, and Market Reforms in Latin America*. New Haven: Yale University Press, 2001.

Murphy, Dale. *The Structure of Regulatory Competition: Corporations and Public Policies in a Global Economy*. New York: Oxford University Press, 2004.

NAFTA. "In the Matter of Cross-Border Trucking Services." Final panel report, February 6, 2001.

Nakamura, Hiryuki, and Toshihiko Yada. "OIE OK's U.S. Beef Exports from Older Cows." *Yomiuri Shimbun*, May 24, 2007.

Narlikar, Amrita. "Developing Countries and the WTO." In *Trade Politics*, edited by Brian Hocking and Steven McGuire. 2nd ed. New York: Routledge, 2004.

National Public Radio. "Why Cars from Europe and the US Just Can't Get Along." *Planet Money*, episode 533, April 18, 2014.

"NCBA Wants Movement on Beef Access before Japan Joins TPP Talks." *Inside U.S. Trade*, January 20, 2012.

Negishi, Mayumi. "Easing Beef Ban Seen as Missing Chance to Let Consumers Rule." *Japan Times*, November 15, 2005.

Negishi, Mayumi. "Oddly, Japan Keeps Tariffs Intact as It Gropes for Beef." *Japan Times*, January 29, 2004.

Neher, Jacques. "EC Emissions Plan in Jeopardy, Danes Press for More Rapid Solution to Question of Small Cars." *Journal of Commerce*, November 6, 1986.

Nesmith, Jeff. "New Rules Aim to Protect U.S. from Mad Cow." *Atlanta Journal-Constitution*, December 31, 2003.

New, William. "Confidential USTR Emails Show Close Industry Involvement in TPP Negotiations." May 6, 2015. http://www.ip-watch.org/2015/06/05/confidential-ustr-emails-show-close-industry-involvement-in-tpp-negotiations/

New, William. "It's Official: TRIPS Health Amendment in Effect, First Ever to a WTO Agreement." *Intellectual Property Watch*, January 23, 2017.

"The New Drug War: Hard Pills to Swallow." *Economist*, January 4, 2014.

Newell, Peter. "Environmental NGOs, TNCs, and the Question of Governance." In *The International Political Economy of the Environment*, edited by Dimitris Stevis and Valerie Assetto (Boulder: Lynn Reinner, 2001).

Newell, Roberto, and Luis Rubio. *Mexico's Dilemma: The Political Origins of the Economic Crisis*. Boulder: Westview, 1984.

"New Japanese Government Divided on Trade Policy Despite Rhetoric." *Inside U.S. Trade*, September 4, 2009.

Nielson, Daniel. "Supplying Trade Reform: Political Institutions and Liberalization in Middle-Income Presidential Democracies." *American Journal of Political Science* 47, no. 3 (2003): 470–91.

"Nine Tons of U.S. Beef Labeled Domestic." *Yomiuri Shimbun*, February 16, 2002.

"Note for the File, Subject: Meeting between Messers. Sutherland, Narjes and Mme. Cresson Minister for External Trade and Industry." February 5, 1985. Historical Archive of the European Union, European University Institute, Florence.

"Novartis Order May Force Pharma MNCs to Change." *Times of India*, April 3, 2013.

Obara, Kakuyu, Michael McConnell, and John Dyck. "Japan's Beef Market." LDP-M-194–01. United States Department of Agriculture, Economic Research Service, August 2010.

"Octane Level Set for Lead-Free Petrol." *European Community Newsletter* (Dublin), October 17, 1984. Historical Archive of the European Union, European University Institute, Florence.

Oda, Takashi. "Ban on U.S. Beef about More Than Just Meat." *Yomiuri Shimbun*, January 25, 2006.

OECD. "Corporate Responsibility: Private Initiatives and Public Goals." 2001.

OECD, WTO, and World Bank. "Global Value Chains: Challenges, Opportunities, and Implications for Policy." Joint report prepared for the G20 Summit, July 19, 2014.

Office of the United States Trade Representative. *2015 National Trade Estimate Report on Foreign Trade Barriers*. March 2015.

Ogawa, Satoshi, and Toshimitsu Miyai. "Election 2009—Battle for Power; U.S. Keeps Close Eye on DPJ Manifesto." *Yomiuri Shimbun*. August 11, 2009.

Ohtsuki, T., Y. Kawasaki, H. Kubota, T. Namiki, T. Iizuka, N. Shionoya, N. Yoshii, et al. "Improvement of Carbon Monoxide Analysis in Fish Meat." *Shokuhin Eiseigaku Zasshi* 52, no. 2 (2011): 130–34. English abstract available at http://www.ncbi.nlm.nih.gov/pubmed/21515968

Oklahoma State University, Department of Agricultural Economics. *Food Demand Survey*. Vol. 2, no. 9, January 16, 2015.

Oliver, John. "Marketing to Doctors." *Last Week Tonight*, February 8, 2015.

"Opposition Jerry Rigs United Front." *Yomiuri Shimbun*, June 26, 2006.

"Opposition Statement: 'We Oppose the Decision to Reopen the Japanese Market to Beef Imports from the United States and Canada.'" Dedicated issue, *Food Safety Citizen's Watch Newsletter* 5, December 2005.

Orme, William. "Brazilian Automakers Forge Deal; U.S. Automakers' Mexican Units Steering Cars North." *Journal of Commerce*, April 9, 1987.

Orme, William. "Ford Motor Will Build New Plant in Mexico." *Washington Post*, January 11, 1984.

Osgood, Iain. "The Breakdown of Industrial Opposition to Trade: Firms, Product Variety, and Reciprocal Liberalization." *World Politics* 69, no. 1 (2017): 184–231.

Ostry, Sylvia. "The Uruguay Round North-South Grand Bargain: Implications for Future Generations." Political Economy of International Trade Law, University of Minnesota, Minneapolis, September 2000.

Ottoviano, Gianmarco. "'New' New Economic Geography: Firm Heterogeneity and Agglomeration Economies." *Journal of Economic Geography* 11 (2011): 231–40.

Panagariya, Arvind. "The Regionalism Debate: An Overview." *World Economy* 22, no. 4 (1999): 477–511.

"Panel: Ease Blanket Testing for BSE." *Yomiuri Shimbun*, March 12, 2005.

Pastor, Manuel, and Carol Wise. "The Origins and Sustainability of Mexico's Free Trade Policy." *International Organization* 48, no. 3 (1994) 459–89.

Pattberg, Philipp. "The Institutionalization of Private Governance: How Business and Nonprofit Organizations Agree on Transnational Rules." *Governance: An International Journal of Policy, Administration, and Institutions* 18, no. 4 (2005): 589–610.

Pattberg, Philipp. "What Role for Private Rule-Making in Global Environmental Governance? Analysing the Forestry Stewardship Council." *International Environmental Agreements* 5 (2005): 175–89.

Pearson, Brendan. "Pressure Builds on Japan to Lift U.S. Beef Import Ban." *Australian Financial Review*, March 19, 2004.

"Penn's BSE Comment Raises Eyebrows." *Yomiuri Shimbun*, January 26, 2006.

"Perception of Safe Beef." *Japan Times*, December 22, 2005.

Perez, Oren. "Between Soft Law and Greenwash: The Compliance Dynamic of Civil Forms of Environmental Regulation." In *Handbook on the Politics of Regulation*, edited by David Levi-Faur. New York: Edward Elgar, 2011.

Perry, James, and Andreas Nolke. "The Political Economy of International Accounting Standards." *Review of International Political Economy* 13, no. 4 (2006): 559–86.

Pew Research Center. "Support in Principle for U.S.-E.U. Trade Pact: But Some Americans and Germans Wary of TTIP Details." April 9, 2014.

Pfeifer, Stuart. "Prescription Drug Spending Jumps 13% to Record $374 Billion in 2014." *Los Angeles Times*, April 14, 2015.

Pharmaceutical Research and Manufacturers of America. "Intellectual Property." Accessed February 11, 2016. https://www.phrma.org/en/Advocacy/Intellectual-Propertyd

"PHRMA Looks to Limit Countries, Diseases Subject to New TRIPS Flexibility." *Inside U.S. Trade*, October 18, 2002.

Poitras, Guy, and Raymond Robinson. "The Politics of NAFTA in Mexico." *Journal of Interamerican Studies and World Affairs* 36 (1994): 1–35.

Pollack, Andrew. "Sales of Sovaldi, New Gilead Hepatitis C Drug, Soar to 10.3 Billion Dollars." *New York Times*, February 3, 2015.

Pollack, Mark, and Gregory Shaffer. *When Cooperation Fails: The International Law and Politics of Genetically Modified Foods*. Oxford: Oxford University Press. 2009.

"Pork Facts." National Pork Producers' Council. Accessed May 1, 2016. http://www.nppc.org/pork-facts/

Porter, Michael. *The Competitive Advantage of Nations*. New York: Free Press, 1998.

Postnikov, Evgeny. "The Design of Social Standards in EU and US Preferential Trade Agreements." In *Handbook of the International Political Economy of Trade*, edited by David Deese. Northampton, MA: Edward Elgar, 2014.

Prakash, Aseem, and Matthew Potoski. *The Voluntary Environmentalists: Green Clubs, ISO 14004, and Voluntary Environmental Regulation*, Cambridge: Cambridge University Press, 2006.

Prasol, Alexander. *Modern Japan, Origins of the Mind: Japanese Traditions and Approaches to Contemporary Life*. New York: World Scientific, 2010.

"Pressure Grows to Lift U.S. Beef Ban." *Yomiuri Shimbun*, May 7, 2006.

"Proof in the Pink: Meat Treated to Give It Fresh Look." ABC News, November 14, 2007.

Public Citizen. "The Trans-Pacific Partnership: Undermining Food Safety." Accessed May 1, 2016. http://www.citizen.org/tpp-food-safety-facts

Pulakkat, Hari. "Number of Cancer Cases in India Predicted to Double in Next 20 Years." *Economic Times*, April 18, 2014.

"Pushing Brazil, Christopher Urges Trade Zone by 2005." *New York Times*, March 4, 1996.

Quark, Amy. *Global Rivalries: Standards Wars and the Transnational Cotton Trade*. Chicago: University of Chicago Press, 2013.

Quark, Amy. "Ratcheting Up Protective Regulations in the Shadow of the WTO: NGO Strategy and Food Safety Standard-Setting in India." *Review of International Political Economy* 23, no. 5 (2016): 872–98.

"Racing down the Pyramid." *Economist*, November 13, 2008.

Radaelli, Claudio. "The Puzzle of Regulatory Competition." *Journal of Public Policy* 24, no. 1 (2004): 1-23.

Raun, Laura. "Dutch Defy Brussels on 'Clean Car' Measure." *Financial Times*, October 14, 1988.

"Regulations Matter: Just Look at Mexico." *Santa Fe New Mexican*, December 9, 2013.

"Resist U.S. Pressure to Lift Beef Ban." *Yomiuri Shimbun*, January 23, 2004.

"Restrictions on U.S. Beef to Be Eased." *Yomiuri Shimbun*, September 6, 2012.

"Review of Blanket Testing for BSE Timely." *Yomiuri Shimbun*, September 7, 2004.

Richardson, R. Jack. "Free Trade: Why Did It Happen?" *Canadian Review of Sociology and Anthropology* 29, no. 3 (1992): 307–28.

Ritchie, Gordon. *Wrestling with the Elephant: The Inside Story of the Canada-U.S. Trade Wars*. Toronto: McFarlane, Walter, and Ross, 1997.

Rivoli, Pietra. *The Travels of a T-Shirt in the Global Economy*. 2nd ed. Hoboken: John Wiley, 2009.

Rodrik, Dani. *The Globalization Paradox: Democracy and the Future of the World Economy*. New York: W. W. Norton, 2011.

Rodrik, Dani. "Why Do More Open Economies Have Bigger Governments?" *Journal of Political Economy* 106, no. 5 (1998): 997–1032.

Rogowski, Ronald. *Commerce and Coalitions: How Trade Affects Domestic Political Alignments*. Princeton: Princeton University Press, 1989.

Rogowski, Ronald, and Mark Kayser. "Majoritarian Electoral Systems and Consumer Power: Price-Level Evidence from the OECD Countries." *American Journal of Political Science* 46, no. 3 (2002): 526–40.

Rohter, Larry. "When a Populist Meets a Complex Issue." *New York Times*, June 15, 2008.

Rohter, Larry, and Jennifer Rich. "Brazil Takes a Stand and Offers a Warning to U.S." *New York Times*, December 19, 2001.

Romero, Simon. "Frustrated, U.S. Will Seek Bilateral Trade Pacts." *New York Times*, November 19, 2003.

Rondinelli, Dennis, and Ted London. "How Corporations and Environmental Groups Cooperate: Assessing Cross-Sector Alliances and Collaborations." *Academy of Management Executive* 17, no. 1 (2003): 61–76.

Roseberg, Tina. "Look at Brazil." *New York Times*, January 28, 2001.

Ross, Philip. "Ford's Catalytic Converter Eliminates Use of Platinum." *New York Times*, December 16, 1988.

Rotter, Julia, Peppi-Emilia Airike, and Cecilia Mark-Herbert. "Exploring Political Corporate Social Responsibility in Global Supply Chains." *Journal of Business Ethics* 125 (2014): 581–99.

Rubenstein, James. *Making and Selling Cars: Innovation and Change in the U.S. Automotive Industry*. Baltimore: Johns Hopkins University Press, 2001.

Rugman, Alan, John Kirton, and Jule Soloway. *Environmental Regulations and Corporate Strategy: A NAFTA Perspective*. New York: Oxford University Press, 1999.

Runge, C. Ford. "Trade Protectionism and Environmental Regulations: The New Nontariff Barriers." *Northwestern Journal of International Law and Business* 11, no. 1 (1990): 47–61.

Ryan, Leo. "Auto Leader Wants Canada to Withdraw from North America Talks." *Journal of Commerce*, April 8, 1992.

Saccomano, Ann. "Sewing Up a Deal." *Journal of Commerce*, April 21, 2003.

Salisbury, Susan. "Where'd the Beef Come From? Gaps Cloud New Food-Labeling Law." *Palm Beach Post*, October 4, 2008.

Sandholtz, Wayne, and John Zysman. "1992: Recasting the European Bargain." *World Politics* 62, no. 1 (1989): 107–14.

Sanger, David. "Dilemma for Clinton on NAFTA Truck Rule." *New York Times*, December 17, 1995.

Sanger, David. "U.S. and Mexico Postpone NAFTA on Truck Crossings." *New York Times*, December 18, 1995.

Scannell, Jack. "Four Reasons Drugs Are Expensive, of Which Two Are False." *Forbes*, October 13, 2015.

Schattschneider, E. E. *Politics, Pressures, and the Tariff*. Englewood Cliffs, NJ: Prentice Hall, 1935.

Schepel, Harm. *The Constitution of Private Governance: Standards in the Regulation of Integrating Markets*. Oxford: Hart, 2005.

Scherer, Andreas, and Guido Palazzo. "The New Political Role of Business in a Globalized World: A Review of a New Perspective on CSR and Its Implications for the Firm, Governance, and Democracy." *Journal of Management Studies* 48, no. 4 (2011): 899–931.

Schiller, Wendy. "Trade Politics in the American Congress: A Study of the Interaction of Political Geography and Interest Group Behavior." *Political Geography* 18, no. 7 (1999): 769–89.

Schlosser, Eric. "The Cow Jumped over the USDA." *New York Times*, January 2, 2004.

Schmit, Julie. "Carbon Monoxide Keeps Meat Red Longer; Is That Good?" *USA Today*, October 30, 2007.

Schoeff, Mark. "SEC Commissioner: DOL Fiduciary Rule Would Create 'a Mess.'" *Investment News*, August 4, 2015.

Schrage, Elliot, and Anthony Ewing. "The Cocoa Industry and Child Labour." *Journal of Corporate Citizenship* 18 (2005): 99–112.

Scott, Ben. "Beef Safety on Stock Show Menu; Cattle Tracking, Testing Discussed." *Denver Post*, January 14, 2004.

Sell, Susan. *Private Power, Public Law: The Globalization of Intellectual Property Rights*. Cambridge: Cambridge University Press, 2003.

Sell, Susan. "TRIPS and the Access to Medicines Campaign." *Wisconsin International Law Journal* 20, no. 3 (2002): 481–522.

Sell, Susan. "TRIPS Was Never Enough: Vertical Forum Shifting, FTAs, ACTA, and TPP." *Journal of Intellectual Property Law* 18 (2011) 447–78.

Sell, Susan, and Aseem Prakash. "Using Ideas Strategically: The Contest between Business and NGO Networks in Intellectual Property Rights." *International Studies Quarterly* 48, no. 1 (2004) 143–75.

Shaffer, Brian, and Amy Hillman. "The Development of Business-Government Strategies by Diversified Firms." *Strategic Management Journal* 21, no. 2 (2000): 175–90.

Shaffer, Greg. "How the World Trade Organization Shapes Regulatory Governance." *Regulation and Governance* 9, no. 1 (2015): 1–15.

Shapiro, Martin. "Administrative Law Unbounded: Reflections on Government and Governance." *Indiana Journal of Global Legal Studies* 8 (2001): 369–77.

Shimbun, Asahi. "U.S. Presses Japan." *Edmonton Journal*, October 4, 2004.

Shoch, James. *Trading Blows: Party Competition and U.S. Trade Policy in a Globalizing Era*. Chapel Hill: University of North Carolina Press, 2001.

Sikkink, Kathryn. "Codes of Conduct for Transnational Corporations: The Case of the WHO/UNICEF Code." *International Organization* 40, no. 4 (1986): 815–40.

Simmons, Beth. "The International Politics of Harmonization: The Case of Capital Market Regulation." *International Organization* 55, no. 3 (2001): 589–620.

Singer, David. "Capital Rules: The Domestic Politics of International Regulatory Harmonization." *International Organization* 58, no. 3 (2004): 531–565.

"Snow Brand Foods Sold Old Meat to Government." *Yomiuri Shimbun*, February 11, 2002.

"Snow Brand Lied about Beef's Origin." *Yomiuri Shimbun*, January 24, 2002.

Sonada, Ryuichi, and Tadashi Isozumi. "Stakes Run High in Resuming U.S. Beef Imports." *Yomiuri Shimbun*, October 24, 2005.

Spar, Deborah, and Lane LaMure. "The Power of Activism: Assessing the Impact of NGOs on Global Business." *California Management Review* 45, no. 3 (2003) 78–101.

"Special 301 Report Stops Short of Naming India PFC; Watch Lists Largely Unchanged." *Inside U.S. Trade*, May 1, 2014.

Spector, Mike, Jeff Bennett, and John Stoll. "U.S. Car Sales Set Record in 2015." *Wall Street Journal*, January 5, 2016.

Staiger, Robert, and Alan Sykes. "International Trade, National Treatment, and Domestic Regulation." *Journal of Legal Studies* 40, no. 1 (2011): 149–203.

Standing Committee on the Food Chain and Animal Health, Section on Toxicological Safety of the Food Chain. Summary record of a meeting under chairperson Patricia Brunko, April 7, 2003. https://ec.europa.eu/food/sites/food/files/safety/docs/reg-com_toxic_summary09_en.pdf

"Starzen Admits Mislabeling Meat." *Yomiuri Shimbun*, March 1, 2002.

Stephen, Roland. *Vehicle of Influence: Building a European Car Market*. Ann Arbor: University of Michigan Press, 2000.

Stigler, George. "The Theory of Economic Regulation." *Bell Journal of Economic and Management Science* 2, no. 1 (1971) 3–21.

Stiglitz, Joseph. *Globalization and Its Discontents*. New York: W. W. Norton, 2002.

Stockton, Nick. "How Prescription Drugs Get So Wildly Expensive." *Wired*, September 23, 2015.

Stolberg, Sheryl. "AIDS Groups Revive a Fight, and Themselves." *New York Times*, March 18, 2001.

Stopford, John, and Susan Strange. *Rival States, Rival Firms: Competition for World Market Shares*. Cambridge: Cambridge University Press, 1991.

Story, Dale. *Industry, the State, and Public Policy in Mexico*. Austin: University of Texas Press, 1986.

Story, Dale. "Trade Politics in the Third World: A Case Study of the Mexican GATT Decision." *International Organization* 36, no. 4 (1982) 767–94.

Stroup, Sarah. *Borders among Activists: International NGOs in the United States, Britain, and France*. Ithaca: Cornell University Press, 2012.

Studer-Noguez, Isabel. *Ford and the Global Strategies of Multinationals: The North American Auto Industry*. New York: Routledge, 2002.

Subramanian, Balaji. "Examining the Rejection of Lee's Saxagliptin CL Application." *Spicy IP*, January 22, 2016.

Sullivan, Becky. "The Trademark Woes of Michael Jordan (and Many Others) in China." National Public Radio, August 16, 2015.

Sutter, John. "Why Beef Is the New SUV?" CNN, November 24, 2015.

Swanson, Ana. "Big Pharmaceutical Companies Are Spending Far More on Marketing Than Research." *Washington Post*, February 11, 2015.

Swarns, Rachel. "Drugmakers Drop South Africa Suit over AIDS Medicine." *New York Times*, April 20, 2001.

Sykes, Alan. "Regulatory Protectionism and the Law of International Trade." *University of Chicago Law Review* 66, no. 1 (1999): 1–46.

"TABD Suggests Harmonization of Auto Safety, Environmental Rules." *Inside U.S. Trade*, April 16, 1996.

Tabuchi, Hiroko. "Fear of Free Trade." *New York Times*, November 12, 2010.

Tagliabue, John. "Germany Fights for Car Pollution Limits." *New York Times*, March 18, 1985.

Takahara, Kanako. "Beef Talks to Resume, Cheney Says." *Japan Times*, April 14, 2004.

Takahara, Kanako. "Japan-U.S. Beef Talks to Continue." *Japan Times*, October 23, 2004.

Takahara, Kanako. "Let Consumers Decide for Themselves: Eatery Lobbyist." *Japan Times*, March 19, 2005.

Takahara, Kanako. "Tentative Accord Reached on U.S. Beef." *Japan Times*, October 24, 2004.

"Taking Pains." *Economist*, September 8, 2012.

Tang, Yixin. "The Future of Patent Enforcement after *eBay v. MercExchange*." *Harvard Journal of Law and Technology* 20, no. 1 (2006): 236–52.

"Tariff h on Beef Lack Justification." *Nikkei Weekly*, August 4, 2003.

"Tesla's Success Sparks China's e-Car Race." *China Daily*, April 26, 2016.

"Text: TABD Final Recommendations." *Inside U.S. Trade*, November 17, 1995.

"Text: U.S.-Japan Statement on Beef." *Inside U.S. Trade*, June 23, 2006.

Thacker, Strom. *Big Business, the State, and Free Trade: Constructing Coalitions in Mexico*. Cambridge: Cambridge University Press, 2000.

Thacker, Strom. "Private Sector Trade Politics in Mexico." *Business and Politics* 2, no. 2 (2000): 161–87.

Thompson, Clive. "How a Nation of Tech Copycats Became a Hub for Innovation." *Wired*, December 29, 2015.

"Thousands Protest Cost of AIDS Drugs." *Toronto Star*, March 6, 2001.

Tilleman, Levi. *The Great Race: The Global Quest for the Car of the Future*. New York: Simon and Schuster, 2015.

Tolbert, Kathryn. "Japan to Test 1 Million Cattle for 'Mad Cow'; Concerns Grow after First Case Botched." *Washington Post*, September 20, 2001.

Tomforde, Anna. "Bonn Flouts EEC with Early Date for Exhaust Control." *Guardian*, September 19, 1984.

Toy Industry Association. "U.S.-EU Free Trade Agreement: Tipping over the Regulatory Barriers." Statement to the House Subcommittee on Commerce, Manufacturing, and Trade, July 23, 2013.

"TPP Enviro Talks Get Bogged Down over MEAs, Conservation, and Biodiversity." *Inside U.S. Trade*, January 17, 2014.

"TPP Partners Invite Mexico and Canada to Join TPP Talks, but Not Japan." *Inside U.S. Trade*, June 22, 2012.

"Tracking Systems Try to Tackle Food Safety." *Japan Times*, May 1, 2002.

Trebilcock, Michael, and Robert Howse. *The Regulation of International Trade*. 3rd ed. New York: Routledge, 2005.

"TRIPS–Public Health Declaration Splits Developing, Developed Nations." *Inside U.S. Trade*, September 28, 2001.

Trumbull, Gunnar. "Consumer Policy: Business and the Politics of Consumption." In *The Oxford Handbook of Business and Government*, edited by David Coen, Wyn Grant, and Graham Wilson. Oxford: Oxford University Press, 2010.

Trumbull, Gunnar. *Strength in Numbers: The Political Power of Weak Interests*. Cambridge, MA: Harvard University Press, 2012.

"Trust and the Food Safety Commission." *Japan Times*, April 22, 2006.

"Trust Not a Given after Mad Cow Debacle." *Japan Times*, May 29, 2003.

Tucker, A. "Trade Associations as Industry Reputation Agents: A Model of Reputational Trust." *Business and Politics* 10, no. 1 (2008): 1–26.

Tuman, John. *Reshaping the North American Automobile Industry: Restructuring, Corporatism, and Union Democracy in Mexico*. New York: Continuum, 2003.

Tybout, James. "Plant and Firm-Level Evidence on 'New' Trade Theories." Working paper 8418, National Bureau of Economic Research, Cambridge, MA, 2001.

Tyfield, David. "Enabling TRIPs: The Pharma-Biotech-University Patent Coalition." *Review of International Political Economy* 15, no. 4 (2008): 535–66.

United Nations. "World Population Prospects: 2015 Revision." Department of Economic and Social Affairs, Population Division, 2015.

United States Chamber of Commerce. "Trans-Atlantic Trade and Investment Partnership." Accessed May 1, 2016. https://www.uschamber.com/issue-brief/trans-atlantic-trade-and-investment-partnership

United States Department of Agriculture, Economic Research Service. Statistics and information. Accessed April 30, 2016. http://www.ers.usda.gov/topics/animal-products/cattle-beef/statistics-information.aspx

United States Department of Agriculture, Office of Inspector General. *Audit Report: Animal and Plant Health Inspection Service Bovine Spongiform Encephalopathy (BSE) Surveillance Program.* Report 50601-10-KC. January 2006.

United States Department of Labor, Bureau of Labor Statistics. "Automotive Industry: Employment, Earnings, and Hours." Accessed May 1, 2019. https://www.bls.gov/iag/tgs/iagauto.htm

United States Department of State, Bureau of Economic and Business Affairs. "2015 Investment Climate Statement—China." May 2015.

United States Environmental Protection Agency, Office of Air and Radiation. "The Benefits and Costs of the Clean Air Act from 1990 to 2020." Final report, April 2011.

United States Meat Export Federation. "U.S. Beef Exports to Japan." Accessed April 28, 2016. https://www.usmef.org/news-statistics/statistics/

"U.S., Australia Float Joint Biologics Text to Other Countries for Vetting." *Inside U.S. Trade*, October 4, 2015.

"U.S., EU Auto Regulators to Cooperate on Seat Belt Anchors, Visibility." *Inside U.S. Trade*, March 18, 2016.

"U.S., EU Officials Say Auto Regulators Making Headway in TTIP Talks." *Inside U.S. Trade*, July 18, 2014.

"U.S., TPP Countries Mull Compromise on Biologics Data Exclusivity." *Inside U.S. Trade*, August 7, 2015.

"U.S. Allows Japan Beef Audits: Japan Eases Inspections." *Inside U.S. Trade*, April 27, 2007.

"U.S. Beef Exporters Must Not Slip Up Again." *Yomiuri Shimbun*, May 21, 2006.

"U.S. Beef Hard Sell: As Concern Lingers, Aussies Fill Void." *Japan Times*, October 5, 2006.

"U.S. Beef Inspections Don't Inspire Much Confidence." *International Herald Tribune*, June 12, 2008.

"U.S. Businesses Back Down from Targeting India as PFC under Special 301." *Inside U.S. Trade*, February 12, 2015.

"U.S. Business Steps Up Fight against Indian Trade Barriers Ahead of Election." *Inside U.S. Trade*, June 14, 2013.

"U.S. Critiques Japan on Familiar Issues at WTO Trade Policy Review." *Inside U.S. Trade*, February 20, 2009.

"USDA Asks Japan to Accept All U.S. Beef in Wake of OIE Finding." *Inside U.S. Trade*, June 1, 2007.

"USDA Unveils Long-Awaited BSE Rule, Says It Will Help Open Foreign Markets." *Inside U.S. Trade*, March 16, 2012.

"USDA Weighs Packer Request to BSE-Test All Cattle." *Reuters*, March 15, 2004.

"U.S. Firms to Push for More IPR Protection in WTO, FTAA Talks." *Inside U.S. Trade*, August 28, 1998.

"U.S. Government Efforts to Negotiate the Repeal, Termination, or Withdrawal of Article 15(c) of the South African Medicines and Related Substances Act." U.S. Department of State, February 5, 1999.

"U.S. Hopeful Africans Coming on Board in TRIPS/Health Dispute." *Inside U.S. Trade*, November 2, 2001.

"U.S. Official Urges Japan to Open Up, Sign FTA." *Japan Times*, December 7, 2007.

"U.S. Senate Mulls Japan Sanctions." *Yomiuri Shimbun*, March 16, 2005.

"U.S.-Seoul FTA Deal May Keep Japan Exporters at Bay." *Yomiuri Shimbun*, December 6, 2010.

"U.S. Shipments of Risky Beef Part Outrage Japanese Consumers." Kyodo News, BBC Monitoring Asia Pacific, January 21, 2006.

"U.S. Should Have Been More Careful." *Aberdeen American News*, January 24, 2006.

"U.S. Steps Up Fight against Moratorium on TRIPS Non-violation Cases." *Inside U.S. Trade*, July 3, 2014.

"U.S. Trade Diplomat Hits Japan's Control on U.S. Beef Imports." Kyodo News, BBC Monitoring Asia Pacific, May 23, 2009.

"USTR Continues TPP Consultations with Japanese Officials in Tokyo." *Inside U.S. Trade*, May 11, 2012.

"U.S. Turning Up Pressure as Japan Continues Beef Ban." *Nikkei Weekly*, March 7, 2005.

Van Alstine, James, and Eric Neumayer. "The Environmental Kuznets Curve." In *Handbook on Trade and the Environment*, edited by Kevin Gallagher. New York: Edward Elgar, 2008.

Van Evera, Stephen. *Guide to Methods for Students of Political Science*. Ithaca: Cornell University Press, 1997.

Van den Bosche, Peter. "NGO Involvement in the WTO: A Comparative Perspective." *Journal of International Economic Law* 11, no. 4 (2008): 717–49.

Van Tulder, Rob, and Denis Audet. "The Faster Lane of Regionalism." In *Cars, Carriers of Regionalism?*, edited by Jorge Carrillo, Yannick Lung, and Rob van Tulder. New York: Palgrave MacMillan, 2004.

Varma, Subodh. "SC Rules for Cheap Cancer Drug." *Times of India*, April 2, 2013.

"vCJD: Variant Creutzfeldt-Jakob Disease." Center for Disease Control and Prevention, U.S. Department of Health and Human Services. Accessed March 8, 2016. https://www.cdc.gov/prions/vcjd/resources.html

"Veneman Out to Demonstrate There's No Beef with U.S. Cattle." *Yomiuri Shimbun*, July 26, 2002.

Verdier, Pierre-Hugues. "Transnational Regulatory Networks and Their Limits." *Yale Journal of International Law* 34 (2009): 113–72.

Viana, Jose Marcos Nogueira. "The Global AIDS Crisis: Intellectual Property Rights, the World Trade Organization and Public Health; The Brazilian Perspective." *Connecticut Journal of International Law* 17 (2002) 311–18.

Vogel, David. "Consumer Protection and Protectionism in Japan." *Journal of Japanese Studies*, 18, no.1 (1992): 119–54.

Vogel, David. "Private Global Business Regulation." *Annual Review of Political Science* 11 (2008): 261–82.

Vogel, David. *The Market for Virtue: The Potential and Limits of Corporate Social Responsibility*. Washington, DC: Brookings Institution, 2005.

Vogel, David. *The Politics of Precaution: Regulating Health, Safety, and Environmental Risks in Europe and the United States*. Princeton: Princeton University Press, 2012.

Vogel, David. "Private Regulation of Global Corporate Conduct." In *The Politics of Global Regulation*, edited by Walter Mattli and Ngaire Woods. Princeton: Princeton University Press, 2009.

Vogel, David. *Trading Up: Consumer and Environmental Regulation in a Global Economy*. Cambridge, MA: Harvard University Press, 1995.

Vogel, David, and Robert Kagan, eds. *Dynamics of Regulatory Change: How Globalization Affects National Regulatory Policies*. Berkeley: University of California Press, 2006.

Vogel, Steven. *Freer Markets, More Rules: Regulatory Reform in Advanced Industrial Countries*. Ithaca: Cornell University Press, 1996.

Vogel, Steven. "When Interests Are Not Preferences: The Cautionary Tale of Japanese Consumers." *Comparative Politics* 31, no. 2 (1999) 187–207.

Vogel, Steven. "Why Freer Markets Need More Rules." In *Creating Competitive Markets: The Politics of Regulatory Reform*, edited by Marc Landy, Martin Levin, and Martin Shapiro. Washington, DC: Brookings Institution, 2007.

"Wag the Cow." *Washington Post*, March 11, 2005.

Wallace, Rick. "Japan Hardliner Hits FTA Hopes." *Australian*, June 9, 2010.

Wallace, Rick. "Japan Raises Hopes of FTA Action." *Australian*, October 14, 2010.

Wallach, Lori, and Michelle Sforza. *The WTO: Five Years of Reasons to Resist Corporate Globalization*. New York: Seven Stories, 1999.

Walter, Andrew. "NGOs, Business, and International Investment: The Multilateral Agreement on Investment, Seattle, and Beyond." *Global Governance* 7, *no. 1* (2001) 51–73.

Walton, Rod. "Animal Risk Status: Much Improved; U.S. Mad Cow 'Controlled.'" *Tulsa (OK) World*, May 23, 2007.

Wang, Shujen. "Recontextualizing Copyright: Piracy, Hollywood, the State, and Globalization." *Cinema Journal* 43, no. 1 (2003): 25–43.

Ward, Andrew, and Amy Kazmin. "Bayer Loses Bid to Block Cheap Version of Cancer Drug in India." *Financial Times*, December 12, 2014.

"Washington Unhappy with Japan's Beef Plan." *Yomiuri Shimbun*, September 12, 2004.

Watanabeand, Tatsuya, and Toru Takahashi. "Beef Ban Dropped to Avoid Political Stew." *Yomiuri Shimbun*, May 21, 2006.

Watts, Jonathan. "Made in China: Tainted Food, Fake Drugs, and Dodgy Paint." *Guardian*, July 5, 2007.

"Ways and Means Republicans Call on USTR to Enhance Beef Access." *Inside U.S. Trade*, July 31, 2009.

Weintraub, Arlene. "Merck's Melanoma 'Game-Changer' Keytruda Likely to Bolster Drug Pricing Debate." *FiercePharma*, September 5, 2014. http://www.fiercepharma.com/pharma/updated-merck-s-melanoma-game-changer-keytruda-likely-to-bolster-drug-pricing-debate/

Weiss, Rick. "FDA Is Urged to Ban Carbon-Monoxide Treated Beef." *Washington Post*, February 20, 2006.

Wellesley, Laura, Anthony Froggatt, and Catherine Happer. "Changing Climate, Changing Diet: Pathways to Lower Meat Consumption." Chatham House, November 24, 2015.

"Where's the Beef From?" *Yomiuri Shimbun*, February 16, 2002.

White, Bob. "The Deal Undermines Canada's Auto Industry." *Toronto Star*, October 19, 1987.

"Why TPP Matters." U.S. Business Coalition for the TPP. Accessed May 1, 2016. http://tppcoalition.org/tpp/

Wijers-Hasagawa, Yumi. "Japan Receives First Batch of U.S. Beef." *Japan Times*, August 8, 2006.

Wilber, Vann, and Paul Eichbrecht. "Transatlantic Trade, the Automotive Sector: The Role of Regulation in a Global Industry, Where We Have Been and Where We Need to Go, How Far Can EU-US Cooperation Go toward Achieving Regulatory Harmonization" in *Systemic Implications of Transatlantic Regulatory Cooperation and Competition*, Simon Evenett and Robert Stern eds., World Scientific Studies in International Economics, London (2011), 165–96.

Williams, Brock. "Trans-Pacific Partnership Countries: Comparative Trade and Economic Analysis." Congressional Research Service, June 10, 2013.

Williams, Glen. *Not for Export: The International Competitiveness of Canadian Manufacturing*. 3rd ed. Toronto: McClelland and Stewart, 1994.

Wilson, James Q. *Bureaucracy: What Government Agencies Do and Why They Do It*. New York: Basic Books, 1989.

Wilson, James Q. *The Politics of Regulation*. New York: Basic Books, 1980.

Winestock, Geoff, and Helene Cooper. "How Activists Outmaneuvered Drug Makers in WTO Deal." *Wall Street Journal*, November 15, 2001.

Winslett, Gary. "Choosing among Options for Regulatory Cooperation." *Global Governance* 25, no. 1 (2019): 100–122.

Wiseman, Paul. "Trade War Looms over Beef Dispute; Japan's Ban Stands amid Mad Cow Fears." *USA Today*, April 20, 2006.

Woll, Cornelia, and Alvaro Artigas. "When Trade Liberalization Turns into Regulatory Reform: The Impact on Business-Government Relations in International Trade Politics." *Regulation and Governance* 1, no. 2 (2007): 126.

Womack, James, Daniel Jones, and Daniel Roos. *The Machine That Changed the World: The Story of Lean Production*. New York: Free Press, 1990.

World Bank. "Global Economic Prospects and the Developing Countries." Washington, DC, 2002.

World Health Organization. "Cancer." Fact sheet, updated September 12, 2018.

World Health Organization. "Cardiovascular Disease." Fact sheet 317, updated May 17, 2017.

World Health Organization. "Diabetes." Fact sheet, updated October 30, 2018.

World Trade Organization, Statistics on Merchandise Trade, 2017, accessed May 1, 2019. https://www.wto.org/english/res_e/statis_e/merch_trade_stat_e.htm

World Trade Organization. "Non-violation and Situation Nullification or Impairment under the TRIPS Agreement." IP/C/W/385. October 30, 2002.

World Trade Organization. "Non-violation Complaints under the TRIPS Agreement: A Communication from the United States." IP/C/W/599. June 10, 2013.

World Trade Organization. *WTO Panel Report on EC Complaint concerning Canada—Patent Protection of Pharmaceutical Products*. WT/DS114/R. March 17, 2000.

World Trade Organization. Statistics Database: Merchandise Trade by Commodity. Accessed May 1 and 16, 2019. https://timeseries.wto.org/

World Trade Organization. "TRIPS and Pharmaceutical Patents: Obligations and Exceptions." Accessed February 16, 2016. https://www.wto.org/english/tratop_e/trips_e/factsheet_pharm02_e.htm#importing

World Trade Organization. *World Trade Report 2012: Trade and Public Policies; A Closer Look at Non-tariff Measures in the 21st Century*,Geneva (2012).

"WTO Awaits U.S. on Disease Limits on TRIPS, Fail to Get Deal on S&D." *Inside U.S. Trade*, December 20, 2002.

"WTO Fails to Bridge Gaps on TRIPS and Health Deal, Sets New Deadline." *Inside U.S. Trade*, December 13, 2002.

Wyles, John. "Tardy Government Catches Up with Green Mood in Italy." *Financial Times*, October 5, 1988.

Yaşar, Mahmut. "Political Influence of Export and Import-Competing Firms: Evidence from Eastern European and Central American Countries." *World Development* 51 (2013): 154–68.

Yates, Charlotte. "Public Policy and Canadian and American Autoworkers: Divergent Fortunes." In *Driving Continentally: National Policies and the North American Auto Industry*, edited by Maureen Molot. Don Mills, Ontario: Carleton University Press, 1993.

Yoshida, Reiji. "Abe to Meet Obama with Hands Tied." *Japan Times*, February 6, 2013.

Yoshimatsu, Hidetaka. "Japanese Economic Policy toward Asia: International Pressure and Domestic Politics." *Electronic Journal of Japanese Studies* 12, no. 2 (2013). https://www.japanesestudies.org.uk/ejcjs/vol12/iss2/yoshimatsu.html

Young, Alasdair. "Not Your Parents' Trade Politics: The Transatlantic Trade and Investment Partnership Negotiations." *Review of International Political Economy* 23, no. 3 (2016): 345–78.

Yu, Peter. 2006. "TRIPS and Its Discontents." *Marquette Intellectual Property Review* 10, no. 2 (2006) 369–410.

Yu, Rose. "China Cars Sales Growth Slows Further." *Wall Street Journal*, January 12, 2016.

Yu, Zhang. "Pricey Pills." *Global Times* (China), January 8, 2015.

Zaun, Todd. "Agreement to Ease Ban on U.S. Beef." *New York Times*, October 24, 2004.

Zirkelbach, Robert. "The Reality of Prescription Medication Costs in Three Charts." Pharmaceutical Research and Manufacturers Association, May 27, 2014. Accessed May 1, 2016. https://www.phrma.org/catalyst/the-reality-of-prescription-medicine-costs-in-three-charts

Index

Note: Page numbers in italics refer to illustrations and tables.